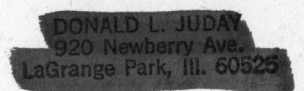

THIS IS A BOOK ABOUT HUMAN COMMUNICATION

DATE DUE

COMMUNICATION INVOLVEMENT: PERSONAL PERSPECTIVES

William W. Wilmot
University of Montana

John R. Wenburg
University of Nebraska

John Wiley & Sons, Inc.
New York London Sydney Toronto

Library of Congress Cataloging in Publication Data:

Wilmot, William W   comp.
  Communication involvement.

   1. Communication—Addresses, essays, lectures.
2. Mass media—Addresses, essays, lectures. I. Wenburg,
John R., joint comp. II. Title.

P87.W5   301.14   73-22181
ISBN 0-471-94957-4

Printed in the United States of America

10-9 8 7 6 5 4 3 2 1

To Charney and Carolyn

PREFACE

All of us wish to be understood and, hopefully, wish to understand others. Consequently, the better part of our lives is involved with the communication process. Since we are so involved with this process, any improvement in its quality has far-reaching results.

We can use effective communication to mold fuller lives for ourselves and others. One way to improve our communication is to observe other people's attempts. Insights into their communication behaviors can be used for reflection about our own encounters. Therefore, materials that can involve the reader in other people's personal perspectives on communication have been selected for this book. These perspectives will assist you in understanding the process of human communication and ultimately will help you to improve your own communication.

This book can be used in many ways. Within the confines of academic courses it can serve as a sole text or can be used in conjunction with other communication textbooks. It can also be used for students engaged in independent course study as a stimulant to their thinking about communication. Whatever the specific application, the selections will stimulate thinking about human communication.

We are grateful to certain students and colleagues who directly influenced our selection of materials. Students Malcolm Parks of the University of Montana, Diane Lee and Larry Christensen of the University of Nebraska, and colleagues Jackson Huntley of the University of Minnesota at Duluth and Duane Pettersen of the University of Montana gave us suggestions for readings or actually supplied articles for our use. Special thanks are also extended to our department chairmen, Dr. Eldon Baker and Dr. John Petelle, who made it possible for us to work together during the academic year. We also appreciate the support of our departmental colleagues who allowed us to work rigorously while we were together and who added needed enjoyment to the visits.

People as inept as we are at typing need the assistance of experts. A much deserved "thank you" is extended to Carolyn Wenburg for typing the working drafts of our original essays and to Michelle Peterson of the University of Montana who typed all of the final copy.

The reviewers of our manuscript were Virginia Bennett of Shoreline Community College; Edward M. Bodaken of the University of Southern California; James Golden of The Ohio State University; Blaine Gross of the University of Oklahoma; William B. Lashbrook of University of West Virginia; Linda Putnam of Normandale State Junior College; and Ronald H. Subeck of Wilbur Wright College. We thank them for their valuable insights and encouragement. Professors Bennett and Bodaken were our major reviewers, and they deserve a special thanks for providing detailed comments about our materials and essays.

It has been a pleasure for us to work with Thomas O. Gay, Editor at Wiley, on this book. We also thank Roger Holloway, Executive Editor at Wiley, who carefully followed this project from its inception.

William W. Wilmot
John R. Wenburg

CONTENTS

1 OUR POINT OF VIEW

2 INTRAPERSONAL COMMUNICATION: TRANSACTING WITH YOURSELF

Intrapersonal Communication   Perception

Intrapersonal Communication   Nonverbal Behavior

Intrapersonal Communication   Barriers

3 INTERPERSONAL COMMUNICATION: TRANSACTING WITH ANOTHER

5 PUBLIC SPEAKING: TRANSACTING WITH A LARGE GROUP

Public Speaking　　　　　　　　　　　　　　Self-Disclosure

Public Speaking　　　　　　　　　　　　　　　　　　Effects

6 MASS COMMUNICATION: TRANSACTING WITH SOCIETY

Mass Communication　　　　　　　　　　　　Perception

Mass Communication　　　　　　　　Nonverbal Behavior

Mass Communication　　　　　　　　　　　　　Barriers

Mass Communication　　　　　　　　　　Self-Disclosure

Mass Communication — Effects

COMMUNICATION INVOLVEMENT: PERSONAL PERSPECTIVES

1

OUR
POINT
OF VIEW

To Begin With

Most of us want to understand ourselves and others better. As a result, we often find ourselves asking questions such as: "Why do I act the way I do?" "Why do I get upset every time I talk with her?" "What does he do that makes me feel so good when I chat with him?" "Why do I fear talking to a group of people even when I am well prepared?" "Why don't my parents understand me?" "Why does he always act like he is thinking about something else when I talk with him?" "Why do people respond to me the way they do?" "Why can't I be more open and honest with people?" Anwers to these and similar questions are often difficult and, at best, tentative. But the important thing is that in asking these types of questions, we are examining our relationships with others.

We believe that a person can make remarkable strides toward understanding himself and others if he engages in a serious examination of human communication behavior. Stop and think for a moment about how much time you spend communicating. You write, speak, listen, or read most of the time. In fact, communicating is so commonplace that it often goes unnoticed. For example, the questions we posed above were communication questions. The answers to those and similar questions can best be found by concentrating your analysis on communication behavior.

This book consists of writings we have found helpful in our attempts to understand communication behavior and in our efforts to help others understand it also. The writings are composed of first-person accounts, pieces of fiction, and interesting summaries of research, which we believe will get you excited about and involved in the study of personal communication. In addition, we have included numerous short statements and aphorisms that we have found stimulating. Your involvement with these materials should lead you to a better understanding of communication and increase your effectiveness as a communication participant.

Communication Arenas

Communication experiences range from private thinking (intrapersonal communication) to situations where you send or receive

3

messages through some form of electronic media (mass communication). To facilitate your understanding of the human communication process, we have organized this book into the five units that we think best represent the way communication experiences can be categorized. We have labeled each category as a communication *arena*. They are the Intrapersonal Communication Arena, the Interpersonal Communication Arena, the Small Group Communication Arena, the Public Speaking Arena, and the Mass Communication Arena. We realize that different authors classify communication arenas in various ways. Some, for example, do not distinguish between interpersonal and small group arenas. Others do not separate communication encounters that take place in the public speaking arena from those that exist in the mass communication arena. Still others choose to classify communication contexts according to the nature of the messages being shared, for example, the degree of personableness of the message. A lengthy, theoretical defense of our classification scheme does not seem necessary or appropriate. The approach we have selected best fits our own conceptualizations of human communication and, based on our experiences as teachers, this approach appears to be useful for students.

We know that separating the communication process into five arenas is artificial. Our intent is to stop the communication process for a moment, make some artificial distinctions, and discuss what we find. We want you to realize that we are separating the process into the different arenas solely for descriptive purposes. We think that the descriptions can ultimately lead to a better overall understanding of the process. Remember, however, that the *arenas are more alike than different.*

Hopefully, realizing that the arenas are more alike than different will help you dismiss some of the fears you might have of being involved in some of the arenas. For example, internalization of the notion that public speaking is merely an extension of small group communication may help you develop a more realistic picture of communication in the public speaking arena. Placed into proper context, public speaking is no longer viewed as a "rare event" in which you stand up, flap your gums, and expose your mind and body to the whole world to criticize. Public speaking is a part of the daily human communication experience. When you are the designated speaker in the arena, the same communication factors are operating as in the interpersonal or small group situations. The emphasis on the factors changes from arena to arena, but the basic factors still exist. If you begin to view public speaking as one integral part of the human communication process, your participation in the arena will probably improve. The same is true of your participation in each of the other arenas. We have, therefore, geared the introductions to the units to give you further information about the characteristics of the arenas.

Communication Factors

A discussion of all of the communication factors that exist in each of the communication arenas is not possible either from a theoretical or practical standpoint. Theoretically, the study of communication is still in its infancy. All of the possible factors simply have not been identified or studied. Practically, time and space limitations do not permit examination of all the factors that have already been identified and studied. Consequently, we have selected five factors that we believe are (1) among those that permeate communication experiences in all of the five communication arenas, and are (2) the most critical in providing insights for a person as he begins to better understand his involvement in communication.

The factors we have selected are Perception, Nonverbal Behavior, Barriers, Self-Disclosure, and Effects. Examination of these communication factors will help you internalize the interrelatedness of the arenas. Nonverbal behavior, for example, is an extremely important factor in all communication transactions. As you will discover, however, it is relied on more heavily in some arenas than in others. Also, what might be perceived as a friendly nonverbal gesture in one arena might be interpreted as a vulgar nonverbal sign in another arena. In terms of communication effects, a message in one arena may create an entirely different type of reciprocal influence than if it were in another arena. Examination of each of the five factors in the arenas should give you a better contextual understanding of communication encounters. Also, your insight into the workings of each of the five factors should be greatly enhanced. Ultimately, by understanding the factors and appreciating the similarities among the arenas, you will become a more informed observer of the human communication experience and a more capable participant.

Thus, the organization of this book is as follows. There are five major units—each unit is one of the communication arenas (Intrapersonal Communication, Interpersonal Communication, Small Group Communication, Public Speaking, and Mass Communication). Each unit is organized around the five factors of Perception, Nonverbal Behavior, Barriers, Self-Disclosure, and Effects. Readings have been selected to develop the factors in each unit. The readings were chosen because they demonstrate the nature of a particular factor as it operates in a given communication arena.

We have provided introductory essays for each of the units and for each of the five factors as they emerge in a unit. We also have written brief introductions to each reading to assist you in realizing how a given selection demonstrates the particular principle being discussed. In addition, we have included short statements or aphorisms at various points in the manuscript. We hope these statements will provide you with further thoughts about communication behavior. We have attempted to place the statements where they have particular relevance to the factor and unit being discussed. We hope you find the aphorisms stimulating.

We are inviting you to study the process of human communication by becoming involved with the material we have selected. Your study will be enjoyable and worthwhile if you are sensitive to the communication behaviors described in the selections.

Communication Defined

The potential for your involvement in human communication exists every second. We define communication as *any attempt to get meaning.*[1] When a person makes an effort, intentionally or unintentionally, to acquire understanding, the person is in the communication process. One axiom of communication is, "One cannot not communicate."[2] Put simply, whenever you are in contact with a person, everything you do or do not do communicates. If a person is aware of your presence in a room, you are communicating with that person whether you realize it or not. The same is true of the other person. If you are aware of the person's presence, he or she is communicating with you whether they realize it or not. Thus, the potential for your involvement in human communication is always present. We cannot conceive of a person being in a situation where at least the potential for communication involvement does not exist.

The effects of communication on your daily life are staggering. They are significant because your involvement in human communication means you are *sharing yourself*—sharing yourself with yourself and with others. Others who are involved in the process, in turn, share themselves with you. The potential impact of this type of involvement and sharing on the quality of your life appears obvious. What can be more significant than your involvement in the human process of sharing and accepting?

The Nature of Human Communication

Human communication is a personal, transactional process. It is "personal" because it is not possible to completely separate yourself from the process. The messages you send and receive are, in part, what they are because of how you perceive yourself and your environment. We can never completely divorce ourselves from our own personal perspective as we engage in communication. In essence, human communication is probably one of the least objective and most personal activities in which man in involved.

[1]John R. Wenburg and William W. Wilmot, *The Personal Communication Process,* Wiley, New York, 1973, p. 7.
[2]Paul Watzlawick, Janet Beavin, and Don D. Jackson, *Pragmatics of Human Communication,* W. W. Norton, New York, 1967, pp. 48–51.

Human communication is also "transactional." It is transactional because all persons in the process are actively involved. Each person is, at any point in time, sending messages. The way we sit, our tone of voice, and our other nonverbal factors make each of us a "source," even when the other person is talking. Obviously, we are also receiving communication messages from others even if we are talking. In short, all participants are sharing in the process. They are each simultaneously sending and receiving messages.

Some people do not view communication as transactional. They see it as interactive. The interactive view would hold, for example, that a speaker says something, the audience reacts (they give him feedback), and he alters his next statement. From this point of view, communication is a series of actions and reactions. We feel that such a view fails to capture the essence of the communication process. From the process point of view, we cannot actually say whether a communication participant is a source or a receiver. He may be a source of the messages to which I am reacting, but at the same time he is receiving the messages I am sending. Which of us is the source? Which of us is the receiver? Again, it depends on where you are in the process.

Thus, labels such as "source," "receiver," "stimulus," "response," and "feedback" are artificial distinctions and should be recognized as such. To capture the essence of communication, we must try to visualize it as a process in which we are a source and, at the same time, a receiver—we encode (send) cues (stimuli) while we are decoding (receiving) other cues. We are not sources, then receivers, then sources, and then receivers. We are involved communicants—we send and receive messages *simultaneously*. When we are engaged in a communication transaction, we are in a duplex relationship in which participation and influence are reciprocal—each of us affects and is affected.

In keeping with the notion that communication is transactional, we say communication is also a process. Where a communication encounter begins and where it ends cannot be determined. Human communication, and your involvement in it, is on-going and cannot be stopped. Where it starts nobody knows. Think for a moment of a recent conversation you had or a speech you gave. When did it begin? Did it begin when you first started talking with the other person or audience? Did it begin when you first realized it was going to take place? Did it begin when you first began forming impressions of the person or persons with whom you communicated? Just where did it begin? Where did it end? When you stopped talking, right? Or was it when you stopped thinking about it? Or, perhaps, when you stopped realizing the direct influence it had on your attitudes or behavior. Just when did it end—or has it? Exactly when the communication process began and where it ended cannot be identified. Communication is a process, an on-going process with an undeterminable beginning and ending. Thus, we see communication as a personal, transactional process. Each of us, when we communicate (attempt to get meaning), is in the process of simultaneously sending and receiving messages—messages to which we attach meaning according to who we are. When we begin communication and when we stop—we cannot specify. We do know, however, that we are involved—involved in a complex behavior—a behavior that each of us can better understand. We hope this book will involve you further into the human communication process.

2

INTRAPERSONAL COMMUNICATION:
TRANSACTING WITH YOURSELF

When you communicate with yourself, you are engaging in intrapersonal communication. The distinguishing characteristic of communication in this arena is that *you are the only participant*. Ultimately, *all* communication can be labeled intrapersonal. It is intrapersonal because all of our communication activities (messages and responses) are processed within us. It is *personal* since, as we noted earlier, our activities in any communication situation are a result of who we are. No two individuals are exactly alike, and consequently, no two people see and hear the same things when they are exposed to a stimulus. Since you can never dismiss your "self" from the processing and interpreting of communication cues, all communication includes intrapersonal communication.

In this section we concentrate on communication that is obviously intrapersonal—the type that exists when a person is definitely communicating with himself. We are primarily concerned with the type of intrapersonal communication that takes place when, for example, you have a dream, meditate, scribble in your personal diary, or just think privately. Hopefully, this section will assist you in your efforts to understand why you see things differently from others, how nonverbal actions can affect communication with yourself, what kinds of factors can become harmful barriers to your intrapersonal communication efforts, how you can get in touch with and accept yourself, and what sorts of effects can result from communication with yourself.

INTRAPERSONAL
COMMUNICATION
PERCEPTION

Twenty-five hundred years ago, it might
have been said that man understood
himself as well as any other part of his
world. Today he is the thing he
understands least. B. F. Skinner

As you will discover throughout this book, perception is a vital issue in all communication arenas. How you perceive yourself, your environment, and others affects all of your reactions. That no two people can ever perceive an object, event, or person in exactly the same manner is a truism with which we are all familiar. Although each of us "knows" it is true, most of us fail to behave that way.

The meaning a person attaches to something depends on his past experiences. In other words, *meanings are in people.* I perceive something the way I do because of *who I am* rather than because of *what it is.* Although people never perceive things in exactly the same way, you can better understand the differences in perception and, as a result, be more tolerant of yourself and others. One place to begin to better understand the perception process is to look at how you perceive things when you are communicating with only yourself.

The following selection by
Rollo May stresses the need
to "experience your body" in
order to be more sensitive of
your own perceptions. As May
says, most of us treat our
bodies as objects to be
controlled, but to understand
ourselves, we need to "listen
to the body." Do you listen to
your body? As you read this
selection, try to think of ways
that you can alter your
perception by becoming more
aware of the experiences your
body encounters.

ROLLO MAY

THE EXPERIENCING OF ONE'S BODY AND FEELINGS

In the achieving of consciousness of one's self, most people must start back at the beginning and rediscover their feelings. It is surprising how many people have only a general acquaintance with what they feel —they tell you they feel "fine" or "lousy," as vaguely as though they were saying "China is in the Orient." Their connection with their feelings is as remote as if over a long-distance telephone. They do not feel directly but only give ideas about their feelings; they are not affected by their affects; their emotions give them no motion. Like Eliot's "Hollow Men," they experience themselves as

Shape without form, shade without colour,
Paralyzed force, gesture without motion.

In psychotherapy when such persons are unable to experience their feelings, they often have to learn to feel by answering the question day after day, Just how do I feel right now? What is most important is not how much one feels, and we certainly do not mean that it is necessary to effervesce; that is sentimentality rather than sentiment, affectation and not affect. Rather what is imporant is the experience that it is "I," the active one, who is doing the feeling. This carries with it a directness and immediacy of feeling; one experiences the affect on all levels of one's self. One feels with a heightened aliveness. Then instead of one's feelings being limited like notes in a bugle call, the mature person becomes able to differentiate feelings into as many nuances, strong and passionate experiences, or delicate and sensitive ones, as in the different passages of music in a symphony.

This also means that we need to recover our awareness of our bodies. An infant gets part of his early sense of personal identity through awareness of his body. "We may call the body as experienced by the infant," says Gardner Murphy, "the first core of the self."* The baby reaches his leg time and again, and sooner or later there is the experience, "Here is this leg; I can feel it and it belongs to *me*." Sexual feelings are particularly significant because they are among the earliest feelings which the child can refer directly to himself. When sexual areas are stimulated in play or by clothing, there is the rudimentary beginning of the experience of feeling one's self. Unfortunately sexual feelings and those connected with toilet experiences have been widely tabooed in the past in our society, and the child has been given to understand that such feelings are "naughty." Since such feelings are a part of his way of identifying himself, the taboo would clearly imply, "Your image of yourself is dirty." This undoubtedly is one important part of the origin of the tendency to despise the self in our society.

The ability to be aware of one's body has a great importance all through life. It is a curious fact that most adults have so lost physical awareness that they are unable to tell how their leg feels if you should ask them, or their ankle, or their middle finger or any other part of the body. In our society the awareness of the different parts of the body is generally limited to some borderline schizophrenics and other sophisticated people who have come under the influence of yoga or other Eastern exercises. Most people act on the principle, "Let hands or feet feel as they may, I must get off to work." As a result of several centuries of suppressing the body into an inanimate machine, subordinated to the purposes of modern industrialism, people are proud of paying no attention to the body. They treat it as an object for manipulation, as though it were a truck to be driven till it runs out of gas. The only concern they give it is a thought each week as perfunctory as a phone call to a relative to ask how he is, but with really no intention of taking the

*Culture and Personality, *eds. Sargent and Smith, p. 19.*

answer seriously. Nature then comes along, if we may speak metaphorically, and knocks the person down with colds or the flu or more severe illnesses, as though she were saying, "When will you learn to listen to your body?"

The impersonal, separated attitude toward the body is shown also in the way most people, once they become physically ill, react to the sickness. They speak in the passive voice—"I *got* sick," picturing their body as an object just as they would say "I *got* hit by a car." Then they shrug their shoulders and regard their responsibility fulfilled if they go to bed and place themselves completely in the hands of the doctor and the new medical miracle drugs. Thus they use scientific progress as a rationalization for passivity: they know how germs or virus or allergies attack the body, and they also know how penicillin or sulfa or some other drug cures them. The attitude toward disease is not that of the self-aware person who experiences his body as part of himself, but of the compartmentalized person who might express his passive attitude in a sentence like, "The pneumococcus made me sick, but penicillin made me well again."

Certainly it is only common sense to avail one's self of all the help science can give, but that is no reason to surrender one's own sovereignty over one's body. When one does surrender autonomy one opens oneself to psychosomatic ills of all sorts. Many disturbances of bodily function, beginning in such simple things as incorrect walking or faulty posture or breathing, are due to the fact that people have all their lives walked, to take only one simple illustration, as though they were machines, and have never experienced any of the feelings in their feet or legs or rest of the body. The correcting of the malfunction of one's legs, for example, often requires that one learn again to feel what is happening when one walks. In overcoming psychosomatic ills or chronic diseases like tuberculosis, it is essential to learn to "listen to the body" in deciding when to work and when to rest. It is amazing how many hints and guides and intuitions for living come to the sensitive person who has ears to hear what his body is saying. To be tuned to the responses throughout one's body, as well as to be tuned to one's feelings in emotional relations with the world and people around him, is to be on the way to a health which will not break down periodically.

Not only do people separate the body from the self in using it as an instrument for work, but they likewise separate it from the self in their pursuit of pleasure. The body is treated as a vehicle of sensation, from which one can get certain gastronomical pleasures and sexual sensations if skillfully handled, just as though one were tuning a television set. The detached attitude toward sex, which we already noted in a previous chapter, is connected with this tendency to separate the body from the rest of the self. The Kinsey report speaks of the sexual partner as a sexual "object," and in the same vein many persons think in terms of "my sexual *needs* require some outlet," rather than "*I* want and choose sexual relations with this particular person." The tendency to separate sexual activity from the rest of the self is, as everyone knows, illustrated on one hand by the Puritan attitudes. But it is not so widely realized that libertinism, the opposite to Puritanism, commits exactly the same error of separating sex from the self.

We are proposing welcoming the body back into the union with the self. This means as already suggested recovering an active awareness of one's body. It means *experiencing* one's body—the pleasure of eating or resting or the exhilaration of using toned-up muscles or the gratification of sexual impulses and passion—as aspects of the acting self. It is not the attitude of "My *body* feels" but "*I* feel." In sex it is the attitude of experiencing sexual desire and passion as one aspect of interpersonal relationships. Separating sex from the rest of the self, indeed, is no more tenable than to isolate one's larynx and speak of "my vocal cords wanting to talk with my friend."

We propose, furthermore, placing the self in the center of the picture of bodily health: it is "I" who grow sick or achieve health. We propose the *active* rather than *passive* voice in illness; the old expression "*I sicken*" is accurate. Fortunately in at least one disease the active verb is still used for the process of getting well—tuberculosis patients say "I *cured*" at such-and-such a sanatorium. We propose that illnesses, whether physical or psychological, be taken not as periodic accidents which occur *to* the body (or *to* the "personality" or "mind"), but as nature's means of re-educating the whole person.

Using illness as re-education is illustrated in a letter a patient with tuberculosis wrote to a friend: "The disease occurred not simply because I overworked, or ran athwart some T.B. bugs, but because I was trying to be something I wasn't. I was living as the 'great extrovert,' running here and there, doing three jobs at once, and leaving undeveloped and unused the side of me which would contemplate, would read and think and 'invite my soul' rather than rushing and working at full speed. The disease comes as a demand and an opportunity to rediscover the lost functions of myself. It is as though the disease were nature's way of saying, 'You must become your whole self. To the extent that you do not, you will be ill; and you will become well only to the extent that you do become yourself.'" We may add that it is an actual clinical fact that some persons, viewing their illnesses as an opportunity for re-education, become more healthy both psychologically and physically, more fulfilled as persons, after a serious illness than before.

Some of the ways that I have kept myself out of touch with by body:

Consulting a clock to see if I have had enough sleep.

Trying to recall how much I have eaten in order to know how much I want to eat now.

Putting on glasses when my eyes hurt (instead of resting them).

Using aspirin and antacids.

Wearing loose clothes so that I won't feel the objectional contours of my body.

Putting thick soles and heels between me and the ground.

Breathing through my mouth (which has no sense of smell).

Using strong chemicals to prevent my body from perspiring and having its natural odor.

Never brushing up against a stranger in a crowd.

Holding myself back from touching people when I talk to them.

Not looking at the parts of another person's body that I want to look at.

H. Prather

The next reading provides us with needed insight about the limitations of our individual perception process. Each of us must rely on the operation of our senses (seeing, feeling, hearing, tasting, and smelling) to perceive things. Johnson highlights the weaknesses of our sense operations and shows that we evaluate all stimuli we receive. Are you aware that you are not objective when you perceive various cues? How can you increase your understanding of yourself by recognizing the personal biases you use as you attach meaning to things?

WENDELL JOHNSON

CERTAIN FUNDAMENTALS OF NONSENSE

One of the most tantalizing truths we know is that there is so much we may never know. Because we can perceive so well the limits of our ability to perceive at all, we know that the most distant regions of our ignorance are destined to remain forever unexplored. We simply cannot overtake the coy horizons of the sea of unawareness that surrounds our modest island of perception. On this fact rests securely the conviction that humility is a vital part of wisdom.

The basic fact to be considered in this connection is that the eyes, ears and other sense organs of the human body are impressively limited in their capacities to respond to stimuli. They are, so to speak, tiny, dusty windows that let in but little of the light of the world. The wave lengths we recognize as light and color are but a small portion of those known plainly and deviously to the physical sciences. The vibrations

From pp. 73–77, 80 ("We have learned . . . thee and me."), and "The Early Morning of the Human Day," Your Most Enchanted Listener, by Wendell Johnson. Copyright © 1956 by Harper & Row, Publishers, Inc. By permission of the publishers.

we register as sound are but a fraction of the full range of air wave frequencies. We smell faintly and erratically, and at the extremes of the narrow range of temperatures to which we are sensitive we quickly die either by freezing or shriveling. Our capacity to discriminate by taste is so slight as to be utterly demoralizing to any but the most tolerant or disillusioned of chefs. And individual peculiarities in these respects are dumbfounding: there are persons who cannot smell a frightened skunk, and others to whom vanilla tastes like strawberries. And all this, of course, is in addition to the fact that a considerable proportion of the human family is either blind or deaf, or nearly so, and large numbers of the rest of us have at least minor sensory impairments. It is as though we were living all our days inside the sealed control room of a spaceship, with vague vibrations from somewhere outside beating faintly and fitfully against our frail antennae.

Moreover, together with the meager direct information we receive from the outside world, we are able to gain through our internal senses only a skimpy set of signals from the complex and continuous events inside our skins. Indeed, we hardly know at any moment what is going on either around us or inside us. The world as we see it, smell it, or sense it in any other way is certainly a patchy picture of the world we would perceive were we equipped with sensory organs responsive to the full range of energy manifestations. Moreover, what little we can sense would appear quite different if only our perceptive apparatus were not so compulsively subject to the laws of illusion.

True, we have indirect inferential knowledge of sorts concerning those portions of energy spectra that we cannot directly sense. We have even learned to make use of many of the unsensed wave frequencies in the operation of radios and other instruments that contribute to our world of sound and sight, or that affect our bodily processes, as in the case of X rays and radioactive isotopes. But to the extent that we take the "naked-eye world" to be reality, we obtain a picture so limited as to be necessarily distorted and untrustworthy. Talking about what we can hear, see, and feel is a far cry from talking about the reality that is independent of our sensory soundings of it.

As a matter of fact, we do not talk much about what we hear, see, or otherwise sense directly. The native Zulu does not see the ghosts he talks about. Nor does the nuclear physicist see the electrons and neutrons about which he speaks. The clergyman has never laid eyes upon the heaven he describes, and no mother has ever directly sensed the "human nature" with which she accounts for the deplorable, or pleasing, behavior of her children.

Even when we do mean to speak about the world as we observe it, we talk largely in terms of our feelings about it or our judgments of it. We do not often *describe* things, persons, and events; we more commonly *evaluate* them as beautiful or good, wise or stupid, ugly or bad. Such words, of course, describe nothing. They express our personal standards and reflect our feelings about whatever we may be responding to.

Not only, then, are we greatly limited in our physical capacity to sense directly the world surrounding us—and the goings-on inside of us—but we also tend to disregard much of what we can, or could, sense. The worlds of words and pictures inside our heads, which we almost always take seriously and to which we feel a nearly deaf and blind loyalty, can hardly be anything other than a mixture of fact and fancy—and we can seldom be quite sure which is which. Moreover, we usually take the "truth" of them so wholly for granted that we rarely wonder, if we ever do, whether they might be misleading and just how they might be made more sane and dependable. As a rule, we speak of the worlds inside our heads with proud confidence that we are talking about the world that is outside.

And we act accordingly. We develop traditions and customs, pass laws, build institutions, formulate foreign policies and personal ways of life based on our largely unexamined mental patchworks. In doing all this we actually create a kind of social reality—a world of stone and steel, national boundaries, international treaties, laws and social customs—which amounts to a great collective self-projection, in which, as it has been said, there is nothing natural about 99 per cent of the things we do [It is a kind of ersatz world in which there is a convincing plausibility about our old codger of a few pages back who said, "Believe in baptism? Of course. I've seen it done."]

A tremendous number of the things we believe in, because we see them done, are done for no other reason except that we believe in them.

It is one of the more curious aspects of all this that, in such a human-made world, common sense involves the delicate art of being just unsane enough to be practical. That is to say, what most clinical psychologists call social adjustment lies in part in the fundamentally negative skill of not making oneself too conspicuous. Good adjustment for any individual, therefore, is generally assumed by these clinical workers to depend more or less on his feeling, thinking, acting pretty much as other people do, of liking what they like, hating what they hate, believing what they believe—and not knowing why. From this point of view, the acquiring of new knowledge and skills, and a heightened consciousness of abstracting and symbolizing, can be hazardous.

It is, in fact, one of the serious risks of education that it tends frequently to alienate the child from his parents, to make it more and more difficult for him to feel at home at home.

To parents as well as teachers, generally speaking, the good child is the one who agrees with them readily and shows no bothersome inclinations to go poking around among the possibilities of making life over into new and unfamiliar designs. Most of us appear to be psychologically discomforted, at least slightly, by appeals from those bent on enlisting us in their missions of social reform. We feel vaguely that slum dwelling, for example, is in some ways more normal than the dissatisfactions its effects arouse in compassionate welfare workers. Even war is evidently widely thought to be more natural than the feeling that it is undesirable. Peace on earth is an ideal to which we contribute generous ceremonial tribute, though not without uneasiness over its disquieting promise of no more fighting.

Believe in Baptism? Of course. I've seen it done.   W. Johnson

---

Edward De Bono has made a major contribution to our understanding of intrapersonal perception. His creative treatment of problem solving is an interesting commentary on our "perceptual prison bars." Most of us approach problems and others with "blinders on our eyes." We use tunnel vision by relying solely on past experiences and impressions for solving problems or making evaluations of others. De Bono asks that we begin approaching experiences and people from a "lateral thinking" perspective. In other words, don't just base all of your impressions on past beliefs—do not just build vertically or "on top" of old ideas. Try to approach experiences in new ways. Be as open minded and accepting as possible—look around, think sideways, be lateral instead of vertical in your approach. The "beautiful teenage daughter" in the following selection serves to illustrate, quite dramatically, De Bono's notions of vertical and lateral thinking.

EDWARD DE BONO

VERTICAL
AND LATERAL
Many years ago when a person who owed
THINKING
money could be thrown into jail, a merchant in London had the misfortune to owe a huge sum to a money-lender. The money-lender, who was old and ugly, fancied the merchant's beautiful teenage daughter. He proposed a bargain. He said he would cancel the merchant's debt if he could have the girl instead.

Both the merchant and his daughter were horrified at the proposal. So the cunning money-lender proposed that they let Providence decide the matter. He told them that he would put a black pebble and a white pebble into an empty money-bag and then the girl would have to pick out one of the pebbles. If she chose the black pebble she would become his wife and her father's debt would be cancelled. If she chose the white pebble she would stay with her father and the debt would still be cancelled. But if she refused to pick out a pebble her father would be thrown into jail and she would starve.

Reluctantly the merchant agreed. They were standing on a pebble-strewn path in the merchant's garden as they talked and the money-lender stooped down to pick up the two pebbles. As he picked up the pebbles the girl, sharp-eyed with fright, noticed that he picked up two black pebbles and put them into the money-bag. He then asked the girl to pick out the pebble that was to decide her fate and that of her father.

Imagine that you are standing on that path in the merchant's garden. What would you have done if you had been the unfortunate girl? If you had had to advise her what would you have advised her to do?

What type of thinking would you use to solve the problem? You may believe that careful logical analysis must solve the problem if there is a solution. This type of thinking is straight-forward vertical thinking. The other type of thinking is lateral thinking.

Vertical thinkers are not usually of much help to a girl in this situation. The way they analyze it, there are three possibilities:

1. The girl should refuse to take a pebble.
2. The girl should show that there are two black pebbles in the bag and expose the money-lender as a cheat.
3. The girl should take a black pebble and sacrifice herself in order to save her father from prison.

From Chapter 1 of **New Think,** *by Edward De Bono, Copyright, 1967 and 1968 by Edward De Bono. Published by Basic Books, Inc., Publishers, New York.*

None of these suggestions is very helpful, for if the girl does not take a pebble her father goes to prison, and if she does take a pebble, then she has to marry the money-lender.

The story shows the difference between vertical thinking and lateral thinking. Vertical thinkers are concerned with the fact that the girl has to take a pebble. Lateral thinkers become concerned with the pebble that is left behind. Vertical thinkers take the most reasonable view of a situation and then proceed logically and carefully to work it out. Lateral thinkers tend to explore all the different ways of looking at something, rather than accepting the most promising and proceeding from that.

The girl in the pebble story put her hand into the money-bag and drew out a pebble. Without looking at it she fumbled and let it fall to the path where it was immediately lost among all the others.

"Oh, how clumsy of me," she said, "but never mind—if you look into the bag you will be able to tell which pebble I took by the color of the one that is left."

Since the remaining pebble is of course black, it must be assumed that she has taken the white pebble, since the money-lender dare not admit his dishonesty. In this way, by using lateral thinking, the girl changes what seems an impossible situation into an extremely advantageous one. The girl is actually better off than if the money-lender had been honest and had put one black and one white pebble into the bag, for then she would have had only an even chance of being saved. As it is, she is sure of remaining with her father and at the same time having his debt cancelled.

Vertical thinking has always been the only respectable type of thinking. In its ultimate form as logic it is the recommended ideal towards which all minds are urged to strive, no matter how far short they fall. Computers are perhaps the best example. The problem is defined by the programmer, who also indicates the path along which the problem is to be explored. The computer then proceeds with its incomparable logic and efficiency to work out the problem. The smooth progression of vertical thinking from one solid step to another solid step is quite different from lateral thinking.

If you were to take a set of toy blocks and build them upwards, each block resting firmly and squarely on the block below it, you would have an illustration of vertical thinking. With lateral thinking the blocks are scattered around. They may be connected to each other loosely or not at all. But the pattern that may eventually emerge can be as useful as the vertical structure.

Lateral thinking is easiest to appreciate when it is seen in action, as in the pebble story. Everyone has come across the sort of problem which seems impossible to solve until suddenly a surprisingly simple solution is revealed. Once it has been thought of, the solution is so obvious that one cannot understand why it was ever so difficult to find. This sort of problem may indeed be difficult to solve so long as vertical thinking is used.

Lateral thinking is not only concerned with problem-solving; it has to do with new ways of looking at things and new ideas of every sort.

If a story like the pebble story is read straight through and the solution given immediately, then the listeners are inclined to wonder what the fuss is about. It is only if there is a pause for the listeners to find the solution for themselves that the difficulty of finding one is appreciated. With the best examples of lateral thinking the solution does seem logically obvious once it has been reached. It is very easy to forget that it has been reached by lateral thinking and not by vertical thinking. Once the solution has been revealed many people are prepared to explain how it could perfectly well have been reached by vertical thinking. In retrospect the logical sequence from the problem to its solution may be quite easy to see.

While in a trance a hypnotized person can be instructed to carry out some bizarre behavior after emerging from the trance. When the time comes the subject duly carries out the hypnotist's instructions, which may have been to put up an umbrella in the drawing-room, to hand everyone a glass of milk, or to drop on all fours and bark like a dog. When asked why he is behaving in this odd way the subject immediately provides a perfectly reasonable explanation. Such an explanation offers an unforgettable demonstration of the powers of rationalization. Everyone present knows the real reason behind the odd behavior and yet the person carrying it out can construct a perfectly reasonable explanation which would convince any late-comer.

There is no harm in rationalizing a vertical-thinking path to the solution after it has been reached by lateral thinking. The danger lies in assuming that because such a path can be constructed in retrospect, all problems can be solved as easily with vertical thinking as they might be with lateral thinking.

One of the techniques of lateral thinking is to make deliberate use of this rationalizing facility of the mind. Instead of proceeding step by step in the usual vertical manner, you take up a new and quite arbitrary position. You then work backwards and try to construct a logical path between this new position and the starting point. Should a path prove possible, it must eventually be tested with the full rigors of logic. If the path is sound, you are then in a useful position which may never have been reached by ordinary vertical thinking. Even if the arbitrary position does not prove tenable, you may still have generated useful new ideas in trying to justify it.

A few people come to like the idea of lateral thinking so much that they try to use it instead of vertical thinking on all occasions. Many more people resent the idea of lateral thinking and insist that vertical thinking is quite sufficient. In fact, the two types of thinking are complementary. When ordinary vertical thinking is unable to find a solution to a problem or when a new idea is required, then lateral thinking should be used. New ideas depend on lateral thinking, for vertical thinking has inbuilt limitations which make it much less effective for this purpose. These limitations of vertical thinking cannot be set aside, for they are its very advantages, looked at from a different point of view.

The functional organization of the mind as an optimizing system makes it interpret a situation in the most probable way. The order of probability is determined by experience and by the needs of the moment. Vertical thinking is high-probability thinking. Without such high-probability thinking, everyday life would be impossible. Every action and every sensation would have to be intensely analyzed and carefully considered—nothing could ever be taken for granted. Like the centipede, confused by self-consciousness, everyone would be incapacitated by complexity. The function of thought is to eliminate itself and allow action to follow directly on recognition of a situation. This is only possible if the most probable interpretation of a situation gives rise to the most probably effective action.

Just as water flows down slopes, settles in hollows and is confined to riverbeds, so vertical thinking flows along the most probable paths and by its very flow increases the probability of those paths for the future. If vertical thinking is high-probability thinking, then lateral thinking is low-probability thinking. New channels are deliberately cut to alter the flow of the water. The old channels are dammed up in the hope that the water will seek out and take to new and better patterns of flow. Sometimes the water is even sucked upwards in an unnatural fashion. When the low-probability line of thought leads to an effective new idea there is a "eureka moment," and at once the low-probability approach acquires the highest probability. It is the moment when the water sucked upward with difficulty forms a siphon and at once flows freely. This moment is always the aim of lateral thinking.

Since lateral thinking is to do with new ideas it would seem to be related to creative thinking. Creative thinking is a special part of lateral thinking which covers a wider field. Sometimes the achievements of lateral thinking are genuine creations, at other times they are nothing more than a new way of looking at things, and hence somewhat less than full creations. Creative thinking often requires a talent for expression, whereas lateral thinking is open to everyone who is interested in new ideas.

In this book creative thinking in the true artistic sense has not been used as an example of lateral thinking because the outcome is too subjective. It is easy to demonstrate the effectiveness of lateral thinking with an invention which either works or does not. It is also easy to decide whether a problem has been effectively solved with lateral thinking. But the value of artistic creative effort is a matter of taste and of fashion.

The further lateral thinking diverges from the rules of reason and vertical thinking, the more it must seem to approach madness. Is lateral thinking only a form of deliberate and temporary madness? Is low-probability thinking any different from the random associations of the schizophrenic? One of the most characteristic features of schizophrenia is the butterfly mind which flits from idea to idea. If one wants to escape temporarily from the obvious way of looking at things, why not use a psychedelic drug? The essential difference is that with lateral thinking the whole process is firmly controlled. If lateral thinking chooses to use chaos it is chaos by direction, not chaos through absence of direction. All the time the logical faculty is waiting to elaborate and eventually judge and select whatever new ideas are generated. The difference between lateral and vertical thinking is that with vertical thinking logic is in control of the mind, whereas with lateral thinking logic is at the service of the mind.

Does a person have a fixed skill in thinking or only as much ability as he has had interest and opportunity to develop? Only a few people have a natural aptitude for lateral thinking, but everyone can develop a certain skill if they set about it deliberately. Orthodox education usually does nothing to encourage lateral thinking habits and positively inhibits them with the need to conform one's way through the successive examination hoops.

Lateral thinking is not a magic formula which can be learned at once and usefully applied thereafter. It is an attitude and a habit of mind. The various techniques described are intended to bring about an awareness of lateral-thinking processes; they are not meant to be used as a problem-solving cook-book. There is no sudden conversion from a belief in the omnipotence of vertical thinking to a belief in the usefulness of lateral thinking. Lateral thinking is a matter of awareness and practice—not revelation.

I hate my daughters' hampsters when
I think about them from my own,
personal viewpoint.

Why?

Because they stink and remind me
of mice and I hate mice—
because they remind me of rats
and I hate rats!

When I think about them from my
daughters' viewpoints, however—
I kinda like the crazy little things.

Why?

Because they remind me of the love
my daughters have for them . . .
J. Wenburg

Jerry and Renny Russell
express a type of "perceptual
freedom" that is refreshing
and moving. By "thinking
laterally" each of us can
experience this type of
perceptual freedom in our
transactions with people as
well as with nature.

JERRY RUSSELL
RENNY RUSSELL

ON THE LOOSE

*Is man the only mourner of wilderness because he is the
    only killer?*
Could we create if we could not destroy?
Would we want knowledge without control?
    Beauty without rape?
Is pastoral man a half-man and love a fiction?
Do I have nothing to blame but the genes in my own body?
Was I just born too late?

NO.
My salvation is that I was not born into the adolescence of my race.
Its beautiful childhood may be gone, but its manhood is now.
Evolution is aware of itself.
*At the last hour of the planting season, the seeds of a universal sanity
    are sown.*

I look at a redwood and don't see board feet.
I look at a river and don't see kilowatt hours.
I look at a lake and don't see an aqueduct.
I look at a marsh and don't see more rotting surplus wheat.
I look at a gorge and don't see a damsite.
I look at a meadow and don't see real estate.
I look at an egret and don't see an absurd feathery hat.

*The early settlers cluck and shake their heads, but the earliest settlers
    are glad.*

INTRAPERSONAL
COMMUNICATION
NONVERBAL BEHAVIOR

I don't want to argue anymore about
how he "is." You see him one way, I see
him another way, he sees himself a third
way. Now if you want to talk about
what how we see him indicates about
us. . . .   H. Prather

From Hugh Prather, *Notes to Myself*. Reprinted
by permission of Real People Press.

Many scholars assert that most of the meaning a person acquires
in a communication transaction is transmitted to him through
nonverbal communication cues. The old adage, "It's not *what* you
say, it's *how* you say it," highlights the importance of nonverbal
cues. We consider nonverbal communication to be all of the cues
other than the actual words that exist in a communication transaction.

Factors such as the way you sit, the way you move, the tone
of your voice, and the way you dress are some of the many nonverbal cues that exist in all oral communication transactions. Although one might not consider these factors to be important in
intrapersonal communication, they can have a definite impact on
the way one communicates with himself. Note, for example, in
the following reading by Richard E. Byrd, how several nonverbal
stimuli such as thirst, pain, and fire completely control his communication with himself.

RICHARD E. BYRD

JUNE I:

DESPAIR
June 1st was a Friday. A black Friday for me. The nightmare left me, and about 9 o'clock in the morning I awakened with a violent start, as if I had been thrown down a well in my sleep. I found myself staring wildly into the darkness of the shack, not knowing where I was. The weakness that filled my body when I turned in the sleeping bag and tried to throw the flashlight on my wrist watch was an eloquent reminder. I was Richard E. Byrd, United States Navy. (Ret.), temporarily sojourning at Latitude 80° 08' South, and not worth a damn to myself or anybody else. My mouth was dry and tasted foul. God, I was thirsty. But I had hardly strength to move. I clung to the sleeping bag, which was the only source of comfort and warmth left to me, and mournfully debated the little that might be done.

Two facts stood clear. One was that my chances of recovering were slim. The other was that in my weakness I was incapable of taking care of myself. These were desperate conclusions, but my mood allowed no others. All that I could reasonably hope for was to prolong my existence for a few days by hoarding my remaining resources; by doing the necessary things *very slowly* and with *great deliberation*. So long as he did that and maintained the right frame of mind, even a very ill man should be able to last a time. So I reasoned, anyway. There was no alternative. My hopes of survival had to be staked on the theory.

But you must have *faith*—you must have faith in the outcome, I whispered to myself. It is like a flight, a flight into another unknown. You start and you cannot turn back. You must go on and on and on, trusting your instruments, the course you have plotted on the charts, and the reasonableness of events. Whatever goes wrong will be mostly of your own making; if it is to be tragedy, then it will be the commonplace tragedy of human vulnerability.

My first need was warmth and food. The fire had been out about twelve hours; I had not eaten in nearly thirty-six. Toward providing those necessities I began to mobilize my slender resources. If there had been a movie camera to record my movements, the resulting picture could have been passed off as slow motion. Every act was performed with the utmost patience. I lifted the lantern—and waited. I edged out of the sleeping bag—and rested on the chair beside the stove. I pulled on my pants, hiking them up a little bit at a time. Then the shirt. Then the socks. And shoes. And finally the parka. All this took a long time. I was shaking so from the cold that, when my elbow struck the wall, the sound was like a peremptory knock at the door. Too miserable to stick it out, I retreated to the sleeping bag; half an hour later the chill in my body drove me into a fresh attempt to reach the stove.

Faintless seized me as I touched foot to the floor. I barely made the chair. There I sat for some minutes, not moving, just staring at the candle. Then I turned the valve, and with the stove lids off waited for the wick to become saturated with the cold, sluggish oil. Thirst continued to plague me. Several inches of ice were in the water bucket. I dropped it on the floor, bottom up. A sliver of ice fell out, which I sucked until my teeth rattled from the cold. A box of matches was on the table. I touched one to the burner. A red flame licked over the metal ring; it was a beautiful thing to see. I sat there ten or fifteen minutes at least, absorbing the column of warmth. The flame burned red and smoky, when it should have been blue and clear; and, studying it, I knew that this was from faulty combustion and was one source of my misfortunes. This fire was my enemy, but I could not live without it.

Thus this never-ending day began. To describe it all would be tedious. Nothing really happened; and yet, no day in my life was more momentous. I lived a thousand years, and all of them were agonizing. I won a little and lost a lot. At the day's end—if it can be said to have had an end—all that I could say was that I was still alive. Granting the conditions, I had no right to expect more. Life seldom ends gracefully or sensibly. The protesting body succumbs like a sinking ship going down with the certificate of seaworthiness nailed fast to the wheelhouse bulkhead; but the mind, like the man on the bridge, realizes at last the weakness of the hull and ponders the irony. If the business drags out long enough, as mine did, the essence of things in time becomes pitifully clear; except that by then it is wadded into a tight little scrap ready to be thrown away, as the knowledge is of no earthly use.

My thirst was the tallest tree in a forest of pain. The Escape Tunnel was a hundred miles away, but I started out, carrying the bucket and lantern. Somewhere along the way I slipped and fell. I licked the snow until my tongue burned. The Escape Tunnel was too far. But in the food tunnel my boots had worn a rut eighteen inches wide and six inches deep, which was full of loose snow. The snow was dirty, but I scraped the bucket along until it was nearly full, then pulled it into the shack, a foot or so at a time.

Snow took a long time to melt in the bucket, and I could not wait. I poured a little into a pan and heated it with alcohol tablets. It was still a soggy mass of snow when I raised it to my lips. My hands were shaking, and the water spilled down the front of my parka; then I vomited, and all that I had drunk came up. In a little while I tried again, taking sips too small to be thrown up. Then I crawled on top of the sleeping bag, drawing a heavy blanket over my shoulders, hoping I should somehow regain strength.

Nevertheless, I was able to do a number of small things, in a series of stealthy, deliberate sorties from the bunk. I attended to the inside thermograph and register, changing the sheets, winding the clocks, and inking the pens. The outlet ventilator was two-thirds filled with ice; I could just reach it from the bunk with a stick which had a big nail in the end. After every exertion I rested; the pain in my arms and back and head was almost crucifying. I filled a thermos jug with warm water, added powdered milk and sugar, and carried the jug into the sleeping bag. My stomach crawled with nauseous sensations; but, by taking a teaspoonful at a time, I finally managed to get a cupful down. After a while the weakness left me, and I felt strong enough to start for the instrument shelter. I reached the hatch and pushed it open, but could go no farther. The night was a gray fog, full of shadows, like my mood. In the shack I lost the milk I had drunk. On the verge of fainting, I made for the bunk.

*

I won't even attempt to recall all the melancholy thoughts that drifted through my mind that long afternoon. But I can say truthfully that at no time did I have any feeling of resignation. My whole being rebelled against my low estate. As the afternoon wore on, I felt myself sinking. Now I became alarmed. This was not the first time I had ever faced death. It had confronted me many times in the air. But then it had seemed altogether different. In flying things happen fast: you make a decision; the verdict crowds you instantly; and, when the invisible and neglected passenger comes lunging into the cockpit, he is but one of countless distractions. But now death was a stranger sitting in a darkened room, secure in the knowledge that he would be there when I was gone.

Great waves of fear, a fear I had never known before, swept through me and settled deep within. But it wasn't the fear of suffering or even of death itself. It was a terrible anxiety over the consequences to those at home if I failed to return. I had done a damnable thing in going to Advance Base, I told myself. Also, during those hours of bitterness, I saw my whole life pass in review. I realized how wrong my sense of values had been and how I had failed to see that the simple, homely, unpretentious things of life are the most important.

Much as I should have liked to, I couldn't consider myself a martyr to science; nor could I blame the circumstances that had prevented staffing the base with three men, according to the original plan. I had gone there looking for peace and enlightenment, thinking that they might in some way enrich my life and make me a more useful man. I had also gone armed with the justification of a scientific mission. Now I saw both for what they really were: the first as a delusion, the second as a dead end street. My thoughts turned to gall and wormwood. I was bitter toward the whole world except my family and friends. The clocks ticked on in the gloom, and a subdued whir came from the register at my feet. The confidence implicit in these unhurried sounds emphasized my own debasement. What right had they to be confident and unhurried? Without me they could not last a day.

The one aspiration I still had was to be vindicated by the tiny heap of data collected on the shelf in the Escape Tunnel. But, even as I seized upon this, I recognized its flimsiness; a romanticized rationalization, as are most of the things which men are anxious to be judged by. We men of action who serve science serve only a reflection in a mirror. The tasks are difficult, the objectives remote; but scholars sitting in bookish surroundings tell us where to go, what to look for, and even what we are apt to find. Likewise, they pass dispassionate judgment on whatever we bring back. We are nothing more than glamorous middlemen between theory and fact, materialists jobbing in the substance of universal truths.

Beyond the fact that I had suffered to secure them, what did I know about the theoretical significance of the records in the Escape Tunnel, of the implications which might differentiate them from a similar heap of records gathered at Keokuk? I really didn't know. I was a fool, lost on a fool's errand, and that was how I should be judged.

At the end only two things really matter to a man, regardless of who he is; and they are the affection and understanding of his family. Anything and everything else he creates are insubstantial; they are ships given over to the mercy of the winds and tides of prejudice. But the family is an everlasting anchorage, a quiet harbor where a man's ships can be left to swing to the moorings of pride and loyalty.

---

*Congenial to other people? It is with
yourself that you must live.*
D. Hammarskjold

Edgar Allen Poe's *Tell-Tale Heart* provides us with a dramatic example of the potential impact that non-verbal cues can have on the intrapersonal communication process. The madman portrayed in this story is insanely obsessed with his own perception of a single nonverbal element in his immediate environment—an old man's eye. Later, he is completely controlled by the imaginary nonverbal stimulus of the "beating of a hideous heart." Can you recall incidents in your own life where some nonverbal cue dominated your intrapersonal communication? Have you, for example, ever been so angry or upset that you were not able to think of anything else?

EDGAR ALLAN POE

THE TELL-TALE HEART

True!—nervous—very, very dreadfully nervous I had been and am; but why *will* you say that I am mad? The disease had sharpened my senses—not destroyed—not dulled them. Above all was the sense of hearing acute. I heard all things in the heaven and in the earth. I heard many things in hell. How, then, am I mad? Hearken! and observe how healthy—how calmly I can tell you the whole story.

It is impossible to say how first the idea entered my brain; but once conceived, it haunted me day and night. Object there was none. Passion there was none. I loved the old man. He had never wronged me. He had never given me insult. For his gold I had no desire. I think it was his eye! yes, it was this! One of his eyes resembled that of a vulture—a pale blue eye, with a film over it. Whenever it fell upon me, my blood ran cold; and so by degrees—very gradually—I made up my mind to take the life of the old man, and thus rid myself of the eye for ever.

Now this is the point. You fancy me mad. Madmen know nothing. But you should have seen *me*. You should have seen how wisely I proceeded—with what caution—with what foresight—with what dissimulation I went to work! I was never kinder to the old man than during the whole week before I killed him. And every night, about midnight, I turned the latch of his door and opened it—oh, so gently! And then, when I had made an opening sufficient for my head, I put in a dark lantern, all closed, closed, so that no light shone out, and then I thrust in my head. Oh, you would have laughed to see how cunningly I thrust it in! I moved it slowly—very, very slowly, so that I might not disturb the old man's sleep. It took me an hour to place my whole head within the opening so far that I could see him as he lay upon his bed. Ha!—would a madman have been so wise as this? And then, when my head was well in the room, I undid the lantern cautiously—oh, so cautiously—cautiously (for the hinges creaked) —I undid it just so much that a single thin ray fell upon the vulture eye. And this I did for seven long nights—every night just at midnight —but I found the eye always closed; and so it was impossible to do the work; for it was not the old man who vexed me, but his Evil Eye. And every morning, when the day broke, I went boldly into the chamber, and spoke courageously to him, calling him by name in a hearty tone, and inquiring how he had passed the night. So you see he would have been a very profound old man, indeed, to suspect that every night, just at twelve, I looked in upon him while he slept.

Upon the eighth night I was more than usually cautious in opening the door. A watch's minute hand moves more quickly than did mine. Never before that night, had I *felt* the extent of my own powers—of my sagacity. I could scarcely contain my feelings of triumph. To think that there I was, opening the door, little by little, and he not even to dream of my secret deeds or thoughts. I fairly chuckled at the idea; and perhaps he heard me; for he moved on the bed suddenly, as if startled. Now you may think that I drew back— but no. His room was as black as pitch with the thick darkness, (for the shutters were close fastened, through fear of robbers,) and so I knew that he could not see the opening of the door, and I kept pushing it on steadily, steadily.

I had my head in, and was about to open the lantern, when my thumb slipped upon the tin fastening, and the old man sprang up in the bed, crying out—"Who's there?"

I kept quite still and said nothing. For a whole hour I did not move a muscle, and in the mean time I did not hear him lie down. He was still sitting up in the bed, listening;—just as I have done, night after night, hearkening to the death watches in the wall.

Presently I heard a slight groan, and I knew it was the groan of mortal terror. It was not a groan of pain or of grief—oh, no!—it was the low stifled sound that arises from the bottom of the soul when overcharged with awe. I knew the sound well. Many a night, just at midnight, when all the world slept, it has welled up from my own bosom, deepening, with its dreadful echo, the terrors that distracted me. I say I knew it well. I knew what the old man felt, and pitied him, although I chuckled at heart. I knew that he had been lying awake ever since the first slight noise, when he had turned in the bed. His fears had been ever since growing upon him. He had been trying to fancy them causeless, but could not. He had been saying to himself —"It is nothing but the wind in the chimney—it is only a mouse crossing the floor," or "it is merely a cricket which has made a single chirp." Yes, he has been trying to comfort himself with these suppositions: but he had found all in vain. *All in vain;* because Death, in approaching him, had stalked with his black shadow before him, and enveloped the victim. And it was the mournful influence of the unperceived shadow that caused him to feel—although he neither saw nor heard—to *feel* the presence of my head within the room.

When I had waited a long time, very patiently, without hearing him lie down, I resolved to open a little—a very, very little crevice in the lantern. So I opened it—you cannot imagine how stealthily, stealthily—until, at length, a single dim ray, like the thread of the spider, shot from out the crevice and fell upon the vulture eye.

It was open—wide, wide open—and I grew furious as I gazed upon it. I saw it with perfect distinctness—all a dull blue, with a hideous veil over it that chilled the very marrow in my bones; but I could see nothing else of the old man's face or person: for I had directed the ray as if by instinct, precisely upon the damned spot.

And now have I not told you that what you mistake for madness is but over acuteness of the senses?—now, I say, there came to my ears a low, dull, quick sound, such as a watch makes when enveloped in cotton. I knew *that* sound well, too. It was the beating of the old man's heart. It increased my fury, as the beating of a drum stimulates the soldier into courage.

But even yet I refrained and kept still. I scarcely breathed. I held the lantern motionless. I tried how steadily I could maintain the ray upon the eye. Meantime the hellish tattoo of the heart increased. It grew quicker and quicker, and louder and louder every instant. The old man's terror *must* have been extreme! It grew louder, I say, louder every moment!—do you mark me well? I have told you that I am nervous: so I am. And now at the dead hour of the night, amid the dreadful silence of that old house, so strange a noise as this excited me to uncontrollable terror. Yet, for some minutes longer I refrained and stood still. But the beating grew louder, louder! I thought the heart must burst. And now a new anxiety seized me—the sound would be heard by a neighbor! The old man's hour had come! With a loud yell, I threw open the lantern and leaped into the room. He shrieked once—once only. In an instant I dragged him to the floor, and pulled the heavy bed over him. I then smiled gaily, to find the deed so far done. But, for many minutes, the heart beat on with a muffled sound. This, however, did not vex me; it would not be heard through the wall. At length it ceased. The old man was dead. I removed the bed and examined the corpse. Yes, he was stone, stone dead. I placed my hand upon the heart and held it there many minutes. There was no pulsation. He was stone dead. His eye would trouble me no more.

If still you think me mad, you will think so no longer when I describe the wise precautions I took for the concealment of the body. The night waned, and I worked hastily, but in silence. First of all I dismembered the corpse. I cut off the head and the arms and the legs.

I then took up three planks from the flooring of the chamber, and deposited all between the scantings. I then replaced the boards so cleverly, so cunningly, that no human eye—not even *his*—could have detected any thing wrong. There was nothing to wash out—no stain of any kind—no blood-spot whatever. I had been too wary for that. A tub had caught all—ha! ha!

When I had made an end of these labors, it was four o'clock—still dark as midnight. As the bell sounded the hour, there came a knocking at the street door. I went down to open it with a light heart,—for what had I *now* to fear? There entered three men, who introduced themselves, with perfect suavity, as officers of the police. A shriek had been heard by a neighbor during the night; suspicion of foul play had been aroused; information had been lodged at the police office, and they (the officers) had been deputed to search the premises.

I smiled,—for *what* had I to fear? I bade the gentlemen welcome. The shriek, I said, was my own in a dream. The old man I mentioned, was absent in the country. I took my visitors all over the house. I bade them search—search *well*. I led them, at length, to *his* chamber. I showed them his treasures, secure, undisturbed. In the enthusiasm of my confidence, I brought chairs into the room, and desired them *here* to rest from their fatigues, while I myself, in the wild audacity of my perfect triumph, placed my own seat upon the very spot beneath which reposed the corpse of the victim.

The officers were satisfied. My *manner* had convinced them. I was singularly at ease. They sat, and while I answered cheerily, they chatted of familiar things. But, ere long, I felt myself getting pale and wished them gone. My head ached, and I fancied a ringing in my ears: but still they sat and still chatted. The ringing became more distinct: —it continued and became more distinct: I talked more freely to get rid of the feeling: but it continued and gained definitiveness—until, at length, I found that the noise was *not* within my ears.

No doubt I now grew *very* pale;—but I talked more fluently, and with a heightened voice. Yet the sound increased—and what could I do? It was *a low, dull, quick sound—much such a sound as a watch makes when enveloped in cotton.* I gasped for breath—and yet the officers heard it not. I talked more quickly—more vehemently; but the noise steadily increased. I arose and argued about trifles, in a high key and with violent gesticulations; but the noise steadily increased. Why *would* they not be gone? I paced the floor to and fro with heavy strides, as if excited to fury by the observations of the men—but the noise steadily increased. Oh God! what *could* I do? I foamed—I raved—I swore! I swung the chair upon which I had been sitting, and grated it upon the boards, but the noise arose over all and continually increased. It grew louder—louder—*louder!* And still the men chatted pleasantly, and smiled. Was it possible they heard not? Almighty God! —no, no! They heard!—they suspected!—they *knew!*—they were making a mockery of my horror!—this I thought, and this I think. But anything was better than this agony! Anything was more tolerable than this derision! I could bear those hypocritical smiles no longer! I felt that I must scream or die!—and now—again!—hark! louder! louder! *louder!*—

"Villains!" I shrieked, "dissemble no more! I admit the deed!— tear up the planks!—here, here!—it is the beating of his hideous heart!"

In the "Need To Be Silent"
excerpt that follows, Dominick
Barbara makes several points
that are related to the
importance of nonverbal cues
in intrapersonal communi-
cation. Each of us can
probably identify with
Barbara's notions about the
need for silence and the
threatening nature of silence.
Being able to cope with
silence, however, can help us
do more than "just listen to
what is said openly"; it can
help us notice the nonverbal
"subtle impressions which are
made upon us" when we
attempt to communicate
intrapersonally.

DOMINICK A. BARBARA

THE
NEED TO BE
SILENT

In our society today, whether to talk or to keep quiet is a most perplexing choice. Silence, to too many of us, is frightening and something to be avoided at all costs, while the urge to talk for talk's sake is a familiar compulsion. We often talk, to repeat, merely for the sake of hearing our own words. We engage in all sorts of verbal pronouncements and discussions about anything and everything. Yet we dread remaining silent!

Silence is golden, yet should you be labeled as a silent person, you may run the risk of being considered as a "quiet type"—a bore. On keeping quiet, Doctor Crane once wrote in his daily newspaper column, "We muff many golden opportunities to gladden the lonely hearts and inflate the ego of deserving folks who are discouraged by lack of friendly praise. . . . God expects all Christians to be good salesmen. And salesmen are not noted for being tongue-tied."

From Dominick A. Barbara, How to Make People Listen to You. Copyright © 1971. Courtesy of Charles C. Thomas, Publisher, Springfield, Illinois.

In conversing with each other and in order to achieve better understanding, it is essential that at times *we keep silent*. Today many of us tend to live on the periphery of our lives because of our *fear of becoming silent* and of having to listen to the realities and to the truth of the matter.

In not being silent, we tend to place a barrage of words between ourselves and any true awareness of reality. We camouflage the true perception of things with falsities and built-up notions. On the other hand, should we become silent, we can then have the courage to search actively and constructively within ourselves for the truth about our actual limitations as well as our real assets and potentialities.

In order to promote inner growth and healthy relatedness, we must become objective enough to develop the capacity and the desire to examine ourselves critically, to understand and to reshape our values, attitudes, and beliefs. To do so, we must have the courage to remain silent so that we listen without distractions and without prejudice, condemnation, or colored judgments. Once we approximate this attitude, we may then be able to experience and perceive the *real truth of the matter as it is, and not as we feel it should be.*

Listening to one's self at times is difficult because of man's aversion to being alone with himself. To many of us a quiet evening at home or time spent in quiet reflection is considered as something to be avoided at all costs. In modern society, the fear of being alone and silent is so frightening that any activity or meaningless pursuit, regardless of its value or purpose, is preferable.

We have been led to believe since early childhood that speech is civilization and that silence isolates. Society is moving so fast nowadays that to pause and reflect on one's self is often misconstrued as falling behind the times. Our uppermost aim in life is action; inactivity or silence is frowned upon.

Silence has a particular healing and is curative in certain intimate situations. Many times, after a most painful emotional experience, words prove inadequate and so we feel forced to remain silent and to meditate. The sudden death of a loved one, the onset of a serious illness to ourselves or to someone near us, an unexpected calamity—any one of which may bring about in us a state of emotional shock and a subsequent need to protect ourselves by withdrawing into ourselves and becoming silent. As H. G. Wells once said, "Words are sometimes only spoken to break the tension of silence, or to evade the conspiracy of silence."

The Bible teaches us to be silent so that we may have an opportunity to listen with the ears of the soul. Silent reverence and meditation is of great importance in many religious groups. A number of monastic orders require their members to maintain complete silence on the assumption that meaningless talk damages the soul. The Quakers, for instance, experience the initial moments of a silence as a unifying element and the revelations of the creative unconscious. To many, the act of prayer is productive only when it takes place in an atmosphere of silence. This is essential to protect us from disturbing noises and thoughts which usually interfere with the necessary and essential penetration into the depths of our "being."

In Buddhism, the ultimate wisdom is Nirvana, which means the bringing of one's self to a minimum of desire and will. The less the will is excited, according to the Buddhists, the less one suffers. However, through silence and meditation, so they believe, "the perfect calm of the spirit, deep rest, and inviolable confidence and serenity" are achieved.

If we are to understand and know ourselves better, we must discipline ourselves to be silent more often and learn how to listen more effectively. In attempting to seek to comprehend the true feelings and communications within ourselves, we must be able to probe further into our inner conscience. To do so, it is not enough to just listen to what is said openly. Instead we must go deeper into our feelings and thoughts, decoding the subtle impressions which are made upon us, and finally attempting to be quiet and alone with our innermost thoughts, feelings, wishes, and desires. In short, the most productive way of penetrating into our secret minds is by remaining silent and by listening holistically. In that way we shall gain a better and more realistic understanding of ourselves, and this stimulates a vital interest and an active curiosity about ourselves and the outside world.

Happy is the hearing man, unhappy the speaking man. As long as I hear the truth, I am bathed by nature. The suggestions are thousandfold that I hear and see. The waters of the great deep have ingress and egress to the soul. But if I speak, I define, I confine, and I am less.   R. W. Emerson

---

The following discussion of
personal space by Julius Fast
seems particularly relevant to
nonverbal communication in
the intrapersonal arena. The
need for personal space is
quite demanding, and the
violation of that space is
extremely disrupting. As you
read this selection, think of
how you handle personal
space and what types of
nonverbal cues you use to
define that space.

JULIUS FAST

HOW WE HANDLE SPACE

A Space To Call Your Own

Among Quakers, the story is told of an urban Friend who visited a
Meeting House in a small country town. Though fallen into disuse, it
was architecturally a lovely building, and the city Quaker decided to
visit it for Sunday meeting although he was told that only one or two
Quakers still attended meetings there.

That Sunday he entered the building to find the meeting hall completely empty, the morning sun shafting through the old, twelve-paned
windows, the rows of benches silent and unoccupied.

He slipped into a seat and sat there, letting the peaceful silence
fill him. Suddenly he heard a slight cough and, looking up, saw a
bearded Quaker standing near his bench, an old man who might well
have stepped out of the pages of history.

He smiled, but the old Quaker frowned and coughed again, then
said, "Forgive me if I offend, but thee art sitting in my place."

The old man's quaint insistence on his own space, in spite of the empty meeting house, is amusing, but very true to life. Invariably, after you attend any church for any period of time, you stake out your own spot.

In his home Dad has his own particular chair, and while he may tolerate a visitor sitting there, it is often with poor grace. Mom has her own kitchen, and she doesn't like it one bit when her mother comes to visit and takes over "her" kitchen.

Men have their favorite seats in the train, their favorite benches in the park, their favorite chairs at conferences, and so on. It is all a need for territory, for a place to call one's own. Perhaps it is an inborn and universal need, though it is shaped by society and culture into a variety of forms. An office may be adequate for a working man or it may be too small, not according to the actual size of the room but according to placement of desk and chair. If the worker can lean back without touching a wall or a bookcase, it will usually seem big enough. But in a larger room, if his desk is placed so that he touches a wall when he leans back, the office may seem to be cramped from his viewpoint.

A Science Called Proxemics

Dr. Edward T. Hall, professor of anthropology at Northwestern University, has long been fascinated by man's reaction to the space about him, by how he utilizes that space and how his spatial use communicates certain facts and signals to other men. As Dr. Hall studied man's personal space, he coined the word *proxemics* to describe his theories and observations about zones of territory and how we use them.

Man's use of space, Dr. Hall believes, has a bearing on his ability to relate to other people, to sense them as being close or far away. Every man, he says, has his own territorial needs. Dr. Hall has broken these needs down in an attempt to standardize the science of proxemics and he has come up with four distinct zones in which most men operate. He lists these zones as 1) intimate distance, 2) personal distance, 3) social distance and 4) public distance.

As we might guess, the zones simply represent different areas we move in, areas that increase as intimacy decreases. Intimate distance can either be *close*, that is, actual contact, or *far*, from six to eighteen inches. The close phase of intimate distance is used for making love, for very close friendships and for children clinging to a parent or to each other.

When you are at *close intimate* distance you are overwhelmingly aware of your partner. For this reason, if such contact takes place between two men, it can lead to awkwardness or uneasiness. It is most natural between a man and a woman on intimate terms. When a man and a woman are not on intimate terms the close intimate situation can be embarrassing.

Between two women in our culture, a close intimate state is acceptable, while in an Arab culture such a state is acceptable between two men. Men will frequently walk hand in hand in Arab and in many Mediterranean lands.

The far phase of intimate distance is still close enough to clasp hands, but it is not considered an acceptable distance for two adult male Americans. When a subway or an elevator brings them into such crowded circumstances, they will automatically observe certain rigid rules of behavior, and by doing so communicate with their neighbors.

They will hold themselves as stiff as possible trying not to touch any part of their neighbors. If they do touch them, they either draw away or tense their muscles in the touching area. This action says, "I beg your pardon for intruding on your space, but the situation forces it and I will, of course, respect your privacy and let nothing intimate come of this."

If, on the other hand, they were to relax in such a situation and let their bodies move easily against their neighbors' bodies and actually enjoy the contact and the body heat, they would be committing the worst possible social blunder.

I have often seen a woman in a crowded subway car turn on an apparently innocent man and snarl, "Don't do that!" simply because the man had forgotten the rules and had relaxed against her. The snarls are worse when a man relaxes against another man.

Nor must we, in the crowded car or elevator, stare. There is a stated time interval during which we can look, and then we must quickly look away. The unwary male who goes beyond the stated time interval risks all sorts of unpleasant consequences.

I rode an elevator down in a large office building recently with another man. A pretty young girl got on at the fourteenth floor, and my friend looked at her absently but thoroughly. She grew redder and redder, and when the elevator stopped at the lobby, turned and snapped, "Haven't you ever seen a girl before, you—you dirty old man!"

My friend, still in his thirties, turned to me bewilderedly as she stormed out of the car and asked, "What did I do? Tell me, what the hell did I do?"

What he had done was to break a cardinal rule of nonverbal communication. "Look, and let your eyes slide away when you are in far intimate contact with a stranger."

The second zone of territory charted by Dr. Hall is called the *personal* distance zone. Here, too, he differentiates two areas, a *close personal* distance and a *far personal* distance. The close area is one and a half to two and a half feet. You can still hold or grasp your partner's hand at this distance.

As to its significance, he notes that a wife can stay within the close personal distance zone of her husband, but if another woman moves into this zone she presumably has designs on him. And yet this is obviously the comfortable distance at cocktail parties. It allows a certain intimacy and perhaps describes an intimate zone more than a personal zone. But since these are simply attempts by Dr. Hall to standardize a baby science, there may be a dozen clarifications before proxemics gets off the ground.

The far phase of personal distance, Dr. Hall puts at two and one half to four feet and calls this the limit of physical domination. You cannot comfortable touch your partner at this distance, and so it lends a certain privacy to any encounter. Yet the distance is close enough so that some degree of personal discussion can be held. When two people meet in the street, they usually stop at this distance from each other to chat. At a party they may tend to close in to the close phase of personal disance.

A variety of messages are transmitted by this distance and they range from, "I am keeping you at arm's length," to "I have singled you out to be a little closer than the other guests." To move too far in when you are on a *far personal* relationship with an acquaintance is considered pushy, or, depending on the sexual arrangement, a sign of personal favor. You make a statement with your distance, but the statement, to mean anything, must be followed up.

INTRAPERSONAL COMMUNICATION
BARRIERS

Anything that affects a communication transaction is a potential communication barrier. We classify those elements that have a negative or disruptive influence on a communication experience as barriers. The existence of a nonverbal cue, for example, can be a communication barrier if it calls too much attention to itself. On the other hand, that same cue might enhance instead of disrupt the process. Thus, virtually all stimuli may be classified as possible communication barriers.

Some factors frequently emerge as barriers in the intrapersonal arena. We have selected readings that discuss several of those factors. The first selection, "The Sweet Uses of Solitude," stresses how the presence of other people may enhance or thwart intrapersonal communication. In the article, Joan Mills stresses the need to be able to be alone at times in order to engage in meaningful intrapersonal communication transactions.

JOAN MILLS

THE SWEET
USES OF SOLITUDE Sometimes it's best to be in company—
sometimes better yet to be alone. I believe in both, and when I am sur-
feited with one, I feel compelled to the other. My pleasures come point-
counterpoint.

Whenever I am locked into a series of days with a friend or relative—beloved, yes, but who will not, will *not*, let go—panic rises in me.
"I must write a letter," I say, fleeing to my room. The other stands outside my door, relentlessly relaying the news about Berlioz, urban re-
newal, corn cures, her analysis. I claw the sheets, or hang out the
window, panting.

Or I am too much alone. No one comes near. No friend is at home
to answer my call or hear me knock, and I need a human contact. I go
to market and engage the vegetable man in a discussion of his broccoli;
I take the car to the gas station where I am called "dearie" and feel
wanted.

In the ordinary rhythm of my life, it's easy to balance society and
solitude. At the far side of every week spent in great part by myself,
there is a weekend overflowing with friends and family. When enough
of that is quite enough, Monday comes. Then everyone is gone but me.

On Monday mornings, I wander through unpeopled rooms, listening to the large, soft silence, giving myself over to being all alone. It is
like a return to having a very private place in which to know oneself,
and grow.

Children make such retreats for themselves. A towering old pine
stands between woods and meadow near our house. Among its
branches, in green obscurity, our two sons long ago built a deck of
boards now weathered black. I imagine—for I never violated that privacy to see—that they created fanciful adventures there, or sprawled,
lax and dreamy, breathing the summer air, sorting sounds, coming to
friendly terms with bugs, and brooding upon the stately drift of clouds.

The loved place of my own childhood was a packing box. A piano
had come in it; then it was painted and installed under a tree. No adult
cared to take the long walk through burs and dusty grass to where it
sat. No other child lived near enough to spy upon, envy or ask to share
its alluring privacy.

Daylight sank through leaves and entered the box by a window my

50

father had cut and I had curtained with thumbtacked squares of chintz. The door was scaled to my size, open often to the sun or shut against the occasional leak of rain down the layers of golden willow.

A quilt within was wadded into lumps that fitted me—its calico pattern dimmed by an overprint of jam and chocolate, pollen smudges, crayon streaks and berry stains. It was a *lived-in* quilt, and tucked into its hollows were many comforts: a rag doll floppily amenable to any scheme of mine, a pair of high heels to wear when I read adult literature, pebbles of satisfying shapes, a magnifying glass that made ants look alarming, and a harmonica that in the house drove my mother mad because I mostly kept it in my mouth and breathed two-notedly through it, in and out, absorbed in other things.

In the packing box, I was free to think about whatever pleased or puzzled me, which was considerable. I hummed homemade tunes, read books soft-spined from loving use. I arranged bouquets of bluets or buttercups in season, and chewed ruminatively on the sweet centers of clover blossoms. I solaced myself for what I did not have by imagining I had it—and thereby learned how little I needed to be happy. Every scent or sound or touch of air or prick of thought lightly reverberated, and added to the sum of me and all I knew.

My children have outgrown their secret, special places—and certainly so have I. But the feel of what those hidey-holes meant to us lingers, incorporated into the privacy we keep intact within ourselves. Even in company, we can withdraw to that when the need is on us: how often have I, deep in my thoughts, been unaware of the blathering of television, the boys racketing up and down the stairs, the girl squealing into the telephone.

Sometimes we move by only a little out of the immediacy of persons. I linger at the window that frames my favorite view or go out to look for mushrooms I daren't pick and eat. My husband skis for the sake of experience enjoyed alone and comes home happy for warmth and sociability. Our daughter takes to her car, the boys to their rooms. Each, in his own time, returns to be with people.

To be with people.

"I cannot bear to be lonely," I say, and it is true. My heart thrives upon the talk—and silences—by which we communicate with a near but always separate and different other. I like to close the distance with a touch of the hand; it reassures me. But I was a solitary child, and the habit of solitude is strong in me, too. I'm grateful that once a year or so my husband grants me a reserve of privacy by taking the children and himself away for a few days.

When they have gone, I neaten the house at once. The setting must be serene for the weightless, ruleless, easeful hours that are mine to spend. Beyond the tidying, I make no plans. That's the glory part.

No one knows if I am up and functioning, or if I am shamelessly snoring at noon. I can type at midnight, and nobody comes to glare and mutter. No one bangs on the bathroom door when I linger long in the tub, turning the hot water on and off with my toes and sloshing deliciously. No critic comments upon my working at crewel through the supper hour and dining much later by the flickering light of the late show.

Ah, my friends, it is grand.

Alone, but not lonely, I postulate philosophies, explore my soul, and, in the modesty of solitude, expose my love and angers, wishes and disappointments. I examine each, and put it in its place. Alone, I redefine my appreciation of the people with whom I live. I remember which child it is that keeps me womanly company when I cook, which it is that has displayed an unexpected tenderness or gallantry. I grin at discovering a boy's snorkeling gear hung beside the bathtub, reminding me that I am not the only one who lives here or, indeed, the only one prone to act out fantasies. Luxuriating in a bed to myself, I think of how companionable it is at other times to have somebody to talk to in the dark.

Time passes. I begin to mind being alone. Not much, at first, but some. Then more. "Well," I think, "maybe I should bake a pie for when they come home." And I do.

Then, suddenly, here they are, filling the house with greetings, belongings, souvenirs and paper bags of laundry. They scatter the pieces of my privacy like dust upon the wind. It's all right. "I'm glad you're back," I say honestly. "I've been missing you."

"I missed you, too," someone says, bending to sniff the pie.

It's separateness that sweetens togetherness—or is it the other way around?

Man fluctuates between a desire for
gregariousness and a desire for solitude.
It is in the moments of aloneness that
we can recharge, take stock of ourselves
and revitalize our energies for further
encounters with others.
N. O'Neill and G. O'Neill

The following is a portion of
a chapter on "Acceptance of
Self and Others" by David
Johnson. The selection helps
us understand how our self-
concept can severely hinder
our intrapersonal com-
munication transactions.
Johnson discusses how you
must be able to accept yourself
before you can hope to
establish mature relationships
with others. Obviously, your
decisions concerning whether
to accept or reject yourself are
made in intrapersonal
transactions.

DAVID JOHNSON

ACCEPTANCE OF SELF AND OTHERS

In this article we focus upon accepting yourself and communicating acceptance to other people. The objectives of this article are to increase your self-acceptance and to increase your skills in expressing acceptance to others.

The Four Positions In Acceptance of Self and Others

Harris (1967) states that there are four possible positions held with respect to yourself and others. They are:

1. *I'm Not O.K., You're O.K.* In this position the person feels at the mercy of other people. He feels a great need for support, acceptance, and recognition. The person in this position hopes that others who are O.K. will give him support and acceptance, and he worries about what he has to do to get others to give him the support and acceptance he needs. He communicates to

David W. Johnson, Reaching Out: interpersonal effectiveness and self-actualization, *copyright © 1972, pp. 103–105. Reprinted by permission of Prentice-Hall, Inc., Englewood Cliffs, New Jersey.*

others that he is self-rejecting and needs their acceptance and support.

2. *I'm Not O.K., You're Not O.K.* In this position there is no source of support and acceptance, not from oneself or from others. Individuals in this position give up all hope of being happy and may withdraw from all relationships. Even if others try to give support and acceptance, the person in this position rejects it because they "are not O.K." He communicates to others both self-rejection and rejection of them.

3. *I'm O.K., You're Not O.K.* The person in this position rejects all support and acceptance from others, but provides it for himself. He feels that he will be all right if others leave him alone. He is ultra-independent and doesn't want to get involved with others. He also rejects the support and acceptance of others because they "are not O.K." He communicates to others that he is fine, but they are not.

4. *I'm O.K., You're O.K.* In this position the person decides that he is worthwhile and valuable and that other people are also worthwhile and valuable. He accepts himself and responds to acceptance from others. He can give acceptance and receive acceptance. He is free to get involved in meaningful relationships. He communicates to others that he appreciates his own strengths and appreciates their strengths. This is the position that everyone should strive to be in. This is the position which facilitates the development of close, meaningful relationships with others.

Every time you relate to another person you are communicating one of the above positions. Most people relate to everyone from the same position; that is, how they feel about themselves and others does not change greatly from relationship to relationship, and it governs everything they do. It is important for you to make the conscious decision that you are going to relate to others from the fourth position and strive to do that. Only when you accept yourself and accept other people can you build and maintain mature meaningful relationships.

Self-Acceptance

Self-acceptance is a high regard for yourself, or, conversely, a lack of cynicism about yourself. Generally, a high level of self-acceptance is reflected in a high level of quality of personal adjustment (see Hamachek, 1971). A person's mental health depends deeply on the quality of his feelings about himself. Just as an individual must maintain a healthy view of the world around him, so must he learn to perceive himself in positive ways. Psychologically healthy individuals see themselves as liked, wanted, acceptable to others, capable, and worthy. Highly self-critical individuals are more anxious, more insecure, and possibly more cynical and depressed than self-accepting individuals. The self-accepting person views the world as a more congenial place than the self-rejecting person and is less defensive towards others and about himself because of it. Carl Rogers (1951) considers self-acceptance to be crucial for psychological health and growth. It is not the individuals who feel that they are liked, wanted, acceptable to others, capable, and worthy who are found in prisons and mental hospitals; it is those who feel deeply inadequate, unliked, unwanted, unacceptable, and unable.

In order for you to grow and develop psychologically, therefore, you must be self-accepting. To help others grow and develop psychologically, you must help others become more self-accepting. To develop your potential for happiness and good relationships you must achieve and maintain a high level of self-acceptance. A self-rejecting person is usually unhappy and unable to form and maintain good relationships.

There is considerable evidence that self-acceptance and the acceptance of others are related (see Hamachek, 1971). Individuals who are self-accepting are usually more accepting of others. This means that if you think well of yourself you are likely to think well of others, and that if you disapprove of yourself you are likely to disapprove of others. In addition, things you try to hide from yourself about yourself you often are very critical of in others. A person who suppresses hostility may be highly critical of people who express hostility. A person who suppresses sexual feelings may be highly critical of individuals who are more open with their sexual feelings. If you recognize and accept your feelings, you are usually more accepting of such emotional expressions in others. The self-accepting person views the world as a more congenial place than the self-rejecting person and is less defensive towards others and about himself because of it. We will, then, be focusing upon how we may increase our self-acceptance and, therefore, become more accepting of others.

Your self-acceptance is built by knowing that others are accepting of you. The acceptance of you by others plays a critical role in increasing your self-acceptance, especially the acceptance of you by those you care about and respect. One of the ways in which you may become more self-accepting is to feel that other people whom you like and respect accept you. We will be focusing upon how to express acceptance towards others in order to help them increase their self-acceptance.

Your self-acceptance can set up self-fulfilling prophecies where your expectations concerning how other people are going to view you are actually confirmed as a result of your behavior. For example, a self-rejecting person expects to be rejected by others and will tend to reject others; as a result of his rejection, the people with whom he is interacting will reciprocate by rejecting him; the person's original expectations are then confirmed. A self-accepting person, on the other hand, will expect to be accepted by others and will tend to accept other people; they, in turn, will tend to reciprocate by being accepting of him; his original expectations are then confirmed. It is through such self-fulfilling prophecies that one may build good relationships or may experience real difficulty in making a friend.

The first and best victory is to conquer self; to be conquered by self is, of all things, the most shameful and vile.
Plato

We must be our own before we can be another's. . . .   J. Millett

---

I say that I accept the way I am, but do I accept it so fully that I am willing to act on it—to actually act the way I am?
H. Prather

From Hugh Prather, *Notes to Myself.* Reprinted by permission of Real People Press.

"How To Be Yourself" by
James W. Felt supports the
conclusions advanced by
David Johnson in the
preceding selection. This
article maintains that in order
to be free, a person must rid
himself of self-rejection
communication barriers. What
are the self-rejection barriers
with which you are
confronted?

JAMES W. FELT

HOW TO
BE YOURSELF
"Be yourself!" Psychologists urge this upon us.
Philosophers stress it. We increasingly recognize that it is profoundly
necessary. But just what does it *mean* to "be yourself"?

In a sense this is a large question, and so I want to focus on just
one sense in which I think "Be yourself" is often *mis*understood. I attack such a misinterpretation, of course, on the basis of what I believe
to be an essential ingredient in what it does mean to "be yourself."

If there is anything we do with relish and at every available opportunity it is make *things* out of *events*. When there is flashing we make
a thing out of it and call it "lightning." When we get a shock we say
there is "electricity" in the wire. When everything has been shaking we
say, "That was an earthquake," just as we might, in another context,
say, "That was an elephant." And this is natural for us, because things
are not only easier to deal with than events, they are also easier to talk
about. Both the language and the logic we inherit from the Greeks put
a premium on the fixed, on the changeless, on *things*.

And so both psychotherapists and their patients spontaneously talk
of "discarding masks," of "peeling off layers," of "uncovering the real
self," as one would uncover the body by disrobing it. The question is,
what can this "real self" signify?

When I "discard a false self" I am obviously not throwing away some *thing* as I would a gum wrapper: I am ceasing to live my life in an unauthentic way. What right, then, do I have to suppose that there is a "true self" waiting to be found under these "masks," as I would expect to find my foot if I took off my sock? But suppose that there is such a "myself" which I am to "be." Suppose, in other words, to "be yourself" means to "live up to your true self (which is already latent within you)." Then what is the nature of that self? The unspoken assumption seems to be that this "true self" was given from eternity or at least from conception, that it has a definite character, that it is just waiting to be filled out, as the acorn is waiting to turn into the oak. My problem in this case is simply to discover, to uncover, my "true self" so that I can live up to it.

Such a view is not far from the Greek idea of fate. We find something like this, I think, in Hermann Hesse's famous novel *Demian.* Its appeal to youth surely lies in its "Be yourself" theme. Hesse himself places on the title page of his work the following lines from its text: "I wanted only to live in accord with the promptings which came from my true self. Why was that so very difficult?"

But at the same time this true self of Hesse's is the self of fate:

"At this point a sharp realization burned within me: each man has his 'function' but none which he can choose himself, define, or perform as he pleases. . . . An enlightened man had but one duty —to seek the way to himself. . . . He might end up as poet or madman, as prophet or criminal—that was not his affair, ultimately it was of no concern. His task was to discover his own destiny—not an arbitrary one—and live it out wholly and resolutely within himself" (Bantam edition, pp. 107–8).

The ideal that Hesse holds up for us is the man who "seeks nothing but his own fate," the man who "only seeks his destiny."

But if, on the contrary, "Be yourself" means simply "Live authentically," then what sort of self is the object of this exhortation? There is just plain old me, the product of all my past experiences, my physical and mental limitations, above all of my past decisions. But this me is never settled nor is it prefabricated. It is always on the way, always in the process of self-creation. At every moment I am creating the me that I choose to be: there is nothing fated here. Whatever my limitations, whatever my past, I hold this me in my hands at every moment, to fashion as I will. Bergson claims we have an immediate experience, if we would only recognize it, "of being creators of our intentions, of our decisions, of our acts, and by that, of our habits, our characters, ourselves." To be myself, then, does not amount to uncovering the sort of me that I was born or fated to be. It means discovering my own true freedom to fashion myself as I can and as I will.

In that sense psychotherapy may often leave off where it should begin. To discover *how* I am the product of my past only fills in the details of the obvious generalization that of course I *am* the product of my past. What I need at this point is to realize that, notwithstanding these limitations of the past, to learn to be myself means precisely to discover that I am in fact free to create my ever-emerging self on my own and in my own way.

If, then, I understand "Be yourself" to mean, "Uncover and live up to that destined self latent in you," I either chain myself to whatever image I evoke of this self, or else I abandon all responsibility for my actions on the grounds that what I do spontaneously lives up automatically to the demands of this hidden true self. But if I am skeptical of the existence of such a prefabricated self, if I take "Be yourself" to mean, "Live authentically, according to values as you yourself grasp them," then I am thrown onto my own responsibility about my life. My fate then consists precisely in the formation of that self which I myself create with every new decision of my freedom. It is I who at every moment decide what sort of man I shall be, and this is my human dignity. To be myself is to be free.

Life is an endless process of self-discovery J. Gardner

The following selection by
James Kavanaugh underscores
how expectations placed on us
by others can be significant
barriers to intrapersonal
development. The emotional
impact of the selection renders
all explanation unnecessary.

JAMES KAVANAUGH

I KNEW THIS KID

I knew this skinny little kid
   Who never wanted to play tackle football at all
But thought he'd better if he wanted
   His daddy to love him and to prove his courage
And things like that.
   I remember him holding his breath
And closing his eyes
   And throwing a block into a guy twice his size,
Proving he was brave enough to be loved, and crying softly
   Because his tailbone hurt
And his shoes were so big they made him stumble.

I knew this skinny little kid
   With sky-blue eyes and soft brown hair
Who liked cattails and pussy willows.
   Sumac huts and sassafras,
Who liked chestnuts and pine cones and oily walnuts,
   Lurking foxes and rabbits munching lilies,
Secret caves and moss around the roots of oaks,
   Beavers and muskrats and gawking herons.
And I wonder what he would have been
   If someone had loved him for
Just following the fawns and building waterfalls
   And watching the white rats have babies.
I wonder what he would have been
   If he hadn't played tackle football at all.

INTRAPERSONAL COMMUNICATION
SELF-DISCLOSURE

Openness and honestry are the primary ingredients in being able to disclose or reveal oneself. Openness and honesty, according to many self-disclosure proponents, are necessary prerequisites to the "good life"—a life in which you experience meaningful relationships with people and nature. In order to develop personal growth, a person must examine himself openly and honestly. This is most easily done in intrapersonal communication transactions. Such encounters, however, can be extremely threatening because one might not like what he discovers. If that is the case, the intrapersonal transactions are being hampered by the self-rejecting barriers that were discussed in the last section. If one can sort through the barriers and engage in open and honest communication with himself, personal growth and awareness will follow.

The short excerpt taken from "It" by Alan Watts contains a good case for engaging in intrapersonal self-disclosure. To Watts, such communication, although difficult, opens the door to becoming sensitive to life's experience.

ALAN WATTS

IT

Just as true humor is laughter at oneself, true humanity is knowledge
of oneself. Other creatures may love and laugh, talk and think, but
it seems to be the special peculiarity of human beings that they reflect: they think about thinking and know that they know. This, like
other feedback systems, may lead to vicious circles and confusions if
improperly managed, but self-awareness makes human experience
resonant. It imparts that simultaneous "echo" to all that we think and
feel as the box of a violin reverberates with the sound of the strings.
It gives depth and volume to what would otherwise be shallow and
flat.

Self-knowledge leads to wonder, and wonder to curiosity and
investigation, so that nothing interests people more than people, even
if only one's own person. Every intelligent individual wants to know
what makes him tick, and yet is at once fascinated and frustrated by
the fact that oneself is the most difficult of all things to know.

From The Book: On the Tabu Against Knowing Who You Are, by Alan Watts,
copyright © 1966. Reprinted by permission of Pantheon Books/A Division of
Random House, Inc.

In the following excerpt from
*I Ain't Much, Baby—But I'm
All I've Got* by Jesse Lair, we
are told that we can each
benefit from intrapersonal self-
disclosure. Lair argues that
such disclosure must take
place before one can
experience personal change.
Furthermore, Lair states that
if one has a desire to change,
he will automatically do so if
he engages in intrapersonal
self-disclosure.

JESSE LAIR

TO BE CONTINUED IN OUR LIVES

The kind of realness that you need daily, continuously, is rigorous emotional honesty with yourself, not about your angers with other people, but rigorous honesty with yourself. I think your anger comes out of your fear, and your fear comes out of your terrible loneliness and your terrible sense of inadequacy.

The minute that you turn and say, I ain't much, baby, but I'm all I got, a lot of that sense of inadequacy goes away because you are able to see that you are no more inadequate than anybody else. And because you are no more inadequate than anybody else, you've got the same tools to work with that anybody else has.

But you've got one great big head start on them in that you know it and you're using your tools because you turned and looked at yourself and the other person hasn't. So much of your fear, then, melts away. As the fear melts away, the anger that comes out of it drops away. So the way to handle your anger is not to spew it around the world and get rid of it by blowing your stack every five minutes but the way to get rid of your anger is to get at your fear. So that you can be at peace with yourself, deep down.

When you are around people who are rigorously honest about

themselves in the sense of their feelings and their motivations, you are warmed and comforted and reassured and you are calmed down. Your fears go away, and with them, your angers. So rigorous personal honesty, mostly about our own feelings and about our own responses to things is tremendously necessary and yet it is very, very rare.

Then there has to be a desire for change. An awful lot of you have a desire for change. Some of you have not, at this moment at least, seen and felt much of a desire to change. The fact that you've been able to minimize your problems, in a sense, says that your own problems aren't that particularly bad and gnawing at you at the moment. But just give them time, friend, and they will. Cause I've never seen anybody yet that was immune from the problems of life.

Now another way of putting it is there are laws of human relations and those laws are just as fundamental as the laws of physics. If you jump off the top of a building, you're going to fall and you're going to break your leg. One of the things that makes the laws of human relationship tougher to understand, tougher to cope with, tougher to figure out, is that the consequences are usually delayed. We don't get that immediate confirmation of right or wrong.

When we bug somebody, it may be a week later before they bug us back. It's very hard to find out what we did to them. But this is the advantage of some of these other things that we are talking about, these good things. Because there is an immediate response to them. There is an immediate reward or an immediate reaction that tells you, "Yes this is right."

Those of you who have had the experience of being blazingly real have seen, man, that really opens up the door to somebody else. And once you've had that experience, you've seen, yah, there is lawfulness out there. The things that are happening in the world around me are not capricious events. It isn't somebody shooting dice and then dealing me whatever breaks there are without any respect for the things I do. Then you have the comfort of knowing: Not only are you not alone in the world, but the world will treat you about as well as you treat it.

An old alcoholic was telling me about his twenty-five years as an alcoholic and as a wino. The way he put it, "I was a big man in wino circles because I was so good at getting money out of people for a bottle. And in the wino circle, when you can get money for a bottle you are a very big man. I was drinking some kind of off brand stuff. When I would panhandle, I'd ask a guy for a quarter and I'd be breathing right in his face. My breath was so bad, that it practically knocked him over. He'd fish out a dollar just to get rid of me."

That's the way that man lived for a long time. He said, "They talk about heaven and hell. I don't know about what heaven is or what it might be like, but I know what hell was like cause that's what I was living for twenty-five years." Then he got rid of alcoholism and got sober. And for the first couple of years that he was sober, he said that being sober and thinking as bad as he was was just as bad as being an alcoholic, in fact maybe worse.

In fact, one alcoholic's wife one time said, "You're off the bottle but I wish you were drinking again because you are so cantankerous and so hard to handle." Because the crux of alcoholism is not the bottle but is the stinking thinking that leads to the drinking. And until you get rid of that stinking thinking you're in trouble. "Oh the world is trying to do me in. Oh, woe is me."

This man was talking about the last twenty years of his life. When he first went dry, he wanted to stay sober and get $10,000 because to him that represented the height of financial security. Well the funny thing is now, he doesn't care about money. He says he doesn't need $10,000 because as long as you've got your thinking right, you don't need any more money than it takes to buy groceries today. The money that it takes to buy groceries tomorrow will take care of itself if you're doing the things that you should be doing. You can make the money that you'll need tomorrow. And if you need an extra thousand dollars or five thousand dollars, all you need to do is just go out and make it. Because you've got the tools all of a sudden to work with.

Now this is how a world that seems completely capricious and unlawful turned into a world of lawfulness. And this man is hanging in there on that kind of thin razor's edge that he has found is the only true way to go.

The curious paradox is that when I accept myself just as I am, then I can change.   C. Rogers

---

The following selection
entitled "Dreams" offers some
specific suggestions about
how, if you want, you might
begin to get in touch with
yourself. You can put your
dreams to work for you in
your efforts at arriving at a
better understanding of
yourself.

GAY LUCE
JULIUS SEGAL

DREAMS

Many psychiatrists now think that we might enjoy better health and
inner peace were we to get in touch with our inner selves by developing the habit of recalling, understanding and acting on our dreams.
If dreams are so important—and all of us dream several hours every
night—why don't we all remember them each morning without effort?
One reason is motivation: Unless dreams become important to you,
you may not bother to recall or even think about them. Often people
entering psychoanalysis suddenly start remembering dreams every
morning to have something to tell their doctor. Similarly, those who
have been paid for dreams in a sleep laboratory have begun to remember more.

Depth of sleep is also a factor in recall; some individuals sleep
very deeply and awaken very slowly. Even in hospital laboratories,
where volunteers could be interviewed as they awakened from dreams,
some people took so long to wake up that the dream evaporated in
the process. The more rapid awakeners recalled more dream events.
Ability to remember dreams may be influenced too by personality
factors. Investigators have found that some people never seem to
remember dreaming, no matter how fast they are awakened. These
people typically are less aware of the hidden aspects of their personalities, out of touch with their own unconscious feelings. They tend to
be conformists and inhibited. By forgetting their dreams, they are
repressing covert tendencies in themselves. There is still another

reason for not remembering dreams: drugs. People who take sleeping pills or tranquilizers may think they get a deep and refreshing sleep. But in fact, the drugs suppress some of the night's precious dream periods and dampen the ability to remember dream life.

Sleep scientists have discovered that dreaming is an important ingredient of everyone's sleep each night—from infancy to old age—and in the animal kingdom too. A cycle of dreaming recurs about every ninety minutes all night long in human beings. This is one reflection of the body's many biological rhythms—a set of internal clocks that makes it possible, for example, for some people to get up at a preset hour without the aid of an alarm clock.

Sleep has a rhythm. When a person first falls asleep, he sinks down in stages into increasingly deep and more oblivious sleep. Then he rises up to lighter sleep again. About seventy minutes after falling asleep the closed eyes begin to move rapidly, as if the person were watching TV. If awakened at once, the person will almost certainly remember a dream. This is known as rapid-eye-movement sleep, or REM sleep. While there is dreaming in other sleep, REM dreams may be more memorable. The first one may last only five to seven minutes and may be a mundane dream about the past day's events. Then the sleeper is likely to turn over and drift into deeper sleep. About ninety minutes later, another REM dream will occur, this one longer, more bizarre and vivid. Such a dream cycle will repeat itself four or five times a night. But the dream we remember upon awakening is likely to be the last one.

During REM sleep the eyes move as if looking at something and the muscles go limp. A sleeping cat will flop her head onto the floor, and her whiskers may twitch. A dog may sleep with eyes partly open and moving rapidly as he woofs or whimpers. The body of the dreamer is limp as a rag, but people struggling to scream or get out of a nightmare may feel they are paralyzed because they cannot move. They are actually superrelaxed and muscle tone will return in a few seconds. REM sleep, despite the surface relaxation of the body, is a time when the heart beats irregularly. Blood pressure and breathing may fluctuate. Males usually have an erection, while in females the clitoris may suggest sexual excitement even though the dream content may be bland and sexless.

This is the period when an infant makes faces, smiles and his fingers twitch. If his eyes are slightly open, you might think he was awake. One of the functions of REM dreaming may be to keep brain tissues in good working order, to restore essential brain proteins, which are needed for memory and learning. Babies spend a huge amount of their sleeping time in REM, but senile people and mentally retarded children spend little. Experiments have shown that both people and animals who are learning a great deal or adapting to a new situation have more than the normal amount of REM sleep. Many people notice that they tend to sleep longer and remember more dreams when they are traveling in a foreign country, going out with a new boy friend, starting at a new school or facing other challenges.

Another function of REM dreaming may be to help us remember, from day to day, all the myriad faces we see and the places and events. Memory is a kind of filing system, but it is neither alphabetical nor numerical. We appear to store memories in a hierarchy of psychological and emotional importance—a hierarchy that begins when we are babies. Sometimes our memories are in symbolic form. Thus the images of our nightly dreams may be a way of storing the day's events so we can remember them later.

Since the 1960's, when scientists found that dreams are universal, nobody is ever again likely to attribute dreaming to eating pickles and chocolate, or insist that dreams come from sickness. Poor eating habits can influence your sleep, cause you to awaken more often, and may even incite unpleasant dreams; but nightmares are usually caused by psychological factors that are deep and difficult to resolve.

Psychologists and psychiatrists found that by waking sleeping volunteers directly out of REM sleep, they could get answers to questions about dreams that man had been asking for centuries. Much of what we had assumed about dreaming was pure myth—and was debunked in the laboratory. For instance, they found that dreams do not usually happen in a flash, as was once believed, but in real time. If you dream of a conversation with your boy friend, it takes about as long to unfold as it would in real life.

Contrary to another popular belief, dreams are often in color. The research suggests that probably everyone dreams in color, but most people apparently pay little attention to it and don't mention it unless asked.

Dreams incorporate outside noises, temperature changes, and other stimuli—but not 100 percent of the time. When a sleeper began to show rapid-eye-movement sleep in the laboratory, a few scientists tried spraying his face with water. Some of the time the person would report dreaming about Niagara Falls, or a rainstorm. Similarly, if a person went to bed thirsty and dehydrated after a spicy meal, he was likely to dream about searching for a drink.

In the laboratory, sleepers talked and mumbled, sighing, whimpering, even singing, in sulky, sarcastic, angry, remorseful and joyful tones. Despite popular fears, sleeptalking is *not* the dangerous avenue for giving away secrets that many people supposed. Most of our utterances during sleep sound like inane fragments from daily conversation. References to gossip, school matters, current events and food are common—so one needn't worry that his innermost secrets will be exposed. It is unlikely.

It is also unlikely that dreams can be premonitions that actually foretell the future. We have all heard of people who "knew" when a distant friend or parent was dying because it happened in a dream, and the next day they received word by telegram. Although we may actually have extrasensory means of knowing about people we love, even at a distance, these are still beyond the realm of present science. Besides, while we all remember the prediction that came true, how many times did we dream of events that never happened? Scientists have studied the images of sensitive volunteers in REM sleep after "senders" thousands of miles away were looking at a specific picture at the right moment. There is no present scientific evidence for telepathy in dreams, perhaps because we have not yet learned how to study a phenomenon so rare and fragile.

Ancient peoples, such as the Egyptians, believed in premonitory dreams and felt that there was a symbolic code for interpreting any dream. Data from psychology and from sleep laboratories indicate the opposite—that there can be no cut-and-dried formula for deciphering dreams.

The way to understand one's own dreams is to remember them, write them down, then face them squarely. Dreams often represent what a person does not dare admit openly. In one New Jersey clinic, for example, it was recently found that children with emotional problems were often trying to communicate with their parents through their dreams. The children were asked to make a drawing of the previous night's dream. When the parents were later shown the drawings, each parent knew at once which drawing came from his or her child. As one mother said, after looking at a sketch of a small dog being squashed by a cow, "I never knew I was pushing so hard." She had had no realization that she was squashing her little boy with constant demands.

About 90 percent of the dreams we recall will be ordinary and uninteresting, but the last dreams of the night tend to be more basic, dramatic and symbolic. Typically, we tend to dream about the relevant aspects of our lives. Pregnant women, for example, dream more about babies. At the onset of menstruation, many girls seem to have dreams of waiting, or about the breaking of an object. Depressed people may dream of frightening or sad experiences, like being abandoned. Thus, our current lives and personalities color and shape our dreams—for our dreams are not separate from our lives. They are part of us. When we "sleep on something" and dream about it, our minds are working just as creatively and purposefully as they do by day.

Many creative persons have known how to use their dreams to solve problems they couldn't solve by day. Robert Louis Stevenson wrote many of his stories from fragments of dreams. One night he dreamed of an escaping criminal who drank a potion that changed his appearance; the dream became *Dr. Jekyll and Mr. Hyde.* Frederich Kekule won a Nobel Prize for finding the molecular shape of the chemical benzene. He had worked long and hard on the problem without success. Then one night he fell asleep and awakened with an image of a snake eating its tail—the benzene ring.

We all solve problems in our sleep. When we go to bed at night we do not know exactly what we will wear the next day or precisely how to arrange the day's activities. When we get up, we do some of these things almost automatically, as if we had already planned them. If one wishes to solve school problems, or even basic life problems, during sleep, there are guidelines that can make it easier to find the solution.

First of all, it is necessary to be steeped in the problem and the relevant facts before going to sleep. Keep a pad of paper near the bed. and write down immediately all the thoughts and dreams that you remember. The effort may take several nights. Usually people discover that part of the solution comes at night, but that it must be translated and made practical by day. More important, however, the written dream will begin to reveal where we stand and what we really want to do about the problem. An understanding of dreams can help us to understand our hidden wishes, fears, motivations. And the person who understands himself is no longer at the mercy of unseen forces, pushed and pulled by the emotions of life, or easily terrified.

Although psychologists used to think of dreams as keys to mental illness, or neurosis, they now realize that dreams are an integral part of every healthy life.

The analysis of dreams for a better understanding of personality began in the early twentieth century. Sigmund Freud, the famed Viennese neurologist, became interested in dreams while treating patients with apparently organic illnesses—headaches, paralysis or blindness—for which neither he nor any other doctor could find any physical cause. He found that when these people remembered forgotten events and feelings their symptoms sometimes vanished. In the process of talking about the repressed events of childhood, patients often re-called a dream. Freud began to examine his own dreams. He found that they were usually a disguised expression of wishes or feelings, or that they might displace a feeling. For instance, if I dream that my brother has hit my little sister, and I am indignant, in actuality I may be mad at my little sister and wish to hit her myself.

Freud also believed that some of our deepest, most basic motives stem from our earliest sexual urges and experiences in infancy, and that we tend to symbolize sexual organs and activities. From this theory came the famous idea of the phallic symbol. In Freud's view any umbrella, mountain, steeple or tree in a dream was a penis symbol, while cabinets, caves and boxes represented female genitals. Rocking, climbing, flying or floating were symbols for sexual intercourse. During the Victorian age in which Freud lived there was a good deal more shame and prudery about sex than there is today, and many more people now dream openly about their sexual desires and hang-ups. If Freudian analysis is overdone, almost anything in a dream can be reduced to a wish fulfillment or a disguise for infantile desires.

The Swiss analyst Carl Jung, once a student of Freud, offered quite a different way of interpreting dreams. While admitting that dreams might conceal some hidden wishes and anxieties, he felt that dreams were actually like letters to oneself, revealing inner thoughts instead of hiding them, and using symbols that are universal to all mankind. Jung felt that each individual should interpret his dreams in the way that was most useful to him. He believed that dreams referred to current life, not infancy. Moreover, he felt that the dream often con-tained elements of deep human wisdom—a universal theme existing in some form in everyone's unconscious. Thus, I may dream of walk-ing into a terrifying dark valley and finally struggling through into a brilliant desert in a burst of joy. Instead of signifying a sexual episode, Jung would say that this dream might represent a universal fear of death and a hope to be reborn. Jung suggested that dreams were at-tempts to search out the dark future, like shining a lamp into the forest and trying to predict the path ahead.

The dream, according to many modern psychologists, is indeed a letter from the dreamer to himself about the state of life at that moment, his or her real feelings about people and about the future as it appears at that time. During the last decade a famous sleep re-searcher, Calvin Hall, collected and analyzed over fifty thousand dream reports. Like Jung, he believes that the dream reveals us to ourselves in clear, economical language—in a picture that is pithier than thousands of words. It is not necessary, Hall feels, to probe back into the sleeper's unconscious in order to understand the dream, for it represents his present situation, his self concept, his relationships with the people close to him, his conflicts or anxieties. Much of the time a sleeping person is working out his worries during sleep.

There are many "authorities" on dreams, but nobody can interpret the "letter" as well as the dreamer, and you should never allow another person to force a dream interpretation on you. A dream of a snake eating its tail can be a creative inspiration, not a phobia or sexual desire. When you become adept at recalling and deciphering your dreams you can sense when a message rings true. You will know when you understand the implications. Then you can apply its message to your waking life.

Members of certain primitive groups—such as the Senoi people of Malaya—have long guided their lives by their dreams. They give their children dream homework to do. If, for example, a Senoi child attacks a friend in his dream, his father may tell him to talk with that friend and take him a gift the next day. After a dream of falling, his father may say, "That's wonderful—where did you fall to?" The child may consider the falling dream frightening and not so wonderful. Through lessons, however, he will learn to convert the fall into a joyful dream of flying.

We can also do dream homework in order to resolve deep-seated anxieties. For instance, a girl kept dreaming that a horribly ugly giant would block her way to school, insulting and threatening her. She told the nightmare to a friend of the family who did exactly what a Senoi Indian would have done. She asked the girl to close her eyes and concentrate deeply until she saw the giant perfectly. Then she asked the girl to look at the giant carefully to see if it reminded her of anyone, and perhaps might be very timid underneath all its swaggering. The girl noticed that the giant resembled her chemistry instructor, who was really very shy. Now, with her eyes closed, she made friends with the giant. The next time she dreamed of him at night he was her friend, taking her on a tour of a strange, futuristic city.

Dreams, like other attitudes, can be remolded and replayed. We can actively change a dream during waking reverie, or we can decide to change our role, or some event in it, before we go to sleep at night. The Senoi, like many psychiatrists, feel that the dreams we have at night are merely the images and fantasies that express the daily process of adapting. Although the Senoi people never developed a written language and never even heard of Freud, they also feel that hostility and conflict appear in dreams, and if not interpreted and dealt with, might make a person sick.

Chronic anxiety, for example, can cause a change in body chemistry and in appearance. We really are what we think, for our brains are the control towers that keep our hearts beating, regulate our chemistry, digestion and metabolism. When we imagine something frightening, we can actually feel butterflies in the stomach, and the effects of adrenalin entering the bloodstream—this is a major chemical change. Some people unconsciously tense their neck muscles and later begin to get stiff necks or headaches. The habits we develop in our reaction to tension may also give us pimples and other symptoms. Perhaps the Senoi were not so far out when they decided that interpreting dreams could improve one's health—for their messages may warn us of tensions of which we are unaware.

Dreams are a precious and fascinating ingredient of everyone's daily life. The fact that they occur during sleep does not diminish their value. Like the Senoi people, by learning to recall and understand your nighttime scenarios, you too can use your dreams to your advantage.

When I get a clear statement about my
life from a dream, it is usually contained
more in the emotions than in what I see.
The visual part of the dream often
appears to be a representation of what
I am feeling during the dream, the
individual images being taken from
situations in my life that have commonly
surrounded those feelings. Usually they
are feelings which I have had recently,
especially that day, and they seem to
always be ones that I brushed over.
Seen in this way my dreams could be
interpreted as saying, "Look what you
were feeling today—you didn't fully
acknowledge it."   H. Prather

INTRAPERSONAL
COMMUNICATION
EFFECTS

Most of us have a tendency to overestimate the effects of communication transactions in all arenas—especially in the public and mass communication arenas. Changes in attitudes and behaviors take place in small increments. Rarely does one experience or witness an actual conversion that results from a single communication encounter. We do change as a result of communication encounters in the various arenas, but that change is slower than many of us realize. All change is part of the process of communication.

The effects of extensive intrapersonal communication, however, can be quite significant over time. The popular short story, "The Secret Life of Walter Mitty," portrays how one rather unusual individual relied almost solely on intrapersonal communication effects to fulfill his needs to escape from reality. As you read the story, try to think about how you fulfill some of your personal needs through intrapersonal communication.

JAMES THURBER

THE SECRET LIFE OF WALTER MITTY

"We're going through!" The Commander's voice was like thin ice breaking. He wore his full-dress uniform, with the heavily braided white cap pulled down rakishly over one cold gray eye. "We can't make it, sir. It's spoiling for a hurricane, if you ask me." "I'm not asking you, Lieutenant Berg," said the Commander. "Throw on the power lights! Rev her up to 8,500! We're going through!" The pounding of the cylinders increased: ta-pocketa-pocketa-pocketa-*pocketa-pocketa*. The Commander stared at the ice forming on the pilot window. He walked over and twisted a row of complicated dials. "Switch on No. 8 auxiliary!" he shouted. "Switch on No. 8 auxiliary!" repeated Lieutenant Berg. "Full strength in No. 3 turret!" shouted the Commander. "Full strength in No. 3 turret!" The crew, bending to their various tasks in the huge, hurtling eight-engined Navy hydroplane, looked at each other and grinned. "The Old Man'll get us through," they said to ane another. "The Old Man ain't afraid of Hell!" . . .

"Not so fast! You're driving too fast!" said Mrs. Mitty. "What are you driving so fast for?"

"Hmm?" said Walter Mitty. He looked at his wife, in the seat beside him, with shocked astonishment. She seemed grossly unfamiliar, like a strange woman who had yelled at him in a crowd. "You were up to fifty-five," she said. "You know I don't like to go more than forty. You were up to fifty-five." Walter Mitty drove on toward Waterbury in silence, the roaring of the SN202 through the worst storm in twenty years of Navy flying fading in the remote, intimate airways of his mind. "You're tensed up again," said Mrs. Mitty. "It's one of your days. I wish you'd let Dr. Renshaw look you over."

Walter Mitty stopped the car in front of the building where his wife went to have her hair done. "Remember to get those overshoes while I'm having my hair done," she said. "I don't need overshoes," said Mitty. She put her mirror back into her bag. "We've been all through that," she said, getting out of the car. "You're not a young man any longer." He raced the engine a little. "Why don't you wear your gloves? Have you lost your gloves?" Walter Mitty reached in a pocket and brought out the gloves. He put them on, but after she had turned and gone into the building and he had driven on to a red light, he took them off again. "Pick it up, brother!" snapped a cop as the light changed, and Mitty hastily pulled on his gloves and lurched ahead. He drove around the streets aimlessly for a time, and then he drove past the hospital on his way to the parking lot.

. . . "It's the millionaire banker, Wellington McMillan," said the pretty nurse. "Yes?" said Walter Mitty, removing his gloves slowly. "Who has the case?" "Dr. Renshaw and Dr. Benbow, but there are two specialists here, Dr. Remington from New York and Mr. Pritchard-Mitford from London. He flew over." A door opened down a long, cool corridor and Dr. Renshaw came out. He looked distraught and haggard. "Hello, Mitty," he said. "We're having the devil's own time with McMillan, the millionaire banker and close personal friend of Roosevelt. Obstreosis of the ductal tract. Tertiary. Wish you'd take a look at him." "Glad to," said Mitty.

In the operating room there were whispered introductions: "Dr. Remington, Dr. Mitty. Mr. Pritchard-Mitford, Dr. Mitty." "I've read your book on streptothricosis," said Pritchard-Mitford, shaking hands. "A brilliant performance, sir." "Thank you," said Walter Mitty. "Didn't know you were in the States, Mitty," grumbled Remington. "Coals to Newcastle, bringing Mitford and me up here for a tertiary." "You are very kind," said Mitty. A huge, complicated machine, connected to the operating table, with many tubes and wires, began at this moment to go pocketa-pocketa-pocketa. "The new anesthetizer is giving way!" shouted an interne. "There is no one in the East who knows how to fix it!" "Quiet, man!" said Mitty, in a low, cool voice. He sprang to the machine, which was now going pocketa-pocketa-queep-pocketa-queep. He began fingering delicately a row of glistening dials. "Give me a fountain pen!" he snapped. Someone handed him a fountain pen. He pulled a faulty piston out of the machine and inserted the pen in its place. "That will hold for ten minutes," he said. "Get on with the operation." A nurse hurried over and whispered to Renshaw, and Mitty saw the man turn pale. "Coreopsis has set in," said Renshaw nervously. "If you would take over, Mitty?" Mitty looked at him and at the craven figure of Benbow, who drank, and at the grave, uncertain faces of the two great specialists. "If you wish," he said. They slipped a white gown on him; he adjusted a mask and drew on thin gloves; nurses handed him shining . . .

"Back it up, Mac! Look out for that Buick!" Walter Mitty jammed on the brakes. "Wrong lane, Mac," said the parking-lot attendant, looking at Mitty closely. "Gee. Yeh," muttered Mitty. He began cautiously to back out of the lane marked "Exit Only." "Leave her sit there," said the attendant. "I'll put her away." Mitty got out of the car. "Hey, better leave the key." "Oh," said Mitty, handing the man the ignition key. The attendant vaulted into the car, backed it up with insolent skill, and put it where it belonged.'

They're so damn cocky, thought Walter Mitty, walking along Main Street; they think they know everything. Once he had tried to take his chains off, outside New Milford, and he had got them wound around the axles. A man had had to come out in a wrecking car and unwind them, a young, grinning garageman. Since then Mrs. Mitty always made him drive to a garage to have the chains taken off. The next time, he thought, I'll wear my right arm in a sling; they won't grin at me then. I'll have my right arm in a sling and they'll see I couldn't possibly take the chains off myself. He kicked at the slush on the sidewalk. "Overshoes," he said to himself, and he began looking for a shoe store.

When he came out into the street again, with the overshoes in a box under his arm, Walter Mitty began to wonder what the other thing was his wife had told him to get. She had told him twice, before they set out from their house for Waterbury. In a way he hated these weekly trips to town—he was always getting something wrong. Kleenex, he thought, Squibb's razor blades? No. Toothpaste, tooth-brush, bicarbonate, carborundum, initiative and referendum? He gave it up. But she would remember it. "Where's the what's-its-name?" she would ask. "Don't tell me you forgot the what's-its-name." A newsboy went by shouting something about the Waterbury trial.

. . . "Perhaps this will refresh your memory." The District Attorney suddenly thrust a heavy automatic at the quiet figure on the witness stand. "Have you ever seen this before?" Walter Mitty took the gun and examined it expertly. "This is my Webley-Vickers 50.80," he said calmly. An excited buzz ran around the courtroom. The judge rapped for order. "You are a crack shot with any sort of firearms, I believe?" said the District Attorney, insinuatingly. "Objection!" shouted Mitty's attorney. "We have shown that the defendant could not have fired the shot. We have shown that he wore his right arm in a sling on the night of the fourteenth of July." Walter Mitty raised his hand briefly and the bickering attorneys were stilled. "With any known make of gun," he said evenly, "I could have killed Gregory Fitzhurst at three hundred feet *with my left hand*." Pandemonium broke loose in the courtroom. A woman's scream rose above the bedlam and suddenly a lovely, dark-haired girl was in Walter Mitty's arms. The District Attorney struck at her savagely. Without rising from his chair, Mitty let the man have it on the point of the chin. "You miserable cur!" . . .

"Puppy biscuit," said Walter Mitty. He stopped walking and the buildings of Waterbury rose up out of the misty courtroom and surrounded him again. A woman who was passing laughed. "He said 'Puppy biscuit,'" she said to her companion. "That man said 'Puppy biscuit' to himself." Walter Mitty hurried on. He went into an A. & P., not the first one he came to but a smaller one farther up the street. "I want some biscuit for small, young dogs," he said to the clerk. "Any special brand, sir?" The greatest pistol shot in the world thought a moment. "It says 'Puppies Bark for It' on the box," said Walter Mitty.

His wife would be through at the hairdresser's in fifteen minutes, Mitty saw in looking at his watch, unless they had trouble drying it; sometimes they had trouble drying it. She didn't like to get to the hotel first; she would want him to be there waiting for her as usual. He found a big leather chair in the lobby, facing a window, and he put the overshoes and the puppy biscuit on the floor beside it. He picked up an old copy of *Liberty* and sank down into the chair. "Can Germany Conquer the World Through the Air?" Walter Mitty looked at the pictures of bombing planes and of ruined streets.

. . . "The cannonading has got the wind up in young Raleigh, sir," said the sergeant. Captain Mitty looked up at him through tousled hair. "Get him to bed," he said wearily. "With the others. I'll fly alone." "But you can't, sir," said the sergeant anxiously. "It takes two men to handle that bomber and the Archies are pounding hell out of the air. Von Richtman's circus is between here and Saulier." "Somebody's got to get that ammunition dump," said Mitty. "I'm going over. Spot of brandy?" He poured a drink for the sergeant and one for himself. War thundered and whined around the dugout and battered at the door. There was a rending of wood and splinters flew through the room. "A bit of a near thing," said Captain Mitty carelessly. "The box barrage is closing in," said the sergeant. "We only live once, Sergeant," said Mitty, with his faint, fleeting smile. "Or do we?" He poured another brandy and tossed it off. "I never see a man could hold his brandy like you, sir," said the sergeant. "Begging your pardon, sir." Captain Mitty stood up and strapped on his huge Webley-Vickers automatic. "It's forty kilometers through hell, sir," said the sergeant. Mitty finished one last brandy. "After all," he said softly, "what isn't?" The pounding of the cannon increased; there was the rat-tat-tatting of machine guns, and from somewhere came the menacing pocketa-pocketa-pocketa of the new flame-throwers. Walter Mitty walked to the door of the dugout humming "Auprès de Ma Blonde." He turned and waved to the sergeant. "Cheerio!" he said. . . .

Something struck his shoulder. "I've been looking all over this hotel for you," said Mrs. Mitty. "Why do you have to hide in this old chair? How did you expect me to find you?" "Things close in," said Walter Mitty vaguely. "What?" Mrs. Mitty said. "Did you get the what's-its-name? The puppy biscuit? What's in that box?" "Overshoes," said Mitty. "Couldn't you have put them on in the store?" "I was thinking," said Walter Mitty. "Does it ever occur to you that I am sometimes thinking?" She looked at him. "I'm going to take your temperature when I get you home," she said.

They went out through the revolving doors that made a faintly derisive whistling sound when you pushed them. It was two blocks to the parking lot. At the drugstore on the corner she said, "Wait here for me. I forgot something. I won't be a minute." She was more than a minute. Walter Mitty lighted a cigarette. It began to rain, rain with sleet in it. He stood up against the wall of the drugstore, smoking. . . . He put his shoulders back and his heels together. "To hell with the handkerchief," said Walter Mitty scornfully. He took one last drag on his cigarette and snapped it away. Then, with that faint, fleeting smile playing about his lips, he faced the firing squad; erect and motionless, proud and disdainful, Walter Mitty the Undefeated, inscrutable to the last.

Find where your main roots lie and do not hanker after other worlds.
H. D. Thoreau

"The Diary of a Madman" by Nikolai Gogol provides an example of how strongly a mentally deranged person relies on the effects of intrapersonal communication to maintain his mental imbalance. Again, a person may rely too heavily on intrapersonal communication effects in order to remain out of touch with reality.

NIKOLAI GOGOL

THE DIARY OF A MADMAN

2000 A.D., *April 43*

This is the day of the greatest public rejoicing! There is a king of Spain! He has been discovered. I am that king. I only heard of it this morning. I must confess it burst upon me like a flash of lightning. I can't imagine how I could believe and imagine myself to be a titular councilor. How could that crazy, mad idea ever have entered my head? It's a good thing that no one thought of putting me in a madhouse. Now everything has been revealed to me. Now it is all as clear as can be. But until now I did not understand; everything was in a sort of mist. And I believe it all arose from believing that the brain is in the head. It's not so at all; it comes with the wind from the direction of the Caspian Sea. First of all, I told Mavra who I am. When she heard that the King of Spain was standing before her, she clasped her hands and almost died of horror; the ignorant woman had never seen a King of Spain before. I tried to reassure her, however, and in gracious words tried to convince her of my benevolent feelings toward her, saying that I was not angry with her for having sometimes cleaned my boots so badly. Of course they are uncultured people; it is no good talking of elevated subjects to them. She is frightened because she is convinced that all kings of Spain are like Philip II.[1]

From The Collected Tales and Plays of Nikolai Gogol, *edited by Leonard J. Kent and translated by Constance Garnett and Leonard J. Kent. Copyright © 1964 by Random House, Inc. Reprinted by permission of Pantheon Books, A Division of Random House, Inc.*

[1] (1527–98), *the king under whom the Spanish Inquisition reached its infamous peak. (ed.)*

But I assured her that there was no resemblance between me and Philip II and that I have not even one Capuchin monk. I didn't go to the department . . . the hell with it! No, my friends, you won't entice me there again; I am not going to copy your horrible papers!

Martober 86 between
day and night

Our office messenger arrived today to tell me to go to the department, and to say that I had not been there for more than three weeks. However, I did go to the department just for the fun of it. The head of our section thought that I should bow to him and apologize, but I looked at him indifferently, not too angrily and not too graciously, and sat down in my place as though I did not notice anything. I looked at all the scum of the office and thought: "If only you knew who is sitting among you!" Good gracious! wouldn't there be a commotion! And the head of our section would bow to me as he bows now to the director. They put a paper before me to make some sort of an extract from it. But I didn't touch it. A few minutes later everyone was in an uproar. They said the director was coming. A number of the clerks ran forward to show off for him, but I didn't stir. When he walked through our room they all buttoned up their coats, but I didn't do anything at all. What's a director? Am I going to tremble before him—never! He's a fine director! He is a cork, he is not a director. An ordinary cork, a plain cork and nothing else—such as you cork a bottle with. What amused me most of all was when they put a paper before me to sign. They thought I should write at the bottom of the paper, So-and-so, head clerk of the table—how else should it be! But in the most important place, where the director of the department signs his name, I wrote "Ferdinand VIII." You should have seen the awe-struck silence that followed; but I only waved my hand and said: "I don't insist on any signs of allegiance!" and walked out. From there I walked straight to the director's. He was not at home. The footman did not want to let me in, but I spoke to him in such a way that his hands fell to his sides. I went straight to her bedroom. She was sitting before the mirror; she jumped up and stepped back when she saw me. I did not tell her that I was the King of Spain, however; I only told her that there was a happiness awaiting her such as she could not imagine, and that in spite of the wiles of our enemies we should be together. I didn't care to say more and walked out. Oh, woman is a treacherous creature! I have discovered now what women are. So far no one has found out with whom Woman is in love: I have been the first to discover it. Woman is in love with the devil. Yes, joking apart. Scientific men write nonsense saying that she is this or that—she cares for nothing but the devil. You will see her from a box in the first tier fixing her *lorgnette*. You imagine she is looking at the fat man with decorations. No, she is looking at the devil who is standing behind his back. There he is, hidden in his coat. There he is, beckoning to her! And she will marry him, she will marry him. And all these people, their dignified fathers who fawn on everybody and push their way to court and say that they are patriots and one thing and another: profit, profit is all that these patriots want! They would sell their father and their mother and God for money, ambitious creatures, Judases! All this is ambition, and the ambition is because of a little pimple under the tongue and in it a little worm no bigger than a pin's head, and it's all the doing of a barber who lives in Gorokhovaya Street, I don't remember his name; but I know for a fact that, in collusion with a midwife, he is trying to spread Mohammedanism all over the world, and that is why, I am told, that the majority of people in France profess the Mohammedan faith.

No date. The day
had no date

I walked incognito along Nevsky Prospekt. His Majesty the Czar drove by. All the people took off their caps and I did the same, but I made no sign that I was the King of Spain. I thought it improper to reveal myself so suddenly before everyone, because I ought first to be presented at court. The only thing that has prevented my doing so is the lack of a Spanish uniform. If only I could get hold of a royal mantle. I should have liked to order it from a tailor, but they are perfect asses; besides they neglect their work so, they have given themselves up to speculating and usually end up being employed in laying pavement. I determined to make the mantle out of my new uniform, which I had only worn twice. And so that the scoundrels should not ruin it I decided to make it myself, shutting the door so that no one might see me at it. I ripped it all up with the scissors because the style has to be completely different.

I don't remember the date
There was no month either
The devil knows what to make of it

The mantle is completely finished. Marva shrieked when she saw me in it. However, I can't make up my mind to present myself at court, for so far the delegation hasn't arrived from Spain. It wouldn't be proper to go without my delegation; there would be nothing to lend weight to my dignity. I expect them any hour.

I am extremely surprised at the lateness of the delegation. What can be detaining them? Can it be the machinations of France? Yes, that is the most malignant of states. I went to inquire at the post office whether the Spanish delegates had not arrived; but the postmaster was excessively stupid and knew nothing. "No," he said, "there are no delegates here, but if you care to write a letter I will send it off in accordance with the regulations." Damn it all, what's the use of a letter? A letter is nonsense. Letters are even written by pharmacists. . . .

And so here I am in Spain, and it happened so quickly that I can hardly believe it. This morning the Spanish delegates arrived and I got into a carriage with them. The extraordinary rapidity of our journey struck me as strange. We went at such a rate that within half an hour we had reached the frontiers of Spain. But of course now there are railroads all over Europe, and ships go very rapidly. Spain is a strange land! When we went into the first room I saw a number of people with shaven heads. I guessed at once that these were either grandees or soldiers because they do shave their heads. I thought the behavior of the High Chancellor, who led me by the hand, extremely strange. He thrust me into a little room and said: "Sit there, and if you persist in calling yourself King Ferdinand, I'll knock the inclination out of you." But knowing that this was only to try me I answered in the negative, whereupon the Chancellor hit me twice on the back with a stick, and it hurt so that I almost cried out, but I restrained myself, remembering that this is the custom of chivalry on receiving any exalted dignity, for customs of chivalry persist in Spain to this day. When I was alone I decided to occupy myself with the affairs of state. I discovered that Spain and China are one and the same country, and it is only through ignorance that they are considered to be different kingdoms. I recommend everyone to try to write Spain on a bit of paper and it will always turn out China. But I was particularly distressed by an event which will take place tomorrow. Tomorrow at seven o'clock a strange phenomenon will occur: the earth will sit on the moon. The celebrated English chemist Wellington has written about it. I must confess that I experience a tremor at my heart when I reflect on the extreme softness and fragility of the moon. You see the moon is usually made in Hamburg, and very badly made too. I am surprised that England hasn't taken notice of it. It was made by a lame barrel maker, and it is evident that the fool had no idea what a moon should be. He put in tarred cord and one part of lamp oil; and that is why there is such a fearful stench all over the world that one has to stop up one's nose. And that's how it is that the moon is such a soft globe that man cannot live on it and that nothing lives there but noses. And it is for that very reason that we can't see our noses, because they are all in the moon. And when I reflected that the earth is a heavy body and when it falls may grind our noses to powder, I was overcome by such uneasiness that, putting on my shoes and stockings, I hastened to the hall of the Imperial Council to give orders to the police not to allow the earth to sit on the moon. The grandees with shaven heads whom I found in great numbers in the hall of the Imperial Council were very intelligent people, and when I said: "Gentlemen, let us save the moon, for the earth is trying to sit upon it!" they all rushed to carry out my sovereign wishes, and several climbed up the walls to try and get at the moon; but at that moment the High Chancellor walked in. Seeing him they all ran in different directions. I as King remained alone. But, to my amazement, the Chancellor struck me with his stick and drove me back to my room! How great is the power of national tradition in Spain!

January of the same year
which came after February

So far I have not been able to understand what sort of a country Spain is. The national traditions and the customs of the court are quite extraordinary. I can't understand it, I can't understand it, I absolutely can't understand it. Today they shaved my head, although I shouted at the top of my voice that I didn't want to become a monk. But I can't even remember what happened afterward when they poured cold water on my head. I have never endured such hell. I was almost going frantic, so that they had difficulty in holding me. I cannot understand the meaning of this strange custom. It's a stupid, senseless practice! The lack of good sense in the kings who have not abolished it to this day is beyond my comprehension. Judging from all the circumstances, I wonder whether I have not fallen into the hands of the Inquisition, and whether the man I took to be the Grand Chancellor isn't the Grand Inquisitor. But I cannot understand how a king can be subject to the Inquisition. It can only be through the influence of France, especially of Polignac.[2] Oh, that beast of a Polignac! He has sworn to harm me to the death. And he pursues me and pursues me; but I know, my friend, that you are the tool of England. The English are great politicians. They

---

[2] (1780–1847), *reactionary prime minister of France in 1830. (ed.)*

poke their noses into everything. All the world knows that when England takes a pinch of snuff, France sneezes.

The twenty-fifth

Today the Grand Inquisitor came into my room again, but hearing his steps in the distance I hid under a chair. Seeing I wasn't there, he began calling me. At first he shouted "Poprischin!" I didn't say a word. Then: "Aksenty Ivanov! Titular councilor! Nobleman!" I still remained silent. "Ferdinand VIII, King of Spain!" I was on the point of sticking out my head, but then I thought: "No, my friend, you won't fool me, I know you: you will be pouring cold water on my head again." However, he caught sight of me and drove me from under the chair with a stick. That damned stick does hurt. However, I was rewarded for all this by the discovery I made today. I found out that every cock has a Spain, that it is under his wings [not far from his tail].[3]

The Grand Inquisitor went away, however, very angry, threatening me with some punishment. But I disdain his impotent malice, knowing that he is simply an instrument, a tool of England.

34 ᴚǝqɯnʌḭ⅄ ⅄ɹɐǝ 349

No, I haven't the strength to endure more. My God! the things they are doing to me! They pour cold water on my head! They won't listen to me, they won't see me, they won't hear me. What have I done to them? Why do they torture me? What do they want of a poor creature like me? What can I give them? I have nothing. It's too much for me, I can't endure these agonies, my head is burning and everything is going around. Save me, take me away! Give me a troika and horses swift as a whirlwind! Take your seat, my driver, ring out, my bells, fly upward, my steeds, and bear me away from this world! Far away, far away, so that nothing can be seen, nothing. Yonder the sky whirls before me, a star sparkles in the distance; the forest floats by with dark trees and the moon; blue-gray mist lies stretched under my feet; a chord resounds in the mist; on one side the sea, on the other Italy; yonder the huts of Russia can be seen. Is that my home in the distance? Is it my mother sitting before the window? Mother, save your poor son! Drop a tear on his sick head! See how they torment him! Press your poor orphan to your bosom! There is nowhere in the world for him! he is persecuted! Mother, have pity on your sick child! . . .

---

[3] *This phrase does not appear in the Academy edition of Gogol's works. Whether or not it belongs to Gogol at all is moot. (ed.)*

And do you know that the Dey of Algiers has a boil just under his nose?[4]

[4] *This line originally read: "The French king has a boil just under his nose." Since the word for boil in Russian, shishka, is a colloquialism for "trouble," the sentence could easily have been interpreted as an irreverent poke at Charles X, who had abdicated in August of 1830, and it is highly probable that Gogol was less than eager to become involved in a postrevolution imbroglio. In its present form, the line refers to the deposal of the last Dey of Algiers, Hussein Pasha, by the French, in 1830. (ed.)*

What happens to a person
when he is isolated from
others for an extended period
of time? The following
fictitious short story gives us
one author's ideas on this
subject. The young lawyer has
nothing but books written by
others and his own
intrapersonal communication
activities to sustain him for
15 years. The effects of his
intrapersonal communication
are rather easy to detect.

ANTON CHEKHOV

THE BET

I

It was a dark autumn night. The old banker was walking up and down
his study and remembering how, fifteen years before, he had given a
party one autumn evening. There had been many clever men there,
and there had been interesting conversations. Among other things they
had talked of capital punishment. The majority of the guests, among
whom were many journalists and intellectual men, disapproved of the
death penalty. They considered that form of punishment out of date,
immoral, and unsuitable for Christian States. In the opinion of some of
them the death penalty ought to be replaced everywhere by imprisonment for life.

"I don't agree with you," said their host the banker. "I have not
tried either the death penalty or imprisonment for life, but if one may
judge *à priori*, the death penalty is more moral and more humane than
imprisonment for life. Capital punishment kills a man at once, but
lifelong imprisonment kills him slowly. Which executioner is the more
humane, he who kills you in a few minutes or he who drags the life
out of you in the course of many years?"

Reprinted with permission of Macmillan Publishing Co., Inc. from The School-
mistress and Other Stories *by Anton Chekhov, translation from the Russian by
Constance Garnett. Copyright © 1921 by The Macmillan Company, renewed
1949 by David Garnett.*

"Both are equally immoral," observed one of the guests, "for they both have the same object—to take away life. The State is no God. It has not the right to take away what it cannot restore when it wants to."

Among the guests was a young lawyer, a young man of five-and-twenty. When he was asked his opinion, he said:

"The death sentence and the life sentence are equally immoral, but if I had to choose between the death penalty and imprisonment for life, I would certainly choose the second. To live anyhow is better than not at all."

A lively discussion arose. The banker, who was younger and more nervous in those days, was suddenly carried away by excitement; he struck the table with his fist and shouted at the young man:

"It's not true! I'll bet you two millions you wouldn't stay in solitary confinement for five years."

"If you mean that in earnest," said the young man, "I'll take the bet, but I would stay not five but fifteen years."

"Fifteen? Done!" cried the banker. "Gentlemen, I stake two millions!"

"Agreed! You stake your millions and I stake my freedom!" said the young man.

And this wild, senseless bet was carried out! The banker, spoilt and frivolous, with millions beyond his reckoning, was delighted at the bet. At supper he made fun of the young man, and said:

"Think better of it, young man, while there is still time. To me two millions are a trifle, but you are losing three or four of the best years of your life. I say three or four, because you won't stay longer. Don't forget either, you unhappy man, that voluntary confinement is a great deal harder to bear than compulsory. The thought that you have the right to step out in liberty at any moment will poison your whole existence in prison. I am sorry for you."

And now the banker, walking to and fro, remembered all this, and asked himself: "What was the object of that bet? What is the good of that man's losing fifteen years of his life and my throwing away two millions? Can it prove that the death penalty is better or worse than imprisonment for life? No, no. It was all nonsensical and meaningless. On my part it was the caprice of a pampered man, and on his part simple greed for money. . . ."

Then he remembered what followed that evening. It was decided that the young man should spend the years of his captivity under the strictest supervision in one of the lodges in the bankers garden. It was agreed that for fifteen years he should not be free to cross the threshold of the lodge, to see human beings, to hear the human voice, or to receive letters and newspapers. He was allowed to have a musical instrument and books, and was allowed to write letters, to drink wine, and to smoke. By the terms of the agreement, the only relations he could have with the outer world were by a little window made purposely for that object. He might have anything he wanted—books, music, wine, and so on—in any quantity he desired by writing an order, but could only receive them through the window. The agreement provided for every detail and every trifle that would make his imprisonment strictly solitary, and bound the young man to stay there *exactly* fifteen years, beginning from twelve o'clock of November 14, 1870, and ending at twelve o'clock of November 14, 1885. The slightest attempt on his part to break the conditions, if only two minutes before the end, released the banker from the obligation to pay him two millions.

For the first year of his confinement, as far as one could judge from his brief notes, the prisoner suffered severely from loneliness and depression. The sounds of the piano could be heard continually day and night from his lodge. He refused wine and tobacco. Wine, he wrote, excites the desires, and desires are the worst foes of the prisoner; and besides, nothing could be more dreary than drinking good wine and seeing no one. And tobacco spoilt the air of his room. In the first year the books he sent for were principally of a light character; novels with a complicated love plot, sensational and fantastic stories, and so on.

In the second year the piano was silent in the lodge, and the prisoner asked only for the classics. In the fifth year music was audible again, and the prisoner asked for wine. Those who watched him through the window said that all that year he spent doing nothing but eating and drinking and lying on his bed, frequently yawning and angrily talking to himself. He did not read books. Sometimes at night he would sit down to write; he would spend hours writing, and in the morning tear up all that he had written. More than once he could be heard crying.

In the second half of the sixth year the prisoner began zealously studying languages, philosophy, and history. He threw himself eagerly into these studies—so much so that the banker had enough to do to get him the books he ordered. In the course of four years some six hundred volumes were procured at his request. It was during this period that the banker received the following letter from his prisoner:

"My dear Jailer, I write you these lines in six languages. Show them to people who know the languages. Let them read them. If they find not one mistake I implore you to fire a shot in the garden. That shot will show me that my efforts have not been thrown away. The geniuses of all ages and of all lands speak different languages, but the same flame burns in them all. Oh, if you only knew what unearthly happiness my soul feels now from being able to understand them!" The prisoner's desire was fulfilled. The banker ordered two shots to be fired in the garden.

Then after the tenth year, the prisoner sat immovably at the table and read nothing but the Gospel. It seemed strange to the banker that a man who in four years had mastered six hundred learned volumes should waste nearly a year over one thin book easy of comprehension. Theology and histories of religion followed the Gospels.

In the last two years of his confinement the prisoner read an immense quantity of books quite indiscriminately. At one time he was busy with the natural sciences, then he would ask for Byron or Shakespeare. There were notes in which he demanded at the same time books on chemistry, and a manual of medicine, and a novel, and some treatise on philosophy or theology. His reading suggested a man swimming in the sea among the wreckage of his ship, and trying to save his life by greedily clutching first at one spar and then at another.

II

The old banker remembered all this, and thought:

"To-morrow at twelve o'clock he will regain his freedom. By our agreement I ought to pay him two millions. If I do pay him, it is all over with me: I shall be utterly ruined."

Fifteen years before, his millions had been beyond his reckoning; now he was afraid to ask himself which were greater, his debts or his assets. Desperate gambling on the Stock Exchange, wild speculation, and the excitability which he could not get over even in advancing years, had by degrees led to the decline of his fortune, and the proud, fearless, self-confident millionaire had become a banker of middling rank, trembling at every rise and fall in his investments. "Cursed bet!" muttered the old man, clutching his head in despair. "Why didn't the man die! He is only forty now. He will take my last penny from me, he will marry, will enjoy life, will gamble on the Exchange; while I shall look at him with envy like a beggar, and hear from him every day the same sentence: 'I am indebted to you for the happiness of my life, let me help you!' No, it is too much! The one means of being saved from bankruptcy and disgrace is the death of that man!"

It struck three o'clock, the banker listened; everyone was asleep in the house, and nothing could be heard outside but the rustling of the chilled trees. Trying to make no noise, he took from a fireproof safe the key of the door which had not been opened for fifteen years, put on his overcoat, and went out of the house.

It was dark and cold in the garden. Rain was falling. A damp cutting wind was racing about the garden, howling and giving the trees no rest. The banker strained his eyes, but could see neither the earth nor the white statues, nor the lodge, nor the trees. Going to the spot where the lodge stood, he twice called the watchman. No answer followed. Evidently the watchman had sought shelter from the weather, and was now asleep somewhere either in the kitchen or in the greenhouse.

"If I had the pluck to carry out my intention," thought the old man, "suspicion would fall first upon the watchman."

He felt in the darkness for the steps and the door, and went into the entry of the lodge. Then he groped his way into a little passage and lighted a match. There was not a soul there. There was a bedstead with no bedding on it, and in the corner there was a dark cast-iron stove. The seals on the door leading to the prisoner's rooms were intact.

When the match went out the old man, trembling with emotion, peeped through the little window. A candle was burning dimly in the prisoner's room. He was sitting at the table. Nothing could be seen but his back, the hair on his head, and his hands. Open books were lying on the table, on the two easy-chairs, and on the carpet near the table.

Five minutes passed and the prisoner did not once stir. Fifteen years' imprisonment had taught him to sit still. The banker tapped at the window with his finger, and the prisoner made no movement whatever in response. Then the banker cautiously broke the seals off the door and put the key in the keyhole. The rusty lock gave a grating sound and the door creaked. The banker expected to hear at once footsteps and a cry of astonishment, but three minutes passed and it was as quiet as ever in the room. He made up his mind to go in.

At the table a man unlike ordinary people was sitting motionless. He was a skeleton with the skin drawn tight over his bones, with long curls like a woman's, and a shaggy beard. His face was yellow with an earthy tint in it, his cheeks were hollow, his back long and narrow, and the hand on which his shaggy head was propped was so thin and delicate that it was dreadful to look at it. His hair was already streaked with silver, and seeing his emaciated, aged-looking face, no one would have believed that he was only forty. He was asleep. . . . In front of his bowed head there lay on the table a sheet of paper on which there was something written in fine handwriting.

"Poor creature!" thought the banker, "he is asleep and most likely dreaming of the millions. And I have only to take this half-dead man, throw him on the bed, stifle him a little with the pillow, and the most conscientious expert would find no sign of a violent death. But let us first read what he has written here. . . ."

The banker took the page from the table and read as follows:

"To-morrow at twelve o'clock I regain my freedom and the right to associate with other men, but before I leave this room and see the sunshine, I think it necessary to say a few words to you. With a clear conscience I tell you, as before God, who beholds me, that I despise freedom and life and health, and all that in your books is called the good things of the world.

"For fifteen years I have been intently studying earthly life. It is true I have not seen the earth nor men, but in your books I have drunk fragrant wine, I have sung songs, I have hunted stags and wild boars in the forests, have loved women. . . . Beauties as ethereal as clouds, created by the magic of your poets and geniuses, have visited me at night, and have whispered in my ears wonderful tales that have set my brain in a whirl. In your books I have climbed to the peaks of Elburz and Mont Blanc, and from there I have seen the sun rise and have watched it at evening flood the sky, the ocean, and the mountain-tops with gold and crimson. I have watched from there the lightning flashing over my head and cleaving the storm-clouds. I have seen green forests, fields, rivers, lakes, towns. I have heard the singing of the sirens, and the strains of the shepherds' pipes; I have touched the wings of comely devils who flew down to converse with me of God. . . . In your books I have flung myself into the bottomless pit, performed miracles, slain, burned towns, preached new religions, conquered whole kingdoms. . . .

"Your books have given me wisdom. All that the unresting thought of man has created in the ages is compressed into a small compass in my brain. I know that I am wiser than all of you.

"And I despise your books, I despise wisdom and the blessings of this world. It is all worthless, fleeting, illusory, and deceptive, like a mirage. You may be proud, wise, and fine, but death will wipe you off the face of the earth as though you were no more than mice burrowing under the floor, and your posterity, your history, your immortal geniuses will burn or freeze together with the earthly globe.

"You have lost your reason and taken the wrong path. You have taken lies for truth, and hideousness for beauty. You would marvel if, owing to strange events of some sorts, frogs and lizards suddenly grew on apple and orange trees instead of fruit, or if roses began to smell like a sweating horse; so I marvel at you who exchange heaven for earth. I don't want to understand you.

"To prove to you in action how I despise all that you live by, I renounce the two millions of which I once dreamed as of paradise and which now I despise. To deprive myself of the right to the money I shall go out from here five hours before the time fixed, and so break the compact. . . ."

When the banker had read this he laid the page on the table, kissed the strange man on the head, and went out of the lodge, weeping. At no other time, even when he had lost heavily on the Stock Exchange, had he felt so great a contempt for himself. When he got home he lay on his bed, but his tears and emotion kept him for hours from sleeping.

Next morning the watchmen ran in with pale faces, and told him they had seen the man who lived in the lodge climb out of the window into the garden, go to the gate, and disappear. The banker went at once with the servants to the lodge and made sure of the flight of his prisoner. To avoid arousing unnecessary talk, he took from the table the writing in which the millions were renounced, and when he got home locked it up in the fireproof safe.

I stopped in the mountains, got out, and climbed to the top. For the first time in twenty years of marriage, I was alone. All alone, just me, and the mountains. I found myself up there. I liked myself. This was three years ago, and ever since, I take time to be alone. I have a sound-proof studio at home, and now I go in, not to play, but just to be alone. I will sit there in my studio and I feel a charge of energy, a self-communication I find nowhere else. Maybe that's what you call liberation. N. O'Neill and G. O'Neill

---

The following paragraphs by
David Johnson clearly
articulate the importance of
self-acceptance—an effect that
can result only from
sustained efforts in the
intrapersonal communication
arena.

DAVID JOHNSON

ACCEPTANCE OF SELF AND OTHERS

To increase your self-acceptance, you must self-disclose in order to let other people know you and to experience acceptance by others. People are not accepting of individuals they do not know—most often they are neutral or indifferent. The relationship among self-acceptance, self-disclosure, and being accepted by other people is important. If you do not self-disclose, you cannot be accepted by others and your self-acceptance will not be increased. Paradoxically, not only is your self-acceptance increased by self-disclosing (and subsequently being accepted by others) but how easy it is for you to self-disclose is related to your level of self-acceptance. The greater your self-acceptance, the easier it will be for you to self-disclose. Self-confidence about your worth reduces the risks involved in self-disclosing. Self-acceptance is the key to reducing anxiety and fears about vulnerability resulting from self-disclosure. If you are afraid to let others know you, or anxious about the reactions others may have to your self-disclosure, you will not be open and disclosing, and, therefore, you will not be able to facilitate the development of good relationships with other people. If you are self-rejecting, you will find self-disclosure very risky.

The deepest conviction a self-rejecting person has is that once he is known he will be rejected and unloved. Before a self-rejecting person can have this conviction dissolved and experience more acceptance from himself and other persons, he must take the risk of disclosing himself. It is important for your self-acceptance that you are honest, genuine, and authentic in your self-disclosing. If you hide information about yourself or selectively try to create an impression on other people, the acceptance they give you may actually decrease your self-acceptance; you will know that it is your "mask" other people like and accept, not your "real" self. Being accepted for a "lie" leads only to self-rejection. It is only as you discover that you are loved for what you are, not for what you pretend to be or for the masks you hide behind, that you can begin to feel you are actually a person worthy of respect and love.

Prayer doesn't change things. It changes people and they change things.   J. Lair

---

3

INTERPERSONAL COMMUNICATION:
TRANSACTING WITH ANOTHER

Whereas intrapersonal communication is communication with oneself, interpersonal communication is communication with another. With the addition of another person, the nature and content of your communication are significantly altered. Your awareness of the presence of another person affects what you say and what you do. Furthermore, because you are aware that the other person is aware of you, you know that your presence affects his behavior. It is necessary that we adjust to the other person and this adjustment makes the communication interpersonal instead of solely intrapersonal. Obviously then, the addition of a second person complicates the nature of the communication. Each person is aware of himself, aware of the other, and also knows the other is aware of him.

Interpersonal communication is significant because communication in this arena is the most frequent and most direct. You can discover more information about each other than you can in the other arenas. You have an equal opportunity for sharing information with one another and your feedback to each other is immediate. Since communication in a dyadic (two-person) situation is so direct, participants are perceived as less manipulative than in communication encounters in the other arenas. Two people involved in communication both share in the communication exchange; they experience a reciprocal bond. With this bond, the interpersonal arena supplies the backdrop for dynamic relationships. Within this arena, significant conflicts can and do arise. But also in this arena, one has the opportunity to treat the other individual as a real person by being truly concerned for his welfare. This arena provides you with an opportunity to form meaningful relationships with other people.

INTERPERSONAL
COMMUNICATION
PERCEPTION

What we look at is not what we see.
W. Johnson

Just as the way we perceive ourselves is a personal thing, the process of viewing someone else is also personal. How can you, for example, *really* know what someone else is like? Your view of another is greatly influenced by *your own* needs and desires. If you have a need to be social and enjoy sitting and talking over coffee, then you may perceive someone who wants to study all the time as rude. On the other hand, a professor who has a need to have an impact on people might perceive that same "studious, rude person" as a valuable student.

We consider ourselves to be inside observers of outside reality. *We expect others to see things the way we do.* If we perceive someone as egotistical, we have a tendency to think he is really egotistical. We all "know" that others may not perceive him as egotistical, but we rarely behave that way. We must constantly remind ourselves that who we are and what our needs are govern what we see. The perception factor is crucial in the interpersonal communication arena. The following selections should help us be more sensitive to our perceptual judgments.

William Schutz says we all
have the interpersonal needs
of inclusion, affection, and
control. We need to feel that
we are significant and
worthwhile (inclusion), that
we are lovable (affection), and
that we are successfully
coming to grips with our
environment (control). The
degree of fulfillment of these
interpersonal needs significantly influences how we
relate to others in the interpersonal arena. For example,
if one is characteristically
undersocial, then he may
perceive a "friendly" person
as overbearing. As you read
the Schutz selection, note how
the descriptions apply to you
and your acquaintances.
Clearly, unfulfilled needs have
powerful impacts on how we
perceive others.

WILLIAM C. SCHUTZ

TYPES OF INTERPERSONAL BEHAVIOR

For each area of interpersonal behav-
ior three types of behavior will be described: (1) defi-
cient—indicating that the individual is not trying directly to satisfy the
need, (2) excessive—indicating that the individual is constantly trying
to satisfy the need, (3) ideal—indicating satisfaction of the need, and
(4) pathological.

In delineating these types it is assumed that anxiety engendered by
early experiences leads to behavior of the first, second, and fourth
types, while a successful working through of an interpersonal relation

leads to an individual who can function without anxiety in the area. For simplicity of presentation the extremes will be presented without qualifications. Actually, of course, the behavior of any given individual could be best described as some combination of behavior incorporating elements of all three types at different times, for instance, the over-social, undersocial, and social.

Inclusion Types

THE UNDERSOCIAL

The interpersonal behavior of the undersocial person tends to be introverted and withdrawn. Characteristically, he avoids associating with others and doesn't like or accept invitations to join others. Consciously he wants to maintain this distance between himself and others, and insists that he doesn't want to get enmeshed with people and lose his privacy. But unconsciously he definitely wants others to pay attention to him. His biggest fears are that people will ignore him, generally have no interest in him, and would just as soon leave him behind.

Unconsciously he feels that no one ever will pay attention to him. His attitude may be summarized by, "No one is interested in me, so I'm not going to risk being ignored. I'll stay away from people and get along by myself." There is a strong drive toward self-sufficiency as a technique for existence without others. Since social abandonment is tantamount to death, he must compensate by directing his energies toward self-preservation; he therefore creates a world of his own in which his existence is more secure. Behind this withdrawal lie anxiety and hostility, and often a slight air of superiority and the private feeling that others don't understand him.

The direct expression of this withdrawal is nonassociation and interaction with people, lack of involvement and commitment. The more subtle form is exemplified by the person who for one reason or another is always late to meetings, or seems to have an inordinate number of conflicting engagements necessitating absence from people, or the type of person who precedes each visit with, "I'm sorry, but I can't stay very long."

His deepest anxiety, that referring to the self concept, is that he is worthless. He thinks that if no one ever considered him important enough to receive attention, he must be of no value whatever.

Closely allied with this feeling is the lack of motivation to live. Association with people is a necessary condition for a desire to live.

This factor may be of much greater importance in everyday interaction than is usually thought. The degree to which an individual is committed to living probably determines to a large extent his general level of enthusiasms, perserverance, involvement, and the like. Perhaps this lack of concern for life is the ultimate in regression: if life holds too few rewards, the prelife condition is preferable. It is likely that this basic fear of abandonment or isolation is the most potent of all interpersonal fears. The simple fear that people are not interested in the self is extremely widespread, but in scientific analyses it, too often, is included as a special type of affectional need. It is extremely useful, however, to make clear the distinction between inclusion and affection.

THE OVERSOCIAL

The oversocial person tends toward extraversion in his later interpersonal behavior. Characteristically, he seeks people incessantly and wants them to seek him out. He is also afraid they will ignore him. His interpersonal dynamics are the same as those of the withdrawn person, but his overt behavior is the opposite.

His unconscious attitude is summarized by, "Although no one is interested in me, I'll make people pay attention to me in any way I can." His inclination is always to seek companionship. He is the type who "can't stand being alone." All of his activities will be designed to be done "together." An interesting illustration of this attitude occurs in the recent motion picture, "The Great Man." José Ferrer, as a newspaper man, is interviewing a woman about her reasons for attending the funeral of a television celebrity.

"Because our club all came together," she replies.
"But," Ferrer persists, "why did you come *here?*"
"I came here because the rest came here."
"Were you fond of the dead man?"
"Not especially," she replies, "but we always do things together."

This scene (the dialogue is from memory) nicely illustrates the importance of being together presumably as an end in itself. The interpersonal behavior of the oversocial type of person will then be designed to focus attention on himself, to make people notice him, to be prominent, to be listened to. There are many techniques for doing this. The direct method is to be an intensive, exhibitionistic participator. By simply forcing himself on the group he forces the group to focus attention on him. The more subtle technique is to try to acquire status through such devices as name dropping, or by asking startling questions. He may also try to acquire power (control) or try to be well liked (affection), but for the primary purpose of gaining attention. Power or friendship, although both may be important (depending on his orientation in the other two interpersonal areas), is not the primary goal.

THE SOCIAL

To the individual for whom the resolution of inclusion relations was successful in childhood, interaction with people presents no problem. He is comfortable with people and comfortable being alone. He can be a high or low participator in a group, or can equally well take a moderate role, without anxiety. He is capable of strong commitment and involvement to certain groups and also can withhold commitment if he feels it is appropriate.

Unconsciously, he feels that he is a worth while, significant person and that life is worth living. He is fully capable of being genuinely interested in others and feels that they will include him in their activities and that they are interested in him.

He also has an "identity" and an "individuality." Childhood feelings of abandonment lead to the absence of an identity; the person feels he is nobody. He has no stable figures with whom to identify. Childhood feelings of enmeshment lead to confusion of identity. When a child is nothing but parts of other people and has not had sufficient opportunity to evaluate the characteristics he observes in himself, he has difficulty knowing who he is. The social person has resolved these difficulties. He has integrated aspects of a large number of individuals into a new configuration which he can identify as himself.

Failure to be included means anxiety over having contact with people. Unsuccessful resolution of inclusion relations leads to feelings of exclusion, of alienation from people, of being different and unacceptable, and usually the necessity of creating a phantasy world in which the nonincluded person is accepted. Inclusion, because it is posited to be the first area of interpersonal relations to be dealt with by the infant, has strong narcissistic elements and other close similarities to the description by psychoanalysts of the interpersonal characteristics in the oral stage. Hence a pathological difficulty in the inclusion area leads to the most regressed kind of behavior, that concerned with belonging to people, being a significant individual. This syndrome is very much like the functional *psychoses*. In Ruth Munroe's description of the Freudian explanation of psychoses (66) these points are made clear:

"The essential feature of Freud's explanation of psychotic conditions may be stated as the greater depth of regression. The adult

never lapses back to infancy all of a piece of course . . . Freud felt, however, that the truly psychotic manifestations, belong to the pre-oedipal period—indeed to the stage of narcissism before the ego has properly developed. The mechanisms of psychoses are the archaic mechanisms of the infant before secure object relations have been established." (p. 288)

The last line of this quotation is especially pertinent to demonstrating the close relations between the Freudian discussion of the psychosis and the area of inclusion. The phrase, "before secure object [interpersonal] relations have been established," certainly bears a close resemblance to the preceding discussion of the problems of becoming included in the social group.

It appears, then, that difficulty in establishing a satisfactory relation with other persons, with regard to inclusion or contact, when difficulty reaches a pathological state, leads to psychosis, especially schizophrenia. This statement does not mean that all conditions now called psychosis are caused by difficulties in the inclusion area, nor does it necessarily mean that all inclusion problems will, if pathological, become psychoses; nor does it even imply that there are "pure" inclusion problems uncontaminated with other areas. It implies only that there is a close relation between disturbance in the inclusion area and psychosis.

Psychosis, especially schizophrenia, appears to be related more to the undersocial pattern than the oversocial. The lack of identity and inability to be alone, if carried to the extreme, would correspond to the pathological extreme of the oversocial.

Control Types

THE ABDICRAT

The abdicrat is a person who tends toward submission and abdication of power and responsibility in his interpersonal behavior. Characteristically, he gravitates toward the subordinate position where he will not have to take responsibility for making decisions, and where someone else takes charge. Consciously, he wants people to relieve him of his obligations. He does not control others even when he should; for example, he would not take charge even during a fire in a children's schoolhouse in which he is the only adult; and he never makes a decision that he can refer to someone else. He fears that others will not help him when he requires it, and that he will be given more responsibility than he can handle. This kind of person is usually a follower, or at most a loyal lieutenant, but rarely the person who takes the responsibility for making the *final* decision. Unconsciously, too, he has the feeling that he is incapable of responsible adult behavior and that others know it. He never was told what to do and therefore never learned. His most comfortable response is to avoid situations in which he will feel helpless. He feels that he is an incompetent and irresponsible, perhaps stupid, person who does not deserve respect for his abilities.

Behind this feeling are anxiety, hostility, and lack of trust toward those who might withhold assistance. The hostility is usually expressed as passive resistance. Hesitancy to "go along" is a usual technique of resistance, since actual overt rebellion is too threatening.

THE AUTOCRAT

The autocrat is a person whose interpersonal behavior often tends toward the dominating. Characteristically, he tries to dominate people and strongly desires a power hierarchy with himself at the top. He is the power seeker, the competitor. He is afraid people will not be influenced or controlled by him—that they will, in fact, dominate him.

Commonly, this need to control people is displaced into other areas. Intellectual or athletic superiority allows for considerable control, as does the more direct method of attaining political power. The underlying dynamics are the same as for the abdicrat. Basically the person feels he is not responsible or capable of discharging obligation and that this fact is known to others. He attempts to use every opportunity to disprove this feeling to others and to himself. His unconscious attitude may be summarized as, "No one thinks I can make decisions for myself, but I'll show them. I'm going to make all the decisions for everyone, always." Behind this feeling is a strong distrust that others may make decisions for him and the feeling that they don't trust him. This latter becomes a very sensitive area.

THE DEMOCRAT

For the individual who has successfully resolved his relations with others in the control area in childhood, power and control present no problem. He feels comfortable giving or not giving orders, and taking or not taking orders, as is appropriate to the situation. Unconsciously, he feels that he is a capable, responsible person and therefore that he does not need to shrink from responsibility or to try constantly to prove how competent he really is. Unlike the abdicrat and autocrat, he is not preoccupied with fears of his own helplessness, stupidity, and incompetence. He feels that other people respect his competence and will be realistic with respect to trusting him with decision making.

CONTROL PATHOLOGY

The individual who does not accept control of any kind develops pathologically into a psychopathic personality. He has not been adequately trained to learn the rules of behavior established for respecting the rights and privileges of others. Ruth Munroe (66) says,

> "The major Freudian explanation for this condition is that there has been a serious failure of superego development. The parental image has not been adequately internalized in the form of conscience but remains the policeman at the corner—an external force. Truly, the behavior of the psychopath is childish without the limited experience of the child. When the resources of adulthood are used without the inner controls of adulthood the resultant behavior is very likely to be deplorable. Object relations generally are poor of necessity since good early object relations would have led to more adequate superego development." (p. 292)

Affection Types

THE UNDERPERSONAL

The underpersonal type tends to avoid close personal ties with others. He characteristically maintains his dyadic relations on a superficial, distant level and is most comfortable when others do the same to him. Consciously, he wishes to maintain this emotional distance, and frequently expresses a desire not to get "emotionally involved"; unconsciously he seeks a satisfactory affectional relation. His fear is that no one loves him. In a group situation he is afraid he won't be liked. He has great difficulty genuinely liking people. He distrusts their feeling toward him.

His attitude could be summarized by the formula, "I find the affection area very painful since I have been rejected; therefore I shall avoid close personal relations in the future." The direct technique for maintaining emotional distance is to reject and avoid people to prevent emotional closeness or involvement actively, even to the point of being antagonistic. The subtle technique is to appear superficially friendly to *everyone*. This behavior acts as a safeguard against having to get close to, or become personal with, any *one* person. ("Close" and "personal" refer to emotional closeness and willingness to confide one's most private concerns and feelings. It involves the expression of positive affection and tender feelings.) Here the dyadic relation is a threatening one. To keep everyone at the same distance obviates the requirement for treating any one person with greater warmth and affection.

The deepest anxiety, that regarding the self, is that he is unlovable. He feels that people won't like him because, in fact, he doesn't "deserve" it. If people got to know him well, he believes, they would discover the traits that make him so unlovable. As opposed to the inclusion anxiety that the self is of no value, worthless, and empty, and the control anxiety that the self is stupid and irresponsible, the affection anxiety is that the self is nasty and bad.

THE OVERPERSONAL

The overpersonal type attempts to become extremely close to others. He definitely wants others to treat him in a very close, personal way. His response may be summarized by the formula, "My first experiences with affection were painful, but perhaps if I try again they will turn out to be better." He will be striving in his interpersonal relations primarily to be liked. Being liked is extremely important to him in his attempt to relieve his anxiety about being always rejected and unlovable. Again, there are two behavioral techniques, the direct and the subtle. The direct technique is an overt attempt to gain approval, be extremely personal, intimate, and confiding. The subtle technique is more manipulative, to devour friends and subtly punish any attempts by them to establish other friendships, to be possessive.

The underlying dynamics are the same as those for the underpersonal. Both the overpersonal and the underpersonal responses are extreme, both are motivated by a strong need for affection, both are accompanied by strong anxiety about ever being loved, and basically about being unlovable, and both have considerable hostility behind them stemming from the anticipation of rejection.

THE PERSONAL

For the individual who successfully resolved his affectional relations with others in childhood, close emotional relations with one other person present no problem. He is comfortable in such a personal relation, and he can also relate comfortably in a situation requiring emotional distance. It is important for him to be liked, but if he isn't liked he can accept the fact that the dislike is the result of the relation between himself and one other person—in other words, the dislike does not mean that he is an unlovable person. Unconsciously, he feels that he is a lovable person who is lovable even to people who know him well. He is capable of giving genuine affection.

AFFECTION PATHOLOGY

Neuroses are commonly attributed to difficulties in the area of affection. Ruth Munroe (66) says,

> *"The early bloom of sexuality, which cannot possibly come to fruition, is called the phallic stage to differentiate it from the true genitality leading to mature mating and reproduction. At this period attitudes are formed which are crucial for later heterosexual fulfillment and good relations with people generally. For this reason it is the stage most fraught with potentialities for neurotic distortion." (p. 199)*

Combining the early experience and present behavior with the pathological classification will provide a more complete picture of the process of personality development and disintegration.

Summary

To summarize, difficulties with initiating interaction range from being uncomfortable when not associating with people ("can't stand to be alone"—the *oversocial*) to not feeling comfortable initiating interaction ("can't stand being with people"—the *undersocial*). Difficulties with controlling others range from not feeling comfortable controlling the behavior of anyone ("can't tell anyone what to do"—the *abdicrat*) to not feeling comfortable when unable to control everyone ("always have to be in charge"—the *autocrat*). Difficulties with originating close, personal relations range from being uncomfortable when unable to establish a sufficiently close, personal relation ("can't get close enough"—the *overpersonal*) to being uncomfortable when getting too close and personal with someone ("don't like to get emotionally involved with people"—the *underpersonal*).

This description could be stated in psychoanalytic terms with little if any difference in meaning. In the struggle between the id and the superego to determine the individual's behavior the excessive response in each area represents the triumph of the id. The restrained response results from the triumph of the superego. The ideal response represents the successful resolution of the id impulses, the demands of the superego, and external reality; it therefore corresponds to the triumph of the ego.

In each of the nonideal (extreme) types described there are anxiety, hostility, and ambivalence. (One outcome of this analysis is to suggest that each of these widely used terms could be divided profitably into three types.) Anxiety arises from a person's (a) anticipation of a nonsatisfying event (for instance, being ignored, dominated, rejected) and (b) fear of exposure, both to self and others, of what kind a person he "really" is—his inadequate self-concept. The anxiety indicates that these behavior patterns are inflexible, since anxiety usually leads to rigid behavior. The threat involved in changing behavior is too great to allow for much flexibility. Hostility also follows from anxiety; so the hostility, too, may arise in three ways.

Finally, ambivalence is also present in the nonideal behaviors, since the behavior pattern being utilized is necessarily unsatisfactory. In many instances an overpersonal individual, for example, will occasionally become underpersonal, and vice versa. Complete reversals are to be expected more than slight modifications, especially for the extreme behavior patterns. The characterization of a person's behavior can desribe only his most usual behavior, not his invariable behavior.

There is a peculiar satisfaction in feeling that one understands another person, and in feeling that one is being understood.
R. D. Laing, H. Phillipson, and A. R. Lee

Laing, Phillipson, and Lee add
a new dimension to
interpersonal perception. They
demonstrate how the
perceptions of communication
participants affect the
relationship between them.
The communication
participants are literally bound
together by their relationship.
One's perception of another
affects the relationship, which
in turn affects the perception
of the other. And it happens
to both participants. The
perception we have of the
other depends on our
experience with him and the
meaning we attach to it. No
two of us perceive another's
behavior identically.

R. D. LAING
H. PHILLIPSON
A. R. LEE

INTERACTION AND INTEREXPERIENCE IN DYADS

In a science of persons, we state as axiomatic that:

1. behavior is a function of experience;
2. both experience and behavior are always in relation to some one or something other than self.

The very simplest schema for the understanding of the behavior of one person has to include at least two persons and a common situation. And this schema must include not only the interaction of the two, but their interexperience.

Thus:

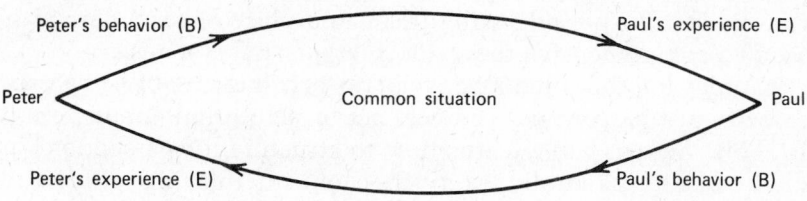

In terms of this schema, Peter's behavior towards Paul is in part a function of Peter's experiences of Paul. Peter's experience of Paul is in part a function of Paul's behavior towards Peter. Paul's behavior towards Peter is in turn partly a function of his experience of Peter, which in turn is in part a function of Paul's behavior towards him. Thus, the behavior of Peter towards Paul, and of Paul towards Peter, cannot be subsumed under an exclusively inter *behavioral* schema (much less any *intra*personal schema) if Peter and Paul are axiomatic persons. For, if Peter and Paul are persons, the behavior of each towards the other is mediated by the *experience* by each of the other, just as the experience is mediated by the behavior of each.

The transformation of Paul's behavior into Peter's experience entails all the constitutional and culturally-conditioned learned structures of perception that contribute to the ways Peter construes his world. Much of this learning has never been open to reflective awareness. To a much greater extent than most of us realize, and any of us wish to believe, we have been "programmed" like computing machines to handle incoming data according to prescribed instructions. Often this has been accompanied by meta-instructions against being aware that we are being thus instructed. This is an additional factor in the frequently great difficulty that many people have in opening their own "programming" to their own conscious reflection.

If each of us carries round a set of criteria by which we judge certain acts as loving and tender or hating and brutal, what may be a loving act to one person may be a hating act to another. For example, one woman may be delighted if her suitor uses a "caveman approach" with her; another woman may think of him as repugnant for just the same behavior. The woman who sees the caveman approach as loving may in turn interpret a more subtle approach as "weak," whereas the woman who is repelled by a caveman approach may see the more subtle approach as "sensitive." Thus behavior even of itself does not directly lead to experience. It must be perceived and interpreted according to some set of criteria. Although these intervening variables are not for the most part explicitly focused upon in this book, this does not mean that we are relegating them to a place of secondary significance in a comprehensive theory of interpersonal systems.

In order for the other's behavior to become part of self's experience, self must perceive it. The very act of perception entails interpretation. The human being learns how to structure his perceptions, particularly within his family, as a subsystem interplaying with its own contextual subculture, related institutions and overall larger culture. Let us take, for example, a situation in which a husband begins to cry. The behavior is crying. This behavior must now be experienced by his wife. It cannot be experienced without being interpreted. The interpretation will vary greatly from person to person, from culture to culture. For Jill, a man crying is inevitably to be interpreted as a sign of weakness. For Jane, a man crying will be interpreted as a sign of sensitivity. Each will react to a greater or lesser extent according to a preconceived interpretive model which she may or may not be aware of. At its simplest level, Jill may have been taught by her father that a man never cries, that only a sissy does. Jane may have been taught by her father that a man can show emotion and that he is a better man for having done so. Frequently such intermediary steps (regulative schemata) that contribute to the determination of the experience are lost to awareness. Jill simply experiences her husband as weak; Jane simply experiences hers as sensitive. Neither is clear why. They might even find it difficult to describe the kinds of behavior which have led them to their conclusions. Yet we must not simply attribute these interpretations to phantasy, as this term is often employed as a form of crypto-invalidation.

Our experience of another entails a particular interpretation of his behavior. To feel loved is to perceive and interpret, that is, to experience, the actions of the other as loving. The alteration of my experience of my behavior to your experience of my behavior—there's the rub.

I act in a way that is *cautious* to me, but *cowardly* to you.
You act in a way that is *courageous* to you, but *foolhardy* to me.
She sees herself as *vivacious*, but he sees her as *superficial*.
He sees himself as *friendly*, she sees him as *seductive*.
She sees herself as *reserved*, he sees her as *haughty and aloof*.
He sees himself as *gallant*, she sees him as *phoney*.
She sees herself as *feminine*, he sees her as *helpless and dependent*.
He sees himself as *masculine*, she sees him as *overbearing and dominating*.

Experience in all cases entails the perception of the act *and* the interpretation of it. Within the issue of perception is the issue of selection and reception. From the many things that we see and hear of the other we select a few to remember. Acts highly significant to us may be trivial to others. We happen not to have been paying attention at that moment; we missed what to the other was his most significant gesture or statement. But, even if the acts selected for interpretation are the same, even if each individual perceives these acts as the same act, the interpretation of the identical act may be very different. She winks at him in friendly complicity, and he sees it as seductive. The act is the same, the interpretation and hence the experience of it disjunctive. She refuses to kiss him goodnight out of "self-respect," but he sees it as rejection of him, and so on.

A child who is told by his mother to wear a sweater may resent her as coddling him, but to her it may seem to be simply a mark of natural concern.

In one society to burp after a good meal is good manners; in another its uncouth. Thus, even though the piece of behavior under consideration may be agreed upon, the intepretation of this behavior may be diametrically disagreed upon.

What leads to diametrically opposed interpretations? In general, we can say interpretations are based on our past learning, particularly within our family (i.e., with our parents, siblings and relatives) but also in the larger society in which we travel.

Secondly, the act itself is interpreted according to the context in which it is found. Thus, for example, the refusal of a goodnight kiss after one date may seem to be perfectly normal for both parties, but after six months' dating a refusal would seem more significant to each of them. Also a refusal after a previous acceptance will seem more significant.

What happens when two people do not agree on the meaning to be assigned a particular act? A very complicated process ensues. If communication is optimum, they *understand* that they differ on the interpretation of the act, and also *realize that they both understand* that they differ in its interpretation. Once this is established they may get into a struggle over whether or not to change the act under consideration in the future. This struggle may take various forms:

Threat—Do this or else.
Coaxing—Please do this.
Bribery—If you do this I will do that in return.
Persuasion—I believe it is a good idea for you to do this because, etc.

However, often in human affairs where there is a disagreement there is also a *misunderstanding* and *failure of realization of misunderstanding*. This may be deliberate, i.e., a simple attempt to ignore the other person's point of view, or it may be an unwitting overlooking of the opposing viewpoint. In either case a disruption of communication occurs. It seems to us that, *for the first time*, our notation makes it possible to characterize and pinpoint levels and pattern of disruption of this kind.

Thus, in the schema on page 113, E and B are categories of variables, each interposed or intervening between the direct impact of B on B and E on E. There is no naked contiguity, as it were, in interpersonal behavior, between the behavior of the one person and the behavior of the other, although much of human behavior (including the behavior of psychologists) can be seen as a unilateral or bilateral attempt to eliminate E from the transaction. Similarly, in this schema it is presumed that there is no direct contiguity or actual conflux of one person's experience with the other. The one person's experience is presumed always to be mediated to the other through the intervening category of the *behavior* (including verbal) of the one person, which in turn has to be perceived and interpreted in order to be experienced by the other. This means that, for the purpose of this enquiry, neither behavior that is the direct consequence of physical behavioral impact (as when one billiard ball hits another) nor experience in the one person generated directly through the experience of another (as in possible cases of extrasensory perception) is regarded as personal.

Now, we know that to different extents in different people and circumstances Peter's view of himself is related to what Peter thinks Paul thinks of him; that is, to Peter's metaperspective and meta-identity. If what Peter thinks Paul thinks of him is not what Peter wants to have thought of him, Peter has, in principle, as a means of controlling the condition that controls him, the option of acting upon Paul to change Paul, or of acting upon his own experience of Paul to change his experience of Paul. By acting on Paul, Peter may intend to act upon Paul's experience of Peter, or he may intend merely to act on Paul's action. If, for instance, he says "Shut up," this injunction may say in effect: "I don't care what you feel about me, just keep it to yourself."

That is, any act may be primarily addressed to the other or to myself, but if perceived it must affect both. If directed to the other, the immediate goal may be to effect change in the other, or to prevent change in the other. Similarly, if directed to self, the immediate aim may be to effect change in self, or to prevent change in self. But in dyadic relationships, any action on the other has effects on me, and any action on self affects the other. I may so act as to induce the other to experience me in a particular way. A great deal of human action has as its goal the induction of particular experiences in the other of one-self. I wish to be seen by the other as generous, or tough, or fair-minded. However, I may or may not know what it is that I have to do to induce the other to interpret my action and experience me as I desire, whether generous or tough or fair-minded. His criteria for making these evaluations may be diametrically opposed to my criteria, and this I may or may not be aware of. Thus a passively resistant person (e.g., a Gandhi) may seem to one person to be tough, whereas to another he may seem to be weak.

Further, the other may wittingly or unwittingly be set to interpret every possible action of mine as indicating a preconceived hypothesis (e.g., that I am hurtful). For example, at a conjoint therapy session a wife interpreted her husband's absence as proof that "he wished to hurt her." When he showed up late she quite calmly assumed that he had finally decided to *come* "in order to hurt her." This is a particularly difficult bind if at the same time the person implies that there is a right course of action that the other just hasn't found. In such a situation the covert operative set is that no matter what he does he intends to hurt, whereas the overt implication is that if he did not intend to hurt he would be doing the right thing.

I therefore tend to select others for whom I can be the other that I wish to be, so that I may then reappropriate the sort of meta-identity I want. This requires that I find another who agrees with my criteria. But such stratagems may entail a remarkable alienation. My center of gravity may become *the other I am to the other*. In such circumstances, in order to achieve the identity that I wish, through being the desired other for the other, the other must be malleable by me, or pervious to me. I must select carefully those others with whom I shall have to interact, acting towards them in such a way that I will be able to be to them what I want to be. I shall be in a serious dilemma, however, if I cannot make the other person regard me as that other that I wish to be for him. I may wish to be a mother to someone who is also wanting to be a mother, or to be generous to someone who insists on seeing me as mean, and so on. Alternatively, under those circumstances I may in desperation adopt the strategy of acting upon my *own* experience of the other, so that in a sense I render my meta-identity independent of the other.

Let us consider this latter strategy in more detail. We see it in one form of self's action on self, namely, Peter's action on his own experience of Paul, under the name of projection. Projection is a form of action directed at one's own experience of the other. It is called a "mental mechanism." This is a very misleading term, since it is neither mental nor mechanical. It is an action whose intentional object is one's own experience of the other. It is to the credit of psychoanalysis that it has brought to light actions of this kind.

Projection is clearly a most important stratagem and may function in different ways in an interpersonal system, but in every case it is one of a class of *actions whose primary object is not the other's experience of me, but my experience of the other.* Secondarily, of course, it must also affect the other's experience of me. For example, when the paranoid individual "projects," he may experience the other as hurting him and not helping him. This in turn forces the other to experience the paranoid as a person who sees him (o) as a hurtful person.

We said above that part of the theoretical problem constantly facing us is that we find it easier to think of each person in a dyad separately, or one at a time, rather than together. This is true, for instance, in terms of the theory of projection. There are a number of different aspects and versions of the concept of projection, not all rendered explicit.

We have already suggested that projection is one way of acting on the other by, paradoxically, not acting directly on him as a real person, but on one's experience of him. But if I convey to the other how I experience him I am certainly influencing him. Indeed, one of the most effective ways to affect the other's experience of me is to tell him how I experience him. Every flatterer knows that, all things being equal, one tends to like someone by whom one is liked. If I am ugly, I am not ugly only in my eyes, I see myself in the looking-glass of your eyes as ugly too. You are the witness of my ugliness. In fact, insofar as ugliness is relative, if you and everyone else saw me as beautiful, I might be ugly no more. If I cannot induce you to see me as I wish, I may act on my experience of you rather than your experience of me. I can invent your experience of me. Many projections, of course, are the apparently compulsive inventions of persons who see themselves as ugly, and wish to extrude this perception from their own self-self relation. At any rate, this is a commonly ascribed motive for projection. All projection involves a simultaneous negation of what projection replaces.

In Zarathustra, the ugliest man abolishes God because he cannot stand an eternal witness to his ugliness, and replaces him with nothing.

Projection refers to a mode of experiencing the other in which one experiences one's outer world in terms of one's inner world. Another way of putting this is that one experiences the perceptual world in terms of one's phantasy system, without realizing that one is doing this. One may seek to make the world actually embody one's phantasy, but this is another story, and projection can occur without so doing.

Pure projection tells us nothing about the other. Projection refers only to one area of the dyadic interaction, namely, the way you act on your own experience of me, or the way I act on my own experience of you, although it will, we know, be influenced by, and will influence, the other areas, since your way of experiencing me interrelates with the way I act towards you, and so on. The way Peter acts towards Paul will have something to do with the way Paul experiences Peter, and with the way Paul, for his part, now acts towards Peter. Unfortunately, there is no systematic theory to guide us here, and a paucity of empirical data. We have no language even to describe various things that can happen in other parts of the dyadic circuit when projection occurs in one section. For instance, how does Paul react to his realization that Peter's experience of Paul is largely projection, and to his realization that Peter's actions are not addressed to the Paul that Paul takes himself to be, but to a Paul who is largely Peter's invention? One way to ease the situation is for Paul systematically to discover the data upon which Peter is constructing him into a person he does not recognize. This is more exacting than to assume that Peter is purely inventing his view of Paul. By this tactic, it becomes Paul's job to discover the criteria by which Peter is coming to his discordant conclusions. These are inevitably there, but they may be hidden or so strange, even to Peter, let alone to Paul, that they are neglected, ignored, or considered insignificant; that is, invalidated in one way or another.

For example, a husband and wife, after eight years of marriage, described one of their first fights. This occurred on the second night of their honeymoon. They were both sitting at a bar in a hotel when the wife struck up a conversation with a couple sitting next to them. To her dismay her husband refused to join the conversation, remained aloof, gloomy and antagonistic both to her and the other couple. Perceiving his mood, she became angry at him for producing an awkward social situation and making her feel "out on a limb." Tempers rose, and they ended in a bitter fight in which each accused the other of being inconsiderate. This was the extent of their report of the incident. Eight years later, however, we were able to tease out some of the additional factors involved. When asked why she had struck up the conversation with the other couple, the wife replied: "Well, I had never had a conversation with another couple as a wife before. Previous to this I had always been a 'girl friend' or 'fiancée' or 'daughter' or 'sister.' I thought of the honeymoon as a fine time to try out my new role as a wife, to have a conversation as a wife with my husband at my side. I had never had a husband before, either." She thus carried into the situation her expectancy that the honeymoon would be an opportunity to begin to socialize as a couple with other couples. She looked forward to this eagerly and joyfully. By contrast, her husband had a completely differing view of the honeymoon. When questioned about his aloofness during the conversation he said: "Of course I was aloof. The honeymoon to me was a time to get away from everyone—a time when two people could learn to take advantage of a golden opportunity to ignore the rest of the world and simply explore each other. I wanted us to be sufficient unto ourselves. To me, everyone else in the world was a complication, a burden and an interference. When my wife struck up that conversation with the other couple I felt it as a direct insult. She was telling me in effect that I was not man enough for her, that I was insufficient to fill her demands. She made me feel inadequate and angry."

Eight years later they were able to laugh at the situation. He could say, "If I had only known how you felt it would have made a great difference." The crucial point is that each interpreted the other's action as inconsiderate and even deliberately insulting. These attributions of inconsiderateness and insult and maliciousness were based on hidden discrepant value systems and discrepant expectations based on these value systems.

Peter's concrete experience of Paul is a unity of the given and the constructed: a synthesis of his own (Peter's) interpretations of his perceptions based on his expectations and his (Peter's) phantasy (projection), and of the distal stimulus that originates from "Paul." The resultant fusion of projection-perception is the phenomenal Paul as experienced by Peter. Thus Paul-for-Peter is neither a total invention nor a pure perception of Peter's, nor a simple duplication of Paul's view of Paul. Paul as actually experienced by Peter will be compounded of perception, interpretation and phantasy. One might speak of a perception coefficient, according to the degree to which perception prevails over projection, or projection over perception. Also, one might speak of a coefficient of mismatching or disjunctive interpretive systems. Now Peter's actions towards Paul may follow from Peter's experience of Paul that is largely projective (has a high phantasy-coefficient) or from mismatched interpretive systems. Peter's experience and consequent actions are likely to be disjunctive with Paul's view of Paul, and with Paul's view of Peter's view of Paul. It is likely that if Peter's view of Paul is very disjunctive with Paul's view of Paul, whether itself highly phantasized or not, then Peter's actions will be addressed to a Paul that Paul does not recognize. Paul may register that Peter treats him with more or less deference than Paul expects, or is too familiar, or is too distant, or is too frightened of him, or not sufficiently so. Paul may find that Peter acts not toward the Paul that Paul takes himself to be, but as a mother, a father, a son, a daughter, a brother, a sister, etc.

All this suggests that Peter cannot perceive himself as Peter if he does not perceive Paul as Paul. If the coefficient of phantasy or of mismatched expectancy systems rises in Peter's experience of Paul, one expcts that Peter's view of himself will become correspondingly mismatched between his self-identity, meta-identity, and Paul's view of Peter, and Paul's view of Peter's meta-identity (not as yet trying to exhaust the different disjunctions) and that this will express itself in the increasingly "strange" way, that, in Paul's eyes, Peter acts towards Paul. It is not necessary to repeat this whole state of affairs, *mutatis mutandis*, exchanging Peter for Paul and Paul for Peter.

What we have to try to understand is how Peter's mismatched interpretations and phantasization[1] of his experience of Peter and Paul effects Paul, and how Paul's experiences of Paul and Peter in turn affect Peter's tendency to experience projectively and to act accordingly.

On might suppose that the easiest part of the circuit to become phantasized by Peter might be what was going on inside Paul, for here there is the minimum of validation available to Peter, except from the testimony of Paul.

Thus, Peter says, "I think you are unhappy inside."

Paul says, "No I'm not."

Peter may, however, attempt to validate his attribution about Paul's relation to Paul by watching the actions of Paul. He may say, "If *I* acted in that way I would be unhappy," or, "When mother acted that way she was unhappy." He may have nothing that he can "put his finger on," but "senses" that Paul is unhappy. He may be correctly reconstructing Paul's experience by succeeding in synthesizing many cues from Paul's behavior, or he may be "wrong" to construe Paul's behavior in his own terms (Peter's) rather than Paul's, or he may put inside Paul unhappiness that he is trying not to feel inside himself. It is not easy to discover criteria of validity here, because Peter may actually make Paul unhappy by "going on" about it. Let us suppose, however, that Peter's view of Paul is disjunctive with Paul's view of Paul over the issue of Paul's relation to Paul. Is Paul unhappy? Peter, wittingly or unwittingly, may register from witting or unwitting cues from Paul's behavior that Paul is unhappy. Paul may be seeking to deny

[1] *The concept of phantasy as a mode of experience in a social system is developed by Laing elsewhere (1961, 1966).*

his unhappiness. On the other hand, Peter may be attributing to Paul what he is denying himself. Furthermore, Peter may seek to avoid feeling unhappy himself by *trying to make Paul unhappy*. One of his ways of doing this may be to tell Paul that he or Paul is unhappy. Let us suppose he does the latter. Paul may accuse Peter of trying to make him unhappy by telling him he is. Very likely, Peter will repudiate this attribution in favor, perhaps, of one of the order, "I am only trying to help you."

Sometimes, what appears to be projection is really a complicated mismatching of expectations, i.e., the interpretation that p gives to o's not fulfilling his expectation. Thus, if Peter becomes upset about something, Paul may hope to help him by remaining calm and detached. However, Peter may feel that this is just the wrong thing for Paul to be doing when he is upset. His feeling may be that a really friendly, helpful person would get upset with him. If Paul does not know this and Peter does not communicate it, Peter may assume that Paul is deliberately staying aloof to hurt him. Paul may then conclude that Peter is "projecting" angry feelings onto him. This, then, is a situation where projection is attributed by Paul to Peter, but it has not actually occurred. This commonly happens in analytical therapy when the analyst (Paul) assumes that a detached mirrorlike attitude is the most helpful stance he can adopt towards the patient (Peter). However, the patient may feel that only an open self-disclosing person could be of help, and if he goes on to interpret the analyst's stance as not only unhelpful in effect but unhelpful in intention, then the analyst may in turn counter-attribute "projection" to the patient. A vicious circle of mismatched interpretations, expectancies, experiences, attributions and counter-attributions is now in play.

It starts to whirl something like this:

Peter:	Paul:
1. I am upset.	1. Peter is upset.
2. Paul is acting very calm and dispassionate.	2. I'll try to help him by remaining calm and just listening.
3. If Paul cared about me and wanted to help he would get involved and show some emotion also.	3. He is getting even more upset. I must be even more calm.
4. Paul knows that this upsets me.	4. He is accusing me of hurting him.

| 5. If Paul knows that his be-havior upsets me, he must be intending to hurt me. | 5. I'm really trying to help. |
| 6. He must be cruel, sadistic. Maybe he gets pleasure out of it, etc. | 6. He must be projecting. |

Attributions of this kind, based on a virtually inextricable mix of mismatched expectations and phantasy and perception, are the very stuff of interhuman reality. One has, for instance, to enter into this realm in order to understand how one person's attributions about others may begin to be particularly disturbing and disjunctive to the others, and come to be repeatedly invalidated by them, so that he may begin to be subject to the global attribution of being mad (Laing, 1961, 1964, 1965).

However, even all-round conjunctions—between Peter's view of Peter and Paul's view of Peter, Peter's view of Paul and Paul's view of Paul, Peter's view of Paul's view of Paul and Paul's view of Peter's view of Paul's view of Paul, Peter's view of Paul's view of Peter and Paul's view of Peter's view of Paul—do not validate a perceptive circle. They achieve all-round "reliability" but not "validity." They "validate" equally readily a *phantasy circle*. These whirling phantasy circles, we suggest, are as destructive to relationships, individual (or international), as are hurricanes to material reality.

To summarize so far. Through my behavior I can act upon three areas of the other: on his experience of me; on his experience of himself; and upon his behavior. In addition, I cannot act on the other himself directly, but I can act on my own *experience* of him.

We see that in a dyadic system, there is no isolated individual person.
R. D. Laing, H. Phillipson, and A. R. Lee

INTERPERSONAL
COMMUNICATION
NONVERBAL BEHAVIOR

What you are speaks so loudly I can't
hear what you say.   R. W. Emerson

In any interpersonal transaction, the things you and the other person say are important, but even more crucial are the nonverbal aspects of the relationship. The glances you exchange, where you sit in relation to each other, the tone of voice you project, and hundreds of other nonverbal stimuli are the stuff from which others get their impressions of you.

While in intrapersonal communication, the primary concern might be with internal nonverbal cues, in interpersonal communication one must be aware of the nonverbal signals he is sending and, in addition, must understand the nonverbal stimuli he receives from others and why he reacts to them the way he does. If, for example, the person you are talking to looks at the floor throughout the conversation, you might conclude a variety of things. You may be offended, you may think he is uninterested in you, or you might even think he is a pensive, thoughtful person. Whatever your reaction, a simple little thing like eye gaze has caused it. The bulk of your reaction might well have been shaped by it and other nonverbal cues. The selections in this unit will hopefully sensitize you to the importance of nonverbal cues in interpersonal communication.

Following are two readings, a
brief one by David Johnson
and a more extensive one
by Nena O'Neill and George
O'Neill, which make it
abundantly clear that nonverbal elements are vital to a
communication relationship.
How nonverbal cues function
and how they join with verbal
cues to convey meaning are
aptly demonstrated. Notice
how lack of agreement or
inconsistency between verbal
and nonverbal signals
affect a communication
relationship.

DAVID JOHNSON

THE NONVERBAL EXPRESSION OF FEELINGS

Although the awareness, acceptance, and expression of feelings is crucial for psychological health
and for the building and maintaining of ful-
filling relationships, many people have great difficulties in clearly and
accurately communicating how they feel to other individuals. Expressing positive feelings such as warmth is a crucial interpersonal skill.
Like all communication, however, feelings are expressed in nonverbal
and behavioral ways as well as verbally. In this article we will focus
upon the skills necessary for effective nonverbal expression of feelings.
The objectives of the article are:

1. To increase your self-awareness of how you communicate feelings to others.
2. To provide skill practice in expressing feelings nonverbally.
3. To remind you of the importance of the congruence between
   your verbal, nonverbal, and behavioral cues in clearly and accurately communicating your feelings to another person.

David W. Johnson, Reaching Out: Interpersonal Effectiveness and Self-Actualization, *copyright © 1972, pp. 103–105. Reprinted by permission of Prentice-
Hall, Inc., Englewood Cliffs, New Jersey.*

Nonverbal Communication

In communicating effectively with other individuals it may be more important to have a mastery of nonverbal communication than fluency with words. In a normal two-person conversation the verbal components carry less than 35 percent of the social meaning of the situation while more than 65 percent is carried by nonverbal messages (Mc-Croskey, Larson, & Knapp, 1971). This may seem surprising to you, but we communicate by our manner of dress, physique, posture, body tension, facial expressions, degree of eye contact, hand and body movements, tone of voice, continuities in speech (such as rate, duration, nonfluencies and pauses), spatial distance, and touch as well as by words. In order to communicate effectively with other persons, therefore, you must be as concerned with the nonverbal messages you are sending as with the verbal ones, if not more so.

By comparison with verbal language, however, nonverbal behavior is very limited. Usually it is used to communicate feelings, likings, and preferences, and it customarily reinforces or contradicts the feelings that are communicated verbally. A major problem in communicating feelings is that feelings are communicated less by words a person uses than by his nonverbal cues. Particularly important in communicating feelings are facial and vocal cues; smiles, for example, communicate friendliness, cooperativeness, and acceptance to other individuals; there appears to be more eye contact between people who like each other than between people who do not like each other; and emotional meanings are communicated quite accurately through vocal expressions.

It is often difficult to know what another person really feels. He says one thing but does another; he seems to like you but never says so; he says he has great affection for you but somehow you don't feel he is sincere. Feelings are often misunderstood and misinterpreted for two major reasons: one, the ambiguity of nonverbal messages, and the other, the frequent contradictions between verbal and nonverbal messages.

Nonverbal messages are inevitably ambiguous; therefore, the receiver is unclear as to what the sender is feeling. The same feeling can be expressed nonverbally in several different ways; for example, anger may be communicated by great bodily motion or by a frozen stillness. Any single nonverbal cue, furthermore, can arise from a variety of feelings; a blush may indicate embarrassment, pleasure, or even hostility. There are wide differences among social groups as to the meaning of many nonverbal cues; standing close to the receiver may be a sign of warmth to a person from one cultural background and a sign of aggressiveness and hostility to a person from another cultural background. In understanding nonverbal messages, the receiver must interpret the sender's actions and, as these actions increase in ambiguity, the chance for misinterpretation increases.

Correct judgments of the feelings of other individuals are often made difficult by the different degrees of feelings, or contradictory kinds of feelings, being expressed simultaneously through verbal and nonverbal messages. We have all been in situations in which we have received or sent conflicting messages on verbal and nonverbal channels. The parent who screams, "I WANT IT QUIET AROUND THIS HOUSE," or the teacher who says, "I've always got plenty of time to talk to a student" while he glances at his watch and nervously begins packing his briefcase, are examples. Sometimes a person may say, "I like you," but communicate nonverbally by a cold tone of voice, looking worried, and backing away, "Don't come close to me." When receiving such conflicting messages through two different channels, we tend to believe the message that we perceive to be harder to fake. This is often the nonverbal channel. You are, therefore, more apt to believe the nonverbal communication than the verbal one. Such contradictory communications are known as "double binds" and can cause anxiety and suspiciousness in the receiver.

Nonverbal messages, in summary, are more powerful in communicating feelings than are verbal messages, but also more ambiguous and difficult to interpret accurately. To communicate your feelings clearly and accurately to another person, you need to be skillful in both the verbal and nonverbal ways of expressing feelings. Above all, you need to make your verbal and nonverbal messages congruent with each other.

NENA O'NEILL
GEORGE O'NEILL

NON-VERBAL
COMMUNICATION

Research has indicated that about 70 percent of our communication with others is carried out on a non-verbal level. The most profound form of non-verbal communication is, of course, sex. But the ways in which your mate walks, stands, holds her head, drums his fingers, smiles or frowns are important, too, and can often tell you far more than words. Every action provides a sensory cue that can be read by others. Some of us are so acutely aware of these cues and responses that we are frequently able to add up the sensory data and then intuit beyond them to another level of understanding, leading us to say we feel "vibrations" from other persons. We can pick up such vibrations from people we've never met but simply exchanged a glance with across a room. Yet in our relationships with those closest to us, we tend to ignore these signals. In many cases we simply become so used to our mate's non-verbal signs that they cease to affect us on a conscious level. Sometimes, too, we deliberately screen them out, either from impatience or because we don't want to recognize the message that is being sent.

Even though body language is often ignored or misread, non-verbal communication is still less complicated than verbal. For this very reason, it should be easier to correct some of our mistakes in this area first. You can make a conscious effort to be receptive to your mate's non-verbal signs and to act according to what they tell you. When Helen comes home from the dentist with a swollen jaw and her eyes dulled with pain, it is sheer sadism to remind her that a pail of dirty diapers has been sitting at the foot of the basement stairs since yesterday.

Timing is a crucial element in life—not only in choosing the right moment to grasp an opportunity, but also in learning when to avoid the wrong moment. If you insist on bombarding your husband with all of your aggravating grievances of the day the moment he comes in the door crumpled from a heat wave and a discouraging day at work, then you are deliberately ignoring non-verbal cues and asking for a fight.

Of course, part of you may be just spoiling for a fight, even though the other half of you would like to avoid it. If you keep your eyes open, and look for the telltale physical signs and body cues that reveal your mate's state of mind, then you will have a much better chance of controlling your responses when your own feelings are divided. Helen's husband, for instance, may indeed feel a degree of unconscious sadism, wondering why the devil he had to marry the woman with the worst teeth in the state, so that he's always up to his neck in dentist's bills. Because he unconsciously wants to upbraid her for something that he consciously realizes she can't possibly help, he seizes on the diapers as a substitute rebuke. But if he opens himself to her non-verbal signals, thus allowing himself to recognize her genuine pain, he will feel sorry for her, and the unconscious urge to hurt her will be squelched.

Discrepant Messages

Learning to read the non-verbal cues of your mate can also help you untangle the confusions caused by discrepant messages. Discrepant messages occur when our verbal and non-verbal forms of communication contradict one another. Bill may say to his wife, "I'm listening, I'm listening," but his body is hunched over attentively in front of the television set. Arthur may tell his wife, "I love you," over and over, but she has good cause to wonder if he means it when he never listens to her attentively, gives her only a peck on the cheek, and is perfunctory in bed.

Whatever we may *say*, it's the *non-verbal message* that usually tells the truth. A verbal lie is all too easy to tell. Controlling your body sufficiently to make it back up your lie is much more difficult. And frequently, even when we ourselves believe our own verbal messages, our bodies may tell a different story.

The discrepancy between a body message and a verbal message may well indicate a problem area in the relationship between husband and wife. Couples who are trying to develop a new openness and move away from the restrictive conditions of a closed marriage may find the pinpointing of discrepant messages in one another a useful method by which to improve communication in general between them. Discovering the contradictions in messages can uncover and bring to light unrecognized needs, feelings and desires.

In the open marriage there should be no need for saying things you don't mean. Bill should not have to say "I'm listening, I'm listening," when he isn't. If he is intently watching television, it is obviously not the time for Mary to start a discussion or rattle on about unimportant matters. However, if her verbal message and a discussion of it is terribly urgent *she* should be able to say so, and Bill should be able to turn off the TV set and listen. If not, *he* should be able to say openly,

"Could we wait till later, Mary?" and Mary can respect his desire to delay the conversation, for she will expect the same kind of consideration from him at another time.

The ability to recognize discrepant messages in one another can provide the couple with important clues as to those areas of the closed marriage that are most restrictive to both. This is not to suggest, of course, that Bill's wife should immediately cry out, "Aha, caught you in the act, you're sending a discrepant message, you don't really want to listen to me at all!" Instead, a frank discussion of the contradictory message that each notices in the other can lead to a much fuller understanding of just how the contract is affecting them. Pinpointing the real message Bill was sending from the TV set could well lead into a discussion of the "your time is my time" clause of closed marriage, and lead to a new respect for each other's privacy.

Creating a Non-Verbal Language

Learning to read your mate's non-verbal signals can help you to understand him or her better, and guide you in choosing the best time for and the best kind of verbal communication. But partners who become aware of the tremendous importance of non-verbal communication can use it as a language in itself. Since our understanding of this type of visible communication is still in its infancy, most of us have been alerted only to *reading* the body messages of others. But body language can, with sensitivity, training and skill, be used as a direct means of communication. From becoming increasingly aware of each other, partners can learn to read, interpret and respond to each other's silent signals. Couples can set up a prearranged system of non-verbal signals for all kinds of situations, such as the golf hat and bandanna we mentioned under Privacy or the signals couples give each other at parties to indicate boredom, silence on certain topics, or "it's time to leave." They can even develop a silent language of their own, a kind of shorthand that cuts across other barriers and which will in the long run become an important aid to better verbal communication.

Sensuality as Communication

Visual communication with body messages is only one kind of nonverbal language. Another method of communicating without words is to use our bodies directly. The need to reach out and *touch* one another, if only for a moment, has created a new national pastime. Sensitivity training and encounter groups flourish from coast to coast. Why their sudden popularity? It is because we desperately need to reawaken our physical senses.

The infant first learns about the world through his sense of touch. His feelings of confidence, trust and warm intimacy are first established by being held, supported, touched, caressed and attended to physically. But in our society this deep need for physical intimacy—the need to reach out and touch, to *feel*—is trained out of us as we grow up. Physical demonstrations of emotion are frowned upon, and we are taught to curb our sensual and erotic sensitivities from earliest childhood. Is it any wonder couples have trouble expressing the simplest affection—or even compassion and sorrow—in a physical way? Is it any wonder that so many couples have difficulty in achieving sexual compatibility? You can't train someone *not* to respond for twenty-five years and then turn around and ask him to perform responsively in bed.

Couples need to relearn the full use of physical expression as a means of intimate communication and to reawaken their sensuality. The dictionary defines sensual as "voluptuous" or "devoted to pleasure of the senses and appetite," and adds, as a final caution, "sometimes lewd." Thus disapproval of sensuality is built right into our language. But sensuality, far from being lewd, is absolutely necessary to good physical communication. The sensuous exchange between partners is the manifest physical expression of caring.

Words are only necessary after love
has gone.   J. Lair

Julius Fast, author of *Body Language*, tells us how one can read, interpret, and utilize body language, which is one form of nonverbal communication. Although Fast is often accused of being non-academic in his attempts to discuss the importance of nonverbal communication, we believe that most readers can grow as a result of exposure to his "gut-level" observations.

JULIUS FAST

THE SILENT LANGUAGE OF LOVE

Stance, Glance and Advance

Mike is a ladies' man, someone who is never at a loss for a girl. Mike can enter a party full of strangers and within ten minutes end up on intimate terms with one of the girls. Within half an hour he has cut her out of the pack and is on his way home with her—to his or her place, depending on which is closer.

How does Mike do it? Other men who have spent half the evening drumming up enough courage to approach a girl, will see Mike come in and take over quickly and effectively. But they don't know why.

Ask the girls and they'll shrug. "I don't know. He just has his antennae out, I guess. I get signals, and I answer them, and the first thing I know...."

Mike is not particularly good looking. He's smart enough, but that's not his attraction. It seems that Mike almost has a sixth sense about him. If there's an available girl Mike will find her, or she will find him.

What does Mike have?

Well, if he hasn't looks or brilliance, he has something far more important for this type of encounter. Mike has an unconscious command of body language and he uses it expertly. When Mike saunters into a room he signals his message automatically. "I'm available, I'm masculine. I'm aggressive and knowledgeable." And then when he zeroes in on his chosen subject, the signals go, "I'm interested in you. You attract me. There's something exciting about you and I want to find out what it is."

Watch Mike in action. Watch him make contact and signal his availability. We all know at least one Mike, and we all envy him his ability. What is the body language he uses?

Well, Mike's appeal, Mike's nonverbal clarity, is compounded of many things. His appearance is part of it. Not the appearance he was born with, that's rather ordinary, but the way Mike has rearranged that appearance to transmit his message. There is, when you look at Mike carefully, a definite sexuality about him.

"Of course," a knowing woman will say, "Mike is a very sexy man." But sexy how? Not in his features.

Pressed further, the woman will explain, "It's something about him, something he has, a sort of aura."

Actually it's nothing of the sort, nothing so vague as an aura. In part it's the way Mike dresses, the type of pants he chooses, his shirts and jackets and ties, the way he combs his hair, the length of his sideburns—these all contribute to the immediate picture, but even more important than this is the way Mike stands and walks.

One woman described it as an "easy grace." A man who knew Mike was not so kind. "He's greasy." What came through as pleasing to the woman was transmitted as disturbing or challenging and therefore distasteful to the man, and he reacted by characterizing the quality contemptuously.

Yet Mike does move with grace, an arrogant sort of grace that could well arouse a man's envy and a woman's excitement. A few actors have that same movement, Paul Newman, Marlon Brando, Rip Torn, and with it they can transmit an obvious sexual message. The message can be broken down into the way they hold themselves, their stance or posture, and the easy confidence of their motion. The man who has that walk needs little else to turn a woman's head.

But Mike has more. He has dozens of little gestures, perhaps unconscious ones, that send out elaborations of his sexual message. When

Mike leans up against a mantel in a room to look around at the women, his hips are thrust forward slightly, as if they were cantilevered, and his legs are usually apart. There is something in this stance that spells sex.

Watch Mike when he stands like this. He will lock his thumbs in his belt right above the pockets, and his fingers will point down toward his genitals. You have surely seen the same stance a hundred times in Western movies, usually not taken by the hero, but by the sexy bad guy as he lounges against a corral fence, the picture of threatening sexuality, the villain the men hate and the women—well, what they feel is a lot more complex than hate or desire or fear, and yet it's a mixture of all these things. With his blatant body language, his leather chaps, his cantilevered groin and pointing fingers he is sending out a crude, obvious but effective signal. "I am a sexual threat. I am a dangerous man for a woman to be alone with. I am all man and I want you!"

On a minor scale, less blatant, Mike sends out the same message.

But his body language doesn't stop there. This much serves to signal his intentions, to create an atmosphere, an aura if you will. This fascinates the available women and interests or even irritates the non-available ones.

Mike himself explained how he proceeded after this. "I size up the women, the ones who want it. How? It's easy. By the way they stand or sit. And then I make my choice and I catch her eye. If she's interested she'll respond. If not, I forget her."

"How do you catch her eye?"

"I hold the glance a little longer than I should, since I don't really know her. I won't let her eyes slide away, and I narrow mine—sort of."

But there is even more to Mike's approach than the insistent eye, as I observed one evening at a party. Mike has an uncanny instinct for sizing up a woman's defensive body language and insistently breaking it down. Are her arms clasped defensively? He opens his. Is her posture rigid? He relaxes as they talk. Is her face pinched and drawn? He smiles and loosens his face.

In short, he answers her body signals with opposite and complementary signals of his own, and by doing this intrudes himself into her awareness. He brushes aside her body language pretenses, and because unconsciously she really wants to open herself up, she opens up to Mike.

Mike moves in on a woman. When he has made signal contact, when his body language gets the message of his availability across, his next step is physical invasion, but physical invasion without touch.

He cuts into the woman's territory or body zone. He comes close enough for her to be uneasy, and yet not close enough for her to logically object. Mike doesn't touch his victim needlessly. His closeness, his intrusion into her territory, is enough to change the situation between them.

Then Mike carries his invasion even further by visual intrusion as they talk. What they say really doesn't matter much. Mike's eyes do far more talking than his voice. They linger on the woman's throat, on her breasts, her body. They linger sensuously and with promise. Mike touches his tongue to his lips, narrows his eyes, and invariably, the woman becomes uneasy and excited. Remember, she's not just any woman, but that particular susceptible woman who has responded to Mike's opening gambit. She has returned his flattering attentions, and now she is in too deep to protest.

And anyway, what could she protest against? Just what has Mike done? He hasn't touched her. He hasn't made any suggestive remark. He is, by all the standards of society, a perfect gentleman. If his eyes are a bit too hot, a bit too bold, this is still a matter of interpretation. If the girl doesn't like it she has only to be rude and move off.

But why shouldn't the girl like it? Mike is flattering her with his attention. In effect he is saying, "You interest me. I want to know you better, more intimately. You're not like other women. You're the only woman here I care about."

For, in addition to his flattering attention to this woman, Mike never makes the mistake of spreading his interest. He narrows his focus and speaks to only one woman, and he makes the impact of his body language all the stronger for it. Half the time, when Mike leaves with the girl of his choice, she hardly needs any persuasion. By that time a simple, "Let's go!" is enough.

Is She Available?

How does Mike single out his victim? What body language does an available girl at a party use to say, "I'm available. I'm interested. I can be had"? There must be a definite set of signals because Mike rarely makes a mistake.

A girl in our society has an additional problem in this game of sexual encounters. No matter how available she may be, it's considered pretty square to let anyone know it. This would instantly put her value down and cheapen her. And yet, unconsciously, she must let her intent be known; how does she do it?

A big part of the way she transmits her message is also in stance, posture or movement. An available woman moves in a studied way. A man may label it posing, another woman, affection, but the movement of her body, hips and shoulders telegraphs her availability. She may sit with her legs apart, symbolically open and inviting, or she may affect a gesture in which one hand touches her breast in a near caress. She may stroke her thighs as she talks or walk with a languorous roll to her hips. Some of her movements are studied and conscious, some completely unconscious.

A few generations ago female availability was broadly burlesqued by Mae West's "come up and see me sometime" routine. A later generation turned to the baby-face and hushed and breathless voice quality of a Marilyn Monroe—a tarnished innocence. Today, in a more cynical age, it is again blatant sexuality. Someone like Raquel Welch spells out the message. But these are the obvious, motion picture messages. On a subtler, living-room level, the level on which Mike operates, the message is more discreet, often so discreet that the man who is ignorant of body language misses it completely. Even the man who knows a little about the subject may be misled. For example, the woman who crosses her arms across her chest may be transmitting the classic signal, "I am closed to any advance. I will not listen to you, or hear you."

This is a common interpretation of closed arms, and it is one with which most psychologists are familiar. As an example of this, there was a recent story in the papers about Dr. Spock addressing a class at the Police Academy. The audience of police were extremely hostile to the good doctor, in spite of the fact that he was responsible for the way most of them and their children had been brought up. They demonstrated their hostility verbally in their discussion, but also much more obviously in body language. In the news photo, every policeman sat with his arms crossed tightly over his chest, his face hard and closed.

Very clearly they were saying, "I am sitting here with a closed mind. No matter what you say I'm unwilling to listen. We just can't meet." This is the classical interpretation of crossed arms.

But there is another equally valid interpretation. Crossed arms may say, "I am frustrated. I am not getting what I need. I am closed in, locked in. Let me out. I can be approached and am readily available."

While the man who knows only a little about body language may misinterpret this gesture, the man well educated in body language will get the correct message from the accompanying signals the girl sends out. Is her face pinched and tight with frustration? Is she sitting stiffly instead of in a relaxed position? Does she avert her eye when you try to catch it?

Nonverbal Behavior 137

All the body signals must be added up to a correct total if a man is to use body language effectively.

The aggressively available woman acts in a predictable fashion too. She has a number of effective tricks of body language to telegraph her availability. As Mike does, she uses territorial intrusion to make her point. She will sit uncomfortably close to the man she is after, taking advantage of the uneasiness such closeness arouses. As the man shifts and fidgets, unaware of why he is disturbed, she will move in with other signals, using his uneasiness as a means of throwing him off balance.

While a man on the make cannot touch the woman if he is to play the game fairly, it is perfectly permissible for a woman on the make, at this stage of the game, to touch the man. This touch can exaggerate the uneasiness of the man into whose territory she has cut.

A touch on the arm can be a disarming blow. "Do you have a match?" Steadying the hand that holds it to her cigarette can allow a moment of flesh-to-flesh contact that may be effectively troubling.

The contact of a woman's thigh, or her hand carelessly brushed against a man's thigh can be devastating if it is applied at just the right moment.

The aggressive approach by a woman can utilize not only body language—the adjustment of a skirt as she sits close, the uncrossing of her legs, the thrusting forward of her breasts, a pouting mouth—it can also utilize smell. The right perfume in the right amount, to give an elusive but exciting scent, is an important part of the aggressive approach.

Is the Face Worth Saving?

But sight, touch and smell are still less than the complete arsenal of the woman on the warpath. Sound is a very definite part of the approach. It is not always what she says, but the tone of her voice, the invitation behind the words, the pitch and the intimate, caressing quality of the sound.

The French actresses understand this well, but French is a language that lends itself to sexuality, no matter what is being said. One of the most amusing off-Broadway revue sketches I have ever seen consisted of án actor and actress doing a "scene" from a French movie. Each recited a list of vegetables in French, but the tone of voice, cadence and vocal innuendo dripped sexuality.

This, as we described earlier in the book, is the use of one communication band to carry two messages. In the area of love and sex it is a very common use. For the aggressively available woman it can serve to throw a man off guard. This is a trick used by both men and women in the aggressive sexual pursuit. If you throw your quarry off balance, make him or her uneasy, moving in for the kill becomes relatively easy.

The trick of using the voice to carry one innocuous spoken message and another more meaningful, and much stronger, unspoken message is particularly effective because the quarry, male or female, cannot protest by the rules of the game. The aggressor, if protest is made, can always draw back and say, with some truth, "But what did I do? What did I say?"

There is a face-saving device in this, for no matter how hot the pursuit of love or sex, it cannot be done with the risk of losing face. For many people, particularly if they are insecure, losing face is a devastating and humiliating occurrence. The sexual aggressor, if he or she is truly successful at the trade, is concerned with face-saving in his victim only as a means of manipulating his quarry. To be sexually aggressive, a man or woman must have enough self-assurance, enough security, to function without the need of face-saving devices.

On the opposite side of the coin, the sexually insecure person, the quarry in the inevitable hunt, desperately needs to avoid humiliation, to save face. This puts her at a tremendous disadvantage in the game. The aggressor can manipulate the quarry, holding loss of face as a threat.

Most of us realize that eye
contact is important. In
"Winking, Blinking and
Nods," Julius Fast details
some of the ways eye contact
communicates. As you read
the selection, you should be
able to recall encounters of
your own that parallel the
ones Fast discusses.

JULIUS FAST

WINKING, BLINKING AND NODS

The Stare that Dehumanizes

The cowpuncher sat his horse loosely and his fingers hovered above his gun while his eyes, ice cold, sent chills down the rustler's back.

A familiar situation? It happens in every Western novel, just as in every love story the heroine's eyes *melt* while the hero's eyes *burn* into hers. In literature, even the best literature, eyes are *steely, knowing, mocking, piercing, glowing* and so on.

Are they really? Are they ever? Is there such a thing as a burning glance, or a cold glance or a hurt glance? In truth there isn't. Far from being windows of the soul, the eyes are physiological dead ends, simply organs of sight and no more, differently colored in different people to be sure, but never really capable of expressing emotion in themselves.

And yet again and again we read and hear and even tell of the eyes being wise, knowing, good, bad, indifferent. Why is there such confusion? Can so many people be wrong? If the eyes do not show emotion, then why the vast literature, the stories and legends about them?

Of all parts of the human body that are used to transmit information, the eyes are the most important and can transmit the most subtle nuances. Does this contradict the fact that the eyes do not show emotion? Not really. While the eyeball itself shows nothing, the emotional impact of the eyes occurs because of their use and the use of the face around them. The reason they have so confounded observers is because by length of glance, by opening of eyelids, by squinting and by a dozen little manipulations of the skin and eyes, almost any meaning can be sent out.

But the most important technique of eye management is the look, or the stare. With it we can often make or break another person. How? By giving him human or nonhuman status.

Simply, eye management in our society boils down to two facts. One, we do not stare at another human being. Two, staring is reserved for a non-person. We stare at art, at sculpture, at scenery. We go to the zoo and stare at the animals, the lions, the monkeys, the gorillas. We stare at them for as long as we please, as intimately as we please, but we do not stare at humans if we want to accord them human treatment.

We may use the same stare for the side-show freak, but we do not really consider him a human being. He is an object at which we have paid money to stare, and in the same way we may stare at an actor on a stage. The real man is masked too deeply behind his role for our stare to bother either him or us. However, the new theater that brings the actor down into the audience often gives us an uncomfortable feeling. By virtue of involving us, the audience, the actor suddenly loses his non-person status and staring at him becomes embarrassing to us.

As I said before, a Southern white may stare at a black in the same way, making him, by the stare, into an object rather than a person. If we wish pointedly to ignore someone, to treat him with an element of contempt, we can give him the same stare, the slightly unfocused look that does not really see him, the cutting stare of the socially elite.

Servants are often treated this way as are waiters, waitresses and children. However, this may be a mutually protective device. It allows the servants to function efficiently in their overlapping universe without too much interference from us, and it allows us to function comfortably without acknowledging the servant as a fellow human. The same is true of children and waiters. It would be an uncomfortable world if each time we were served by a waiter we had to introduce ourselves and indulge in social amenities.

A Time for Looking

With unfamiliar human beings, when we acknowledge their humanness, we must avoid staring at them, and yet we must also avoid ignoring them. To make them into people rather than objects, we use a deliberate and polite inattention. We look at them long enough to make it quite clear that we see them, and then we immediately look away. We are saying, in body language, "I know you are there," and a moment later we add, "But I would not dream of intruding on your privacy."

The important thing in such an exchange is that we do not catch the eye of the one whom we are recognizing as a person. We look at him without locking glances, and then we immediately look away. Recognition is not permitted.

There are different formulas for the exchange of glances depending on where the meeting takes place. If you pass someone in the street you may eye the oncoming person till you are about eight feet apart, then you must look away as you pass. Before the eight-foot distance is reached, each will signal in which direction he will pass. This is done with a brief look in that direction. Each will veer slightly, and the passing is done smoothly.

For this passing encounter Dr. Erving Goffman in *Behavior in Public Places* says that the quick look and the lowering of the eyes is body language for, "I trust you. I am not afraid of you."

To strengthen this signal, you look directly at the other's face before looking away.

Sometimes the rules are hard to follow, particularly if one of the two people wears dark glasses. It becomes impossible to discover just what they are doing. Are they looking at you too long, too intently? Are they looking at you at all? The person wearing the glasses feels protected and assumes that he can stare without being noticed in his staring. However, this is a self-deception. To the other person, dark glasses seem to indicate that the wearer is always staring at him.

We often use this look-and-away technique when we meet famous people. We want to assure them that we are respecting their privacy, that we would not dream of staring at them. The same is true of the crippled or physically handicapped. We look briefly and then look away before the stare can be said to be a stare. It is the technique we use for any unusual situation where too long a stare would be embarrassing. When we see an interracial couple we use this technique. We might use it when we see a man with an unusual beard, with extra long hair, with outlandish clothes, or a girl with a minimal mini-skirt may attract this look-and-away.

Of course the opposite is also true. If we wish to put a person down we may do so by staring longer than is acceptably polite. Instead of dropping our gazes when we lock glances, we continue to stare. The person who disapproves of interracial marriage or dating will stare rudely at the interracial couple. If he dislikes long hair, short dresses or beards he may show it with a longer-than-acceptable stare.

The Awkward Eyes

The look-and-away stare is reminiscent of the problem we face in adolescence in terms of our hands. What do we do with them? Where do we hold them? Amateur actors are also made conscious of this. They are suddenly aware of their hands as awkward appendages that must somehow be used gracefully and naturally.

In the same way, in certain circumstances, we become aware of our glances as awkward appendages. Where shall we look? What shall we do with our eyes?

Two strangers seated across from each other in a railway dining car have the option of introducing themselves and facing a meal of inconsequential and perhaps boring talk, or ignoring each other and desperately trying to avoid each other's glance. Cornelia Otis Skinner, describing such a situation in an essay, wrote, "They re-read the menu they fool with the cutlery, they inspect their own fingernails as if seeing them for the first time. Comes the inevitable moment when glances meet, but they meet only to shoot instantly away and out the window for an intent view of the passing scene."

This same awkward eye dictates our looking behavior in elevators and crowded buses and subway trains. When we get on an elevator or train with a crowd we look briefly and then look away at once without locking glances. We say, with our look, "I see you. I do not know you, but you are a human and I will not stare at you."

In the subway or bus where long rides in very close circumstances are a necessity, we may be hard put to find some way of not staring. We sneak glances, but look away before our eyes can lock. Or we look with an unfocused glance that misses the eyes and settles on the head, the mouth, the body—for any place but the eyes is an acceptable looking spot for the unfocused glance.

If our eyes do meet we can sometimes mitigate the message with a brief smile. The smile must not be too long or too obvious. It must say, "I am sorry we have looked, but we both know it was an accident."

INTERPERSONAL COMMUNICATION
BARRIERS

*We may never hope to understand fully
what we say so long as we think we
already do.*   W. Johnson

---

*Whenever I find myself arguing for
something with great passion, I can be
certain I'm not convinced.*   H. Prather

From Hugh Prather, *Notes to Myself*. Reprinted
by permission of Real People Press.

Barriers or obstacles to effective communication come in many
forms. In all interpersonal encounters, elements are constantly
present that can cause participants frustration, anger, or resentment. People misunderstand one another, time remarks incor-
rectly, cause defensive reactions, misread the other's intent, and
do hundreds of other things that cause conflict. While it may be
that conflict is good, especially if it is later resolved, few of us
find conflict pleasing in and of itself. If you better understand the
barriers that damage relationships, you might be able to avoid
unnecessary conflict. The following readings were selected to
provide you with a better understanding of the barriers that create
conflict and interfere with communication in the interpersonal
arena.

Nena O'Neill and George
O'Neill suggest five principles
of effective communication
that can be used to overcome
barriers to interpersonal
communication. The inter-
personal relationships to
which the O'Neill's refer are
marital relationships. The
application of their five
principles to all dyadic (two-
person) communication
relationships, however, is
quite apparent.

NENA O'NEILL
GEORGE O'NEILL

SELF-DISCLOSURE
AND FEEDBACK Self-knowledge, self-disclosure, and honesty—
these comprise sound psychological foundations for good communications between mates. To build upon this foundation, we suggest the
use of the following five principles of effective communication.

1. Understand the context
2. Timing
3. Clarity
4. Open listening
5. Feedback

We will discuss each of these principles in turn.

Understand the Context

Every communicative exchange takes place within a web of circumstances which determine the meaning of what is said. We have already
seen how similar comments about a wife's appearance can take on
different meanings in different contexts—in one case a harsh putdown,
in the other a shared joke. Another example involves the use of the

word "scatterbrain." When Harry says, "Hi, scatterbrain," and pulls Pam down onto the couch with him, the word is a term of endearment: But if he uses it when she arrives home from the supermarket without the charcoal briquettes he asked her to buy for the barbecue, she may well take offense.

Rose is a great kidder. It's a quality her husband Ben is well able to appreciate most of the time, but unfortunately she doesn't know when to stop. Even when he is genuinely concerned about something, a problem at work or the number of unpaid bills in the desk drawer, she goes right on making her little jokes. She may only be trying to cheer him up, but under the circumstances it seems to him that she is belittling him for taking his problems so seriously. What is meant to be helpful thus comes out seeming like criticism.

Such examples may seem trivial. But a large part of any relationship with a marital partner does in fact consist of what can only be called trivia. And if you can't get along with your mate on the level of trivia, you are certainly headed for larger problems. Many misunderstandings and disagreements can be avoided if you simply pay attention to the context, and are sensitive to the conditions under which you are attempting to communicate. Sometimes the context is obvious, as when Pam forgot the charcoal. At other times, the *real* context may become apparent only if you read your mate's non-verbal signals.

You may at first feel self-conscious, even foolish, in attempting to become aware of the context. But if you make a genuine effort to increase that awareness, it will in time become second nature to you, something to which you do not even need to give conscious attention. Most of us have bad habits in this regard; we ride roughshod over the context when talking to people in general and particularly to our mates. In correcting, or giving up, any bad habit, whether it is excessive smoking or talking a blue streak at breakfast (when all your mate wants to do is read the paper in silence), there will be a period of self-consciousness. But in the long run the benefits will prove worth it.

Timing

Timing is allied to context. As you become more aware of context, and attune yourself to your mate's non-verbal signals, you can set about timing your verbal communications on difficult matters accordingly. Instead of letting yourself in for unnecessary and unpleasant confrontations, you can hold off for the proper moment to speak. The time to tell your wife she's shooting the budget to pieces with the amount she spends on clothes is not when she comes rusing home full of pleasure with a new purchase. Since she's going to have to deny herself future pleasures, there's no point in spoiling her present pleasure as well. That merely adds insult to injury.

The art of timing is really a simple one. Children make use of it constantly, although in a negative way. The savvy kid reads his parents' moods and saves his confessions of wrongdoing or his requests for extra money until he thinks the circumstances favor him. He zooms in when you're harassed or confused, knowing perfectly well that you'll say "yes" just to get rid of him; and if he's lost another pair of gloves, he'll be sure to tell you when there's company present, since you're much less likely to bawl him out in public.

This negative, manipulative approach is one that many people unfortunately never grow out of. As adults, they discover that the restrictive clauses of the closed marriage contract make it necessary for them to try to manipulate their mates just as they did their parents. Open marriage, however, makes such maneuvering unnecessary. When it is possible to communicate openly and honestly with your mate, there is no need to trick him into giving you your way. "Your way," in fact, is something that will be freely granted you, provided that it does not involve restricting your mate's way. But timing remains important as a positive technique. You read your mate's non-verbal cues not in order to choose the best moment in which to manipulate him, but rather in order to pick out the best moment in which to fully and openly discuss the question that concerns you. In the closed marriage the art of timing is too often used to disguise one's real desires; in open marriage it is used positively to further the chances of honest communication.

Clarity

Verbal communication is very complex, at best. We add greatly to its complexity, and to the possibilities for misunderstanding, by being unclear in what we say. Sometimes we say one thing when we actually mean another. "Did you pick up the laundry today?" Mary asks Bob. Since Bob has arrived home without the laundry, Mary's question didn't even have to be asked. But what she was really saying was, "Why are you so late? You damn well didn't pick up the laundry!" Or Bob may say to Mary, after spending the evening at the home of friends, "Alice certainly comes up with unusual meals, doesn't she?"

What he really means, of course, is, "Why don't you cook a few more interesting dishes?"

Some spouses may understand what is really meant in such situations, but if they do they are likely to react with hostility. For almost always when we say one thing and mean another the message we actually want to get across is a criticism of some sort. Try to think before you speak, making sure exactly what it is you really want to say. If it sounds rude or unpleasant when directly, clearly expressed, then it's probably better left unsaid. On the other hand, if it seems upon reflection something that must be said, even though unpleasant, try to hold back for the moment, and bring it up for discussion at an appropriate time.

There are occasions, of course, when you are so angry or upset that you must say something immediately. But instead of making some snide comment, full of hidden meaning, or shouting a muddled accusation, say exactly what the fact of the matter is: "I'm very angry." When you are emotionally upset, you are less likely than ever to be able to express yourself clearly. The chances of unnecessarily hurting your mate, or further confusing the issue are very great. If at such a moment you must say something, to relieve the pressure, start out by stating how *you* feel, instead of by accusing your *mate* of wrongdoing. In many cases, your mate will know immediately what it is that he has done to upset you, and will apologize. If you begin by attacking him, however, probably hurting him in the process, his natural reaction will be to either defend himself (even though he may know he is wrong) or to strike back.

What we are describing here is a technique modeled on the principles of communication that Dr. Haim Ginott has delineated in his best-selling book, *Between Parent and Child*. Although his concepts have been popularized as "childrenese," they are nevertheless applicable in a reciprocal type of communication between husband and wife (which could be termed "matese"). The principles he outlines are sound advice for good communication between any two people, no matter what age. Dr. Ginott's directions (which can be interpreted in the simplified motto: say what you see, tell what you feel, but do not criticize) are based on respect, consideration and what he calls extending "emotional hospitality" to others. Although his methods involve many other aspects of good communication in interpersonal relations, we can stress only a few of them here, in terms of clarity and consideration in communication between mates.

If you think your husband is giving the plants too much water, if you think your wife is stirring the martinis too much, don't say,

"Here, dear, this is the way to do it." That sounds perfectly clear, even polite, but in fact it implies that your way of doing it is right and your mate's is wrong. Whenever there is a hidden message, you are not being as clear as you can be. And whenever there is a hidden message, the possibility of an altercation lurks. You may not in fact be right. Everyone is wrong some of the time. So work at avoiding criticism. Say, "I usually only give that plant half a glass. Do you think it needs more?" That gives your husband a chance to say, "Well, it was drooping a lot this morning," if he has a reason for what he is doing, and an opportunity to retreat with grace if he doesn't have a reason.

The technique of "saying what you see and telling what you feel without criticizing the other" makes it possible to state your own point of view, when it is at variance with your mate's. The main idea is to avoid accusation and destructive criticism of the other. If you make a direct attack on your mate, impugning his judgment or taste, you are invading his *ego territory* and you must expect a counterattack. Using these principles allows you to delineate the boundaries of your own ego territory, by clearly stating what you think and feel, while at the same time acknowledging the boundaries of your mate's ego territory by refraining from direct attack. It may require patience, skill and practice, but if you can get out of the habit of criticism and attack, we believe you will find that you can sharply reduce the number of domestic confrontations. At the same time, of course, you will be taking another step toward granting your mate the full right to his own identity.

A different application of "telling what you feel" develops in respect to the communication of your deeper feelings and emotions. In our adherence to good manners and the niceties of convention, we have lost the intimate language of feeling. We tend to leave it to the poet—or the songwriter—to express our joy, frustration, despair or exaltation. A few of us, because of our ethnic background or a particularly outgoing personality, are more expressive than others, but by and large the language of emotion, having been sacrificed on the altar of conformity, now lies buried beneath it in a casket of purest embarrassment.

The feelings are still there below the surface, but they seldom make themselves fully known except when we explode in anger—moments which find us at our most incoherent. Men in particular are taught to believe that they should not express their feelings, that to do so is somehow unmanly. In fact, the very opposite is true—what could be more cowardly than to be afraid to admit what one most deeply feels? It is important to fight the embarrassment that prevents us from saying what we feel. Unless we say it out, clearly, our mates cannot know that we feel it. And if we will not tell them how we feel, how can we expect them to respect those feelings?

Open Listening

Open, clear expression of what we feel is vital to a healthy relationship between marital partners. But it will go for nothing unless it is complemented by open listening. Most husbands and wives seldom really listen to one another at all. They conduct what the philosopher Abraham Kaplan has called a duologue. In a duologue two people dutifully take turns expounding their separate lonely litanies. Everyone knows how such "conversations" go: Susan and Mark discuss the activities of the day, Susan talking about the fact that their son Bobby is going to have to have braces, Mark wondering aloud about the rumors that his company may be involved in a merger. Each is listening to himself rather then to the other. Susan is concerned about the cost of the braces, as well as their nuisance value, and Mark is concerned about what a merger might mean to his position in the company. Since Mark will have to pay for Bobby's braces, and since Susan will also be affected if Mark's job situation changes, they will eventually have to stop their separate soliloquies, and start all over again asking one another to repeat what has already been said. We have all been through it a thousand times.

In open marriage if you really do not want to listen, at a given moment, it is possible for you to make that desire known to your mate, and you can expect to have your desire respected. But if your mate is going to continue to respect your desire for such moments of privacy, then you must be prepared really to listen when you indicate a willingness to do so. You must be prepared to enter into a *dialogue*, as opposed to a duologue. Kaplan describes the true dialogue, in which both parties listen and respond to one another, as communion rather than communication. In a true dialogue, each partner is, certainly, communicating with the other, but because he is also listening, and responding to what he hears, the final result is a form of communion. Good communication, when coupled with open listening, results in communion.

Open listening requires that you become, in effect, transparent, thus letting the other in. You cannot respond properly unless you open yourself completely to what is being said to you. Unless you listen, actively, you cannot hear. Unless you hear you cannot enter into a dialogue. And no true meeting of a husband and wife can occur unless they both enter willingly into such a dialogue.

Feedback

Your response to someone's attempt to communicate with you can be as simple as a nod of the head. Sometimes that is enough. But too often, when a fuller response is really necessary, we settle for that nod, for a mere "uh huh," or a "yes, dear." You cannot create a dialogue with your mate unless you provide a lot more than a few grunts in the way of feedback.

Feedback is a term that is part and parcel of the new computer technology. In technical terms it can be described as the automatic furnishing of information on a machine's output to a control device, so that errors can be corrected. Thus a feedback system is self-correcting. In more human terms, when a man sets a glass down on a table, his nervous system provides him with the visual and sensory feedback necessary to guide his hand. This is the hand-eye-brain feedback system at work. If the man is drunk, the feedback is likely to be incorrect, so that the man drops the glass on the floor. This concept of feedback can easily be applied to communication between human beings. You can give your mate feedback by paraphrasing his statement to make sure you understand it, by asking questions, or by making your own responsive statement that tells how you feel about the matter.

You need open and honest feedback from your mate in order to know that he has understood you, in order to discover how he feels, and in order to adjust your own feelings or perceptions in light of his. Many husbands and wives short-circuit the feedback cycle, through deception or overt criticism, or by withholding their response altogether. Sullen silence might be described as negative feedback; like a failed monitoring system on a moon rocket, it tells you that *something* is wrong, but it doesn't go very far toward telling you what. Unless you indicate what is wrong, through positive feedback, your mate will not know how to proceed further.

For couples who need to learn feedback on an elementary level, there is a simple exercise called "completing the communication," as described by Lederer and Jackson in *Mirages of Marriage,* that they can make use of. While it may seem unnatural and even rather silly at first, it will get you in the habit of providing feedback and increase your sense of the importance of responding to your mate. There are three elementary steps to the exercise: Person I makes a statement. Person II acknowledges the statement. Person I confirms the acknowledgment.

For example:
MARY: Did you pick up the laundry?
DICK: No, I didn't. No parking space.
MARY: Maybe I can do it tomorrow, then.

Or:
DICK: I ran into Bob Bartlet today.
MARY: How is he these days?
DICK: He seemed fine.

The two initial statements made by Mary and Dick above are of the sort that frequently evoke no more than a word. Other simple statements (such as "What a beautiful sunset") evoke no more than a nod, a grunt or a mumble. But each one, when you begin these exercises, should be acknowledged and have the acknowledgment confirmed. Making a specific meaningful response to such minor statements is a step toward improving your ability to provide feedback in other more important situations. It will also help stimulate you to open listening. Open listening is, of course, absolutely essential to providing proper feedback.

With feedback established, you can approach real self-disclosure that will implement growth. We change and grow by *re-forming* our concepts of ourselves and the other through our own disclosures and through our mate's feedback to us.

All five of the principles of good communication that we have discussed in this chapter—Understanding the Context, Timing, Clarity, Open Listening and Feedback—are vital to open and honest communication. As you have seen, each of them reinforces the others. Your timing cannot be improved unless you understand the context. All the clarity in the world means nothing unless your mate is committed to open listening. And proper feedback both depends upon and aids the exercise of the other four principles. With these interrelated principles as a background, we will discuss in our third and last chapter on communication some additional techniques that can be of help to you in achieving truly open verbal and non-verbal exchange.

---

*Filling our own ears with all we have
learned to say, we are deaf to what we
have yet to hear.* W. Johnson

Copyright © 1972 Jules Feiffer. Courtesy Publishers-Hall Syndicate.

As the preceding cartoon demonstrates, one prominent barrier to good interpersonal communication is that we are not usually as concerned for the other person as we are for ourselves. The following article from *Time* magazine emphasizes some of the effects of not truly engaging the other person. How about you, are your interpersonal communication transactions "duologues"? Do you frequently participate in interpersonal conversations that are best described as "dialogues of the deaf"?

TIME

THE ART OF
NOT LISTENING
Everybody knows that somebody listening to a joke is not really listening; he is impatiently awaiting his turn to tell a joke of his own. Everybody knows that husbands give half an ear to the discourse of their wives—and vice versa. Why do these highly disciplined attempts at human dialogue fail? The reason, says Abraham Kaplan, a professor of philosophy at the University of Michigan, is that they are not really dialogues at all. Before a conference on human and animal communication at Minnesota's Gustavus Adolphus College this month, Kaplan introduced his own word for all those human occasions when everybody talks and nobody listens. He calls them "duologues."

Kaplan applies his coinage widely. "Duologue," he says, "takes place in schools, churches, cocktail parties, the U.S. Congress and almost everywhere we don't feel free to be wholly human." In his view, a duologue is little more than a monologue mounted before a glazed and exquisitely indifferent audience, as in the classroom: "First the professor talks and the students don't listen; then the students talk or write and the professor doesn't listen or read."

The duologue has its unforgiving rules: "You have to give the other his turn, and you give signals during his turn, like saying 'uh huh' or laughing at what he says, to show that he is having his turn. You must also refrain from saying anything that really matters to you as a human being, as it would be regarded as an embarrassing intimacy." A near-perfect example of duologue is the televiewer, transfixed by that mesmeric eye. A truly perfect duologue would be two TV sets tuned in and facing each other.

OPEN TO YOU. The prevalence of the duologue saddens Philosopher Kaplan, a devoted student of the late Jewish philosopher Martin Buber, whose I-thou philosophy was based on the conviction that each man defines himself by genuinely engaging others; humanity is a meeting. Kaplan applied this notion to the laryngeal noise that fills humanity's crowded corners and rooms. An honest dialogue, says Kaplan, is never rehearsed. "I don't know beforehand what it will be. I don't know beforehand who I will be, because I am open to you just as you are open to me." Dialogue involves serious listening—listening not just to the other, but listening to oneself. This rare and wondrous event Kaplan calls "communion" instead of communication.

"It seems to me impossible," he says, "to teach unless you are learning. You cannot really talk unless you are listening." The student is also the professor; the joke teller should also be part of the audience. To Kaplan, there is nothing lonelier than two humans involved in a duologue—and nothing more marvelous than two genuinely engaged listeners. "If we didn't search so hard for our own identities but occupied ourselves with the other, we might find precisely what we were not seeking. If we listen, it may be that we will find it at last possible to respond: 'Here I am.' "

All I want is for you to accept me as I am.

Yes, and all I want is for you to accept my not accepting you.   H. Prather

---

From Hugh Prather, *Notes to Myself.* Reprinted by permission of Real People Press.

The following poem by Diane Lee expresses a communication barrier produced by a type of identity crisis. If a professor is in such a state or if students perceive him to be in such a state, can you see how that would produce a barrier between him and students?

DIANE LEE

NOTES ON AGING PROFESSORS

Gray-haired inadequacy and a
  brief case of trivia
    clutched tightly in the anxious hand
Searching for a universal word
  in some paperback excuse for teaching.
Wondering
  when he finds it someday
  the world will find a
  word big enough
  for him to fall into
  like
  the old elephant
  finally come to the eternal
    resting place,
  tripping
  into the ditch of
    soft scholarly oblivion
  comfortable
  at last in being ignored.
Wondering
  if anyone will take the time
  to notice
he's finally gone.

157 *Reprinted with permission of the author.*

Probably the most common, most destructive, and hardest communication barrier to overcome is hostility toward another person. This barrier is especially prominent in the interpersonal communication arena. When we are upset with another person, our decisions seem justifiable. The other person seems to have wronged us, and we are morally indignant. The hostility can, however, be contained and actually used in a constructive manner.

MILTON LAYDEN

HOSTILITY—
A BIG EXPENSE
YOU CAN AVOID

Hostility causes more misery, inefficiency, loss of work time and financial drain than any other problem in industry. In the form of anger, resentment and hurt feelings, it is a principal cause of mental, nervous and physical illness on the job.

Ask yourself how often you become resentful during the work day.

How do you deal with this emotion?

Discussing the question with businessmen in the United States and abroad convinces me that hostility is one of the most mismanaged problems in business.

What sort of trouble does it cause?

It is governed by Newton's Law: "To every action there is an equal and opposite reaction."

This means that one's hostility is always returned. The object of our anger turns against us and becomes unreceptive to our ideas and persuasion.

No matter how hard we try to conceal anger, it shows anyway,

Reprinted from Nation's Business, *September 1970, copyright © 1970, by Na-*tion's Business.

thus antagonizing the other person. Many blunders are entirely caused by resentful feelings. Hostility always generates anxiety; together they comprise the essential ingredients of nervous and mental disturbances. When we try to hide anger—that is, to suppress it—serious mental and physical changes occur. Mentally, the individual becomes anxious, tense, irritable, indecisive, forgetful, careless and confused.

Over a period of time, suppressed hostility helps cause physical exhaustion, headache, virus diseases, ulcers, high blood pressure, heart disease, arthritis, allergies, diabetes and many other ailments.

Deleting hostility does not mean eliminating fight, firmness and resolution. Quite the contrary.

Without it, one becomes cool under fire, unflinching and firm. This was pointed out by Bernard Baruch, who took boxing lessons from Jim Jeffries.

Mr. Baruch related that the fighter told his pupils: "Try to put your fist right through your opponent's body, but don't get mad at him."

He had learned that much of a boxer's skill and judgment are lost when he becomes angry.

As an example of the harm wrought by hostility, let us consider this typical situation. Bill Calkins presents a plan to his boss, John Jones, who subconsciously resents his subordinate. Mr. Jones rejects Mr. Calkins's plan because he believes it lacks merit. He does not realize that his resentment is responsible for the rejection, rather than any fault in the plan.

Mr. Calkins, sensing his boss's attitude, becomes bitter and uncooperative. He does not dare express his anger, and therefore tries to conceal it. However, it is quite apparent to his boss. Thus, he unwittingly insures the rejection of any of his proposals.

How to Cure Your Hostility

If Mr. Jones knew how to dissolve his hostility, he would be able to see the value of his subordinate's plan. Mr. Calkins would then become more cooperative, creative and better motivated.

Each would be able to work more efficiently with the other. Even if only one of them knew how to rid himself of his resentful feelings, it would erase the enmity of the other.

Here is what you need to know to rid yourself and your associates of hostility.

All of use have a need to feel that we are liked and appreciated. If we are not, we suffer a biological deficiency in the mental realm as real as lack of food in the physical.

Our invariable response to this deficiency is anxiety and a sense of inferiority. With it goes a mirage-like vision in which we see ourselves as superior to the other fellow. To free ourselves from the feeling of inferiority, the mirage causes us to see him as the one who is to blame.

Hostility is generated as a reaction to the feelings of inferiority.

Here are five simple steps which will enable you to rid yourself and your associates of hostility.

1. Awareness: Look carefully for any trace of irritation in your feelings.
2. The IH Principle: I = Inferiority; H = Hostility.
   If you detect any hostility, ask yourself what is causing you to feel inferior.
3. Overcome your inferiority; Your concept of yourself as inferior is the result of hostile, belittling attitudes of your parents and, to a lesser extent, of brothers, sisters and teachers.
   In addition, you often react with inferiority to disrespect, rebuffs and complaints received from your wife, children and associates. Recognize that such attitudes do not necessarily reflect on you, and that a man is no less for being blamed.
4. Apply the IH principle to the other fellow: Like the rest of us, he, too, may have become hostile only because he felt inferior.
5. Overcome the other fellow's inferiority: Your understanding that he is the innocent victim of the attitudes of others and perhaps of yourself will dissolve your hostility. The deeper your hostility, the more you must repeat these steps.

The Hidden Conflict

In analyzing your relationship with anyone, you must take into account that there is something going on between you that is far more significant than the subject being discussed. This is the vying for superiority. It is perceived by both parties, in spite of the most elaborate attempts at concealment.

For example, suppose the boss is suppressing the resentment he feels about a mistake by a staff member. Many signs make this resentment apparent. The eyes become narrow and menacing, the mouth

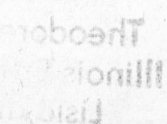

tightens and some facial redness appears. On the phone, the tone of voice is a dead giveaway.

This transmission of hostility causes the staff member to make more mistakes. Don't approach him with a flat "You're wrong." The resentment generated would only blind him to your correction.

How can you correct his mistakes?

First, dissolve your hostility.

This can be done by asking him questions about the issue and mentioning how he has helped you on other matters. Then relate how you made a similar mistake. Humility is not degrading. Since it elevates the other fellow's self-esteem, he respects you more. Now that you have raised his esteem, he will be much more receptive to your correction.

The boss can openly vent his complaints and blow his top. But his employees, because of fear of demotion or dismissal, are likely to suppress their rage. Thus they are much more apt to develop serious illness or alcoholism.

Damage wreaked by hostility may spread like a turnpike chain collision. Witness the boss who is provoked by his wife's criticism at breakfast. At the office, he laces into his sales manager. The sales manager transmits his anger to 200 salesmen at the sales meeting. The salesmen then carry their irritations to their assorted customers.

And to think that this entire chain reaction originated with some trivial remark by the boss's wife.

And it could have been avoided.

Industry is being called on increasingly to apply the knowledge of science to environmental pollution. Concentration on this problem must not divert us from that of mental pollution—poisoning our minds with man's chief enemy, hostility.

Whenever you know you are right,
that's when you are in trouble.
W. Wilmot

INTERPERSONAL
COMMUNICATION
SELF-DISCLOSURE

It takes two to speak the truth—
one to speak and another to hear.
H. D. Thoreau

In interpersonal communication, to self-disclose is to let the other person know you. You disclose part of yourself to the other so he, in turn, can respond to the real you. In our contemporary society, establishing open and honest relationships is much more difficult than most of us are willing to admit. We hurry past one another in our quests for money, security, and happiness. We meet one another, have relationships for years, and then when tragedy strikes we discover we did not know anything about one another. We have a best friend, move to a different town, and find we have nothing to say to him because we said nothing when we were together.

In order to reach out and let others know us, we need to first be open and honest with ourselves. But intrapersonal self-disclosure is not enough; one has to open up to others as well as be honest with himself. It is important to remember that interpersonal self-disclosure is more than a one-shot affair. We cannot be open and honest once and then stop. We must continually strive for authentic relationships. As in the intrapersonal arena, self-disclosure in this arena is extremely threatening. The actual rewards, however, will probably outweigh the potential danger.

The poem "Will You Be My Friend?" by James Kavanaugh and the following excerpt from a First Presbyterian Church bulletin demonstrate the need for people to be touched by others in genuine relationships. No matter who you are or what your interpersonal affiliations might be, you need authentic relationships.

JAMES KAVANAUGH

WILL YOU BE MY FRIEND?

Will you be my friend?
There are so many reasons why you never should:
I'm sometimes sullen, often shy, acutely sensitive,
My fear erupts as anger, I find it hard to give,
I talk about myself when I'm afraid
And often spend a day without anything to say.
  But I will make you laugh
  And love you quite a bit
  And hold you when you're sad.
I cry a little almost every day
Because I'm more caring than the strangers ever know,
And, if at times, I show my tender side
(The soft and warmer part I hide)
  I wonder,
    Will you be my friend?
A friend
  Who far beyond the feebleness of any vow or tie
  Will touch the secret place where I am really I.
  To know the pain of lips that plead and eyes that weep,
  Who will not run away when you find me in the street
  Alone and lying mangled by my quota of defeats
  But will stop and stay—to tell me of another day
  When I was beautiful.

Will you be my friend?
There are so many reasons why you never should:
Often I'm too serious, seldom predictably the same,
Sometimes cold and distant, probably I'll always change.
I bluster and brag, seek attention like a child,
I brood and pout, my anger can be wild,
> *But I will make you laugh*
> *And love you quite a bit*
> *And be near when you're afraid.*

I shake a little almost every day
Because I'm more frightened than the strangers ever know
And if at times I show my trembling side
(The anxious, fearful part I hide)
> *I wonder,*
> *Will you be my friend?*

A friend
> *Who, when I fear your closeness, feels me push away*
> *And stubbornly will stay to share what's left on such a day,*
> *Who, when no one knows my name or calls me on the phone*
> *When there's no concern for me—what I have or haven't done—*
> *And those I've helped and counted on have, oh so deftly run,*
> *Who, when there's nothing left but me, stripped of charm and*
> *sublety,*
> *Will nonetheless remain.*

Will you be my friend?
> *For no reason that I know*
> *Except I want you so.*

A friend is one who always is.   J. Lair

CHURCH BULLETIN

. . . we have good biblical warrants for asserting that it is not good for man to be alone. Aloneness is not the will of God either in ordinary life or the Christian Life. People need fellowship, and it is God's will that they should have it. Bruce Larson, the leader of 'Faith at Work' movement, sees an indication of this fundamental human need in the popularity of the tavern:

The neighborhood bar is possibly the best counterfeit there is to the fellowship Christ wants to give His Church. It's an imitation, dispensing liquor instead of grace, escape rather than reality, but it is an accepting and inclusive fellowship. . . . You can tell people secrets and they usually don't tell others or even want to. The bar flourishes not because most people are alcoholics, but because God has put into the human heart the desire to know and be known, to love and be loved, and so many seek a counterfeit at the price of a few beers. Christ wants this Church to be unshockable—a fellowship where people can come in and say, "I'm sunk! I'm beat! I've had it!" Our churches too often miss it.

Then the Lord God said:
It is not good for man to be alone. . . .
Genesis 2, 18

Reprinted from First Presbyterian Church Newsletter, *Mt. Pleasant, Michigan,* **166** *February 28, 1973.*

Sidney Jourard is one of the
foremost proponents of self-
disclosure. From his point of
view, interpersonal self-
disclosure is prerequisite to
getting to know yourself.
Whether you believe that you
have to know yourself before
you can know others or that
you have to know others
before you can know yourself,
self-disclosure is important.
One person may have to
engage in intrapersonal self-
disclosure before he can
openly relate to another, yet
the next person may need to
do the reverse. Jourard's
preference is quite clear:
Interpersonal self-disclosure
is a prerequisite to self-
knowledge. Have you
experienced such com-
munication relationships?

SIDNEY M. JOURARD

SELF-DISCLOSURE AND THE MYSTERY OF THE OTHER MAN

If I look naively at my fellow man, I see him doing all manner of things, and I have no way of predicting or understanding why he does what he does. In fact, I may fear him, as I fear anything which acts with caprice. I may impute motives like mine to him, as primitive man imputed human motives to animals, the sea, plants, and the weather. I may engage in magic, ritual, or other superstitious practices, as primitive men did, in order to get others to help me or leave me alone.

But when man learned the conditions which were responsible for the behavior of the weather, the sea, plants, and animals, he feared them less and became more able to enlist their collaboration for the pursuit of his ends. He no longer imputed characteristics to these things which they did not possess, but strove, rather, to ascertain their real characteristics and to understand the forces which moved them. Man's fear changed then to respect.

With his fellow, however, man continues to behave much as he did in earlier times with plants, animals, and elements. His concepts and beliefs about the other man are usually based on insufficient or emotionally distorted evidence, and they are thus often false. Consequently, a man may find himself living in a world of strangers whose actions are either misunderstood or misinterpreted. And he becomes afraid.

The other man is a mystery. He is opaque. We cannot know in advance what he will do. We do not know his past, and we do not know what is "going on inside him." Consequently, we remain on guard when we are in his presence. Naive observation will show that the other man behaves predictably some of the time in the ritual of social living. He clothes himself, goes to work, tips his hat to ladies, utters polite conversation, and in short, seems "normal"—unless he is a foreigner, a psychotic, or a child. In the latter instances, we may be frank in admitting we don't know what he is thinking, and even if he tells us, we may not understand because we don't know his language. Or, erroneously, we may assume that we know his motives, thoughts, and reactions. But even with "normal" people, most of us feel rather uneasy, because we do not always know what they are thinking. In fact, if "normal" people tell us what they are thinking, what they feel, believe, or day-dream about, many of us feel, with a certain un-ease, that we are being "snowed"—the man isn't leveling with us. He is telling us what he thinks we want to hear. Often, he is doing just that. Because he may mislead us in telling us what he is like, we become shocked when we read that Mr. Jones, without warning, took a hatchet and butchered his family, whom he seemed to love so well.

> "Things are seldom what they seem,
> Skim milk masquerades as cream."
> "Externals don't portray insides,
> Jekylls may be masking Hydes."

Let me apologize for such atrocious verse and then point up an empirical fact. Man, perhaps alone of all living forms, is capable of *being* one thing and *seeming* from his actions and talk to be something else. Not even those animals and insects and fishes which Nature expertly camouflages can do this "seeming" at will; they do it reflexly.

Now, let me mention another truism. If Mr. Jones, the one who butchered his family, had *frankly* disclosed his inner thoughts, feelings, and plans to you, then news of his butchery would have come to you as no surprise. You would have understood it. Perhaps you could have predicted it and then interfered, thus saving the lives of his "loved ones."

It is a simple, patent fact that when a man discloses his self, his inner experience to another, fully, spontaneously, and honestly, then the mystery that he was decreases enormously. When a man discloses himself to me, I find all my preconceptions and beliefs about him becoming altered, one after the other, by the facts as they come forth—unless, of course, I have a vested interest in continuing to believe untruths about him.

In the general scheme of things, what consequences follow when men disclose their real selves one to the other? Here are some of the more obvious outcomes:

They learn the extent to which they are similar one to the other, and the extent to which they differ from one another in thoughts, feelings, hopes, reactions to the past, etc.

They learn of the other man's needs, enabling them to help him meet them or else to ensure that they will not be met.

They learn the extent to which this man accords with or deviates from moral and ethical standards for being and behaving. Here we may have a reason why people are reluctant to disclose themselves: they dread the moral judgment of their friends, family, minister, or the law.

I don't want to belabor the point, but I think it is almost self-evident that you cannot love another person, that is, behave toward him so as to foster his happiness and growth, unless you know what he needs. And you cannot know what he needs unless he tells you.

You cannot collaborate with another person toward some common end unless you know him. How can you know him, and he you, unless you have engaged in enough mutual disclosure of self to be able to anticipate how he will react and what part he will play?

Why do we disclose ourselves, and why do we not? Answers to this question are of enormous importance, since ignorance between man and man seems to be partly at the root of just about all current world problems. We do not know the Russians, for example, though I suspect we have disclosed ourselves much more to them than vice-versa; furthermore, through an effective spy service, they have learned much about us that we would not freely disclose. Possibly, the Russian leaders want to prevent us from disclosing ourselves fully to the Russian people because they fear that such disclosure will show the

Russian man-in-the-street that we have much in common with him regarding life's goals. But we have often tried to block teachers' disclosures of what they know and think about Russian life, political system, etc., because we *want* young people to have prejudiced concepts of "the Russian."

Researches that I have been undertaking point strongly to the likelihood that a person will disclose himself, permit himself to be known, only when he believes that his audience is a man of good will. To put this another way, self-disclosure follows an attitude of love and trust. If I love someone, not only do I strive to know him, so that I can devote myself more effectively to his well-being; *I also display my love by letting him know me.* At the same time, by so doing, I permit him to love me.

But loving is a scary business because when you permit yourself to be known you expose yourself, not only to a lover's balm, but also to a hater's bombs! When he knows you, he knows just where to plant them for maximum effect.

In a poker game, no man discloses the content of his hand to the other players. Instead, he tries to dissemble and bluff. If he holds four aces, he tries to get the others to believe his hand is empty, until it is time for the showdown. If he holds nothing, he tries to seem as if he holds four aces in order to get something for nothing. In a society which pits man against man, as in a poker game, people do keep a poker face; they wear a mask and let no one know what they are up to. In a society where man is *for* man, then the psychological iron curtain is dropped.

But now a paradox, turned up through research. Surely within the family, where love is expected to prevail, and people will *be* themselves, we find much evidence for dissembling, for the lack of mutual disclosure. Children do not know their parents; fathers do not know what their children think, or what they are doing. Husbands and wives often are strangers one to the other to an incredible degree.

We are said to be a society dedicated, among other things, to the pursuit of truth. Yet, disclosure of the truth, the truth of one's being, is often penalized. Impossible concepts of how man ought to be— which, sadly enough are often handed down from the pulpit—make man so ashamed of his true being that he feels obliged to seem different, if for no other reason than to protect his job. Probably the "tyranny of the should" is a factor which keeps man from making himself known as he is. Yet, when a man does not acknowledge to himself who, what, and how he is, he is out of touch with reality, and he will sicken and die; and no one can help him without access to the facts.

And it seems to be another empirical fact that *no man can come to know himself except as an outcome of disclosing himself to another person*. This is the lesson we have learned in the field of psychotherapy. When a person has been able to disclose himself utterly to another person, he learns how to increase his contact with his real self, and he may then be better able to direct his destiny on the basis of knowledge of his real self.

But outside the clinic, disclosure of man to man, honest, direct, uncontrived, is the necessary condition for reducing the mystery that one man is for another. It is the empirical index of an I-Thou relationship, which I, agreeing with Buber, see as the index of man functioning at his highest and truly *human* level rather than at the level of a thing or animal. It is the means by which people become able to collaborate or else to learn that in reality they are far too different one from the other to collaborate in this particular enterprise. Disclosure of man to man appears to be the most direct means by which we can all learn wherein we are identical with our fellow man and wherein we differ. Such knowledge, suitably evaluated, then provides us with the basis for action which can either destroy man or meet his needs for more abundant and human living. Self-disclosure, my communication of my private world to you, in language which you clearly understand, is truly an important bit of behavior for us to learn something about. You can know me truly only if I let you, only if I *want* you to know me. Your misunderstanding of me is only partly your fault. If I want you to know me, I shall find a means of communicating myself to you. If you want me to reveal myself, just demonstrate your good will— your will to employtyour powers for my good, and not for my destruction.

Whatever my secrets are, remember
when I entrust them to you, they are part
of me.   J. Powell

In order to interpersonally
self-disclose, you literally
have to *give yourself away.*
David Dunn argues forcefully
that working at giving
ourselves to others can have
positive results.

DAVID DUNN

TRY
GIVING YOURSELF
AWAY

Jammed into a New York subway in rush
hour recently, swaying dangerously with the mass of my
fellow standees, I considered how inhuman the city is. A moment later,
as the train rocketed toward Grand Central, the emergency brakes
grabbed. If we hadn't been so tightly packed in, all of us would have
been thrown to the floor. As it was, my feet were stepped on, one arm
was twisted and my back jabbed so hard by an elbow that I thought
my spine would crack.

Irritated, I turned to the owner of the elbow. As I started to speak
he murmured, "Terribly sorry, my friend." Then, in a voice loud
enough to be heard down the car, he announced, "Unscheduled stop.
All change for Good Nature."

There was a spontaneous burst of laughter. In no time there was
almost a carnival spirit in that subway car. My friend of the sharp elbow had given all of us a glimpse of New York as it *might be*—good-
natured, friendly, human.

The reason people crowd into cities is that cities provide jobs and
educational opportunities, support libraries, museums, theatres, the
makings for truly rewarding living. The trouble is, when we come to
a large urban area, we forget to bring with us the most precious ingredient of life in a small place—humanness.

What priceless opportunities we are offered daily to make our
cities pleasant places. Recently, driving to work, I noticed a metal hoop
lying in the road. I started to steer around it—until something prodded
me into action. Pulling to the curb, I got out and tossed the hoop into
a trash receptacle so that its sharp edges would not cut some motorist's
tire. Half an hour later a stranger came up to me in the parking lot. "I

saw you pick up that hoop," he said. "Thanks for waking me up. I've often driven past such hazards, but I'm not going to again."

It's an old saying that what is everybody's business is nobody's business. City officials, the police, clubs, churches, schools and newspapers can't do all that's needed to make a town livable. They can help, but it is we ordinary citizens—all of us together—who create the spirit of a community, whether it be New York or Eastport, Maine.

Ralph Waldo Emerson once wrote: "The only gift is a portion of thyself." If, like many of us, you earn a living through some talent, skill or craft, why not share it? A printer in a Western town was annoyed by the crude, hand-lettered signs in the windows and on the doors of many businesses. On his own he printed sets of commonly used signs—"Open for Business," "Closed Wednesday Afternoon," etc. —and sent a set to each merchant. The last I heard he was looking for other ways he could use his printing talents to dress up the town.

A splendid word which has come into common use in the last few years is "empathy." It means *entering into the feelings or needs of others; putting oneself in another's place.* An example might be the case of a dying woman in our town. She lived on a heavily traveled street and, every time a heavy truck went over a hump in front of her house, the vibration shook her bed and caused acute distress. Hearing of her plight, I called the commissioner of streets and explained the situation. Before nightfall a paving crew had leveled that hump. Not only the patient but her neighbors and friends were relieved, for they had suffered with her.

Empathy also prompts us to give credit—credit for a job well done, for an idea suggested, for prompt service. Your wife makes a tasty omelet. Do you tell her so? Your child gets a good mark on an examination. Do you show your appreciation by going over the paper with him? A salesgirl shows unusual courtesy. Do you mention it? You criticize an elected official when what he does displeases you. Do you also commend him for actions you approve?

Wrapped up as most of us are in our own concerns, we tend to resist when others demand our attention, try to take us into their lives. Yet how happy each of us is to find a "good listener," a sharer, one who will "give up" his own pursuits to enter our world wholeheartedly. I tried the giving-up principle one evening when my wife and I were invited to dinner at the home of a man whose hobby is collecting postage stamps. I had always been bored with stamp collections. But instead of paying polite, perfunctory attention when he talked stamps, I determined to give him the pleasure of having a really *interested* listener. Drawing on his broad knowledge of stamps and their history and geography, he held me fascinated. When we parted, his face was aglow with pleasure—and so was mine.

The giving-up principle is at work in any willingness to share, to concede—giving up one's place in a line, one's seat on a train or, as a retired friend of mine does, passing up a parking place near the supermarket entrance in order that a young mother with a heavy bag of groceries to carry may have a shorter distance to walk.

I've adopted another form of "giving up." I now try, whenever I find myself in disagreement with someone, to probe conversationally until I find a point on which we do agree. And I let him know as enthusiastically as I can that I agree. Disagreeing, even vehemently, on other points later is much less painful if we have agreed on *something* at the start. What miracles might be wrought in these difficult times if controversial issues between young and old, black and white, violent and non-violent could be examined honestly and constructively, for at least *some* points of agreement.

Is a personal program of giving away always successful? Hardly. You may be self-conscious at first. You may be misunderstood, even rebuffed. You will have to swallow your pride at times. What of it? You will soon learn how to give yourself easily and gracefully. As a matter of fact, what every community probably needs first and foremost is to be *thawed out*. When enough of us start giving ourselves, the thaw will start—and suspicion, cynicism and rebuffs will go out of fashion.

When I'm worried, or generally low in spirits, a conscious effort to give myself away works wonders. I don't mean this in a goody-goody sense, but I do believe that the flush of pleasure-giving actually quickens the circulation and produces a healthy glow. I find myself more alert, somehow *savoring* life around me, enjoying its color and variety. The gift should, of course, be given with *no thought of reward*. "There is no grace," said one of the ancients, "in a benefit that sticks to the fingers." Giving a "portion of oneself" is to sip happiness—at the same time that one contributes one's own small share toward a better, kindlier, more livable world.

But if I tell you who I am, you may not like who I am, and it is all that I have.   J. Powell

---

The readings to this point
have demonstrated the need
for and benefits of interpersonal self-disclosure. It
would be easy to think that
all you have to do is to want
to self-disclose to another and
bingo! It's done! That,
however, is not the case. It is
work and it takes much
concentration. This last
selection on interpersonal
self-disclosure brings us two
people who are desperately
trying to say something
meaningful to each other. It
becomes obvious that opening
up to another is not an easy
thing to do, yet it may be
what we need most.

JOHN GLIDEWELL

ON LOVE—
SOUGHT AND
OFFERED

Over the years I have known many people trying hard to express warm and tender feelings. I have
seen men and women at work devise all sorts of clever incentive plans
to offer material rewards for effort and involvement in the work. They
would very rarely say that the incentives were expressions of their
warm feelings of gratitude and affection to their fellows who shared
their involvement in the work. But, I think, it was their way, a most
poorly understood and often defeated way, of expressing both gratitude
and affection toward their fellows who shared their involvement in the
work. A simple, straightforward expression of gratitude and affection
would have been seen as an unfair attempt to control—to gain power
—based on sentiment rather than on competence. It is fair, it seems, to
allow others to hold power by their competence to guide the work but
unfair to allow others to hold power based upon mutual affection for
involvement in the work. It is fair, it seems, to accept stock options for

Reprinted from Choice Points *by John Glidewell by permission of The M. I. T.
Press, Cambridge, Massachusetts. Copyright © 1970 Massachusetts Institute of
Technology.*

work accomplishment, but it is unfair to accept affection options for work accomplishment.

For women it is especially hard. Once I was much concerned because an attractive woman colleague whose husband was out of town found suddenly that she must enter a hospital alone, under a frightening threat of a possible serious illness. I expressed my concern and offered to take her to the hospital, to stay with her until she was settled and under good nursing care. I said, "I'm too fond of you to let you go alone." She was both pleased and embarassed, and I said, "I thought you knew I was fond of you." Her eyes turned toward the floor, and she said, "I had hoped you liked me for my work." Then I knew how hard it must be for an attractive woman to accept warm feelings from men with whom she works. I knew how hard it must have been for my friend to be sure her men colleagues respected her competence at work and were not just attracted to her appeal as a woman. Surely I both respected her competence and delighted in her attractiveness. How was she to know which was which?

I have seen adolescents so tangled up in their affections and vulnerabilities that they just sat down and cried. I have seen grown men and women of long and happy marriages jockey around on the long distance telephone, each trying to get the other to say "I love you" first. I have seen good friends among vigorous men punch and shove each other about to avoid any appearance of weakness or feminity in their feelings for each other. Very few of us object to being loved, but to accept love with simple trust requires a special sensitivity, a special strength, and a special courage. At some terrible times, when I have felt deeply affectionate or have felt the deep affection of another, I have found myself all wound up in myself, in a way strangely foreign to the simple deep warmth I felt. And I remember an evening a long time ago.

I was visiting an old friend, the resident head of a girls' dormitory in a traditional women's college. It was a cold winter's night. We had been sitting before the fire in big, high-backed chairs at one end of one of those large, lobby-like living rooms so typical of girls' dormitories. My friend had left to attend to some duty or other in her office. As I sat waiting I heard the voices of two youngsters approaching, then stopping. I became aware that they had taken seats on a couch, back to back with me. They didn't know I was behind them. Their voices had a familiar quality. The casual way in which they tossed off their comments wasn't quite consistent with the pitch of their voices. I smiled wisely at first, but then I recognized myself. When I was at college age, it was acutely important to me to be sophisticated, to be hardened against the wounds I had suffered when naïvely I had exposed my needs to young extortionists. The young need affection most acutely and exploit affection most cynically. I remembered how it was for me. Simply to offer open love was too naïve. What I didn't understand then was that it was too dangerous. I might get hurt. My reverie was interrupted as the couple started their conversation again. I was too closely identified not to eavesdrop.

"You look tired," she was saying.

"Yeah. Been drinking a lot. Can't seem to break the cycle. Bunch of fellows go out on the prowl every night, you know, liquor and girls, all part of it." He had that familiar note again, the phony defensive callousness.

"You do look thinner," she maintained the mood.

"Can't seem to eat right."

"Yeah." She added in a bored tone. They were quiet for a time until he turned the conversation toward her.

"Guess college is OK, huh?"

"It's a bore."

"For you?"

"I have these spells," she said in the same tone of the hardened victim of fate.

"Spells?" He showed a little surprise.

"I get wild."

"How you mean, wild?"

"Wild, I scream."

"You mean here, at school?" He was clearly surprised. She had him now.

"Everybody worries about me."

"Wild spells. That's new for you."

"Yeah, no more sweet little Betty."

"Yeah, Betty, the psycho!" He was willing to be impressed, and he moved quickly into her mood of ill-starred destiny. He said sadly,

"We're a mess."

"Aren't we?"

For a long time they said nothing. I could feel two real people under all that exchange of sad destiny, straining every fiber of their being to offer love, and in every straining act they were holding each other at bay.

"Your note," he began again. "You wanted to see me."

"I did. I did. I said I did." She was upset now.

"I wasn't really sure."

"I was clear enough. What do you want for an invitation?"

"It was a long time before your note. You didn't write. Months."

"Damn you!" It was a whisper but she conveyed all the force of a shout in it. "I want to see you. I said it. Twice I wrote for you."

"Oh, I . . . It's clear. I just wasn't sure you wanted to see me the way I am now." His voice carried his pain. "No, no. . . ." he began again, and stopped.

"I wanted to see you, sure, I . . ." He could not continue.

She sighed. "We are—we are a mess— a stinking mess."

"Your spells, are they bad for you—I mean your feelings?"

"I scream."

"Often?"

"Often."

"I see."

They stopped again. It was as if they had come quite close to what each wanted to say, too close and they were running away again.

"You have to study much?"

"I don't study."

"You used to."

"How can I study?"

I heard him move. He had moved toward her on the couch.

"You seem sad," he said very quietly.

"You do, too."

"Yeah, I'm not the man you once knew."

"You're thinner."

"Yeah, it's rough on me."

"What is?"

"Drinking, not sleeping, running . . ."

He trailed off in silence. No one moved a muscle.

"You really are sad," she whispered.

"Yeah."

"Both of us are."

"Yeah."

There followed one of the longest periods of silence I think I ever lived through. They sat perfectly still. I sat perfectly still. Finally, he broke the silence.

"When do I have to leave the dorm?"

"It closes at ten."

"Soon, huh?"

"Yeah, I guess so." I could hardly hear her. The struggle had ended. I came within an inch of walking round my chair and just putting her in his arms. But I was caught by the same powerful emotional force that was keeping them apart. Fear. Fear and embarrassment. I knew it well. I could not break out of it.

They rose. She stood quite still.

"Good night, Betty," he said.

"Good night, Mark," she whispered. He left her standing there. She stood still by the couch for a long time and, finally, walked away.

After a time my friend returned. "I saw Betty and her friend saying goodbye and I waited a bit."

"Is Betty ill in any way? I heard her say she had spells."

"Betty? No." She answered. "Betty is a brilliant student, charming girl, but lately she has been rather sad."

I, too, left the dormitory soon. As I walked out the gate to the street, I was struck by the appearance of a young man sitting on a bench at the bus stop. I stopped in the shadows, and I heard racking sobs just breaking through the fierce manly restraints. It may have been the most painful crying I have ever heard.

By now I have lived a long time with people I love deeply and dearly, people who love me deeply and dearly. By now I have known some magnificent moments of feeling and expressing a free and open love just for the joy of the expression—and love has been simple uncomplicated joy. But rarely. Very, very rarely.

Feelings can be held in, restrained,
left unexpressed in any open way, and
they become not much good to anyone.
J. Glidewell

People need people.
Laurie was about three when one night
she requested my aid in getting undressed.
I was downstairs and she was upstairs,
and . . . well.
"You know how to undress yourself," I
reminded.
"Yes," she explained, "but sometimes
people need people anyway, even if they
do know how to do things by
theirselves." W. Schutz

Love is essentially a relationship.
J. Powell

INTERPERSONAL
COMMUNICATION
EFFECTS

To change ourselves, reach others, and modify personal behaviors, we must have communication transactions with others as well as ourselves. The effects of interpersonal communication usually outreach any effects on others due to public speeches or exposure to mass messages. Awareness of the effects of interpersonal communication is both exciting and frightening. It is exciting because in interpersonal communication we can reach out and establish close, personal bonds with the other person, and frightening because interpersonal contacts can be used to harm others. This section is designed to demonstrate that interpersonal encounters do have their consequences.

In "Shame," by Stephen
Crane, both the negative and
positive effects of interpersonal communication are
highlighted. Being cut off from
friends because they think
something you do is funny or
weird is a devastating
experience for most of us. The
hurt and shame felt because
we have been excluded can
only be cured when someone
takes the time and effort to be
interested in us.

STEPHEN CRANE

SHAME

When he arrived in the outskirts of the grove he heard a merry clam-our, and when he reached the top of the knoll he looked down the slope upon a scene which almost made his little breast burst with joy. They actually had two camp-fires! Two camp-fires! At one of them Mrs. Earl was making something—chocolate, no doubt—and at the other a young lady in white duck and a sailor hat was dropping eggs into boiling water. Other grown-up people had spread a white cloth and were laying upon it things from baskets. In the deep cool shadow of the trees the children scurried, laughing. Jimmie hastened forward to join his friends.

Homer Phelps caught first sight of him. "Ho!" he shouted; "here comes Jimmie Trescott! Come on, Jimmie; you be on our side!" The children had divided themselves into two bands for some purpose of play. The others of Homer Phelps' party loudly endorsed his plan. "Yes, Jimmie, you be on our side." Then arose the usual dispute. "Well, we got the weakest side."

"Tain't any weaker'n ours."

Homer Phelps suddenly started and, looking hard, said, "What you got in the pail, Jim?"

Jimmie answered, somewhat uneasily, "Got m'lunch in it."

Instantly that brat of Minnie Phelps simply tore down the sky with her shrieks of derision. "Got his lunch in it! In a pail!" She ran screaming to her mother. "Oh, mamma! Oh, mamma! Jimmie Tres-cott's got his picnic in a pail!"

Now there was nothing in the nature of this fact to particularly move the others—notably the boys, who were not competent to care if he had brought his luncheon in a coal-bin; but such is the instinct of childish society that they all immediately moved away from him. In a moment he had been made a social leper. All old intimacies were flung into the lake, so to speak. They dared not compromise themselves. At a safe distance the boys shouted, scornfully: "Huh! Got his picnic in a pail!" Never again during that picnic did the little girls speak of him as Jimmie Trescott. His name now was Him.

His mind was dark with pain as he stood, the hang-dog, kicking the gravel, and muttering as defiantly as he was able. "Well, I can have it in a pail if I want to." This statement of freedom was of no importance, and he knew it, but it was the only idea in his head.

He had been baited at school for being detected in writing a letter to little Cora, the angel child, and he had known how to defend himself, but this situation was in no way similar. This was a social affair, with grown people on all sides. It would be sweet to catch the Margate twins, for instance, and hammer them into a state of bleating respect for his pail; but that was a matter for the jungles of childhood, where grown folks seldom penetrated. He could only glower.

The amiable voice of Mrs. Earl suddenly called: "Come, children! Everything's ready!" They scampered away, glancing back for one last gloat at Jimmie standing there with his pail.

He did not know what to do. He knew that the grown people expected him at the spread, but if he approached he would be greeted by a shameful chorus from the children—more especially from some of those damnable little girls. Still, luxuries beyond all dreaming were heaped on that cloth. One could not forget them. Perhaps if he crept up modestly, and was very gentle and very nice to the little girls, they would allow him peace. Of course it had been dreadful to come with a pail to such a grand picnic, but they might forgive him.

Oh no, they would not! He knew them better. And then suddenly he remembered with what delightful expectations he had raced to this grove, and self-pity overwhelmed him, and he thought he wanted to die and make every one feel sorry.

The young lady in white duck and a sailor hat looked at him, and then spoke to her sister, Mrs. Earl. "Who's that hovering in the distance, Emily?"

Mrs. Earl peered. "Why, it's Jimmie Trescott! Jimmie, come to the picnic! Why don't you come to the picnic, Jimmie?" He began to sidle toward the cloth.

But at Mrs. Earl's call there was another outburst from many of the children. "He's got his picnic in a pail! In a pail! Got it in a pail!"

Minnie Phelps was a shrill fiend. "Oh, mamma, he's got it in that pail! See! Isn't it funny? Isn't it dreadful funny?"

"What ghastly prigs children are, Emily!" said the young lady. "They are spoiling that boy's whole day, breaking his heart, the little cats! I think I'll go over and talk to him."

"Maybe you had better not," answered Mrs. Earl, dubiously. "Somehow these things arrange themselves. If you interfere, you are likely to prolong everything."

"Well, I'll try, at least," said the young lady.

At the second outburst against him Jimmie had crouched down by a tree, half hiding behind it, half pretending that he was not hiding behind it. He turned his sad gaze toward the lake. The bit of water seen through the shadows seemed perpendicular, a slate-coloured wall. He heard a noise near him, and turning he perceived the young lady looking down at him. In her hand she held plates. "May I sit near you?" she asked, coolly.

Jimmie could hardly believe his ears. After disposing herself and the plates upon the pine needles, she made brief explanation. "They're rather crowded, you see, over there. I don't like to be crowded at a picnic, so I thought I'd come here. I hope you don't mind."

Jimmie made haste to find his tongue. "Oh, I don't mind! I like to have you here." The ingenuous emphasis made it appear that the fact of his liking to have her there was in the nature of a law-dispelling phenomenon, but she did not smile.

"How large is that lake?" she asked.

Jimmie falling into the snare, at once began to talk in the manner of a proprietor of the lake. "Oh, it's almost twenty miles long, an' in one place it's almost four miles wide! an' it's deep too—awful deep— an' it's got real steamboats on it, an'—oh—lots of other boats, an'— an'—an'—"

"Do you go out on it sometimes?"

"Oh, lots of times! My father's got a boat," he said, eyeing her to note the effect of his words.

She was correctly pleased and struck with wonder. "Oh, has he?" she cried, as if she never before had heard of a man owning a boat.

Jimmie continued: "Yes, an' it's a grea' big boat, too, with sails, real sails; an' sometimes he takes me out in her too; an' once he took me fishin', an' we had sandwiches, plenty of 'em, and my father he drank beer right out of the bottle—right out of the bottle!"

The young lady was properly overwhelmed by this amazing intelligence. Jimmie saw the impression he had created, and he enthusiastically resumed his narrative: "An' after, he let me throw the bottles in the water, and I throwed 'em 'way, 'way, 'way out. An' they sank, an'—never comed up," he concluded, dramatically.

His face was glorified; he had forgotten all about the pail; he was absorbed in this communion with a beautiful lady who was so interested in what he had to say.

She indicated one of the plates, and said, indifferently: "Perhaps you would like some of those sandwiches. I made them. Do you like olives? And there's a deviled egg. I made that also."

"Did you really?" said Jimmie, politely. His face gloomed for a moment because the pail was recalled to his mind, but he timidly possessed himself of a sandwich.

"Hope you are not going to scorn my devilled egg," said his goddess. "I am very proud of it." He did not; he scorned little that was on the plate.

Their gentle intimacy was ineffable to the boy. He though he had a friend, a beautiful lady, who liked him more than she did anybody at the picnic, to say the least. This was proved by the fact that she had flung aside the luxuries of the spread cloth to sit with him, the exile. Thus early did he fall a victim to woman's wiles.

"Where do you live?" he asked, suddenly.

"Oh, a long way from here! In New York."

His next question was put very bluntly. "Are you married?"

"Oh no!" she answered gravely.

Jimmie was silent for a time, during which he glanced shyly and furtively at her face. It was evident that he was somewhat embarrassed. Finally he said, "When I grow up to be a man—"

"Oh, that is some time yet!" said the beautiful lady.

"But when I do, I—I should like to marry you."

"Well, I will remember it," she answered; "but don't talk of it now, because it's such a long time; and—I wouldn't wish you to consider yourself bound." She smiled at him.

He began to brag. "When I grow up to be a man, I'm goin' to have lots an' lots of money, an' I'm goin' to have a grea' big house, an' a horse an' a shotgun, an' lots an' lots of books 'bout elephants an' tigers, an' lots an' lots of ice-cream an' pie an'—carmels." As before, she was impressed; he could see it. "An' I'm goin' to have lots an' lots of children—'bout three hundred, I guess—an' there won't none of 'em be girls. They'll all be boys—like me."

"Oh, my!" she said.

His garment of shame was gone from him. The pail was dead and well buried. It seemed to him that months elapsed as he dwelt in happiness near the beautiful lady and trumpeted his vanity.

At last there was a shout. "Come on! we're going home." The picnickers trooped out of the grove. The children wished to resume their jeering, for Jimmie still gripped his pail, but they were restrained by the circumstances. He was walking at the side of the beautiful lady.

During the journey he abandoned many of his habits. For instance, he never travelled without skipping gracefully from crack to crack between the stones, or without pretending that he was a train of cars, or without some mumming device of childhood. But now he behaved with dignity. He made no more noise than a little mouse. He escorted the beautiful lady to the gate of the Earl home, where he awkwardly, solemnly, and wistfully shook hands in good-bye. He watched her go up the walk; the door clanged.

On his way home he dreamed. One of these dreams was fascinating. Supposing the beautiful lady was his teacher in school! Oh, my! wouldn't he be a good boy, sitting like a statuette all day long, and knowing every lesson to perfection, and—everything. And then supposing that a boy should sass her. Jimmie painted himself waylaying that boy on the homeward road, and the fate of the boy was a thing to make strong men cover their eyes with their hands. And she would like him more and more—more and more. And he—he would be a little god. . . .

A friend is one whose coming always brings pleasure, and whose going is always a source of regret. J. Millett

---

Obviously, one of the most
common interpersonal
situations is marriage. And,
while marriage entails a legal
obligation, it is also very
similar to any interpersonal
relationship where the
participants are emotionally
committed to one another. If
an interpersonal relationship
is one that lasts for an
extended period of time,
conflict will naturally arise.
The article "Is Your Marriage
a Fighting Affair?" discusses
the important effects that
conflict can have on a
marriage. The same principles
of conflict can obviously be
applied to other interpersonal
relationships.

CHANGING TIMES

IS
YOUR MARRIAGE
A FIGHTING
AFFAIR?

Last night both of you went at it again, a regular scene from *Who's Afraid of Virginia Woolf?* right there in your own home. Sure, the brickbats you threw were only words, but they were the cruelest words you could think of and you threw them as hard as you could. Now that it's over, you feel guilty and ashamed. You wonder what, if anything, was won or lost.

As you try to recall how the fracas started this time, maybe you ask yourself why your marriage can't be more like the placid union of the Smiths, who never seem to have a cross word for one another.

Possibly Mr. and Mrs. Smith are not the perfect models you think they are. The truth is that most really intimate married people do fight,

although many won't admit it. What's more, the marriage without quarrels may be faltering from emotional starvation.

"Contrary to folklore, the existence of hostility and conflict is not necessarily a sign that love is waning," say Dr. George R. Bach and Peter Wyden in their book, *The Intimate Enemy.* "Indifference to a partner's anger and hate is a surer sign of a deteriorating relationship than is indifference to love." In other words, if you care, you probably fight.

"Marriages are not made in heaven," says Dr. Melvin Gravitz, a Washington, D. C., psychologist and family counselor. "They evolve out of two persons' needs. When their needs conflict, there is bound to be difficulty."

Sad to say, few couples marry realizing that the tenderness and rapture of their courtship is mortal. When they find themselves fighting for the very first time, they may become alarmed by their anger and ease off before anything is settled, setting the stage for a long, dangerous cold war. If they see that first quarrel through to the end, though, it may add strength rather than weakness to their marriage.

Not that every marriage should become an open battlefield with no holds barred. Quarreling in which the partners never level with each other about their true complaints—maybe the husband takes out on his wife a smoldering, unspoken resentment against an unreasonable boss—can wreck a marriage. The healthy kind of conflict, experts advise, uses words not to kill but to dig out what's bothering each of you deep down. Then bottled-up tensions are released naturally.

Wrong Way, Right Way

In domestic conflict, as in most things, there is a right way and a wrong way to proceed. Consider these contrasting modes of combat:

DESTRUCTIVE CONFLICT

This is the gloves-off variety, in which the participants specialize in scathing criticism aimed at destroying their partner's ego. "You're no man," the wife may shout. To which he replies, "If you were only a lady. . . ." Frequently, such negative bickering flares into a white heat, only to sputter out pointlessly, leaving behind more wounds than there were before.

PRODUCTIVE CONFLICT

Advocates of successful quarreling advise, "Get it off your chest, but do it fairly." Have a specific issue and argue it through to a settlement, keeping your partner's character out of the debate. You don't have to mince words, either. If it's your style, talk at the top of your voice. But stay with the issue.

Most married people suffer a communication gap of one kind or another. Or sly innuendo may substitute for truth. One way to improve communications is simply to start listening to each other and responding candidly, much as it may hurt at first. Dr. Bach, who teaches the art of fair fighting in his California clinic, says a typical noncommunicating encounter might go something like this:

HE: You're pretty nervous about your mother coming, aren't you?
SHE: What makes you think so?
HE: Well, you don't usually spend so much time cleaning house.
SHE: Oh, so you think I'm a lousy housekeeper! Boy, you just don't understand me!
HE: (shrugging) Here we go again.

After training, however, the couple might be able to listen to each other instead of attacking, like this:

HE: You're pretty nervous about your mother coming, aren't you?

SHE: I'm not nervous about her. I'm nervous about how you're going to get along with her. By the way, what made you think I'm nervous about it?

HE: Because of the way you've been cleaning around here.

SHE: You're pretty sharp.

Of course, we all can't go into fight training or settle every spat with such simple diplomacy. But you can examine your customary ways of dealing with everyday grievances and ask how your tactics are working. You might be slipping into a destructive pattern of conflict without realizing it.

FAVORITE ISSUES TO FIGHT ABOUT

Just as you suspected, money is what married folks disagree about most often. When University of Pennsylvania researchers asked 300 couples to rate their conflicts in order of frequency, the top ten were:

1. finances
2. household management
3. personality disagreements
4. sexual adjustment
5. sharing household tasks
6. children
7. recreation
8. husband's mother
9. personal habits
10. jealousy

Researchers got answers from two groups of couples—200 who had once sought counseling help and 100 confident enough of their marriage to pit their wedded bliss against other contenders in a national "representative families" contest. Oddly, both groups ranked their conflicts in essentially the same order. The difference was in the intensity of the disagreements.

Getting the Most from a Fight

To see where your own quarreling habits may be leading you, take this brief test:

☐ Do you find yourself spoiling for a quarrel more often than you did a year ago?

☐ Do you frequently turn a deaf ear when your spouse complains?
☐ Do you store up injuries to be redressed at each fault-finding session?
☐ Do you often threaten retribution you are unlikely to carry out?
☐ Can you easily list five of your mate's worst faults and did you mention most of them during your last quarrel?
☐ Were you the winner?

If your honest answer to any of these questions is yes, you need to do some serious thinking about the way you deal with marital discord. If you replied yes to the last one, you are on particularly shaky ground. You have gone for the knockout, a sure sign of an unfair fighter. As William J. Lederer and Dr. Donald Jackson put it in *The Mirages of Marriage,* "When one spouse yields to the other's blandishments, he does so primarily so that he will be yielded to in turn." As heady victor, you miss the point of constructive combat.

Smart couples admit that disputes will occur, then form rules for arguing their differences through to a conclusion. Here are some of the guides others have used to avoid unfair tactics. Give them a fair trial. At the very least, you may get a chip off your shoulder without doing lasting damage to your marriage.

IS THIS FIGHT NECESSARY?

It's human to exaggerate. When you find yourself using a sledge hammer to drive in a thumbtack of a point, take time to ask yourself, "Do I have a real beef? What will I accomplish with a quarrel now?" If you can't convince yourself that any good will come from a showdown, better back down.

PICK A TIME AND PLACE

Farfetched as it sounds, make an appointment to air your next grievance. Don't excuse yourself as the type who simply gets mad and blows up. Explosions only open deeper wounds that take longer to heal. Advance notice will give both of you time to get your cases in order coolly and logically. One caution: If you make a date to quarrel and don't keep it, don't expect your gripes to be taken seriously.

GET TO THE POINT

One young couple fought a series of devastating quarrels that put their marriage in jeopardy. Usually, the fights occurred near the end of each month with the arrival of the bank statement. She complained

"You're mad about something, right?"

bitterly that he never told her how much to spend just so he could criticize her spendthrift ways. Invariably, he replied that she wouldn't keep to a budget if she had one.

With outside counsel, they learned that what the wife really wanted was for her husband to ask for a raise. He, in turn, resented her apparent disregard for stashing away some rainyday money. The couple improved their relationship by agreeing not to fight about money matters unless there was some new information they could introduce to show how they felt about the issue. To seal the bargain, he opened a separate checking account for her.

Thus a fundamental rule for productive quarreling: Say what's on your mind, rather than trying to use words to disguise the real issue at hand.

DRAW THE LINE

Everybody has an Achilles' heel, some tender spot where he is vulnerable. Janet has a college diploma; Joe graduated from high school. So when tempers flared she would snap out this unfair punch, "No wonder you don't understand me—with your education!"

It may take a little doing to resist the telling slur, but the effort is worth a try. Once taboo topics are recognized, you can keep them out of your quarrels.

MAKE UP

Be sure the fight is finished with questions like, "Have you said all you want to on the subject?" If somebody has to spend some time in the doghouse, so be it. But don't prolong the punishment—or the penance —unduly. The longer either drags on, the more difficult reconciliation becomes.

No fight is really over until the combatants have made up. And, as everybody knows, apologizing doesn't come easy. If you've never been one for saying "I'm sorry," try it for a change. You will find there are no better words for ending a successful quarrel.

---

*Women who can clean, look good and
mother children are a dollar a dozen,
but a woman who can make a man
feel his uniqueness is worth the world
to him.*
J.,
The Sensuous Woman

The importance of inter-
personal relationships to our
lives has been pointed out
previously. It is true that most
of our attitudes and values
are formed in interpersonal
contexts. Therefore, when the
nature of interpersonal
relationships changes the
effects may be extremely far
reaching. Alvin Toffler's best-
selling book, *Future Shock*, is
a provocative treatment of the
changes evolving in interpersonal relationships.

ALVIN TOFFLER

PEOPLE: THE MODULAR MAN

Each spring an immense lemming-like migra-
tion begins all over the Eastern United States. Singly and in
groups, burdened with sleeping bags, blankets and bathing suits, some
15,000 American college students toss aside their texts and follow a
highly accurate homing instinct that leads them to the sun-bleached
shoreline of Fort Lauderdale, Florida. There, for approximately a week,
this teeming, milling mass of sun and sex worshippers swims, sleeps,
flirts, guzzles beer, sprawls and brawls in the sands. At the end of
this period the bikini-clad girls and their bronzed admirers pack their
kits and join in a mass exodus. Anyone near the booth set up by the
resort city to welcome this rambunctious army can now hear the
loudspeaker booming: "Car with two can take rider as far as Atlanta
. . . Need ride to Washington . . . Leaving at 10:00 for Louisville . . ."
In a few hours nothing is left of the great "beach-and-booze party"
except butts and beer cans in the sand, and about $1.5 million in the
cash registers of local merchants—who regard this annual invasion
as a tainted blessing that threatens public sanity while it underwrites
private profit.

What attracts the young people is more than an irrepressible passion for sunshine. Nor is it mere sex, a commodity available in other places as well. Rather, it is a sense of freedom without responsibility. In the words of a nineteen-year-old New York co-ed who made her way to the festivities recently: "You're not worried about what you do or say here because, frankly, you'll never see these people again."

What the Fort Lauderdale rite supplies is a transient agglomeration of people that makes possible a great diversity of temporary interpersonal relationships. And it is precisely this—temporariness—that increasingly characterizes human relations as we move further toward super-industrialism. For just as things and places flow through our lives at a faster clip, so, too, do people.

The Cost of "Involvement"

Urbanism—the city dweller's way of life—has preoccupied sociology since the turn of the century. Max Weber pointed out the obvious fact that people in cities cannot know all their neighbors as intimately as it was possible for them to do in small communities. Georg Simmel carried this idea one step further when he declared, rather quaintly, that if the urban individual reacted emotionally to each and every person with whom he came into contact, or cluttered his mind with information about them, he would be "completely atomized internally and would fall into an unthinkable mental condition."

Louis Wirth, in turn, noted the fragmented nature of urban relationships. "Characteristically, urbanites meet one another in highly segmental roles . . ." he wrote. "Their dependence upon others is confined to a highly fractionalized aspect of the other's round of activity." Rather than becoming deeply involved with the total personality of every individual we meet, he explained, we necessarily maintain superficial and partial contact with some. We are interested only in the efficiency of the shoe salesman in meeting our needs: we couldn't care less that his wife is an alcoholic.

What this means is that we form limited involvement relationships with most of the people around us. Consciously or not, we define our relationships with most people in functional terms. So long as we do not become involved with the shoe salesman's problems at home, or his more general hopes, dreams and frustrations, he is, for us, fully interchangeable with any other salesman of equal competence. In effect, we have applied the modular principle to human relationships. We have created the disposable person: Modular Man.

Rather than entangling ourselves with the whole man, we plug into a module of his personality. Each personality can be imagined as a unique configuration of thousands of such modules. Thus no whole person is interchangeable with any other. But certain modules are. Since we are seeking only to buy a pair of shoes, and not the friendship, love or hate of the salesman, it is not necessary for us to tap into or engage with all the other modules that form his personality. Our relationship is safely limited. There is limited liability on both sides. The relationship entails certain accepted forms of behavior and communication. Both sides understand, consciously or otherwise, the limitations and laws. Difficulties arise only when one or another party oversteps the tacitly understood limits, when he attempts to connect up with some module not relevant to the function at hand.

Today a vast sociological and psychological literature is devoted to the alienation presumed to flow from this fragmentation of relationships. Much of the rhetoric of existentialism and the student revolt decries this fragmentation. It is said that we are not sufficiently "involved" with our fellow man. Millions of young people go about seeking "total involvement."

Before leaping to the popular conclusion that modularization is all bad, however, it might be well to look more closely at the matter. Theologian Harvey Cox, echoing Simmel, has pointed out that in an urban environment the attempt to "involve" oneself fully with everyone can lead only to self-destruction and emotional emptiness. Urban man, he writes, "must have more or less impersonal relationships with most of the people with whom he comes in contact precisely in order to choose certain friendships to nourish and cultivate . . . His life represents a point touched by dozens of systems and hundreds of people. His capacity to know some of them better necessitates his minimizing the depth of his relationship to many others. Listening to the postman gossip becomes for the urban man an act of sheer graciousness, since he probably has no interest in the people the postman wants to talk about."

Moreover, before lamenting modularization, it is necessary to ask ourselves whether we really would prefer to return to the traditional condition of man in which each individual presumably related to the whole personality of a few people rather than to the personality modules of many. Traditional man has been so sentimentalized, so cloyingly romanticized, that we frequently overlook the consequences of such a return. The very same writers who lament fragmentation also demand freedom—yet overlook the unfreedom of people bound together in totalistic relationships. For any relationship implies mutual demands and expectations. The more intimately involved a relationship, the greater the pressure the parties exert on one another to fulfill these expectations. The tighter and more totalistic the relationship, the more modules, so to speak, are brought into play, and the more numerous are the demands we make.

In a modular relationship, the demands are strictly bounded. So long as the shoe salesman performs his rather limited service for us, thereby fulfilling our rather limited expectations, we do not insist that he believe in our God, or that he be tidy at home, or share our political values, or enjoy the same kind of food or music that we do. We leave him free in all other matters—as he leaves us free to be atheist or Jew, heterosexual or homosexual, John Bircher or Communist. This is not true of the total relationship and cannot be. To a certain point, fragmentation and freedom go together.

All of us seem to need some totalistic relationships in our lives. But to decry the fact that we cannot have *only* such relationships is nonsense. And to prefer a society in which the individual has holistic relationships with a few, *rather than* modular relationships with many, is to wish for a return to the imprisonment of the past—a past when individuals may have been more tightly bound to one another, but when they were also more tightly regimented by social conventions, sexual mores, political and religious restrictions.

This is not to say that modular relationships entail no risks or that this is the best of all possible worlds. There are, in fact, profound risks in the situation, as we shall attempt to show. Until now, however, the entire public and professional discussion of these issues has been badly out of focus. For it has overlooked a critical dimension of all interpersonal relationships: their duration.

The Duration of Human Relationships

Sociologists like Wirth have referred in passing to the transitory nature of human ties in urban society. But they have made no systematic effort to relate the shorter duration of human ties to shorter durations in other kinds of relationships. Nor have they attempted to document the progressive decline in these durations. Until we analyze the temporal character of human bonds, we will completely misunderstand the move toward super-industrialism.

For one thing, the decline in the *average* duration of human relationships is a likely corollary of the increase in the number of such relationships. The average urban individual today probably comes into contact with more people in a week than the feudal villager did in a year, perhaps even a lifetime. The villager's ties with other people no doubt included some transient relationships, but most of the people he knew were the same throughout his life. The urban man may have a core group of people with whom his interactions are sustained over long periods of time, but he also interacts with hundreds, perhaps thousands of people whom he may see only once or twice and who then vanish into anonymity.

All of us approach human relationships, as we approach other kinds of relationships, with a set of built-in durational expectancies. We expect that certain kinds of relationships will endure longer than others. It is, in fact, possible to classify relationships with other people in terms of their expected duration. These vary, of course, from culture to culture and from person to person. Nevertheless, throughout wide sectors of the population of the advanced technological societies something like the following order is typical:

LONG-DURATION RELATIONSHIPS

We expect ties with our immediate family, and to a lesser extent with other kin, to extend throughout the lifetimes of the people involved. This expectation is by no means always fulfilled, as rising divorce rates and family break-ups indicate. Nevertheless, we still theoretically marry "until death do us part" and the social ideal is a lifetime relationship. Whether this is a proper or realistic expectation in a society of high transience is debatable. The fact remains, however, that family links are expected to be long term, if not lifelong, and considerable guilt attaches to the person who breaks off such a relationship.

MEDIUM-DURATION RELATIONSHIPS

Four classes of relationships fall within this category. Roughly in order of descending durational expectancies, these are relationships with friends, neighbors, job associates, and co-members of churches, clubs and other voluntary organizations.

Friendships are traditionally supposed to survive almost, if not quite, as long as family ties. The culture places high value on "old friends" and a certain amount of blame attaches to dropping a friendship. One type of friendship relationship, however, acquaintanceship, is recognized as less durable.

Neighbor relationships are no longer regarded as long-term commitments—the rate of geographical turnover is too high. They are expected to last as long as the individual remains in a single location, an interval that is growing shorter and shorter on average. Breaking off with a neighbor may involve other difficulties, but it carries no great burden of guilt.

On-the-job relationships frequently overlap friendships, and less often, neighbor relationships. Traditionally, particularly among white-collar, professional and technical people, job relationships were supposed to last a relatively long time. This expectation, however, is also changing rapidly, as we shall see.

Co-membership relationships—links with people in church or civic organizations, political parties and the like—sometimes flower into friendship, but until that happens such individual associations are regarded as more perishable than either friendships, ties with neighbors or fellow workers.

SHORT-DURATION RELATIONSHIPS

Most, though not all, service relationships fall into this category. These involve sales clerks, delivery people, gas station attendants, milkmen, barbers, hairdressers, etc. The turnover among these is relatively rapid and little or no shame attaches to the person who terminates such a relationship. Exceptions to the service patterns are professionals such as physicians, lawyers and accountants, with whom relationships are expected to be somewhat more enduring.

This categorization is hardly airtight. Most of us can cite some "service" relationship that has lasted longer than some friendship, job or neighbor relationship. Moreover, most of us can cite a number of quite long-lasting relationships in our own lives—perhaps we have been going to the same doctor for years or have maintained extremely close ties with a college friend. Such cases are hardly unusual, but they are relatively few in number in our lives. They are like long-stemmed flowers towering above a field of grass in which each blade represents a short-term relationship, a transient contact. It is the very durability of these ties that makes them noticeable. Such exceptions do not invalidate the rule. They do not change the key fact that, across the board, the *average* interpersonal relationship in our life is shorter and shorter in duration.

The interchange of feelings is very different from the interchange of objects. Give your friend an object and you don't have it anymore. You can't use it anymore. Give your friend an idea or a feeling and you haven't lost it. You still have it, often with greater understanding and control of it.   J. Glidewell

4

SMALL GROUP COMMUNICATION:
TRANSACTING WITH OTHERS

Everywhere you turn, small groups of people are present. At work, play, and school, we all are members of groups. Whether we are playing cards with a group of friends, attending a family reunion or committee meeting, or are a member of a bowling league, our immediate small group is important to us. Whether one's group affiliations are formal, such as a committees, or informal, such as several people who meet for coffee, they are important to our lives. Small groups exist in every culture and every land because humans seem to have a need to belong. As a result, small groups are ever-present.

Small groups play important roles in shaping decisions. The old adage "Two heads are better than one" is sometimes very appropriate. We can "bounce our ideas" off others and, in the process, discover new solutions to problems. Groups can, also, of course, suppress creative ideas if the members approach the task with a negative attitude. Clearly, groups are important forces in the shaping of ideas. Perhaps more importantly, however, groups serve social needs. For example, most people join card groups, craft classes, bowling groups, and similar organizations because forming and maintaining interpersonal relations in groups is satisfying.

Small group transactions are extensions of basic two-person interchanges. The presence of additional persons, however, magnifies the complexity of the communication transactions. The nature of the relationships is primarily interpersonal, because all participants should have an equal opportunity to share in the encounter, feedback is immediate, and it is still possible to deal directly with others and treat them as unique individuals.

SMALL GROUP
COMMUNICATION
PERCEPTION

Perceptions in a small group become more complicated than perceptions in interpersonal situations because of the addition of more individuals. How one perceives his role in the group, how he sees the others in the group, how he sees the importance of the group as a whole, and his notions of other competing groups are all part of his viewpoint.

Viewing yourself as a leader or follower in a group quite clearly affects your communication. If, for example, you think you have nothing to offer a committee of which you are a member, you probably will miss meetings, talk very little, and generally become uninvolved in the group process. If, on the other hand, you have skills to offer a group that values them, you will undoubtedly be an active member who forms meaningful friendships in the group. Likewise, your view of the importance of the group, of its role compared to other groups, affects your communication. The readings in this section highlight some of the varied perceptions one can have in small group transactions.

The following short selection by Howard Lane and Mary Beauchamp highlights the need to belong that we all have. How about you? Can you identify with the family members in this article who, because of the nature of the chores they are assigned, feel they are not needed?

HOWARD LANE

MARY BEAUCHAMP

NEED
TO BELONG
We need to belong to something—a gang, a group, a club, a family, a church, a team, a political party, or some other unit. Little children seek this belongingness by participating in whatever mother and father are doing. If mother is baking a cake, four-year-old Jane will be making one, too. If father is building a cabinet, little Sam will be hammering boards together. He, too, is making a cabinet. Children in their play reveal their reaching out for belonging to the adult world. They play house, going to the doctor's office, buying groceries, having babies, caring for the children, playing bridge, and so on.

As the child grows, his group identification becomes more and more important until, by the time he is an adolescent, his own age group is more powerful in setting standards, codes of behavior, and modes of dress than are the adults in his life. This is a step in growth that should be welcomed. Instead it is frequently resisted by adults— teachers and parents alike. A sorry world this would be if our young did not learn to make and stand by their own decisions. Psychiatrists' offices are cluttered today with middleaged men and women who still are tied to mom's apron strings. Let's remember this as we lament the apparent stubborn defiance in adolescent conduct. Redl has much of value to say on this subject.

We need to be needed. To belong, we have to be able to carry our own weight. We have to contribute something. We have to be needed because of what we have to give. One of the problems of present-day living is to find important ways in which children can belong to the family in a dynamic, real sense. The modern home does not need much contribution from children. Nothing is more

"Phooey!"

demoralizing than to spend one's time doing "phoney" work or work that doesn't need to be done. The ten-year-old who was given the task of sweeping out the garage each morning generated an ample store of resentment with each sweep of the broom, for he knew there was no sense to his work, no need for it. It contributed nothing to the happiness or the effectiveness of the home. It did make the boy resentful, skeptical of the judgment of adults and of the authority they wield.

One of the clearest statements
of the positive aspects of
small groups is offered
in "Group Life Is to Enhance
Individual Dignity." The
selection contrasts the
unique features of democratic
and authoritarian views of
small groups.

HOWARD LANE
MARY BEAUCHAMP

GROUP LIFE IS TO ENHANCE INDIVIDUAL DIGNITY

The critical philosophical difference between democracy and authoritarianism in all its form is that the ends for which we wish the goods of life are diametrically opposed. Both ideologies profess a concern with feeding the hungry, sheltering the cold, running trains on time, bringing health to the diseased and peace to the warring. Both philosophies profess to be their brother's keeper, to be concerned with all men everywhere. Both philosophies promise an improved way of living to the deprived, the miserable, and the oppressed.

The authoritarian purpose, the motivation for its concerns, stems from the belief that *the group is the supreme end.* The group is self-selected, self-perpetuating, and maintains an elite of its individuals. The will of this elect few at the top is then handed down to local groups through whatever prevailing machinery may exist—secret police; local committees on production, distribution, allocation. The individual's life, his goods, his produce are used to fulfill the quotas established by the group. The individual's welfare is at every point and in all realms tied irrevocably to group decision, and the individual must be trained to understand, feel, and accept at all times the supremacy of the group, and his own subservience to it. He must never question the wisdom of the group. He votes, he participates in decision-making, he elects officers, he has choices—all in a framework of circumscribed conditions and of preconditioned responses. Thus the individual exists for purposes of manipulation by others. He is trained

Howard Lane and Mary Beauchamp, Human Relations in Teaching: The Dynamics of Helping Children Grow, *copyright © 1955. Reprinted by permission of Prentice-Hall, Inc., Englewood Cliffs, New Jersey.*

from birth to be group-minded. He is a creature whose mechanisms can be put to use for those purposes deemed expedient by the governing group. Accepting this doctrine infers accepting that man is a mechanistic organism that can be conditioned to respond in predetermined ways appropriate to group supremacy. The doctrine is supported by a psychology of conditioned reflexes, by a physics of static matter, by a materialistic, mechanistic concept of man. Our times have produced at least two great satires describing this way of life—*Nineteen Eighty-four*[1] by Orwell and *Brave New World*[2] by Huxley. Many centuries ago Plato commented: "A slave is one who gets his purposes from somebody else."

Democracy's purpose, the motivation of concern with man, stems from the belief that individual dignity and well-being are the supreme end of group endeavor, that man's associations are for the purpose of enhancing, strengthening, making more operative that dignity. This presupposes that man has the inherent capacity for dignity, that living can be so managed—regardless of its specifics—that dignity pervades. Democracy states a faith in the individual's being able to make wise choices without benefit of coercion, deceptive persuasion, propaganda machines, or other manipulative devices. Democracy believes in not only the right but also the duty of the individual to examine the validity of majority decisions.

Examining the differences between authoritarian and democratic

---

[1] *George Orwell*, Nineteen Eighty-four *(New York: Harcourt, Brace & Company, 1949)*.

[2] *Aldous Huxley*, Brave New World *(New York: Harper & Brothers, 1932)*.

THE GROUP LIFE

concepts of *man* is a significant way of distinguishing between these two pervading ideologies. Man as a tool for the group versus the group as an expression of man's unique, individual dignity seems a clear mark of distinction between the two ideologies.

The quality of group life directed to the enhancement of individual living is the focus of this chapter. We are seeking to draw the dimension of Lindeman's words: "The good man knows how to work in and through groups but steadfastly refuses to become collectivized."[3]

[3] *Lecture made on occasion of William H. Kilpatrick's Eightieth Birthday by Eduard C. Lindeman at Hotel Commodore, November 17, 1951.*

Vance Packard details how
status perceptions of other
groups operate. The perceived
differences between groups
have significant effects on the
communication transactions
that are formed and
maintained. If there are
perceived differences between
groups, then associations
across the "lines" are difficult
and infrequent. Do you
perceive other groups as
different from our own? In
what ways?

VANCE PACKARD

WHO CAN BE A FRIEND?

The people who ask us back to dinner are almost always those who regard us as approximate equals in social prestige. I'm referring here to the social evenings that are relaxed and spontaneous. For better or worse, most people feel more at ease with their own kind. An early sociologist, F. H. Giddings, developed a concept to explain this, which has become known as "consciousness of kind." Certainly it is true that many people find that trying to socialize across class barriers can be a strain, because ingrained habits, outlooks, tastes, and interest, especially if they are people of low curiosity, typically differ by class. Sociologist Joseph A. Kahl has stated that the fellow who owns a yacht is likely to think he cannot have much fun with a townsman who owns a rowboat. When people find themselves in a cross-class social situation, they are likely to put on their best behavior and strain to make pleasant conversation.

Furthermore, most of us confine our socializing to members of our own social class because we feel that status is attached to the act of socializing. What will people think if we are seen at so-and-so's house? People a notch higher than we are, socially, may hesitate to come to our house, despite all our charming qualities, because someone might interpret this as meaning they had slipped down to our social class. Thus it is that we usually end up confining our socializing to our own kind of people.

In Hollingshead's Elmtown, an informant, Mrs. Daniels, told about her neighbors, the Joseph Stones, whose home backed up to her own. The Stones, she said, "are above us socially" in a clique known as The Little Eight. She said, "We talk back and forth as neighbors in the yard," and she added that Mrs. Stone had invited her for some afternoon bridge, but then she remarked, "Mr. Daniels and I have never been invited to any of their parties, and we never invite them here." Another family in the neighborhood was the Hewitts, who belonged to a still higher social clique, The Big Eight. The Hewitts, she felt, were downright snooty. "We have been neighbors for seven years, but she has never asked me to one of her parties, and she has them all the time."

Actually, Elmtown is an old-fashioned community, where people of the different classes do at least see each other around the neighborhood. Even this is becoming unlikely in the newer, stratified development-type communities. There, we see only people whose husbands make an income close to our own—within a quite narrow band, say $6,500 to $8,250. Such a family rarely sees the family of a factory worker, an industrialist, or even a schoolteacher.

The people we are willing to declare are our "friends" persistently come from our own social stratum. Some years ago, a fund-raising campaign in Boston ran aground because of this fact. The women's auxiliary of the Boston Philharmonic Orchestra conceived the idea of using a chain letter to raise money. Each woman in the auxiliary was supposed to write a letter to ten "friends." It was assumed that, in no time at all, such a chain letter would swirl over Boston and produce a windfall of dollars. Unfortunately, that didn't happen at all. The women in the auxiliary were all upper-class women, and the chain letters to "friends" never got out of the relatively small upper class, and down into the city's other classes.

At the bottom of the scale, much the same situation prevails regarding friends. The majority of textile workers in Paterson, New Jersey, reported that they had no friends in any social class but their own.

Perhaps the most illuminating study of friendship patterns is that conducted by Bevode McCall in a study of the social structure of his

Georgia Town.[1] He concluded: "The way people choose their friends is a part of the functioning of social class." In his Georgia Town, at least, few mutual friendships crossed the lines of the classes he found there. McCall asked more than 2,000 persons to name their "three best friends." Many people named one of two bank presidents as their best friend. A druggist and an eighty-year-old lady also were named as "best friend" by many people. With the exception of the very bottom class, the people in each class named as "best friends" more people in their own class than in any other.

Altogether, McCall had 5,200 choices listed for "three best friends." He sorted out all the cases where a "best friend" was named across a class line. Then he checked the list of the persons named to see if the feeling was mutual. (Often it was not.) He found only 140 cases out of the 5,200 where there was a mutual choice across class lines—or less than 3 per cent!

The stratification of our socializing patterns is seen most vividly in situations that parallel the company town. I have in mind those socializing systems confined to employees of one company, or to people of a military base, a university campus, or a one-industry town such as Hollywood. Let us look at examples of the four in order.

Company Entertaining

Management officials of a company, living in the same area, will almost always devote most of their home entertaining to one another. Partly, perhaps, this is "consciousness of kind" at work. Partly it results from a deliberate encouragement by management of off-hour socializing to promote, it hopes, team spirit. Also, it reflects an anxiety on the part of the officials to keep an eye on one another even during off hours. And much of it is a reflection of ambition. One account of Neil McElroy's rise up through the echelons of Procter & Gamble states that he and his wife, both ambitious for higher things, "limited their entertaining primarily to important P & G people. . . ."[2]

The *Wall Street Journal*, in a study of executive entertaining, noted that men are quick to deny they have fallen into any corporate

[1] *Bevode C. McCall, "Social Class Structure in a Small Southern Town" (doctoral dissertation, University of Chicago Library).*

[2] Time, *January 13, 1958, p. 12.*

mold or "just live for the company." One young sales executive, who made that protestation, stated a few minutes later, however: "My wife and I decided a long time ago not to waste too much of our leisure time with casual entertaining. When we have people out to the house, it has to be those who may be important to me as contacts."

Some companies not only encourage home entertaining within their ranks, but have some pretty explicit rules on how it must be done. The *Wall Street Journal* quoted the wife of a middle-management executive of a great chemical concern as griping: "I know of at least four couples who have left our company recently because of the unwritten rules of protocol that must be observed when entertaining company officials. We can never entertain anyone higher or lower in rank than my husband; when the husband of a friendly couple receives a promotion, then we can no longer socialize; except for formal open houses, or yearly cocktail parties, higher officials never entertain anyone below them."

The vice-president of a sizable company in a small western Pennsylvanian town told me of an awkward social problem he had. He brought in, from the "field," a promising man of Hungarian extraction to head up a sales department under him. The man persisted in asking the vice-president and his wife to his house for dinner. Each time the vice-president and his wife begged off, pleading other engagements. The president, similarly invited, also declined. After three months, although he was performing brilliantly at his job, the new subordinate grumbled to associates that the local "society" situation was too sticky for him and quit.

Recently, *Nation's Business* carried an article, "Friendship Can Ruin Your Business," by a business writer who cautioned executives to keep a sharp eye on fraternization patterns developing around the office to prevent fraternization from becoming "excessive." He cited positive values such as "group spirit," but his concluding paragraph pointed out that precautionary watchfulness "will prevent an up-and-coming manager from carrying around his neck a millstone of personal commitments, loyalties and friendships . . ." and help him perform his job better.

Below the management level of companies, you find somewhat similar stratification in entertainment. Although members of the white-collar force may work only a few yards from blue-collar workers, they almost never intermingle with them, either on or off the jobs. As for the blue-collar workers, they apparently just want to get home. They rarely invite their colleagues to come to their houses for supper;

and most of them wouldn't dream of asking their foreman to their houses. It is not that they would be afraid to. The idea simply would not occur to them.

Military Towns

Officers in the regular services, of course, are accustomed to putting the business of behaving according to one's rank openly and precisely on the line. They aren't inhibited by the requirement imposed on corporate officers to maintain, ostensibly, democratic forms. Actually, there is quite a bit of unofficial intermingling at the casual level across the lines of rank. In any social event of consequence, however, the lines are drawn firmly by rank; and seating is by date of rank. An invitation that comes from a higher-ranking officer, or his wife, has the force of a command. And, if it is a large affair where both tea and coffee are to be poured, the officer's wife invited to pour the coffee must outrank the wife invited to pour tea. This, apparently, derives from England, where coffee is regarded as a higher-status symbol than tea.

A perceptive young wife, who has just completed a tour of several years' duty as an Air Force lieutenant's wife, relates that as an Air Force wife she had to forget her ideas about democratic sociability. And the Air Force social pattern is not as rigid as that of the older services. She and her husband dutifully attended an orientation course during which they were warned of the dangers of familiarity with men of lower rank—or the men's wives.

While stationed in Enid, Oklahoma, this couple lived next door to a sergeant and his wife. They talked affably across the few feet of yard many hundreds of times—but never did they have supper together or play cards together. The wife explains, "Between enlisted men's families and officers' families there is no social passing. You do not invite them to your house and you do not go socially to theirs."

Whenever the base commander gave a party or reception, she added, attendance was mandatory. Every officer was required to leave his calling card (as proof of attendance). If the couple neglected to attend, the husband had to fill out an RBI (reply by endorsement) and that went into his permanent record.

My informant has concluded that wives of superior officers are more likely to "wear their rank" than the husbands. The line at the commissary always gave way when the colonel's wife appeared. My informant relates that, unfortunately for her, she and the colonel's wife became pregnant at approximately the same time. As the delivery dates approached, she found that her appointments to see a base doctor—which always involved an exhausting wait in line—fell on the same day as those of the colonel's wife. The colonel's wife asserted her prerogatives and was always ushered directly into an inner office whenever she appeared. My informant waited an average of two hours each visit. The colonel's wife never spent more than fifteen minutes at the clinic.

University Towns

For all their broad-mindedness, college professors are almost as careful about observing rank in social matters as the most anxious corporate executive. They have their own tight hierarchical structure for socializing, especially if the college dominates the community. Associate professors, on many campuses, are people who still haven't arrived; assistant professors are a big step further away from arriving; and teaching fellows at the bottom of the scale have no status at all. They might as well be janitors. A man who went to the University of Michigan, at Ann Arbor, from the West Coast, as a full professor, expressed pleasant surprise to an associate professor in the same department at the speed with which he and his family had been accepted socially in the community. He attributed it to the community's democratic spirit. The associate professor sourly suggested it was more likely due to the fact that he came with the rank of full professor.

A former faculty member, who served as an associate professor at Michigan for some years, told me he made several overtures to seek membership in a "discussion and drinking" faculty club on the campus. More than two hundred faculty members belong. He kept receiving evasive responses to his overtures. Finally, a friend, a full professor, advised him: "You need to be a full professor, or the equivalent in status, to belong."

Even the full professor has his social limitations. He would not invite a dean to his house socially, or the president or the vice-president. However, he might invite a department head if it was a large affair. At larger, more official, parties, where a dean is the top ranking guest invited, he or she will be careful to be the last to arrive and the first to leave. That situation prevails at Michigan. Some time ago, while visiting Penn State University, I found myself being escorted to a party by a dean. I mentioned to him, good-humoredly, that at Michigan deans were expected to arrive last and leave first. He laughed, and said they didn't believe in that sort of fancy protocol at Penn State. He went on to say, however, that at some colleges where he had served they had simply frightful rules of etiquette regulating social intermingling. When we arrived at the party, I noted that the party was in full progress. I noted, further, that no guest arrived after we did. We had been at the party for what seemed a short time when the dean came up to me and said he was ready to leave any time I was. There were about sixty people there. We were the first to leave.

Students, too, at the universities are evidently showing keen interest in being seen only with the right people. *Parade* magazine quotes one of the biggest men on campus at Iowa State University as stating: "You have to be careful not to associate with the wrong clan of people, an introvert group that isn't socially acceptable, guys who dress in the fashion of ten years ago, blue serge suits and loud ties. These people are just not accepted. And if you associate with them, you're not accepted either." This man, who was on the Student Council, said he aspired after college to go to work for a large corporation. As for the secret of his success in becoming a campus leader: "You've always got to be in there pitching and smiling."

Hollywood

My informant here is a high-ranking, creative artist who has been in Hollywood more than twenty years, and has attended "hundreds" of Hollywood parties. "Hollywood is the most class-conscious place in the world, and getting worse," he said. "It's brutal." Surprisingly, to me, it is not the stars who throw their rank around. They tend, he said, to be rather naïvely democratic. He called them "jay walkers." Rather, it is the movie makers (producers, writers, technicians, and staff people, etc.) who draw the lines. A $120-a-week secretary would not think of associating with a $70-a-week one. "A $1,000-a-week writer will not associate with a $2,000-a-week writer," he said. "If they associated when they both made $1,000, they stop associating. The man being promoted in income may associate once or twice after the promotion with his old $1,000 friend—he doesn't want to seem an utter heel—but no more." All creative artists, such as composers and writers, who are permitted to work at home, are automatically of higher status than those who are expected to report in regularly at studios.

Anyone giving a party in Hollywood, he said, draws the guests from his social level. He indicated four of the major levels by listing the kind of people you inevitably see at the parties of each of the four levels:

First level: "Your party here will be made up of directors, producers, a couple of stars (probably of pre-1940 vintage), a famous columnist, perhaps the wife of a famous writer, now dead. You will never find a cameraman, important as he is, at this level, nor a set designer unless he is awfully famous, brought in especially for a film from New York."

Second level: "Most of the composers, writers, top cameramen, set designers. I'm at this level. I've been to hundreds of parties and I've never seen a cutter, even though he makes more money than many of us, and can be terribly important—some say the most important—in making or breaking a picture. He's not 'creative.' "

Third level: "The cutters, top electricians who handle the lights, skilled technicians of all kinds, the 'effects' men who make the miniatures. When the Oscars are handed out each year, these effects men are the two little guys who run up early in the evening, when no one is paying any attention, to get their prize."

Fourth level: "The lower levels of prop men, the higher level of secretaries, etc."

As with the faculty people of universities, the Hollywood motion-picture people, from top to bottom, socialized almost exclusively within their own fantasy-building world. The outside butcher, brakeman, and candlestick manufacturer may pass them every day, but are seen only as blurred figures.

To return to the over-all view, ideas about what constitutes a good party vary from class to class. At the upper-class level, the cliques tend to prefer a good deal of relaxed informality, with the emphasis on sociability laced with whisky rather than show. Food typically is offered casually. There may be amiable and fairly open flirting, and talking. Weaving figures may offer toasts. Other parties at this level are carried on with quiet decorum. It depends on the personalities. Publicity, in the newspapers, in either case is not sought. It is considered a sign of social weakness to seek publicity. The people having the party at the upper level usually aren't trying to prove anything.

At the semi-upper-class level, members of the cliques frequently are trying to prove something, and it shows. More thought and effort go into decorations and food preparation. Allison Davis and Burleigh B. and Mary R. Gardner, describing party life in a Southern town they studied, noted that, at the upper-middle-class level (as they call it), there was a great deal of vying to serve the most unusual delicacies, and a great deal of preoccupation with decoration and display of status symbols.[3] There is less emphasis on drinking or flirting. There may be card playing, or some cultural treat such as a Tchaikovsky recording just acquired. The hostess will often see to it that news about her party will somehow reach the attention of the local society editor.

Clique parties in homes of the still lower limited-success class are likely to be even more decorous, if less ostentatious. These are the people who show the greatest fondness for church suppers, and when they have parties at their homes prefer the same type of festivity. Frequently, at least in smaller communities such as Elmtown, each couple will bring a dish. They call it "potluck," but when the hostess gets around to writing her piece for the local paper, as she is very likely to do, it will become a "covered dish party."

At the working-class level, most of the socializing is done with siblings, siblings-in-law, or very near neighbors, and is quite random. The parties are often spur-of-the-moment affairs. In fact, the clique, as we've known it in the above classes, a pack of people running together, virtually disappears at the working-class level. A study of fifty working-class couples in the New Haven area disclosed that only two out of the fifty couples belonged to a clique of non-relatives who took turns giving parties. And two fifths of these working-class couples confined their intimate friendships entirely to kinfolk. At this level we see, too, the beginning of a tendency of the sexes to split up in their socializing. The women have their auxiliaries and their "hen" circles. The men get away from their wives by chatting or drinking with male friends and relatives.

The real-lower-class people depend even more than the working class on relatives for companionship. Their idea of festivity is to idle on Main Street Saturday nights, chatting with people they know, or to congregate in the taverns. In any case, the tendency for the sexes to split up in their chatting becomes even more marked.

One interesting way people reveal their class status in a simple act of socializing is the way that two married couples, on their way to a festivity, get into an automobile. If they are from one of the two lower classes, the men will climb into the front seat together and the women in the back. If they are from the limited-success class, where respectable behavior is cherished, each man will typically get in beside his wife. If

[3] *Allison Davis, Burleigh B. and Mary R. Gardner,* Deep South *(Chicago: University of Chicago Press, 1941).*

they are from one of the two top classes, each husband will most likely, with a show of gallantry, get in with the other man's wife.

They are playing a game. They are playing at not playing a game. If I show them I see they are, I shall break the rules and they will punish me. I must play their game, of not seeing I see the game.   R. D. Laing

The following poem
reveals how individual
perceptions among group
members can vary. In this
case, the group is a peer
group of grandmothers—a
delightful lot; but they suffer
from the same perception
problems as the rest of us.

ANONYMOUS

"GRANDMOTHERS"

They say that all grandmothers
Are inclined to brag a-bit
And that there is some truth
  in that I frankly must admit.

For since I've reached that stage—
And all my friends have too—
I'm floored by all the bragging
These other grandmothers do.

Yet when I see these boys and girls,
Their grandmothers' pride and joy,
Each seems to me to be
Quite an ordinary girl or boy!

Of course I humor them along
And say I think they're fine,
But you can see the difference
If you've ever noticed mine.

My own are so much cuter, smarter,
  Handsomer than theirs,
I can afford to humor them
  When they put on such airs.

I'm really glad that I don't brag
Like other grandmas do
I've so much more to brag about
  If I just wanted to.

SMALL GROUP
COMMUNICATION
NONVERBAL BEHAVIOR

*Nonverbal communications signal to
members of your own group what kind
of person you are, how you feel about
others, how you'll fit into and work in a
group . . .   E. Hall and M. Hall*

With the addition of persons to a communication transaction, more and more cues are present. Seating arrangement, vocal expressions, eye contact, and the other numerous nonverbal cues from all members are abundant. Each person is having an impact on all the others, perhaps most forcefully with nonverbal cues.

Nonverbal behavior of participants indicate two dimensions of interpersonal behavior. A vast array of research in small group and interpersonal contexts leads us to the following conclusion. Our relationships with others indicate dominance-submission and hostility-warmth. Put simply, we have a degree of control over others (and they over us), and we communicate affection, which can range from hostility to warmth. While one could easily supply different labels such as control-submission and love-hate, the dimensions remain unchanged.

Furthermore, while nonverbal behavior within groups is important, it also signals things to other groups. The desk arrangement, arrival time at work, the kinds of cars we drive, and other nonverbal trappings of a group have an effect on other groups. Relations between groups are affected nonverbally because we communicate to others everything our group stands for and against.

In "Styles of Leadership,"
James Kinder focuses on the
dimensions of leadership
behavior in small groups.
These same dimensions bridge
the transactions among all
participants. As you read this
selection, think of how you
and others in your small
groups are affected by
dominance-submission and
hostility-warmth as bases for
evaluation. If a group member
is nonverbally aggressive—
talks loudly, takes control,
uses an authoritative tone
of voice—what effect does he
have on your group?

JAMES F. KINDER

STYLES OF
LEADERSHIP
Many of us take leadership for granted and yet it is essential to business, government and the voluntary organizations that shape the way we live, work and play.

Each one of us is some way involved in leading others whether we happen to be the Prime Minister, president of our own company, chairman of a voluntary committee, or head of a family. The problems of leadership are important whether we have many subordinates, one subordinate or whether we are trying to influence members of our peer group.

Leadership is more than an appointed position—it's more than the personal qualities of the leader—it's more than just having authority over someone. Leadership is the process of influencing others so that they, along with you, reach a mutually acceptable goal in a way that is satisfying to all.

Implied in the discussion of leadership are the motives of the leader. Presumably a leader is interested in influencing others, in striving for effective results and in providing achievement satisfaction for himself and others.

The concept of leadership is usually analyzed in terms of the

Reprinted by permission of James F. Kinder and the Canadian Personnel Journal, May, 1971, pp. 35–41.

leader, those whom he is leading, and the situation in which leadership takes place. Our discussion focuses on the behavior of the leader and the reaction of the followers to his behavior.

Our focus then is on behavior: the behavior of the leader as it is *seen* by the persons he is leading. The key word here is *seen*. All of us tend to react to others in terms of the behavior which we observe. We do not usually make allowances for behavior which is unacceptable to us unless we have known an individual over many years, and most of our work associations are of relatively short duration. We interact with others in terms of observable behavior. As a subordinate I am concerned with *what* you do to me, not in what you *intended* to do.

In the study of leadership it is important then that we analyze various types of behavior initiated by the leader or to put it another way—the analysis of leadership styles.

A helpful way of identifying leadership styles is through the use of a behavioral model. For example, one of the earliest models portrays the implications of the use of democratic as opposed to autocratic leadership. Other models combine a leader's concern for production and his concern for people and describe four or five leadership styles.

There are many behavioral analysis models but all have one thing in common—they are concerned with how a leader gets the job done and how he handles people in getting that job done.

Lawrence Appley, retired President of the American Management Association once said that the world is composed of four kinds of people:

- ☐ those who make things happen
- ☐ those to whom things happen
- ☐ those who watch things happen
- ☐ those who do not even know that things are happening

This is one way of indicating that various "styles" of behavior exist.

The model to be used in our discussion combines four basic behavioral traits—Dominance, Submission, Warmth and Hostility. It may be shown visually this way:

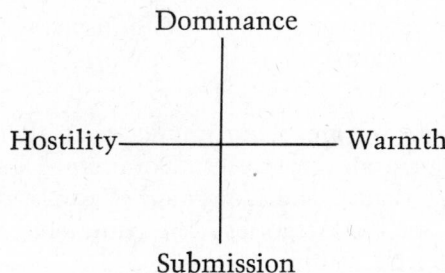

The evidence of dominance is shown by a person who leads, advises, directs, initiates, takes over situations, organizes, believes in structure, volunteers, and generally takes responsibility.

A person who is submissive is willing to accept others' leadership and guidance. In fact, he enjoys following others and tends to be a low risk-taker. In situations that require leadership he tends to nominate others for the task.

Individuals who show warmth have a genuine concern for others. They tend to be confident, friendly, approachable, cheerful, have a sense of humor and, on occasion, can be self-sacrificing.

Hostile individuals tend to be cold, indifferent, competitive and intolerant of other people's ideas. A hostile person is self-centered, does not listen to others and has very little sense of humor.

Using the four basic behavioral traits we can identify four leadership styles in our model.

An individual who combines the traits of dominance and hostility we call Dominant-Hostile and identify with the symbol L1.

The other three styles may be identified as follows:

Submissive-Hostile — L2
Submissive-Warm — L3
Dominant-Warm — L4

The symbols L1, L2, L3 and L4 are useful to us in discussing the implications of the model. They are useful in the sense that we can establish almost instant understanding of the type of behavior we are seeking to understand.

Our model can now be shown as follows:

Dominant- Hostile		Dominant- Warm
	L1	L3
	L2	L4
Submissive- Hostile		Submissive- Warm

The style model we are using implies that all behavior may be analyzed in four separate categories: Dominant-Hostile, Submissive-Hostile, Submissive-Warm, and Dominant-Warm and that each of us fits neatly into one of the categories. Unfortunately human behavior is much more complex than this.

For example—a person who is usually Dominant-Warm will at times show evidence of submissiveness and/or hostility. Sometimes the submissive worm turns and shows flashes of leadership. On occasion the hostile person will show warmth toward certain people.

The point is that behavior should be analyzed in terms of what is happening in the current situation, not that a certain style once identified will always be used.

The purpose of behavior analysis through a style model is not to categorize but to be able to recognize here-and-now behavior in understandable terms.

With this purpose in mind, it might be helpful to illustrate briefly how the four styles may be recognized.

L1. Dominant-Hostile

The Dominant-Hostile leader is usually perceived as one who puts the immediate task above all other considerations. He is ineffective in that he makes it obvious that he has no concern for others' feelings and has little confidence in the efforts of other people. While this attitude promotes fear it also produces dislike and thus people are motivated to work only when the Dominant-Hostile is present. The Dominant-Hostile cannot understand why so many people are unco-operative; he does not fully realize that co-operation to him means doing it his way.

Further understanding may be achieved by considering the leader's action in handling certain managerial situations.

For example:

Control of Work Assignments
"Do it this way and do not change it unless you check with me."

Mistakes Made by Others
"Who is responsible for this?"

Decision Making
"My mind is already made up; do not confuse me with facts."

Attitude to Meetings
"Committees are a waste of time, the fastest way to get things done is to do it yourself."

Attitude to Suggestions Made by Others
"We've tried that before and it does not work."

L2. Submissive-Hostile

The Submissive-Hostile leader is seen as one who often shows his lack of interest in both task and relationships. He is less effective not only because of his lack of interest but also because of his effect on others' morale. He may be seen not only as shirking his own duties but also as hindering the performance of others through intervention or by withholding information.

Likely to be resistant to change or accepts change and then sabotages it—withholds information, aims at minimum output, impedes others, lowers morale.

Control of Work Assignments
"I don't care how you do it, as long as it's done."

Mistakes Made by Others
"Forget it—we all make mistakes."

Decision-Making
"It's entirely up to you."

Attitude to Meetings
"Another meeting!—let's get it over with as soon as possible."

Attitude to Suggestions Made by Others
"Good idea. I'll pass it on to Bill."

L3. Submissive-Warm

The Submissive-Warm leader is basically a kindly soul who puts happy relationships above all other considerations. He is ineffective because his desire to see himself and be seen as a "good guy" prevents him from risking even mild disagreement in order to improve production.

He believes that happy people produce more and that production is less important than good fellowship. He strives to create a warm, pleasant, social atmosphere where an easygoing work tempo may be maintained.

He spends much of his time trying to find ways to make things easier for his people.

Control of Work Assignments
"How are things going, Charlie?"

Mistakes Made by Others
"Ah! forget it, we all make mistakes; better luck next time."

Decision Making
"I had nothing to do with the decision but it seems fair so I think we should go along with it."

Attitude to Meetings
"Yeh, the meeting may not accomplish much but it gives all of us an opportunity to get to know each other better."

Attitude to Suggestions Made by Others
"Wonderful idea, Joe, never thought of doing it that way. I'll discuss it with the others."

L4. Dominant-Warm

The Dominant-Warm leader is perceived as one who sees his main task as maximizing the effort of others toward both short and long term goals. He sets high standards for production and performance but recognizes that because of individual differences he will have to treat everyone a little differently. He is effective, in that his commitment to both task and people is evident to all and acts as a powerful motivating force.

He welcomes disagreement and conflict as they relate to the task. He sees such behavior as necessary, normal and appropriate.

He believes that differences can be worked through, that conflict can be resolved, and that commitment will result.

Control of Work Assignments
"Go ahead, Bill, I'll keep in touch to see if I can be helpful if you run into difficulty."

Mistakes Made by Others
"Let's see if we can determine *what* went wrong so it isn't likely to happen again."

Decision Making
"Let's discuss it before we proceed. I'd like your opinion."

Attitude to Meetings
"Tomorrow?—*great*, it will give us all an opportunity to express our views and decide on action."

Attitude to Suggestions Made by Others
"Sounds like a good idea; let's talk it over and see if it can be implemented."

A leader might ask himself—

What are some of the practical applications of behavior at work?

What does a study of behavior mean to me?

Is my leadership behavior consistent?

Is there a "best" style of leadership?

What are my assumptions about people and how they work?

Can I really change my behavior?

The answers to some or all of these questions may be found in studying the model.

Research seems to indicate that we are basically consistent in our behavior and therefore we show a predominant style over a period of time. Our actions are a result of our value system about people and how work gets done. For example, if we believe that people are lazy, indifferent and irresponsible and therefore they will have to be pushed, coerced or ordered to do a job we will use a Dominant-Hostile style (L1).

There also seems to be some evidence that in most situations a style which involves others in planning and goal setting, that is, Dominant-Warm (L4), is the best style to use for effective results.

An understanding of behavior in style terms enables the leader to better understand the actions of others. For example, if a leader operates in a Dominant-Hostile fashion he should not be surprised if he gets either a Dominant-Hostile reaction or, worse still, a Submissive-Hostile attitude.

No behavior change in either the leader or the subordinate can take place until there is some understanding of what behavior choice is available; until there is some understanding of the results of a behavior choice; until there is some belief that by changing behavior a more effective result will be achieved.

In our society we tend to over-complicate issues and leadership is no exception. There have been guidelines in the past on good leadership practice. One of the best was stated by Lao-Tzu, a Chinese philosopher in the 6th Century, B.C. It is entitled "The Way of Life According to Lao-Tzu" and goes like this:

"A leader is best
When people barely know that he
*   exists,*
Not so good when people obey
*   and acclaim him,*
Worst when they despise him.
Fail to honor people,
They fail to honor you;

But of a good leader, who talks
little,
When his work is done, his aim
fulfilled,
They will all say, "We did this
ourselves."

A leadership style well worth adopting.

I don't want to listen to just what you
say. I want to feel what you mean.
H. Prather

From Hugh Prather, *Notes to Myself*. Reprinted by permission of Real People Press.

We turn again to Vance
Packard, this time for his
insights into the nonverbal
facets of group behavior. In
"Pecking Orders In Corporate
Barnyards," Packard shows
the numerous nonverbal cues
that certain group members
use to demonstrate their
uniqueness. What about your
own groups? Do you have
special handshakes, dress
styles, or other nonverbal
behaviors that set you apart
from other groups?

VANCE PACKARD

PECKING ORDERS IN CORPORATE BARNYARDS

The headlong trend toward large organizational structures in America—not only in business but in government, labor, and education—has in the past decade produced new built-in stratification systems across the landscape. Nowhere is this more apparent than in the great corporation, which can often impose its hierarchy of ranks—and symbols of differential status —upon the social structure of the surrounding community.

These hierarchical ranks are becoming as explicit as those of the United States Civil Service or those of the armed forces. Each corporation has its hierarchy of the "line" (first-line foreman, assistant general foreman, general foreman, assistant department superintendent, department superintendent, divisional superintendent, assistant plant manager, plant manager, and others responsible for production) and its vertically parallel hierarchy of staff specialists (such as designer, assistant supervisor, supervisor, general supervisor, assistant staff head, staff head). Topping these twin jungles of titles are the elect of "advanced management" or "elite nucleus."

Mabel Newcomer, in comparing the lives of modern business executives with those at the turn of the century, was deeply impressed by the fact that while two thirds of the executives in 1900 had once run their own enterprises, only 1 in 10 of the mid-century executives had; and the number who had spent their entire careers within the walls of one corporation had tripled.

One result of the growth of corporate bureaucracy is the intense preoccupation that has developed in the past decade with symbols of status. The *Wall Street Journal,* after a nation-wide study of business trends, reported on its page 1: "At an increasing number of concerns, the corporate caste system is being formalized and rigidified." And *Time* magazine reported on its business pages that the "trappings of power and rank are normal incentives in U.S. business life." It quoted a Cleveland president as saying that "often the little privileges that go with an office are more important to an executive than a raise. You'd expect executives to be more mature, but they frequently aren't."[1] *Time* added that the trend is toward "more instead of less luxury" in executive trappings. (A corporation executive who read this present chapter suggested only that I make it clear I'm not being facetious, that status symbols have indeed come to play a most serious role in corporate incentive systems.)

This preoccupation with prerogatives—or "perks" as the British call them—reflects the special problems posed by bigness. In a small company, everybody knows who is who, and where the power resides. An executive can charge about in shirt sleeves issuing orders and use a battered desk in an open room as his office. In my search for men who had made at least $10,000,000 in the last twenty years, I found that almost all made their fortunes by starting and running their own companies (which makes them look a little like dinosaurs in this modern managerial era); and I found the ways of operating of these lone wolves startlingly different from the hundreds of corporate executives I have interrogated, over the years, behind their neat, polished desks. Several of the entrepreneur-multimillionaires worked in such modest cubicles that I couldn't believe I had reached my destination when I faced them. One shared a secretary with his two assistants. Another had odds and ends of furniture; a third had a "board" room less than ten feet square. Most impressive, at least eight relaxed by putting up their feet on their desks as they talked. I have strained my memory and I can remember only one executive of a large corporation who ever did that. He was a president, and even he did it uneasily.

In the large corporation, just as in the Army, the executive feels a need for highly visible signs of his authority, even though he feels a

---

[1] Time, *"Executive Trappings," January 24, 1955, p. 80.*

need simultaneously to act out the American Creed by showing what a nice, regular fellow he is.

The result is that the office managers of many corporations are trained in the nuances of status and systematize the apportioning of "perks."

First, there is the physical problem of assigning office space. This is often done by rule. Crown Zellerbach Corporation, in planning its move to a new twenty-story building, has arranged walls so that offices for executives of equal rank can "all be built to within a square inch of one another in size."[2] In a typical corporation, the head of the hierarchy assigned to a floor gets the corner office with the nicest view, and the offices of his subordinates branch out from his corner in descending order of rank. Physical closeness to the center of power is considered evidence of status; and nobody wants to be put out "in left field."

Desks, too, typically are categorized by rank. Mahogany, of course, outranks walnut; and walnut outranks oak. The man who is entitled to wall-to-wall carpeting is likely to have a water carafe, which has replaced the brass spittoon as a symbol of flag rank, and also probably has a red-leather couch. An executive with a two-pen set on his desk clearly outranks a man with a one-pen set. At one broadcasting company, executives above a certain level—and only they—are entitled to electric typewriters for their secretaries.

Several of the automobile-making corporations have highly formalized systems for bestowing status symbols. Here is how the *Wall Street Journal* described the ascent of one former Ford executive: "As his position improved, his office grew larger, his furniture fancier, his name went on the door, he received a rug for the floor and a spot in the indoor garage. Then came keys to executive washrooms, country club membership at company expense, and finally a free car." One of the added benefits of gaining a key to the executive washroom was that in it he could enjoy showers and the use of electric shavers and free cologne. In the town of Darien, Connecticut, where executives tend to congregate, 65 per cent of the membership fees of one local country club are paid by companies.

The private washroom, in many companies, is reserved for vice-presidents and up. Some have gold faucets. At a Midwestern oil firm, however, a fine line is drawn. The vice-presidents, like the president, have a private washroom; but it is literally that. Their washroom has no toilet, as the president's has.

[2] Wall Street Journal, *"Status Symbols,"* October 29, 1957, p. 1.

An invitation to use the executive dining room is another "perk" that comes only when the employee passes a certain level on the company's hierarchical chart. At a steel plant I visited near Pittsburgh, there were two executive dining rooms side by side for different levels of executives. The one with tablecloths was for the higher group. A New York insurance company has, in its building, five dining rooms in ascending elegance, and personnel are assigned by rank. The democratic custom of eating with rank-and-file employees at a common dining hall has become so rarely observed by corporate executives that the president of a medium-sized company in Northeast City boasted to me that he did that. It helped morale, he felt.

The circumstances under which an employee arrives for work also are highly indicative of status. Does the employee have to punch a time clock or not? Does he or she come through the plant gate or the office door? At what time does he or she arrive in relation to others? Bosses typically make it a practice to arrive either earlier or later than their flock. In England, a government proposal to ease the rush-hour traffic by persuading some business firms to start their day a half hour earlier encountered a snob barrier. White-collar workers of one large company that was considering opening a half hour earlier (at 8:30) vehemently objected. When questioned, they reluctantly made the point that factory employees commonly started their work at 8:30, so that for them to do so would involve a loss of social prestige. . . .

Where your office is located also seems to be a factor of importance. Being on the same floor with the people at the "head office," so that you can be seen, helps. Other things being equal, you are far more likely to be advanced than a status equal whose office happens to be in another floor, another building, or (worse) another city.

Home life, too, is important. An advertising executive who stated publicly that he and his family couldn't live on $25,000 a year also stated why: "There is no denying that when a man starts to make a certain amount of money how he lives becomes a matter of concern to his employers. And the advertising business is an Ivy League, where clothes, manners and gracious living are an essential part of doing business."[3] So, evidently, is the gracious wife. A top official of a Midwestern concern states: "Entertaining is one of the best ways to determine if the wife is good enough to enable a man to become a well-rounded executive."[4] A member of a management-consulting firm in

[3] Ladies' Home Journal, *February 1958.*
[4] Wall Street Journal, *November 13, 1957.*

the Midwest recently found himself being considered for a top spot in one of the nation's larger food corporations. The scrutiny of him went on for what he felt was an indecently long period. Finally, he and his wife were invited to dine at an elite downtown Chicago restaurant with the president and the president's wife. The candidate and his wife dressed and behaved the very best they knew how. Two days later, without any further evidence of screening, he was advised that he had been hired. He had passed the final test.

If a man takes off his sunglasses, I
can hear him better.   H. Prather

From Hugh Prather, *Notes to Myself.* Reprinted by permission of Real People Press.

SMALL GROUP COMMUNICATION
BARRIERS

Communication transactions within small groups can be affected by numerous barriers. If the individuals in the group have low self-respect, if the members fail to support one another, or if the communication climate is ridden with conflict, the outcome of the group will probably be less than satisfactory. A barrier to small group transactions is anything that hinders successful task completion or interferes with personal relationships. Barriers can preclude a group from performing its assigned task and can damage interpersonal relationships.

Because barriers arise within (and, of course, across) groups does not mean that they are to be avoided at all costs. Many conflicts arise spontaneously and may, in fact, not be barriers. They may serve valuable functions. If one group member is confused on an issue, and he stops a pending vote, his confusion may cause a necessary relook at the policy. Our task is to be sensitive to barriers so we can deal with them wisely and more fully comprehend and participate in the small group process.

Howard Land and Mary Beauchamp crisply demonstrate how the absence of self-respect can interfere with interpersonal relations in a group. One cannot feel he is a worthwhile member of a group if he has low self-respect.

HOWARD LANE
MARY BEAUCHAMP

NEED FOR
SELF-RESPECT
All of us need to think well of ourselves always. We go to all lengths to rationalize our behavior, regardless of its irrationality, so that we may tell ourselves that we are all right. To be thoroughly shamed is to be stripped of our ability to face the world, to relate to other human beings. The tragedy of Nick in *Knock on Any Door* is that, as he heard his counsel tell the jury how society had made him a killer, he was deeply ashamed of himself. And he sat with his head bowed, too ashamed to look up, shoulders slumped, staring at his hands, no swagger, no hard-boiled grin. All of Nick was defeated from that moment on.

No constructive living can come from a person who lacks self-respect. Self-respect is the cement of mental health. The admonition, "Love thy neighbor as thyself," is sound psychological advice. But how difficult it is to love the self that is so often reminded of shortcomings, of selfish motivations, of smallness of spirit. We are reminded of the cry that came from the ten-year-old who was being told to be a good girl and to be happy but not to pinch brother or use bad language or get dirty, "My ears don't seem to be a part of me!" He who undermines another's self-respect does violence.

A major task of the teacher is to help each child build and maintain self-respect. Many children are continually shamed at home, are drilled in self-depreciation from morning to night. In one day's listening we heard these remarks addressed to children in one family.:

"Aren't you ashamed of yourself?"

"Look at that face!"

"How many times do I have to tell you to comb your hair before coming to the table?"

"Shut up! Who cares what you think?"

"Daddy will be so ashamed of you!"

"You know your mother doesn't like you when you suck your thumb."

"I'm not interested in your side of the story. Just go to your room, you naughty boy!"

More than likely the child who needs to have help in developing his self-respect is one who hasn't had much chance to develop unique-

Howard Lane and Mary Beauchamp, Human Relations in Teaching: The Dynamics of Helping Children Grow, *copyright © 1955. Reprinted by permission of Prentice Hall, Inc., Englewood Cliffs, New Jersey.*

"Aren't you ashamed?"

ness or whose uniqueness hasn't been appreciated. Self-respect does not feed well upon the shortcomings of others. Our job is to help each one feel valued because he is himself, and therefore is of special worth to the group.

Loneliness is being in a roomful of people and not being able to trust any of them.   J. Lair

---

One barrier in small
groups that is frequently
unrecognized is the inability
to see how much we depend
on others. Often, we fail to see
the impact of others'
contributions and exclude
them by failing to give them
proper credit for their efforts.
Ideas or solutions they help
you develop suddenly become
"your" ideas. Excluding
others in this way can cause
disruption in a group. Some
member(s) begin to resent
the person who takes all the
credit. We must remember
that each individual group
member needs to feel wanted,
unique, and worthwhile. In
the following selection, John
Glidewell tells how important
it is to feel wanted, unique,
and worthwhile.

JOHN GLIDEWELL

ON LOVE AND BEING HELPFUL

In the groups I have studied, the acts more sorely missed by the members were supportive acts, expressing interest, attraction, respect, approval. Leaders most often complain that members don't work or that they withdraw after just one effort to participate. Even a brief look at the activities of the group shows that neither the leader nor the member has made even a small move to offer any support for the one effort. Leaders will study for hours to find provocative questions or issues or incentives to stimulate participation. I am pretty confident that a single supportive act can

Reprinted from Choice Points *by John Glidewell by permission of The M. I. T. Press, Cambridge, Massachusetts. Copyright © 1970 Massachusetts Institute of Technology.*

stimulate more work than a battery of provocative questions, hot issues, or attractive incentives.

In trying to listen to groups in search of support for their participants, I often get the impression that supportive acts are as awkward as offers of love, because perhaps they are a way of expressing one kind of love. Our preoccupation about astute bargaining and about not being taken in by confidence men may have impaired our ability to offer or accept genuine support when it is felt. To support may mean to make our resources too readily available, to make our positive feelings vulnerable to exploitation. If all bargaining must be a fight for advantage, our bargaining constrains human resources, including authentic supportive feelings. How can I offer my support without exposure to exploitation? Very probably, never.

Once having offered love, I can never take it back. If I have exposed myself to unfair demands or if I have made unfair demands on others for the return of love they can't express, I have strained a relationship and I can never return to the old one. But I can maintain the encounter. I can try new ways and times of expressing my positive feelings and watch for your response and the cues it gives us for building a new relationship, not too close, not too distant, for the interchange of the support we both feel and can express.

Once in 1960 a group of my fellows and I were engaged in work in a temporary laboratory in which we were trying to train ourselves and others to be more genuinely and humanly supportive to one another. It was not easy work, but we felt it was important. We were making a little progress, and we decided to take a weekend off.

One of us was a remarkable young lady. She was young and competent and bright and attractive and single. It is a rare combination, and she was a rare person. All of us had come to share the kind of friendship that comes from having worked hard at a trying task. In the spirit of friendship, she told us of her plans for the weekend off. She was going into nearby Washington to meet a friend for dinner and the theater. He was, she said, a man of whom she was very fond and he was quite an eligible bachelor. He was one of those surprised millionaires who found themselves unexpectedly rich on their electronic inventiveness and the electronic adventures in space. He was, she said, also attractive, personable, and vigorous, and she was thinking very seriously about marrying him. Her fellow staff members were happily married, but the men were just a little jealous and the women just a little envious as she left for the weekend.

All of us returned from our recreation on Sunday evening for dinner together. All of us made various kinds of talk and all of us were marking time until Claudia told us about her weekend. In good time, she did.

It was Saturday at dinner, she said, that he had been upset and sad. He and his two partners in the electronic firm had been having a fight. One of the partners had been kicking up all kinds of trouble. It seemed that, from the friend's point of view, the one partner had become so obstinate and obstructionistic that the tension was unbearable. They had decided to dissolve the partnership. "There is," he said, "no alternative."

Claudia thought, "I'm supposed to be learning new things and developing new skills in being supportive and helpful to people. If help is love made useful, perhaps I can be helpful to him. I'm going to try." So it was that she asked him to tell her more about the problem, to explain to her the when, and where, and how, and who of the conflict.

It was all he needed. He explained at length. Claudia asked at times for clarification, at times for elaboration, at times for explanation, at times for information, consciously avoiding offering opinions or suggestions. And, Claudia thought, it went very well. He was seeing new angles, remembering facts he had forgotten before, checking his biases. All through dinner, during intermission at the theater, while snacking after the show, at brunch on Sunday, and in the park on Sunday afternoon, his views were widening, new ideas were developing, and new feelings were emerging.

It was on that Sunday afternoon in the park that he mentioned, "It's been one of the best weekends of my life. It's been a long time since I've thought through a problem so thoroughly. And, say, I do appreciate your being such a good listener while I talked so much and thought out loud so much."

Claudia was pleased, and in her joy she asked, "How did it happen?"

"Well, it just shows you how important it is to take the time to think about these things. I use time at work to think about electronic problems, but I don't use any time at all to think about problems between people. This weekend I did. I just took the time to think. Time to think, that's how it happened."

Claudia was beginning to be less pleased. "You think," she asked "that did it, huh? Time to think."

"Yep, that was it. I'll know better now just how important it is to take the time to think." He really meant what he was saying.

By now Claudia wasn't pleased at all. "I was thinking *I* might have had something to do with it," she said, as quietly as she could.

"Oh, you did! You did. I know how hard it is to be a good listener, and you were a very, very good one. I am really deeply grateful." And he was.

Claudia looked around at us and stopped telling the story for a minute. Then, she said, "I think I did a pretty good job of helping him with his problem. I *am* struck by what can be accomplished when it doesn't matter who gets the credit. But I'm not sure that I am really proud of my work. I do like him and I do know now how close we can be."

"Are you going to marry him?"

Claudia smiled slowly and wistfully and said, "No. No, the man I marry must know the difference between what I do and what he does. That's how he will know the difference between him and me."

Claudia's wistful wisdom made crystal clear the insight I had been seeking. I knew before then that love was giving and receiving, and I knew that people in love sometimes found themselves so close that they often couldn't tell who was feeling what, offering what, getting what. To accept the love of my wife, a real living unique person, must be to know quite sensitively and precisely what she gives and what I take. In our exchange of our love and ideas and motives and feelings and skills, all the resources get transformed into new forms of human life. I am a little different each day, and my wife is a little different each day, partly because of what we interchange and transform in our interaction. But as I grow in the art of accepting her love, I become more and more sensitively, more and more lovingly aware of what she has contributed—and what she has become. Each of us has become more fully, more distinctly in my mind, a unique person. But I don't grow in my love so very fast. I still get the two of us confused.

It is quite easy to see members
of another group as all the
same. Such stereotyping is
a barrier to effective
intergroup transactions. If
a college student group sees
professors as "absent-minded"
or if a faculty group sees
students as "lazy," these
stereotyped views of the other
create instant barriers. In
"Out of Tensions, Progress,"
Robert Goheen spells out
several types of intergroup
barriers that exist within
university settings.

ROBERT GOHEEN

OUT OF TENSIONS, PROGRESS

Universities are increasingly in the news today, not only because of student unrest and enlarging campus populations, but also because the role of universities as centers of teaching and research has been getting more pervasive and more critical in myriad aspects of our national life. In Washington and in the state capitals, in city offices, on farms, and in homes, people find reason to give heed to the once-sequestered halls of higher learning.

Ironically, as more attention is paid and more people are involved, there seems to be less understanding of what a university *is*, other than simply a training ground. Everyone apparently has a pretty clear idea of what a hospital is for and how it works, or a law court, or a school; but despite the torrents of printed words about universities these days, there seems to me to be a vast amount of misunderstanding about them. And along with this misunderstanding, there is questioning—often with the wrong questions being asked—and there is distrust.

The purpose of this volume is to try to shed some light on certain essential aspects of the university, generically viewed. The objective is not to set down guidelines for the handling of protesting students, or for dealing with disaffected faculty members, or troublesome trustees, or even political figures who nowadays, increasingly, show an inclination to tell the university how to conduct its affairs. I would hope, though, that light shed on the university's basic nature might help to illuminate these and other problem areas.

In many ways, a university is a loose and peculiar association of persons, assembled for the pursuit of knowledge and understanding. Misunderstanding grows at least in part out of the tendency so many of us have to see others only as stereotypes—even in a day of instant and wide communications. Thus we hear pronouncements about university faculties as if they walked in lock-step and could be uniformly labeled. It has been my observation that if you gather a hundred professors together, you have a hundred individualists. Professors may kick—often do—but seldom with unisoned precision.

Another stereotype is applied to college students—as if over six million young men and women engaged in higher education in this country could be categorized simply! I have known a good many of them and I see few signs of a common stamp.

Then there is the alumnus. If anyone harbors the notion that the alumni of any university form a solid, homogenized phalanx of nostalgic, reactionary "old grads," let him read my mail for a week. As for trustees, I can only say that if those of my own university are a fair example, they are certainly no clutch of corporate tycoons, as the stereotype would have them. From physicians to scientists, to clergymen, to lawyers, to publishers, to educators—as well as to bankers and businessmen—the trustees I have seen at Princeton and elsewhere tend to be a cross-section of the leadership in American life. As such, they rarely agree unanimously—as I well know. What they do have in common is considerable experience beyond the university and a willingness to give to her generously of their time and effort, without reward and with little recognition.*

As the constituent groups within a university embrace human differences and individualities, so do universities themselves vary widely—in the base of their support, in the range of their activities,

---

* In a move that both evidenced its present flexibility and promised even greater flexibility in the future, Princeton's Board of Trustees voted in 1969 to provide for the election each spring of a Trustee from the graduating class to serve a 4-year term. Election will be by the junior and senior classes and alumni from the two most recent graduating classes.

and in the way they are organized. From their beginnings in the western world, the universities have persistently resisted pressures to uniformity.

In this country, some are public, some are private, some are a bit of both; some are large, some small; some are church-related, some not; some are confined to one campus, some spread out to many. Universities also differ in the range of their efforts. Some extend themselves widely in programs of direct service for community and state; others tend to stick closely to the traditional business of instruction and scholarship.

Finally, universities are variously organized. One can point to the oligarchic self-governance enjoyed by the professors in European universities, or to monarchical presidencies that appeared in certain late nineteenth-century American institutions, or to the many forms of academic organization to be found on today's campuses—none quite like the other. Whether one sees the presidency or the faculty as weak or strong, the governing board as involved or remote, the decision-making as more, or less, democratically based—seems to depend mainly upon what institution one is looking at and at what time.

Today it is clear that there is a marked desire among many students and many faculty members to have an effective role in the direction of their universities. And what is more important, they seem willing —in principle, at least—to devote time and effort to it. This was not always so, and may not be again. As long as faculty and students *are* inclined to effective participation, it is in everyone's best interest, I believe, to draw on what they can contribute. For when decisions are discussed widely and hammered out jointly among the principal parties of interest, they tend to be sounder institutional decisions, and the additional time and effort required to achieve them that way is usually justified by the wider, readier acceptance they are likely to find.

None of this is to suggest that a university can be run on the principle of one man, one vote. As I shall say repeatedly in this volume, the university's main objective is the advancement of learning and of thought—not its own governance or any other activity. It is not a political entity and not intended to be one. Nevertheless, in my view, if the procedures for student as well as faculty participation are soundly conceived, if responsibility is seriously assumed, and if everyone concerned will work together for the common good with forebearance and mutual respect, the power and authority of the university can be widely and effectively shared.

Yet in this as in most matters, universities may differ greatly. Why should they not?

But if universities are first of all associations of human beings, diverse and variously organized, they nevertheless have significant things in common. All are basically concerned with the advancement of learning. All seek to carry on their proper work in an atmosphere of freedom: freedom to pursue the truth wherever it leads, and *to talk about it*. All are optimistic enterprises, presupposing that man's lot on earth may be improved, albeit slowly, bit by bit. They share, besides, many of the attributes of the human creature. Thus, they are sites of both reason and emotion. They are complex, changeable, but also resistant to change. At their best, they are laudable; at their worst, disappointing; most of the time, both of these at once.

Such is the nature of a university—its human nature. I once saw an abandoned college campus. The broken windows, crumbling brick, cobwebs, and caved-in roofs expressed more eloquently than many words the simple truth that an educational institution does not essentially consist of walls and ivy, but of the human beings who make it up. And just as that which most distinguishes human from other vocal and gregarious forms of life is man's capacity for reasoned thought, so, I submit, a basic commitment to the life of the mind most properly marks the university. It does not seek victories; it does not work for profits; its production is not measurable. Its truest goals are not precise targets, but high deals—the enrichment of the minds and lives of its students, the advancement of knowledge, the increase of understanding among men, and the unending search for truth.

Obviously, in this imperfect world the loftiness and rightness of a university's aims do not guarantee harmony or insure against disintegration. Much depends upon a subtle, hard-to-define set of human relationships within it, organic filaments of mutual trust and at least minimal friendliness. These are easily broken. When emotion gets astride of reason, when invective displaces argument, when suspicion erodes trust, then the filaments may snap and the university may fall into pieces—into hostile cliques. Or, disturbed by too much discord on campus, outsiders may invite themselves in to "straighten things out" —with results that can only be injurious.

I do not suggest for a moment that there should be no disagreements, no strong feelings, no righteous indignation. Teaching and research do not preclude passion or emotion. On the contrary, scholarly inquiry is often prompted by passion, and scholarly research often helps to clarify men's deepest convictions and make them effective. At the same time, thoughtful examination and reasoned argument must be defended in the university against all who would substitute force and coercive types of protest, or else the university loses its prime function.

There may be causes worth shattering a campus for, but when it happens, a very high price is paid.

Like a human being, a university can suffer bruises, be pushed around and temporarily damaged, while yet preserving its basic strength and capacities. Like a human being, it can learn from experience and is adaptable—more adaptable than some would have use believe. But like a human being also, it can suffer irreparable wounds. It can be crippled or even destroyed when attacks are pressed too far against its fundamental nature, which is to be a site and stimulus for the free-ranging, uninhibited, judicious, impartial action of the mind.

As a one-time classicist I am naturally inclined in viewing the university to take my starting point in the distant past. Frequently in recent years my thoughts have been drawn back there—in particular to two of the pre-Socratic philosophers, both men of the early fifth century before Christ.

One was Parmenides of Elea in southern Italy. Perhaps because conditions in the western Greek world of his time were relatively stable, but for other reasons too, Parmenides centered his attention on the permanence of things—or, better, the permanence within things. He banished, as matters of illusion and unsteady opinion (doksa), the flux and uncertainties of experience, the transitoriness of events. Against them he set a vision of the real as something without beginning or end, single, constant, motionless, final, complete. All the diversity of nature and of history exist, he said, only "in name"; reason leads us not to them, but to a steady, unchanging world order.

At the other extremity of the Greek world, where the westward thrust of the Persian Empire was being felt, a slightly older contemporary of Parmenides was meantime expounding a very different view of the world and of life. He was Heraclitus of Ephesus. For him movement, tension, and strain were fundamental; "everything comes about by strife and necessity"; "all is flux, nothing is stationary"; the universe is an unending conflict of opposites.

Heraclitus' favorite images were the bow and the lyre. The tension of the bow, the strain put on its opposite ends, gives the arrow force to carry firmly to a mark. In the playing of a lyre, harmony results only where there is contrast—when there is interplay among tones at variance with one another.

Need we ask ourselves which of these men speaks to us today in terms that strike home? Surely it is Heraclitus. A large array of compeling and competing demands bears on every American university to force historic choices. Almost everywhere we look we encounter forces making for change and strain, and this is no less true in the supposedly tranquil halls of higher learning than in the multitudinous, shifting, shrinking world of human affairs. For the American university of today is very much a part of these affairs both at home and abroad, and increasingly it is subject to heightened and to spreading calls for service —and for change—from the society and the world of which it is a part.

In some this situation evokes dismay; and in most of us no doubt the wish for a calm, stable ordering of things runs strongly. Nevertheless, what we should see plainly is that, within the strains and tensions that confront and involve us, there lies the hope of progress, with great potential benefits to the nation and to mankind. Indeed, as they bend their efforts to respond with vigor and with purpose, our institutions of higher education are likely, I believe, to drive to higher levels of beneficial accomplishment than ever before.

Twice in my life I thought it possible
that I was about to die. Both times
the prospect compelled me to seek what
I have left undone. Both times I knew
that I had failed to find a way to show
my love; both times I knew that those I
loved most would never really feel
and know how much, how tenderly, how
deeply I loved them. Should I die today,
it would be the same. I still have not
found a way to let my loved ones know
how much I love them. That is the great
tragedy of the life I live.   J. Glidewell

SMALL GROUP
COMMUNICATION
SELF-DISCLOSURE

*I can only know that much of myself
which I have had the courage to confide
to you. J. Powell*

Self-disclosure also takes on new elements in small group situations. While on one hand it becomes more difficult to be open and honest with added numbers of people, the presence of others can often facilitate self-disclosure. Some, for example, may feel that there is more anonymity in a small group setting than in a dyadic situation, or that the group climate is supportive so he can disclose to others and have some assistance in doing it. If you are in a group when another discloses, you can see first hand some of the benefits of disclosure.

Self-disclosure can be viewed as an action one can use to break some of the barriers to communication that exist in a small group situation. There are numerous sensitivity groups, encounter groups, T-groups, and awareness groups that rely on self-disclosure to break down communication barriers among people. In recent years there has been considerable interest in the use of these types of small groups. Some individuals claim that they experience extensive personal growth in encounter and sensitivity training groups. At the same time, other individuals maintain that such group experiences have been damaging to them. There are many complex and sensitive issues to be examined when we look at self-disclosure in the small group arena. The readings in this section, rather than being examples of disclosure, discuss the types and effects of small group disclosure.

In the following reading,
Gerard Egan examines the
types and functions of
self-disclosure in small groups.
As you read the essay, think
about groups to which you
belong. Do individuals self-
disclose? In what type of
disclosure do they (you)
engage? Does the disclosure
have impact on the group?

GERARD EGAN

SELF-DISCLOSURE IN THE CONTEXT OF THE GROUP

One of the reasons why self-disclosure appears so frightening to many is that it is often
depicted as an end in itself. Out of context self-disclosure *is* frightening. In a laboratory in interpersonal relations, however, it should always be kept in context; that is, it should always be related to the
goals of the group and the individual goals of the participants. There is
a world of difference between "secret dropping" (self-disclosure out of
context) and self-revelation as one of the means used to establish and
develop relationships of some closeness or intimacy with other group
members (the procedural goal of the encounter group).

What to Disclose in the Encounter Group

If I am a participant in an encounter group, there are, broadly speaking,
two categories or sources of self-revelation: (1) what is going on inside
me during the group itself—that is, how I feel, what I think about myself and the other members of the group, and (2) my experience and
behavior in the past (the "then") and my experience and behavior
outside the group (the "there"). Let's take a look at each source
separately.

From Face To Face: The Small-Group Experience and Interpersonal Growth *by*
Gerard Egan. Copyright © 1973 by Wadsworth Publishing Company, Inc. Re-
printed by permission of the publisher, Brooks/Cole Publishing Company,
Monterey, California.

My Experience Inside the Group.

The more freely you and the other participants reveal what is going on inside you during the group meetings, the more effective your contact with one another will be. Consider the following examples:

- ☐ I'm a very short-tempered person and you are really getting under my skin.
- ☐ I like you, but I feel a bit foolish putting it that baldly.
- ☐ I've been bored this past hour, but I think I deserve my boredom because I've done nothing about it.
- ☐ I think my behavior here shows that I'm pretty self-centered.
- ☐ I'm confused. I'm not sure whether you are saying that you like me or that you dislike me.
- ☐ I'm curious about you, John, about what you are like. I can't say that that is friendship, much less love, but somehow I feel that it is something very positive.

These disclosures are attempts on the part of the participants to deal immediately with their relationships to others or to what is happening in the group. This kind of self-disclosure is extremely important in any group. No trust can be built up in a group if the participants feel that there are members who are keeping things to themselves. The silent member and the guarded one, then, hang like dead weights around the neck of the group. It is extremely difficult to risk trusting the silent or the overly guarded member.

PAST BEHAVIOR AND BEHAVIOR OUTSIDE THE GROUP:
THE "THERE-AND-THEN"

I can also talk about my past experience and behavior (whether inside the group or outside) and what I do and experience outside the group. Since the purpose of self-disclosure in encounter groups is not merely to retail information about myself, disclosure of there-and-then experience and behavior should be related to the purpose of the group (establishing relationships with others, increasing interpersonal skills). Here are some examples of how there-and-then material is related to the group both poorly and effectively:

Unrelated self-disclosure	Related self-disclosure
My dad and I don't get along. He's usually down on my brother, too. It makes living	I'm reacting to you just the way I do to my dad. He doesn't listen to me, nor do

Unrelated self-disclosure	Related self-disclosure
at home difficult. Sometimes I just feel like getting an apartment on my own.	you. I feel like turning my back on you, like I feel like getting my own apartment. You're older, but I don't think that has anything to do with it.
I'm homosexual. I don't think society is fair to the homosexual. But then society is uptight about a lot of things. People have to fit in, to do things like everybody else.	I think I trust you people enough to tell you that I'm homosexual. The reason I'm telling you is not to have you counsel me. I feel that some of you might reject me, but I'm hoping you won't. Since my sexual identification is something big on my mind and since I fear rejection, I felt I had to bring it up.
I don't communicate much with my wife and children but they let me alone.	I don't communicate much with my wife and children at home, and I'm falling into the same pattern here, except you challenge me whereas they don't. I should begin to challenge myself.
I have many fears. I'm afraid of strong men. I'm afraid of those who don't like me. I'm afraid I will not succeed.	I have many fears. For instance, I'm afraid of strong men, Bill, and I see you as strong. I fear rejection, and, Jane, I feel you don't like me. I'm afraid of failure and I think I am making a mess of this group experience. Well, it's out in the open now.

What, then, should you disclose in the encounter group? The answer is simple: anything that helps you and the other members pursue the goals of the group. In other words, self-disclosure should be organic—related to the goals of the group. The depth of a person's self disclosure should be related to the process of establishing and developing relationships and should arise naturally from the give-and-take of the group process. As indicated in one of the examples above, I have seen participants reveal something as sensitive as their homosexuality *not* because they wanted to engage in secret dropping but because they needed to know that they would not be rejected in the group because of their sexual identification. They did not spend a great deal of time subsequently dealing with their homosexuality, for that was not a here-and-now issue for the group. But dealing with it briefly improved their ability to communicate with *these* people in *this* situation. Once this obstacle was overcome, they felt free to go about the business of developing relationships with other participants.

You, the individual participant, are in charge of your own disclosure. You should take the initiative to reveal yourself at whatever level you think you should in order to pursue the goals of the group. While you should resist any individual or group effort to claw your secrets out of you, still you should take some reasonable risks in the group. The purpose of the group is not to throw your defenses to the winds (and uncontrolled self-disclosure is one way of doing precisely that), but you should be willing to experiment with a reasonable lowering of your defenses. One way of doing this is to risk revealing yourself and your feelings if you think it will help you establish and develop relationships in the group, *even* if you fear some rejection on the part of some group members. First of all, most rejection fears in high-level encounter groups are unfounded (for there is a climate of support), and, second, you may also learn that you can live on, even though some people cannot approve of certain aspects of your personality or behavior. Most of the outstanding figures of history had to face a great deal of rejection precisely because they had the courage to tell the world who they were and where they stood.

The Quality of Self-Disclosure: "Story" versus "History"

The *way* in which a person reveals himself in the group is very important. In a sense it is even more important than the content of the revelation, for content, no matter how intimate in itself, can lose its intimacy and its meaning in the telling. I propose two styles or modes of self-disclosure: "history," the mode of noninvolvement, and "story," the mode of involvement.

HISTORY

A recent television documentary showed excerpts from a marathon group experience conducted at Daytop Village, a rehabilitation center for addicts. During the early hours of the marathon a young addict began talking about himself and his past life. His self-revelation was almost totally history. I was disturbed to think that what he was doing was considered acceptable group process; that is, I was disturbed until one of the group leaders finally spoke up and confronted the speaker. In effect he said: "You have been engaging in history rather than story, and mere history in this group experience is meaningless."

History is pseudo-self-disclosure. It is actuarial and analytic, and usually has a strong "there and then" flavor. It clicks off the facts of experience and even interpretations of this experience but leaves the person of the revealer relatively untouched; he is accounted for and analyzed, but unrevealed. The person relates many facts about himself, but the person within still remains unknown. History is often a long account. It is long and often steady because it fears interruption. Interruption might mean involvement, and a person engages in history to avoid, rather than invite, involvement. History has a way of saying "Be quiet" or "Don't interrupt," but these are dodges to keep others at bay. The steady clicking off of facts keeps the group focused on the revealer but does not allow the members to involve themselves with him.

In history the manner of self-revelation is usually somewhat detached. There is little ego-involvement and thus little risk. The speaker deals with himself as object rather than as subject. Intimate life details might be revealed, but the intimacy has no particular meaning. The details are just facts. On the other hand, history might be a string of generalities—generalities poorly disguised by the first-person pronoun. But whether history consists of intimate details or generalities, the message is always the same: "Keep your distance." It is as if the revealer were trying to intimate to others that he is rather invulnerable: "This is not really affecting me; I don't see why it should affect you." Sometimes sheer quantity of intimate information about self is divulged because the historian implicitly realizes that if he relates enough, quickly enough, the others will not be able to react effectively to any particular part of it. History is also self-centered. The leader in the Daytop Village marathon took the young addict to task for his egocentricity. He told him that he had been talking a long time and had not even mentioned that he had a wife who had feelings.

Historical information does not unite speaker and listeners. Rather, the information sits there as an obstacle between them. It is a barrier rather than a bridge. It sometimes even has an "I dare you to do anything about this" aura. Even when the information disclosed is intimate, it is usually boring. The historian exudes an "I don't really care" attitude that is readily picked up by the other members of the group.

The information *is* boring, because it is divorced from the person. It is flat; there is no human drama about it. History is "computorial," and, as such, calls for feedback rather than human response. In McLuhan's (1964) terms, history is a "hot" modality, high in definition and low in involvement. Its high definition refers not to just sheer quantity but to its "there it all is and there is really nothing to do about it" quality.

STORY

Story lies at the other end of the continuum. It is authentic self-disclosure, for it is an attempt to reveal the person within; and more than that, it is an attempt to get him involved with his listeners. Story is an invitation for others to come in; it is an opening of the door. In group growth experiences, as in the rest of life, others often stand around waiting to come in. Story is a signal for others to move into one's presence.

Story is not actuarial; it is rather selective in detail, for the revealer intuits that it is not the transmission of fact that is important but the transmission of self. It does not avoid detail, but the choice of detail is secondary to the act of communication. Story usually avoids interpretation, too; it allows experience to remain unintellectualized and thus speak for itself. The storyteller, even if he leaves out detail, is graphic and specific, he does not hide behind generalities disguised by the first-person pronoun. Facts are selected for their impact value, for their ability to reveal the person as what he is now through what he has experienced.

The storyteller is taking a risk and he knows it. Therefore, story is always an implicit request for human support. The revealer has come to trust the group to a certain degree, but he still feels his vulnerability; his act of self-revelation is akin to Kierkegaard's "leap of faith," which is always a leap of trust. But he takes this leap because he wants to relate to the other members of the group and relate more fully to himself. He realizes that story is the way of involvement and the way of discovery, and he wants both. And so he comes to the point. He does not wander around in the there and then but manages to make the past, the "there," and even the future define him as he is in the here and now. Story, then, is not analytical and discrete. It is synthetic; it attempts to present a totality, the complex totality that is the person himself, who takes shape out of the complexity of his experience.

The one who tells his story—if that story is not computorial and therefore not a request for feedback in a dehumanized sense—is looking for human response. Story, of its very nature, is dialogue and merits such response. Because story is not computorial and monologic, it is inevitably engaging, even when someone who is usually a bore adopts it. Some people are constantly talking about themselves, and most others find this terribly boring. Such people are boring because they are usually engaging in history rather than story. First of all, they are really saying nothing about themselves, and second, they care little for the objects of their monologue and would find real response, such as self-disclosure and confrontation, frightening. Bores speak in generalities poorly disguised under the pronoun "I." But story, on the other hand, is always engaging, for it means that the speaker has to "blow his cover," lower his defenses, and stand somewhat naked in his own eyes and in the eyes of others. People are seldom, if ever, bored with sincere self-revelation, because they intuitively realize its importance for the one revealing himself and respect him for what he is doing. The person who engages in story is one who stops complaining about how much he *hurts* and begins admitting who he *is*. I think perhaps that it might be impossible to dislike someone who engages in story, for it is an act of humility, a manifestation of a need to move into community, and a surrender of egocentricity (or at least a beginning of surrender).

In McLuhan's terminology, story is a "cool" modality, low in definition and high in involvement. It is low in definition not just because it is selective of detail and thus allows others to fill in the gaps in information, but because the information transmitted is seen as a medium, a bridge instead of a barrier. Story has high impact value; it tends to change both speaker and listener. It draws the listener out of himself and toward the speaker; it changes the speaker in that it calls forth emotions that are authentic and therefore perhaps unfamiliar to the revealer. Story, then, is not maudlin, but it is short through with emotion; it is not sensational, but it has drama in the same way that a life fully lived has drama.

When I repress my emotions, my stomach keeps score.   J. Powell

---

The numerous types of small
groups that are currently
utilizing self-disclosure and
openness are outlined by Ted
J. Rakstis in the next selection.
His assessment of the values
and limitations of such
groups will greatly assist you
in seeing them from a balanced
perspective.

TED J. RAKSTIS

SENSITIVITY TRAINING: FAD, FRAUD, OR NEW FRONTIER?

High on a mountainside overlooking the Pacific Ocean in northern California, 25 strangers gather at the Esalen Institute for a five-day adventure into "self-discovery." At the outset, several members of the group are openly hostile. But after a week of nude sulphur baths, dream analysis, and pull-no-punches dialogues, the one-time adversaries warmly embrace and leave filled with at least temporary love for each other and the world.

In a Chicago suburb, 65 people walk in off the street and pay $6 each to attend a three-hour "microlab" conducted by an amateur psychologist who assures them that they will "find a beautiful feeling, a sense of being connected to their fellow man." They touch one another's faces, grope around while blindfolded, and lie in a circle and ramble on about the happiest moment in their lives.

And in Boston, a dozen hard-bitten businessmen meet for three days under the guidance of an expert in group dynamics. Following a test to measure their attitudes toward group inclusion, affection, and the need to control, one executive's profile nails him as a corporate tyrant. A subordinate tells him bluntly: "It's no wonder we can't communicate on the job—you're uptight and you bug everyone around you."

In one form or another, all these people are undergoing sensitivity training, an anything-goes human relations movement whose major precepts are "do your own thing" and "tell it like it is." Sensitivity training sessions also are known as encounter groups, personal growth labs, T-groups ("T" for training), awareness experience, confrontation

From Sensitivity Training: Fad, Fraud, or New Frontier? *by Ted J. Rakstis. Reprinted by permission from the January 1970 issue of* Today's Health, *published by the American Medical Association.*

groups, training laboratories, organizational development, and, collectively, the human potential movement. Whatever it may be called, the phenomenon is attracting hundreds of thousands of Americans of all ages to programs run by persons who may be either skilled professionals or rank amateurs.

The tangle of sensitivity training nomenclature suggests that not even the experts can clearly define it. It incorporates elements of psychiatry, sociology, philosophy, education, religion, and community organization, and its practitioners number people from these and other fields. Depending upon his professional background and personal bias, each person who conducts a sensitivity group has a different focus.

Most sensitivity sessions, however, share several common attributes. The programs are designed to place people in a group situation. Through a mixture of physical contact games and no-holds-barred discussions about each other's strengths and failures, each group member hopefully will feel less constricted. He will become more open, readily able to understand himself and others. If he is a member of an organization, it may enable him to become a more persuasive and influential participant in group decisions.

But these goals can be achieved only if the person is willing to accept the rules of the group and its trainer. He must *want* to be sensitized and must be prepared to deal with the frank criticism that the group may engender. Unless he is willing to "open up," he will be wasting his time and may run the risk of psychological punishment. In short, sensitivity training is not for everyone.

Sensitivity training has been around since 1947, when three social psychologists formed an organization bearing the cumbersome title of National Training Laboratories Institute for Applied Behavioral Science (NTL). Yet only in the past three years has the movement really begun to explode. "Growth centers," emulating the highly experimental work of Esalen Institute, now are found throughout the nation, and countless independent entrepreneurs are running sessions that seek to "turn on" participants through sensory awareness rather than drugs.

During a time when Americans are torn with conflict and beset by fear, loneliness, and alienation, many are searching for something of meaning. Says Thomas Bennett, Ph.D., director of graduate studies for George Williams College and a fellow of NTL: "In our culture, it's extremely difficult to find experiences with other people which provide a degree of freedom and intimacy and a real opportunity to deal with persons at a fairly intense level. A lot of that has led to the growth in sensitivity training."

The supporters of sensitivity training call it a new frontier in social psychology, a means of making people more innovative, honest, trusting, and free. It is not a form of psychoanalysis, they say, but a significant outgrowth of adult education rooted in the emotions rather than the intellect. Numerous organizations—corporations, universities, churches, government agencies—view it as a method of helping people to break the communication barrier.

Skeptics term it "the acidless trip" or "instant intimacy." Right-wing political groups have tried to link sensitivity training with Communism, brainwashing, and sexual promiscuity. More responsible critics, including some in the medical profession, question the wisdom of stripping a person's emotions to the core in a group setting. They challenge the use of unskilled trainers, the frequent absence of pre-screening to keep psychotics out of the programs, and the problem of returning to an essentially insensitive world after an emotion-charged group experience.

The sensitivity training boom has come so quickly and assumes so many forms that most of the experts have been caught off guard. Neither the American Psychiatric Association nor the American Psychological Association has an official position, and the American Medical Association's Council on Mental Health offers this middle-of-the-road viewpoint:

"Although sensitivity training is an issue of current concern, it is not an accepted part of medical practice. The Council believes that the procedures employed are not well enough defined to lend themselves to objective evaluation. It urges that particular caution be taken against participating in sessions conducted by leaders who are not professionally trained and qualified, in view of reports of psychotic and neurotic sequelae [consequences]."

It is difficult, however, to define "qualified trainer." At present, there are no laws controlling trainer certification. National Training Laboratories, based in Washington, D.C., with several branch offices across the nation, has the most stringent standards. NTL requires that its trainers have a Ph.D. or master's degree in psychology, social work, or one of the other related "helping professions" and that trainer candidates take advanced laboratory training. But NTL represents only one branch of the field. Some "trainers" have virtually no education whatever. Says one: "Who needs a degree? I know I'm a good trainer because I've got a 'gut' feeling for people."

The motivations of persons enrolling in sensitivity groups vary as widely as the caliber of the trainers. Some are making an honest attempt to discover themselves; others want a quick emotional "high" and a chance to meet members of the opposite sex; many attend only because their job requires it. A few use it as a cheap substitute for group psychotherapy. Oron P. South, Ph.D., director of the Midwest Group for Human Resources, a division of NTL, warns: "This is learning, not therapy. It is not intended for sick people, but for the 'normal neurotic' who wants to get more out of his relations with people."

Just as the quality of programs and trainers defies easy categorization, "sensitivity training" in itself is an omnibus label that means little. Despite the profusion of names and the frequent overlapping of techniques, there are really three distinct styles.

One is the encounter group, sometimes called a "personal growth lab," which focuses on the individual and seeks to instill in him a sense of self-awareness. Since it relies heavily on nonverbal ("touch and feel") methods, this is actually sensitivity training in the most commonly accepted use of the term.

The T-group, an older method, uses more verbal exercises and emphasizes the "here and now"—the relationship of each group member to what is happening in the group at that particular time. It allows the participant to know what others think of him, to be granted the wish once expressed by Robert Burns: "Oh wad some power the giftie gie us To see oursels as others see us!"

A third basic form is a T-group offshoot known as organizational development. Somewhat less personal than either the encounter session or the T-group consisting of strangers, its goal is to help members of an organized body—a business, school, or church—learn to work better as a team.

There also are several different time lengths for sensitivity programs. The shortest form is a three-hour "microlab." More often, encounter or T-group labs run from two days to two or more weeks, and yet another version is the "marathon," a continuous, exhaustive session that may last for 24 or 48 consecutive hours. Because of the emotional and physical fatigue that may result, NTL and most other responsible training groups usually avoid the marathon.

Esalen Institute, at Big Sur, California, developed the encounter method. Founded in 1962 by Michael Murphy, a 39-year-old psychology graduate of Stanford University, Esalen attracts some 25,000 awareness seekers each year to Big Sur and a branch in San Francisco. At Big Sur, the site of a former health spa, 75 people pay $60 each to attend weekend meetings, and 25 more spend up to $175 on in-depth, five-day sessions.

The Esalen pilgrims are a mixed lot—business and professional people, teachers, movie stars, housewives, hippies. Unlike NTL, Esalen conducts no programs for organizations. "You do things in a personal growth lab that you could never try with a bunch of IBM executives," explains Stuart Miller, Ph.D., the Institute's vice president.

Philosophy, psychology, the meditative aspects of Eastern religions —these and dozens of other approaches are tried at Esalen. "Our techniques demand the total involvement of participants and, like the experiences of an LSD trip, are intensely personal and extremely difficult to describe in conventional language," says Murphy. Miller further terms Esalen as "experiential and experimental, a forum for the exploration of human potential."

The Esalen enrollee may find himself hugging strangers of both sexes, pounding pillows to release aggressions, telling the group his deepest secrets, acting out all the characters in his dreams, or taking an imaginary trip through his own body and relating the experience. William Schutz, Ph.D., one of the Institute's leading figures, says that the goal is to find "joy," and, appropriately, he has written a book titled *Joy.*

The most controversial phase of the Esalen program has been its mixed nude bathing, an idea conceived in 1967 by Paul Bindrim, a Los Angeles psychologist. Bindrim, who emphasizes that his approach is totally nonsexual, explains: "If a participant disrobes physically, he might gain the freedom to also disrobe emotionally." Since Bindrim introduced the nude swimming at Esalen, he has traveled extensively to other growth centers across the nation to carry on similar programs.

Persons who have gone to Esalen often say they were wary and nervous when the sessions began. The most antagonistic members of some groups frequently find Schutz placing them in a situation of direct physical or verbal confrontation. In most cases, the hostility melts into trust or even affection. By the end of a week, says one writer who entered Esalen full of doubt, "I found myself hugging everyone, behaving like the idiots I had noticed on first arriving."

Esalen has 15 full-time associates on its staff. Ten have advanced degrees, but several never have graduated from high school. "We consider experience, talent, and creativity far more important than formal education," says Stuart Miller. Similarly, the outsiders who come to Esalen to conduct workshops may be psychotherapists, historians, Hindu mystics, or LSD apostles.

Some 90 growth centers—Miller calls them "little Esalens"—have sprung up across the United States. A year ago, there were only 40, and five years ago they were almost unknown. Among them are Kairos, in San Diego; Oasis, in Chicago; Espiritu, in Houston; and the

Center for the Whole Person, in Philadelphia. Many were founded by persons trained at Esalen and closely follow the Big Sur methods.

A number of solo practitioners also are operating encounter groups. One such man is Jorge Rosner, a Chicagoan who tries to help people overcome their "mini-fears" through weekly three-hour "Adventures Into Being," at a place called The Center. Rosner, a product of Esalen, admits that he has no degree but feels that his background in experimental theater qualifies him at a trainer.

"In this field, a college education is not important," he maintains. "People with degrees get too hung up on intellectual aspects. Psychiatrists, particularly, are used to working with people on a one-to-one basis and can't get with it in a group situation."

Esalen and its disciples are part of the free-wheeling, eclectic West Coast encounter movement. The East Coast school, exemplified by National Training Laboratories, is more scientific, oriented toward research and organizational work, insistent upon education and experience in its trainers. NTL is the father of the T-group.

In a sense, the T-group is as unstructured as the encounter group. There is no agenda; the leader lets the group swing on its own momentum. The session revolves around the "here and now" rather than the "then and there." Group members, usually 10 or 12 in number, often know each other only by their first names. Their occupations, home problems, and childhood experiences are irrelevant. What matters is what is happening within the group.

Like encounter groups, T-groups often play many non-verbal games. People may shout, crawl around the floor, chant arm in arm, or hug each other. But there also is considerable talk, centered upon how the group is behaving. For those who enjoy cocktail banter, a T-group experience can be painful. Masks are torn away and emotions exposed; a person may face a torrent of comments like, "I perceive that you're acting phony," or "You're a nonperson; you really turn me off."

The T-group has a peculiar lingo, a mixture of hippie talk and social science jargon. People are always "hungup" or "uptight," trying to discover "where I'm at." They don't talk; they "have a dyad." In one exercise, half the group listens to the others and then gives its impression of what it has heard. But this is not talking and criticizing —it is known as "input" and "feedback." (Some sophisticated T-groups get "feedback" through videotaped replays.)

Despite the esoteric terminology, the T-group to some extent shares with its cousin, the encounter group, a basic disdain for intellectual solutions. Trainers speak about a need to elevate the "affective domain" over the "cognitive domain," to trust the senses more and the intellect less. A common T-group remark is: "Don't *think—feel!*"

The T-group theory is that criticism will develop honesty, self-understanding, and trust in others. However, it also can result in conflict, and for this reason a skilled trainer is a requisite. Jerry Spiegel, an active NTL trainer in Chicago, observes: "In most cases, a poor trainer will simply create a dull group. But there's always the chance that two people will really get into a major conflict—or that a participant may be on the verge of real emotional difficulty—so the trainer must be prepared to intervene. T-group training is like fire. It can warm the house and make it comfortable, or it can burn the damn thing down."

Besides drawing together an assortment of strangers, the T-group also can be used as a training tool for homogeneous groups. Spiegel's wife, Eleanor, who also is an NTL trainer, has been involved in working with a series of all-female T-groups where the major emphasis has been issues of femininity. The techniques range from the more nonverbal aspects of sensitivity training to written tests that evaluate such perceptions as the need for affection. Many NTL trainers also conduct sessions for married couples, single people, and family groups.

Nearly 75 percent of the work of most NTL trainers is with organizations, and business has become a strong booster of T-group learning, which it sometimes terms organizational development. Among the companies that have sponsored programs for their employees are General Electric, Standard Oil of New Jersey, Syntex Laboratories, Humble Oil and Refining, and Texas Instruments. One of the corporate pioneers is TRW, Inc., a Cleveland aerospace contractor that has offered training to executives in its four divisions since 1963. Some companies force their employees into T-groups. TRW makes attendance optional, yet about 90 percent of those who are eligible accept.

"You've got to make T-group instruction voluntary," says Thomas A. Wickes, Ph.D., director of personnel development for TRW and an NTL trainer. "This program is not for everyone, and the guy who is compelled to attend is likely to resist. He may even suffer emotional damage. We also give our men three or four 'checkout' points when they can drop out. T-groups make our men more human executives. But, unfortunately, those who benefit the most are the ones who need it the least . . . and vice versa."

Many companies have discovered that T-group experience enables executives to talk matters out more freely. In an era in which the autocratic and arbitrary rule of a few men at the top of the corporate pyramid has given way to consensus decisions made by committees, the T-group is designed to bring forth the best skills that each man can contribute.

One T-group conceptualization describes personality traits and shows that most people fall into one of three categories—the "Tough Battler," the "Friendly Helper," and the "Objective Thinker." The lesson is that any decision-making group needs each of these types if it is to function as a representative body. Through T-groups, companies have uncovered men who are highly valuable but who previously were never noticed and thus never consulted.

Besides helping to build functional management teams, business has found the T-group useful in reducing potential employee conflict. When Scott Paper Company hired 30 disadvantaged persons—primarily black—for its plant in Chester, Pennsylvania, it put 300 workers through 16 hours of T-group training to help them understand the problems of slum-dwellers. Company officials later said that the program averted what could have been an explosive transition.

Schools have employed the T-group for similar purposes. In Pontiac, Michigan, a community filled with racial tension, the school board recently allocated $25,000 for a program for parents, students, teachers, and administrators throughout the school system. After black students boycotted Proviso East High School in Maywood, Illinois, early in 1969, NTL was called in to organize a teacher-student lab. "The NTL project opened up lines of communication so that students and teachers began talking to each other," notes one Proviso East teacher. "Things came out in the open."

State and municipal bodies—including the police forces in Los Angeles, Houston, and Grand Rapids, Michigan—have experimented with T-groups. Some physicians are trying it as a means of improving patient relationships, and the University of Alabama Medical Center recently began an organizational program for some 100 medical personnel. Many people in the creative arts, notably the theater, have turned to T-groups and encounter programs.

A number of churchmen also are adopting the technique. In Chicago, for example, the Rev. Owen F. McAteer, associate pastor of St. Dorothy's Catholic Church, has organized a group of 25 priests and nuns and set up sensitivity training under the auspices of the Archdiocese of Chicago. "The program is helping nuns and priests to communicate better with their parishioners, to come down a bit off their pedestals," says Father McAteer. "This can be one of the most effective of all methods to achieve the goals of Christianity."

As sensitivity training spreads throughout America, attitudes polarize. Proponents call it one of the major learning discoveries of this century, but opposition develops on many fronts. It has become a prime target of the same ultraconservative groups that oppose sex education in the schools, such as the John Birch Society and the American Independent Party. A Chicago group called Let Freedom Ring recently issued a manifesto branding sensitivity training as "a Communist brainwashing technique" and "a grotesque, mind-bending program." Yet not all the critics are of this fanatical breed; even responsible medical men are troubled by abuses.

At a school district in Jackson, Michigan, a sensitivity training program that mixed teachers with teen-agers became so controversial that the Michigan State Medical Society launched a statewide study. The Society's Committee on Mental Health, in probably the strongest statement yet issued by a major American medical body, concluded that sensitivity training is acceptable only when conducted by professionals in the field of mental health.

"These programs are being run by unskilled and unqualified lay individuals," declares Benjamin Jeffries, M.D., a Detroit psychiatrist who is chairman of the committee. "As a result, participants are experiencing emotional problems beyond their capacity to control. I personally feel that the only people who should be doing this type of training are psychiatrists, psychologists, and psychiatric social social workers."

The medical profession is sharply divided over whether encounter and T-groups actually constitute psychiatry in disguise. Howard P. Rome, M.D., senior consultant and professor of psychiatry at the Mayo Graduate School of Medicine and a member of the AMA Council on Mental Health, feels that sensitivity training is outside the field of medicine.

"People in the behavioral sciences other than psychiatry are most valuable in conducting these programs," Doctor Rome asserts. "With the nation facing a critical health manpower shortage, we must use all available resources."

NTL officials state that less than one percent of the persons who have been in their sessions have suffered psychological damage and that most of those already had emotional problems. Although most reputable trainers try to screen out persons with psychiatric disorders, some occasionally slip through. When an unqualified trainer is presiding, the problem can become acute.

The vice president of one Midwest corporation suffered a complete mental breakdown in a T-group and was forced to enter a hospital. In New York, a mentally ill woman enrolled in a growth center and soon started to organize her own sessions. And in Evanston, Illinois, after an untrained high school teacher tried to sensitize his students, one girl went into screaming hysterics and a boy later was found wandering the streets in a stupor.

"Sensitivity training can all too easily become insensitivity training," contends Dana L. Farnsworth, M.D., director of health services for Harvard University and chairman of the AMA Council on Mental Health. "There can be great danger for the person who has psychotic difficulties or who is involved in any sort of acute crisis."

Moreover, laboratory training is viewed by most experts as essentially a program for adults. In many communities, some of the strongest opposition to T-groups has come after teachers participated with youths and trainers utilized some of the more deeply personal techniques of sensitivity training. "When teenagers are involved, you've got to be very careful in what you do," says NTL trainer Jerry Spiegel. "A T-group is a learning process, not a way to get an emotional kick."

Perhaps the greatest potential danger occurs when an inexperienced person who has been "turned on" at a session tries to help others find the same route. So far, there is little evidence of outright fraud in the sensitivity training field, but there is a proliferation of misguided do-gooders. A number of teachers, for example, have been known to begin programs for their students on the basis of a single weekend's encounter experience. Their intentions may have been honest, but the results sometimes were disastrous. As Doctor Farnsworth puts it: "Compassion without competence soon becomes quackery."

Another major problem is the inability of many people to cope with an insensitive society once they have left the sanctuary of the group. The T-group hangover has been particularly troublesome for business. A *Wall Street Journal* survey of companies sponsoring T-groups reported that many persons have returned to their jobs disillusioned with office policies and personnel, tried for a more open environment, and then were either fired or quit in frustration. Although a T-group may alter an individual's personality, it is likely to have little effect upon the organization he works for.

The encounter session or T-group can become an emotional crutch for the person who finds it difficult to adjust to the world around him. "You see a number of people coming back year after year; they're called T-group bums," says Morton Leiberman, Ph.D., associate professor of psychiatry at the University of Chicago. "They have a strong need for this kind of relatedness and they aren't getting it outside in real life."

There is also mixed opinion over whether people derive any meaningful long-term benefits from laboratory training. Although NTL claims that two-thirds of the persons who have taken T-group instruction have improved their skills, there as yet are no scientific studies to support this. It is highly doubtful whether sensitivity training can conquer both heredity and environment and create a new person, but it can make him think and perhaps modify his behavior.

"T-groups can't change your personality," Jerry Spiegel observes. "However, they can make you acutely aware of the impact you have on others—and their impact on you. The training session furnishes you with the information, the sort of things your friends won't tell you. What you do with that information is up to you."

For good or ill, sensitivity training appears to be more than a mere passing fad. In its more bizarre forms, as a means of providing thrill seekers with a quick emotional jolt, it may fade into obscurity once the novelty has worn off and the publicity has subsided. But as a means of learning to cope in a group, of discovering and capitalizing upon hidden inner strengths, its potential appears limitless.

"Sensitivity training will settle down and find its rightful place," Doctor Rome predicts. "Hopefully, we will see the day when instruction in human relations will be as much a part of the school curriculum as the three R's. When properly used, sensitivity training can help to educate our young people to live in a pluralistic society as better, more understanding citizens. It can be a powerful tool in creating a better world."

SMALL GROUP
COMMUNICATION
EFFECTS

We form many of our attitudes on the basis of our small group memberships. For example, a college student's friends usually have much more influence on him than his parents do. Students spend more time with friends and are more sensitive to the advice and evaluation of their friends than that of their parents. Earlier in their lives, however, these same students existed almost entirely in the small group of the family. At that time the family unit had a lasting effect on their basic values and approach to life. Clearly, our small groups shape and maintain our attitudes.

Small groups can exert another type of influence, namely, helping us resist change. If you are a member of a study group on religion or transcendental meditation and someone tries to change your beliefs by attacking them, you will probably try to locate your fellow group members who will support you. This will enable you to resist the persuasive efforts designed to change you. The social support of others helps us to resist change. Small groups, therefore, are instrumental in promoting changes and in warding off effects from others.

Dorwin Cartwright's comprehensive essay supplies an overview of the study of groups and details the effects of groups both as agents of change and as the target for change attempts. Even though the content of this article is difficult, as you read the essay, stop periodically and think of your own small groups. Are they primarily inducing changes in you or do they serve to minimize the effects on you from people outside the group?

DORWIN CARTWRIGHT

ACHIEVING CHANGE IN PEOPLE: SOME APPLICATIONS OF GROUP DYNAMICS THEORY

What principles of achieving change in people can we see emerging? To begin with the most general proposition, we may state that the behavior, attitudes, beliefs, and values of the individual are all firmly grounded in the groups to which he belongs. How aggressive or cooperative a person is, how much self-respect and self-confidence he has, how energetic and productive his work is, what he aspires to, what he believes to be true and good, whom he loves or hates, and what beliefs and prejudices he holds—all these characteristics are highly determined by the individual's group memberships. In a real sense, they are properties of groups and of the relationships between people. Whether they change or resist change will, therefore, be greatly influenced by the nature of these groups. Attempts to change them must be concerned with the dynamics of groups.

In examining more specifically how groups enter into the process

Dorwin Cartwright, "Achieving Change in People: Some Applications of Group Dynamics Theory" from Human Relations, *Vol. 4, 1951. Reprinted by permission of Plenum Publishing Corporation.*

of change, we find it useful to view groups in at least three different ways. In the first view, the group is seen as a source of influence over its members. Efforts to change behavior can be supported or blocked by pressures on members stemming from the group. To make constructive use of these pressures the group must be used *as a medium of change*. In the second view, the group itself becomes the *target of change*. To change the behavior of individuals it may be necessary to change the standards of the group, its style of leadership, its emotional atmosphere, or its stratification into cliques and hierarchies. Even though the goal may be to change the behavior of *individuals*, the target of change becomes the group. In the third view, it is recognized that many changes of behavior can be brought about only by the organized efforts of groups *as agents of change*. A committee to combat intolerance, a labor union, an employers association, a citizens group to increase the pay of teachers—any action group will be more or less effective depending upon the way it is organized, the satisfactions it provides to its members, the degree to which its goals are clear, and a host of other properties of the group.

An adequate social technology of change, then, requires at the very least a scientific understanding of groups viewed in each of these ways. We shall consider here only the first two aspects of the problem: the group as a medium of change and as a target of change.

The Group as a Medium of Change

Principle No. 1. If the group is to be used effectively as a medium of change, those people who are to be changed and those who are to exert influence for change must have a strong sense of belonging to the same group.

Kurt Lewin described this principle well: "The normal gap between teacher and student, doctor and patient, social worker and public, can . . . be a real obstacle to acceptance of the advocated conduct." In other words, in spite of whatever status differences there might be between them, the teacher and the student have to feel as members of one group in matters involving their sense of values. The chances for reeducation seem to be increased whenever a strong we-feeling is created (5). Recent experiments by Preston and Heintz have demonstrated greater changes of opinions among members of discussion groups operating with participatory leadership than among those with supervisory leadership (12). The implications of this principle for classroom teaching are far-reaching. The same may be said of supervision in the factory, army, or hospital.

Principle No. 2. The more attractive the group is to its members the greater is the influence that the group can exert on its members.

This principle has been extensively documented by Festinger and his co-workers (4). They have been able to show in a variety of settings that in more cohesive groups there is a greater readiness of members to attempt to influence others, a greater readiness to be influenced by others, and stronger pressures toward conformity when conformity is a relevant matter for the group. Important for the practitioner wanting to make use of this principle is, of course, the question of how to increase the attractiveness of groups. This is a question with many answers. Suffice it to say that a group is more attractive the more it satisfies the needs of its members. We have been able to demonstrate experimentally an increase in group cohesiveness by increasing the liking of members for each other as persons, by increasing the perceived importance of the group goal, and by increasing the prestige of the group among other groups. Experienced group workers could add many other ways to this list.

Principle No. 3. In attempts to change attitudes, values, or behavior, the more relevant they are to the basis of attraction to the group, the greater will be the influence that the group can exert upon them.

I believe this principle gives a clue to some otherwise puzzling phenomena. How does it happen that a group, like a labor union, seems to be able to exert such strong discipline over its members in some matters (let us say in dealings with management), while it seems unable to exert nearly the same influence in other matters (let us say in political action)? If we examine why it is that members are attracted to the group, I believe we will find that a particular reason for belonging seems more related to some of the group's activities than to others. If a man joins a union mainly to keep his job and to improve his working conditions, he may be largely uninfluenced by the union's attempt to modify his attitudes toward national and international affairs. Groups differ tremendously in the range of matters that are relevant to them and hence over which they have influence. Much of the inefficiency of adult education could be reduced if more attention were paid to the need that influence attempts be appropriate to the groups in which they are made.

Principle No. 4. The greater the prestige of a group member in the eyes of the other members, the greater the influence he can exert.

Polansky, Lippitt, and Redl (11) have demonstrated this principle with great care and methodological ingenuity in a series of studies in children's summer camps. From a practical point of view it must be emphasized that the things giving prestige to a member may not be those characteristics most prized by the official management of the group. The most prestige-carrying member of a Sunday school class may not possess the characteristics most similar to the minister of the church. The teacher's pet may be a poor source of influence within a class. This principle is the basis for the common observation that the official leader and the actual leader of a group are often not the same individual.

Principle No. 5. Efforts to change individuals or subparts of a group which, if successful, would have the result of making them deviate from the norms of the group will encounter strong resistance.

During the past few years a great deal of evidence has been accumulated showing the tremendous pressures which groups can exert upon members to conform to the group's norms. The price of deviation in most groups is rejection or even expulsion. If the member really wants to belong and be accepted, he cannot withstand this type of pressure. It is for this reason that efforts to change people by taking them from the group and giving them special training so often have disappointing results. This principle also accounts for the finding that people thus trained sometimes display increased tension, aggressiveness toward the group, or a tendency to form cults or cliques with others who have shared their training.

These five principles concerning the group as a medium of change would appear to have readiest application to groups created for the purpose of producing changes in people. They provide certain specifications for building effective training or therapy groups. They also point, however, to a difficulty in producing change in people in that they show how resistant an individual is to changing in any way contrary to group pressures and expectations. In order to achieve many kinds of changes in people, therefore, it is necessary to deal with the group as a target of change.

The Group as a Target of Change

Principle No. 6. Strong pressure for changes in the group can be established by creating a shared perception by members of the need for change, thus making the source of pressure for change lie within the group.

Marrow and French (9) reports a dramatic case-study which illustrates this principle quite well. A manufacturing concern had a policy against hiring women over 30 because it was believed that they were slower, more difficult to train, and more likely to be absent. The staff psychologist was able to present to management evidence that this belief was clearly unwarranted at least within their own company. The psychologist's facts, however, were rejected and ignored as a basis for action because they violated accepted beliefs. It was claimed that they went against the direct experience of the foremen. Then the psychologist hit upon a plan for achieving change which differed drastically from the usual one of argument, persuasion, and pressure. He proposed that management conduct its own analysis of the situation. With his help management collected all the facts which they believed were relevant to the problem. When the results were in they were now their own facts rather than those of some "outside" expert. Policy was immediately changed without further resistance. The important point here is that facts are not enough. The facts must be the accepted property of the group if they are to become an effective basis for change. There seems to be all the difference in the world in changes actually carried out between those cases in which a consulting firm is hired to do a study and present a report and those in which technical experts are asked to collaborate with the group in doing its own study.

Principle No. 7. Information relating to the need for change, plans for change, and consequences of change must be shared by all relevant people in the group.

Another way of stating this principle is to say that change of a group ordinarily requires the opening of communication channels. Newcomb (10) has shown how one of the first consequences of mistrust and hostility is the avoidance of communicating openly and freely about the things producing the tension. If you look closely at a pathological group (that is, one that has trouble making decisions or effecting coordinated efforts of its members), you will certainly find strong restraints in that group against communicating vital information among its members. Until these restraints are removed there can be little hope for any real and lasting changes in the group's functioning. In passing it should be pointed out that the removal of barriers to communication will ordinarily be accompanied by a sudden increase in the communication of hostility. The group may appear to be falling apart, and it will certainly be a painful experience to many of the members. This pain and the fear that things are getting out of hand often stop the process of change once begun.

Principle No. 8. Changes in one part of a group produce strain in other related parts which can be reduced only by eliminating the change or by bringing about readjustments in the related parts.

It is a common practice to undertake improvements in group functioning by providing training programs for certain classes of people in the organization. A training program for foremen, for nurses, for teachers, or for group workers is established. If the content of the training is relevant for organizational change, it must of necessity deal with the relationships these people have with other subgroups. If nurses in a hospital change their behavior significantly, it will affect their relations both with the patients and with the doctors. It is unrealistic to assume that both these groups will remain indifferent to any significant changes in this respect. In hierarchical structures this process is most clear. Lippitt has proposed on the basis of research and experience that in such organizations attempts at change should always involve three levels, one being the major target of change and the other two being the one above and the one below.

These eight principles represent a few of the basic propositions emerging from research in group dynamics. Since research is constantly going on and since it is the very nature of research to revise and reformulate our conceptions, we may be sure that these principles will have to be modified and improved as time goes by. In the meantime they may serve as guides in our endeavors to develop a scientifically based technology of social management.

In social technology, just as in physical technology, invention plays a crucial role. In both fields progress consists of the creation of new mechanisms for the accomplishment of certain goals. In both fields inventions arise in response to practical needs and are to be evaluated by how effectively they satisfy these needs. The relation of invention to scientific development is indirect but important. Inventions cannot proceed too far ahead of basic scientific development, nor should they be allowed to fall too far behind. They will be more effective the more they make good use of known principles of science, and they often make new developments in science possible. On the other hand, they are in no sense logical derivations from scientific principles.

I have taken this brief excursion into the theory of invention in order to make a final point. To many people "group dynamics" is known only for the social inventions which have developed in recent years in work with groups. Group dynamics is often thought of as certain techniques to be used with groups. Role playing, buzz groups, process observers, post-meeting reaction sheets, and feedback of group observations are devices popularly associated with the phrase "group dynamics." I trust that I have been able to show that group dynamics is more than a collection of gadgets. It certainly aspires to be a science as well as a technology.

This is not to underplay the importance of these inventions nor of the function of inventing. As inventions they are all mechanisms designed to help accomplish important goals. How effective they are will depend upon how skillfully they are used and how appropriate they are to the purposes to which they are put. Careful evaluative research must be the ultimate judge of their usefulness in comparison with alternative inventions. I believe that the principles enumerated in this paper indicate some of the specifications that social inventions in this field must meet.

REFERENCES

1. Cartwright, D. Some principles of mass persuasion: Selected findings of research on the sale of United States war bonds. *Human Relations*, 1949, 2(3), 253–67.

2. Cartwright, D. *The research center for group dynamics: A report of five years' activities and a view of future needs.* Ann Arbor: Institute for Social Research, 1950.

3. Coch, L. and French, J. T. P., Jr. Overcoming resistance to change. *Human Relations*, 1948, 1(4), 512–32.

4. Festinger, L., et al. *Theory and experiment in social communication:* Collected papers. Ann Arbor: Institute for Social Research, 1950.

5. Lewin, K. *Resolving social conflicts*, p. 67. New York: Harper & Bros., 1951.

6. Lewin, K. *Field theory in social science*, pp. 229–36. New York: Harper & Bros., 1951.

7. Lewin, K., Lippitt, R., and White, R. K. Patterns of aggressive behavior in experimentally created "social climates." *Journal of Social Psychology*, 1939, 10, 271–99.

8. Lippitt, R. *Training in Community Relations*. New York: Harper & Bros., 1949.

9. Marrow, A. J. and French, J. R. P., Jr. Changing a stereotype in industry. *Journal of Social Issues*, 1945, *1*(3), 33–37.

10. Newcomb, T. M. Autistic hostility and social reality. *Human Relations*, 1947, *1*(1), 69–86.

11. Polansky, N., Lippitt, R., and Redl, F. An investigation of behavioral contagion in groups. *Human Relations*, 1950, *3*(4), 319–48.

12. Preston, M. G. and Heintz, R. K. Effects of participatory vs. supervisory leadership on group judgment. *Journal of Abnormal and Social Psychology*, 1949, *44*, 345–55.

5

PUBLIC SPEAKING:
TRANSACTING WITH A LARGE GROUP

Earlier we noted that most of us have a tendency to become apprehensive when we think about performing in the public speaking arena. We think that giving a speech is completely different from participating in intrapersonal, interpersonal, or small group communication. Actually, communication in the public speaking arena is more alike than different from communication in these arenas. The primary distinguishing characteristic of this arena is that one individual has the major responsibility for presenting a verbal message to a group of receivers. This characteristic forces us to think of the public speaking arena as more formal and less personal. Increased formality and decreased personableness, however, are not inherent in a public speaking encounter. The essence of a public speaking situation is transactional communication. All participants are simultaneously sending and receiving communication cues. The more a public speaker can generate the feeling of a personal, transactional relationship with his audience members, the more successful he will be. Put simply, a successful public speaker communicates *with* his audience members rather than speaking *at* them. Communication in the public speaking arena is naturally more premeditated and more representative of a monologue than of an interpersonal dialogue, since it is also characterized by more restrictive feedback (verbal feedback is usually nonexistent); it is a difficult arena in which to create informality and personableness.

Communication factors are altered when they exist in this arena. For example, the importance of a nonverbal cue will be different. What may be perceived as an acceptable, friendly gesture in the interpersonal arena may appear crude or vulgar in the public speaking arena. Also, self-disclosure becomes more difficult and less common.

Obviously, communication in this arena is different from the other arenas. We believe, however, that when one realizes and admits that it is less different than he might have originally thought, participation in public speaking can become less threatening and more enjoyable. The essence of communication in this area is participants transacting with each other in the personal communication process. It is a part of the personal communication process—it is not a rare event to be feared and avoided. It is only an extension of the other communication arenas. The readings in this unit were selected to provide you with insight into how the factors of perception, nonverbal behavior, communication barriers, self-disclosure, and communication effects operate in public speaking transactions. Hopefully, this will help you in your attempts to improve your own participation in this arena.

PUBLIC
SPEAKING
PERCEPTION

The difference between talking "at" and talking "with" is the difference between touching, and touching and being touched.
H. Prather

From Hugh Prather, *Notes to Myself*. Reprinted by permission of Real People Press.

As in all the other communication arenas, perception in the public speaking arena is extremely selective. One audience member's perception of a stimulus will be different from another audience member's perception of the stimulus. Furthermore, your perception of a stimulus while you are talking with a large group will probably be very different from your perception of an identical stimulus while you are talking with a small group or with a single individual. For example, negative nonverbal cues directed at you by a friend will probably be much more disruptive if you are presenting a speech to a large group than if you are talking with the friend in an interpersonal situation.

Other perception changes also occur. For example, you will perceive a "speaker" differently if you listen to him in the public speaking arena than if you listen to him in another arena. Following is a brief excerpt from the chapter "The Sender's Influence: Source Credibility," which appears in the book, *The Personal Communication Process,* which we coauthored. This excerpt should help you internalize how your perception operates differently when you are a participant in this communication arena. How does the way you perceive a speaker affect the impact his message has on you?

JOHN R. WENBURG
WILLIAM W. WILMOT

THE SENDER'S INFLUENCE: SOURCE CREDIBILITY

Source Credibility Defined

The first term to be clarified is "source." A source is an encoder who sends the message cues that we focus on for the purpose of description.[1] Source credibility is the degree of believability or acceptability a receiver gives to a source. The degree of believability or acceptability may range from high to low. Thus, source credibility is not a concept that is restricted to just "high" credibility sources.

Whether we are primarily sources or receivers, we are all concerned with source credibility. In the role of a source, each of us is concerned with his own image.[2] Also, as sources, what we perceive to be the credibility of our receivers (the "sources" who give us feedback) affects our communication behavior. In the receiver role, each of us is concerned with credibility because the amount of credibility we give to a source has an impact on our own responses to him. The information we receive is almost always colored by the feelings we have about the source of the information. He may be telling us the "truth," but if we do not trust him, we will not accept it. In the other hand, if we do trust him, we are much more reluctant to question the validity of the information.[3] Also, as receivers, the credibility that a source confers on us as "sources of feedback" will affect the way the source communicates with us.

Dynamics of Credibility

It should be apparent from the above discussion that source credibility is a receiver phenomenon. According to Brooks, "the fact that thou-

From The Personal Communication Process by Wenburg and Wilmot. Copyright © 1973, John Wiley & Sons, Inc., New York, New York.

[1] See, for example, Wallace C. Fotheringham, Perspectives on Persuasion, Allyn and Bacon, Boston, 1966, p. 261.

[2] Kenneth E. Andersen, Persuasion: Theory and Practice, Allyn and Bacon, Boston, 1971, p. 245.

[3] George Borden, An Introduction to Human Communication Theory, Wm. C. Brown, Dubuque, 1971, p. 58.

sands of years of study and more than thirty-five years of empirical research have brought little improvement to our understanding of the basis of source influence was due in part to a false assumption that source credibility is an inherent property of the speaker."[4]

The assumption that credibility is an inherent property of the speaker is incorrect. It denies the whole notion of process and individual differences in perception, attitudes, needs, and desires. Source credibility is a dynamic, not a static, notion. It is subject to constant reevaluation and change. In fact, it changes from receiver to receiver, from time to time, from topic to topic, and from setting to setting.

RECEIVER TO RECEIVER

A source does not "possess" credibility; it is conferred upon him by his receiver(s).[5] Often we hear the statement, "He really has high credibility." Such a statement says more about the person making the statement than the person toward whom the comment is directed. A source simply does not *have* high credibility. Some people may evaluate him as a highly credible source; in fact, a large majority of people may evaluate him as such, but this does not mean that he *has* high credibility. In another's eyes, he may be a lowly credible source. For example, a college or university president may be perceived as highly credible by the board of trustees, the administration of his institution, the majority of his faculty members, most of the student population, and the general public. Whether he "has" high or low credibility cannot be measured, however, until he is confronted with a specific receiver(s). If the receiver is any of the preceding, he will probably have high credibility. If the receiver is a leading campus radical or a faculty member who has recently been dismissed from his position, it is quite likely that he will have low credibility.

TIME TO TIME

Source credibility changes from time to time in the same manner that it changes from receiver to receiver. Time changes can be seen both *during* a given communicative transaction (internal changes) and *between* various communicative acts (external changes).

[4] *William D. Brooks*, Speech Communication, *Wm. C. Brown, Dubuque, 1971,* p. 163.

[5] *Gerald R. Miller*, Speech Communication: A Behavioral Approach, *Bobbs Merrill, Indianapolis, 1966,* p. 39.

INTERNAL CHANGES. In any given communicative act, a communicator's credibility will constantly undergo changes that may be moderate, but are definitely changes. This changing status of source credibility demonstrates the transactional nature of communication. All cues during a communication transaction, that is, public, private, and behavioral (verbal and nonverbal) cues, affect our continual assessment of another's credibility. Empirical support for the varying nature of credibility is reported by Brooks in a summary of a series of studies. In these investigations, people were asked to evaluate a source with whom they were familiar, such as Malcolm X, James Hoffa, Richard Nixon, or Martin Luther King, Jr. They were then exposed to a brief recorded passage from one of the sources. After exposure to the brief passage, the people were asked to evaluate the sources again. Brooks summarized the results by stating, ". . . the results of these studies produce this limited conclusion: Audiences whose initial evaluations of speakers are clearly favorable or clearly unfavorable tend to shift in the opposite direction after a brief exposure to the source's recorded speech."[6]

This finding leads us to speculate that one's evaluation of a source changes throughout the communication situation. For description, the labels "pretransaction," "transactional," and "posttransaction" can be used to discuss the internal credibility changes.

Pretransaction credibility is a receiver's assessment of another person *before* a communication transaction begins. Determinants of pretransaction credibility may be our previous experiences, direct or vicarious, with the source; facts we know about the source, particularly those which provide us with information about his group memberships; knowledge of how others perceive the source; and the immediate stimuli leading to the actual communication transaction.[7] The college president we referred to earlier would automatically have some level of credibility conferred on him by some receivers before a given communication situation merely by virtue of his office and reputation. Status and reputation are two examples of many possible pretransaction determinants. Remember, however, although some of us may evaluate certain status and reputation elements in a positive way, others may evaluate them negatively.

Transactional credibility is a receiver's assessment of another per-

---

[6] *Robert D. Brooks, "The Generality of Early Reversals of Attitudes Toward Communication Sources,"* Speech Monographs *(June 1970), VII, 154.*

[7] *Andersen, pp. 225–226 (cited in footnote 2).*

son, produced *during* a communication transaction. Factors, such as language usage and tone serve to alter our perception of a person's pretransaction credibility.

Posttransaction credibility is a receiver's assessment of another person existing at the *completion* of a communication transaction. The changes from pretransaction to transactional credibility produce posttransaction credibility. Some refer to this concept as "source-message" interaction. That is, before a communication encounter, we have expectations about the potential source (pretransaction credibility). During a communication encounter, our previous expectations serve as a basis of evaluation. Where our expectations are not fulfilled or are exceeded by the source, our assessment of the source's credibility changes (transactional credibility). All of these alterations become a basis on which we give our concluding assessment of the source (posttransaction credibility). Portions of this final image are activated in the receiver's mind and serve as *one* basis for the source's pretransaction credibility in the next communication encounter.[8] And, in that next encounter, the credibility will change again.

EXTERNAL CHANGES. As credibility changes *during* a communicative act, it also changes *between* communicative acts. A source's posttransaction credibility in one situation is only one determinant of his pretransaction credibility in the next encounter. As our own goals, desires, values, and knowledge change, our evaluations of other people change. What is admirable to us today may not be as admirable tomorrow. As we change, our attitudes, positions on issues, and methods of dealing with people change. We all undergo personal changes that affect our evaluations. The college president referred to earlier will be perceived differently by us two years from now than today—even if we are communicating with him in the same place and on the same topic.

TOPIC TO TOPIC

Topical changes also alter perception and credibility. These changes, however, are less significant than the other changes we have discussed. For example, according to most people, especially nonsmokers, the United States Surgeon General is an extremely credible source on the topic of smoking and lung cancer. He probably is not perceived as quite so credible, however, on the topic of United States foreign policy. It is virtually impossible to be highly knowledgeable on all topics. Thus,

---

[8] *George A. Borden, Richard B. Gregg, and Theodore G. Grove,* Speech Behavior and Human Interaction, *Prentice-Hall, Englewood Cliffs, 1969, p. 200.*

when one is perceived as being less knowledgeable on one topic than on another, perception of his credibility should change. Some of us do, however, assess others as being highly credible on many divergent topics. If we are impressed by the status of "United States Surgeon General," per se, our perception of his credibility will be affected in all situations. This tendency to generalize credibility across many unrelated topics is called the "halo-effect." For example, if you have an extremely good biology teacher, you may perceive him as highly credible on many topics, such as civil rights, until he proves otherwise. Although credibility is influenced by topical changes, these changes may be quite minor.

SETTING TO SETTING

Changes in setting alter our perception of another's credibility. Some of the reverence of a minister's words are lost, for example, in a fishing boat. Changes from one communication arena to another serve to alter credibility perceptions. We normally perceive a person's credibility differently on a one-to-one basis than in a public speaking situation. For example, think how a personal conference with a professor alters your perception of his credibility. After such a conference, your perception of him in the classroom will be different from before. You have all heard statements such as, "He's a pretty good guy once you get a chance to talk with him personally."

Thus, credibility is an unstable phenomenon. It changes like the wind. It is different after a communication act than it was before, it is different between communication acts, it is different from one topic to another, from one place to another, and most importantly it is different from one person to another. We do not "have it," it is "given to us" by others in a multiplicity of ways for many different reasons.

Dimensions of Credibility

CREDIBILITY IN PUBLIC SPEAKING SETTINGS

Aristotle suggested that source credibility is composed of three separate dimensions, character, sagacity (intelligence), and goodwill. Although the Aristotelian dimensions have been challenged, no one has denied the assumption that credibility has more than one dimension. Before we examine some of the specific ideas about the various components of source credibility, make a list of words that you would use in de-

Credibility Dimensions

Aristotle	Intelligence	Character	Goodwill
Hovland, Janis, and Kelley	Expertness	Trustworthiness	Intention

Figure 1

scribing a person whom you perceive as highly credible in a given situation. What words do you come up with? Probably words such as knowledgeable, sincere, understanding, concerned, impressive, articulate, expert, and friendly. If you analyze your list, you may discover that most of the words can be placed under the three dimensions set forth by Aristotle.

Hovland, Janis, and Kelley speculate that a source's credibility consists of expertness, trustworthiness, and intention toward the receiver as perceived by the receiver.[9] Notice how closely their speculations mirror Aristotle's ideas. "Expertness" is another word for intelligence, "trustworthiness" is related to character, and "intention toward the receiver" is another way of labeling perceived goodwill. Figure 1 shows the close relationship between the dimensions of Aristotle and Hovland, Janis, and Kelley.

Recently, with the use of computerized factor analysis, researchers have examined the dimensions more carefully, though perhaps not more accurately. Andersen found that two major dimensions were employed in making credibility judgments about sources. He identified

Credibility Dimensions

Aristotle	Intelligence	Character	Goodwill	
Hovland, Janis, and Kelley	Expertness	Trustworthiness	Intention	
Andersen	Evaluation			Dynamism

Figure 2

[9] Carl I. Hovland, Irving L. Janis, and Harold H. Kelly, *Communication and Persuasion*, *Yale University Press*, New Haven, 1953, pp. 19–55.

Credibility Dimensions

	Intelligence	Character	Goodwill	
Aristotle	Intelligence	Character	Goodwill	
Hovland, Janis, and Kelley	Expertness	Trustworthiness	Intention	
Andersen	Evaluation			Dynamism
Berlo and Lemert	Qualification	Safety		Dynamism

Figure 3

these dimensions as evaluation and dynamism. It should be noted, however, that the respondents in the Andersen research were assessing "potential" sources. They were not actually exposed to messages delivered by the sources.[10] Figure 2 illustrates Andersen's research, as compared to previous theorizing.

Berlo and Lemert discovered three dimensions of source credibility. They labeled them "safety," "qualification," and "dynamism."[11] Notice how closely safety resembles the character dimension of Aristotle, the trustworthiness dimension of Hovland, Janis, and Kelley, and a large portion of the evaluative dimension found by Andersen (Figure 3). Also, the qualification dimension is similar to the sagacity dimension forwarded by Aristotle, the expertness factor stated by Hovland, Janis, and Kelley, and the other portion of the evaluative dimension found by Andersen. The dynamism dimension duplicates the dynamism dimension set forth by Andersen. In a later study Berlo, Lemert, and

[10] *Andersen, pp. 221–222 (cited in footnote 2). The bipolar adjective scales that Andersen discovered that were descriptive of the evaluative dimensions were honest-dishonest, moral-immoral, fair-unfair, sympathetic-unsympathetic, good-bad, reasonable-unreasonable. Scales that were descriptive of the dynamism dimension were interesting-uninteresting, strong-weak, fast-slow, aggressive-nonaggressive, and active-passive. From this list, one can see that scales relevant to both character and intelligence went together to constitute Andersen's evaluative dimension. For example, honest-dishonest, moral-immoral, sympathetic-unsympathetic, and good-bad constitute a description closely related to character, whereas fair-unfair, and reasonable-unreasonable more closely resemble an intelligence or expertness dimension.*

[11] *James B. Lemert, "Dimensions of Source Credibility." Paper presented to the Association for Education in Journalism, August 26, 1963.*

Credibility Dimensions

Aristotle	Intelligence	Character	Goodwill	
Hovland, Janis, and Kelley	Expertness	Trustworthiness	Intention	
Andersen	Evaluation			Dynamism
Berlo and Lemert	Qualification	Safety		Dynamism
McCroskey	Authoritativeness	Character		

Figure 4

Mertz discovered that the dynamism factor was quite unstable and did not account for much of the overall source assessment.[12]

McCroskey, in an impressive series of studies designed to develop better credibility scales, found two dimensions. He labeled them as character and authoritativeness (Figure 4).[13]

COMPARISON OF CREDIBILITY DIMENSIONS

The two pieces of research, by Andersen and Berlo and Lemert, found dynamism as a "new" dimension of credibility. In McCroskey's research, however, dynamism did not emerge as a third dimension (Figure 4), because when the dynamism of a source was changed, it affected the other two dimensions. McCroskey found that a dynamic source was consistently perceived to be more competent, and usually more trustworthy, than a nondynamic source. He concluded that the dy-

[12] David K. Berlo, James B. Lemert, and Robert J. Mertz, "Dimensions for Evaluating the Acceptability of Message Sources," Public Opinion Quarterly (Winter, 1969–1970), XXXIII, 562–576. The scales that delineated the safety dimension were just-unjust, kind-cruel, honest-dishonest, and so forth. Some of the scales indicative of the qualification dimension were trained-untrained, qualified-unqualified, and informed-uninformed. The dynamism dimension was exemplified by such scales as aggressive-meek, emphatic-hesitant, and energetic-tired.

[13] James C. McCroskey, "Scales for the Measurement of Ethos," Speech Monographs (1966), XXX, 65–72.

namism of a source is important, but that it affects the other dimensions of credibility, and, therefore, may not be a separate credibility dimension. Figure 4 also demonstrates that the goodwill or intention toward the receiver dimension no longer appears, although it was set forth by Aristotle, and Hovland, Janis, and Kelley.

The lack of consistency between the goodwill and dynamism dimensions is, on the surface, very confusing. We attribute these inconsistencies to the ways in which the studies were conducted. The scales used to measure the dimensions of credibility in the research were constructed on an a priori basis. They were developed by having people describe qualities they liked or disliked in sources. The people were rating sources outside of any particular communication event. People were not exposed to a source in an actual communication transaction and then asked to describe the qualities they perceived in the source.

We have reason to believe that scales need to be developed specifically for the measurement of posttransaction credibility. Given the phenomenon of source-message interaction, there is a need to develop scales that assess a person's credibility *after* a communication transaction occurs. Such scales might (1) show a goodwill dimension emerging, and (2) demonstrate that dynamism is much more important than previously thought. Both goodwill and dynamism depend upon a transaction actually taking place. They might emerge if scales are designed to measure posttransaction credibility. In short, goodwill and dynamism are probably constituents of credibility in an oral interchange.

At any rate, there are at least two dimensions of source credibility that we as receivers in a public speaking situation use to evaluate a source; those dimensions are character and authoritativeness. Only further research will illustrate whether we are correct about the importance of goodwill and dynamism.

It is possible and it is common to see what one believes only because one believes it.   W. Johnson

---

"Know what I think? He levels least when he raps most."

Drawing by Richter; © 1972 The New Yorker Magazine, Inc.

PUBLIC
SPEAKING
NONVERBAL BEHAVIOR

The less people speak of their greatness,
the more we think of it.   F. Bacon

Nonverbal behavior is important in all communication transactions. Encounters in the public speaking arena certainly are not exceptions to this rule. A speaker's nonverbal behavior, for example, affects how the audience members perceive his verbal message. In turn, the nonverbal behaviors of audience members can affect a speaker's performance and the speaker's perception of the audience. As participants in this arena, it is important that we understand how nonverbal behavior affects the communication transactions.

"Listen to What You Can't Hear" by Norman B. Sigband helps us become more sensitive to the nonverbal cues that are directed toward us. Sigband stresses, listen "both to what is said and what isn't said" because the nonverbal messages in this arena are often more informative than the verbal.

NORMAN B. SIGBAND

LISTEN
TO WHAT YOU
CAN'T HEAR

Today's executive spends roughly 40 per cent of his work day just listening. The higher he rises in the management hierarchy, the greater that percentage is apt to be, thanks to more meetings, as well as to interviewing, counselling, exchanging of information and decision making.

To the manager, it is vital to listen as the effective salesman must listen—to determine what the "prospect" will buy.

The manager must "sell" his ideas to his superiors; he must persuade his subordinates; he must inform his associates. But in every case he will not be aware of what to sell, how best to persuade, and in what areas to inform, if he first does not listen to those around him.

He must not only listen, he must try to hear what is not said.

Take the case of Supervisor Galvin. Joe has just approached him to report:

"Well, Mr. Gavin, I finally locked up the Bahr Co. order. Boy, was it a mess! But you said it was an emergency job, and I saw to it that it went out today—right on the button. You know, I've been here every night this week and almost all last weekend to tie that darned thing up. Bahr's specifications are ridiculous, but the order is on its way, even though my wife may throw me out. And let me tell you, if I never see another job as tough as that, I'll be plenty happy. It really required blood, sweat and tears."

If Mr. Galvin should answer, "Great, Joe. Now let's get to work on the Sunnyvale order," he hasn't really been listening.

What was Joe really saying? We'll never be sure, but he was not simply saying the Bahr order was difficult. He probably was saying, "How about giving me a pat on the back, Mr. Galvin?" or "Why do you give me all the problem jobs?" or "I hate to work nights."

The sensitive, effective manager will hear what the other fellow often is inhibited from stating directly, due to ego, emotions, position held, or what have you.

Let's tune in on Supervisor Jackson's interview with extremely conscientious Jim Cantonelli, who has just been offered a promotion to section chief.

"I sure appreciate the offer, boss, but I don't think I can handle it. You know I only been in the States seven years, I murder the language, I don't write well. What am I goin' to do about the weekly reports? And

 Reprinted from **Nation's Business,** *June, 1969, by permission.*

Vital image

I'm not too hot on the reading angle; wow, all those instructions that come down. And the guys laugh now when I try to talk; how can I hold meetings? And you know yourself that all I know about switching systems, I picked up around here."

If Supervisor Jackson continues to press, and points out the increased salary, new title, and other ego satisfying factors, Cantonelli may accept. This, however, may place a hard-working production man in a position over his head and result in failure for him, decreased morale in the department, and financial loss to the firm.

What should Jackson have perceived from Cantonelli's reaction to the offer? He probably should have heard him saying, "I'm not ready for the job, I'm afraid to take it on, I don't think the men will be with me."

Obviously a supervisor can't back away from every worker who appears reluctant to accept promotion. Many such promotions work out very well. But when a manager hears a Cantonelli say what he said, that is the time to perceive correctly.

You Have to Concentrate

One basic barrier to effective listening is simply inability to concentrate, which causes facts and ideas to be lost.

What's he really saying?

Lack of concentration may have several roots. Most of us speak at about 140 words per minute, but we can comprehend at a much faster rate. This permits us to take mental excursions into other areas as we listen.

For a few seconds, the listener thinks about that faulty car transmission; then he returns to the speaker's topic; then he is off again. This time he wonders about the football game: Will it be worth $5.50 per ticket? And again back to the speaker. But what about vacation? Two weeks in September should be O.K. And back to the speaker.

But now the speaker is too far ahead; the listener has missed something vital on one of his excursions. Besides, the topic seems very complex. Oh, well, not concentrating is easier than trying to concentrate. And another listener now is just hearing.

Opinions and prejudices can also cause poor concentration. When a statement the listener doesn't like is made, he may figuratively reach up into his brain and turn the communicator off. Or he may concentrate on a statement with which he disagrees, allowing other statements to go unheard.

The style of the speaker's clothes, the look on his face, his posture, his accept, the color of his skin, his mannerisms, or past experiences with him may also cause the listener to react emotionally and tune him out.

Try to put aside your preconceived ideas or prejudices. The man who is speaking may have a new concept that is worth putting into practice.

And if you want to concentrate, don't try to do something unrelated to the discussion while the man you wish to listen to is talking.

Also, by the way, make him realize you are concentrating. Look directly at him, and sit up straight. Don't protest that you listen best when you are relaxed, hands clasped behind your head and feet propped on the desk. This may be true, but the speaker may see lack of interest and perhaps discourtesy on your part. The result would be a barrier to clear communication.

Listening for Facts

The good listener makes a definite attempt to listen to every statement for facts and for feelings.

In listening for facts, you should first attempt to perceive the theme or the thesis of the presentation. In a speech, this may be stated in the first few minutes. It probably will be noted in different words several times during the talk, and may well serve as a concluding statement.

The basic ideas should then be recognized. What are the four key points in the entire talk? The alert listener will be able to perceive them, even if the speaker doesn't label each specifically. Facts to support the ideas should be assimilated. But once the ideas are firmly fixed in your mind, they will help you recall specific facts.

If you listen analytically, you can recognize major ideas and separate them from minor ones. Of course this requires your full effort. Effective listening is hard work.

Sometimes, you find yourself listening to someone who hasn't organized his ideas too well. He seems to be going in circles. He repeats himself. He barely mentions a key fact. It's up to you to organize his presentation in your mind, as he talks.

Taking notes during the talk will help you retain ideas and facts. But you should never become so absorbed in the task of taking notes that you lose the ideas being transmitted. And if the talk goes on for any length of time, the good listener occasionally will hastily review in his mind the ideas and facts which have already been cited.

All in all, to perceive the facts that are stated, you need to be attentive and analytical, and to develop an ability to be retentive.

Don't outrun speaker

Listening for Feelings

Listening for feelings is more difficult.

Here you must try to perceive what is really behind a seemingly obvious statement. You must give, insofar as you are able, the same connotations to words that the other fellow gives. You must also try to recognize his biases and his frame of reference. You must try to remember his salary level and his desires.

When a slow, easygoing man says, "We must get on this job right away," you interpret "right away" as "in a week or two." When an employee you know to be conscientious and slow to give praise calls another a "hard worker," your connotation probably will be very similar to his.

You must constantly "listen" to the other person's nonverbal communications. His inflections, his gestures, his finger tapping, the look in his eyes, and the changing lines in his brow.

If his words say, "Well, it really isn't very important to me anyway," but his posture is stiff, his knuckles white, his eyes hopeful and his forehead glistening with perspiration, you had better hear the nonverbal message. If you don't, communication will not be effective.

Here is a situation similar to one which may have occurred to you or one of your salesmen just yesterday. Mr. Big, President of the Acme

Co., is very proud of the newly completed offices for his five immediate subordinates. They had been scattered in different sections of the plant; now they all will be on the same floor with him.

You are trying to sell him office furniture and you tell him you have an especially good buy for his company on five beautiful executive walnut desks. Mr. Big is unimpressed.

"They don't seem quite right," he says. "They're very modern and they look terribly short of drawer space. Of course they are beautiful, but they don't have file drawers. And holy smokes, why does our controller or purchasing head need so much surface area? Why, these desks must be twice as big as mine!"

Now, if you know Mr. Big at all, you should be able to tell what he is really saying.

There is no point in pressing him about how inexpensive, or beautiful or functional the five desks are. For what he is telling you is, "I don't want my subordinates to have bigger, more beautiful desks than mine. It hurts my ego."

Of course, he can't say that. Nevertheless, you must hear what he does not say and respond tactfully to it. If you don't—no sale.

The Results

Effective listening on your part produces many salutary results.

First, there will be more effective listening on the other person's part. When he notes that you are sincerely and carefully listening, and not merely waiting for him to pause and inhale so you can jump in, he does not feel threatened. Thus, after he has had his complete say, he is ready to listen carefully to you.

Second, the speaker presents more information which may benefit you. Your careful listening usually will motivate him to cite as many facts as he can. Then you are in a better position to make correct decisions.

Third, your relationship with the speaker often is improved, and you understand him better. He has an opportunity to get facts, ideas and hostilities off his chest. And you may recognize that one man requires frequent praise, while another does not; that one responds favorably to counselling, while another resents it; that he is an extrovert, while she is an introvert.

Everyone wants understanding—with or without agreement—and there is no better way of giving it than through sensitive listening.

A fourth product of careful listening often will be unexpectedly easy solutions to problems. When the other person is permitted to speak in an unthreatening environment, and feels he has the listener's complete attention and respect, he may hear himself more clearly. As a result, solutions may come through to him or you more clearly.

All in all, effective listening, both to what is said and what isn't said, can bring major benefits to a businessman. Too often, the business manager says, "I don't have time to listen carefully." The only reply to that is, "You don't have time NOT to listen carefully."

To understand people, I must try to hear what they are not saying, what they perhaps will never be able to say.
J. Powell

The following excerpt from
Speech and Man by Charles
Brown and Charles Van
Riper reinforces the points
about nonverbal communi-
cation stressed in the last
reading. The authors stress
how the contradictory nature
of verbal and nonverbal
messages often create confusion in the public speaking
arena.

CHARLES BROWN
CHARLES VAN RIPER

SPEECH
FOR COMMUNICATION

Another of the chief misunder-
standings about the nature of communication results from the illusion
that most of the meaning people have for each other is the work of
words. It is true that words are important. Without them we could not
communicate as human beings, but much of the essential message is
sent by postures, gestures, and facial expressions.

To hear the nonverbal broadcast one does not listen to what the
speaker says, but to the way he says it. We react to his voice, to the
way he stands, to his mannerisms, and to the expressions that fleet like
shadows across his face. A person tells about his feelings, motives, and
conflicts in this second broadcast. The listener has to imagine himself
speaking with the feelings and the actual posture of the speaker in
order to be able to decode and translate the message into English.

> *A student was presenting to a class the view that verbal lan-*
> *guage in the main, disguises the speaker, and that the real burden*
> *of communication is sent in the nonverbal broadcast. This he il-*
> *lustrated with a story not to be forgotten. He said he was driving*
> *on a super-highway one morning at dawn, and an automobile ap-*
> *proaching at a high speed began to sway crazily from one side of*
> *the road to the other. It eventually plunged off the road, crashed*
> *into a concrete pole which broke off and fell over the automobile,*

Charles T. Brown and Charles Van Riper, Speech and Man, *copyright © 1966.*
303 *Reprinted by permission of Prentice-Hall, Inc., Englewood Cliffs, New Jersey.*

bringing it to a halt. The student stopped and ran to the man's aid. The victim was hanging out of his automobile, apparently dead, his face covered with broken windshield glass. The student began to lift the glass from the man's face and the man shook his head slowly. Without opening his eyes, he mumbled, "Give me your hand." The student took the man's hand and in a few minutes the man died. The student said, "In those moments I was told about death as no words will ever tell me."

Of course, what the dying man communicated was that in the last moments of life the important thing was to be close to another human. At this point he was not concerned about who the other person was. The other was human and that was enough. It was not important to see him or to hear him, but to touch him. "Give me your hand." One is entitled to hear many things in this communication, but it is difficult to escape the point that much of the power of the communication rests in the perfect compatability of the verbal and nonverbal communication—a man sprawled, dying, asks for another's hand.

This compatability is not always to be found. Indeed, much of the confusion in communication is the felt conflict between the two broadcasts. A boy asks a girl to go to the prom. She says, "Oh, I'm so sorry. I do wish you had asked earlier. I have made other plans that I just can't alter now. Please excuse me, I have a class in ten minutes." And the boy feels that her departure was abrupt or that she had overexpressed her disappointment or that her eyes appraised him too carefully as the words gushed. People "give themselves away" in nonverbal communication unless they have learned to monitor even their voices and faces, and then they wear expressionless masks which arouse the suspicion of the listener, and even closer inspection of the nonverbal cues.

The American psychiatrist Harry Stack Sullivan makes the point that almost all of us in our culture send conflicting messages in the two broadcasts. What we put into words is always somewhat monitored. (Even your best friends won't tell you, you know.) One does not get up in class and say, except perhaps in fun, "I'm going to give the best speech you will hear today. Indeed, I shall show you I am a pretty exceptional fellow." But these things and a multitude of other unmentionables are thought of in the course of a communication and are very often said nonverbally.

But Sullivan's point about conflicting messages goes deeper, into more troubled waters. Each of us has been penalized since childhood for revealing unacceptable attitudes and feelings such as "I don't like you," "You always make me feel stupid when I talk to you," "Why do you let your hair hang in your face?" Polite society does not allow these things to be said, so they are repressed, and they are repressed so habitually, so unconsciously, that they escape from our control. Thus our nonverbal transmitters secretly send the message. As people grow into middle life, their faces and postures tell the unspoken thoughts and feelings that dominate their lives. A truly great artist, like Andrew Wyeth, best known perhaps for his "Christina," captures these subtle nonverbal messages and puts them on canvas.

It is little wonder that the art of understanding what a person says is so incredibly difficult to acquire. There are always the lyrics and the music, and they do not always match. Worse, part of the music is unconsciously composed. And perhaps toughest of all—no meaning can be transmitted; it can only be aroused.

In the "Dynamics of a Black
Audience," Annette Powell
Williams presents a vivid
description of potential
differences in the nonverbal
behaviors of black and white
audiences. The selection
demonstrates how a speaker
who fails to predict certain
nonverbal behavior differences
may fail miserably when
attempting to speak to an
audience composed of
members of a race different
from the race he is accustomed
to addressing. Clearly, nonverbal behavior considerations
are crucial in the public
speaking arena.

ANNETTE POWELL WILLIAMS

DYNAMICS OF
A BLACK AUDIENCE
In *Thinking on Your Feet*, Louis Nizer
advises his readers that "the art of persuasion is a complex combination of psychology, hope, prejudice, emotion, fear, facts, purpose, and
beauty. The vehicle on which they are all propelled is rhythm." According to Nizer, a speaker can expect certain conduct from his audience. It is considered improper to do anything that disturbs either the
speaker or your fellow listeners. Included in the infractions are such
things as talking to your neighbors, slouching in your seat, and laughing or snickering when the speaker has made a mistake embarrassing
to himself.

Such "courtesy" is expected and is generally given to speakers by
white audiences. It is not the case with black audiences. What constitutes courtesy to a white person may not, in fact, constitute courtesy
to a black person. Courtesy is relative to the group one finds oneself
with. To turn one's back when greeting an old friend is a courtesy to a
black person; it acknowledges that the two friends still maintain a

From Rappin' and Stylin' Out, *edited by Thomas Kochman. Copyright © Uni-*
306 *versity of Illinois Press, 1972.*

binding trust with one another. Such a gesture to a white person would be discourteous.

Very often, if a white speaker appears before a black audience, he experiences anxiety and frustration. He finds that the audience does not respond in the usual, courteous manner. An examination of the audience would reveal a good deal of activity during the speech. Commenting to neighbors, constant adjustment of the position in the seat, and turning around are frequent.

This kind of activity constitutes inattention and disrespect to the white speaker, the worst thing that could happen. To a black speaker it means something else. It means that he is communicating with his audience and that they are communicating with him. He is stirring their emotions and they are reacting to what he has to say.

In examining a black audience, certain patterns seem to unfold. Before the program begins, the audience is relaxed. Many people are sitting with their arms and/or legs crossed; they are conversing with friends and neighbors. They may be found walking, talking, or just standing along the sides looking at others.

When it is time for the program to begin, the audience composes itself. Conversations with neighbors and friends cease. People begin to find the seats they previously selected for themselves. Those seated unfold their arms, sit up straight in their seats, and uncross their legs. For the most part this movement is self-directed. As the appointed hour approaches, the ritualistic activities cease out of respect for the occasion. If one arrives at the point when most of the people are seated and quiet, then he knows the program is about to begin.

The movement which follows depends on what the speaker has to say and how he says it. Black audiences react to speakers more with their movements than with their applause; this is more prevalent when the person speaking is unfamiliar to them. If the opening remarks made by the speaker antagonize his audience, they react by keeping their arms folded during the entire speech. Some will not applaud. Some will cross their legs again, slouch in their seats, and wait until the speech is over.

When what a speaker has to say is acceptable to most members of the audience, they sit forward in their seats, or bend forward slightly. Some have their arms resting on their legs and their hands folded. In this position a person can watch the expression of others sitting around him. It is also a position which indicates that he is giving his full attention to the speaker.

Certain positions assumed by black people have their special reasons and meanings. Black people carry expressions on their faces which communicate acceptance or rejection, boredom, agreement or disagreement, embarrassment, indecisiveness, belief or disbelief. Most black people can read these facial expressions, and it is therefore important to them to be in a position where they can watch others. This probably accounts for most black people's preference for sitting in the middle of the audience.

Black people have many ways of indicating boredom. For example, cupping the chin in one's hands can signal that attention is being given —or it might indicate boredom, depending on the facial expression. Another indication of boredom appears in a person who is observed with his head slightly to the side, arms folded, in a statue-like position. Still another is in a person who repeatedly turns his head up to the ceiling and sighs an extended sigh.

Black people show agreement by nodding the head—but then, most people do. But if a speaker brings out a point that that person has never thought about, the nodding is replaced by a change of position in the seat, arms are folded, and the person rocks back and forth before assuming his original position. Before this person resettles himself, he will glance around the audience to see how others are reacting.

Some people close their eyes to indicate agreement. Others look at the persons next to them. If the person smiles at his neighbor, it indicates approval of what has been said. If the neighbor does not smile back, it indicates that he did not approve of what was said, or that he did not agree with it.

When something said sounds ridiculous to a black person, he generally will turn to another black person and give him a very hard stare when he catches his eye. Such stares translated into words would say, "Does this sound real to you?" or, "That's a bunch of shit!" or, "This cat is out of his mind!" Usually this movement is simultaneous, which makes it a source of amusement between the parties, as well as indicating that the two are of the same mind.

When a speaker says something that is embarrassing to himself, certain movements are elicited from black people. Many of them will slowly bring their hands up to rest on their cheeks until the embarrassing moment is over. Others will bend their heads back, touch their cheeks, and close their eyes. Still others will change their positions in their seats, turning around at the same time to look at the other members of the audience. In doing this, they can catch the eyes of several people and communicate a thought.

When black people are not sure whether what the person has said is believeable, some of them give one another very quick glances to ascertain what others think about that point.

When the audience does not understand what a speaker is discussing, most of them turn around nervously, glancing from side to side. An indication of total rejection is shown by turning one's head away from the speaker with eyes closed.

Cultural "understanding" can only come about after a long period of involvement with a group. The subtle ways in which black people communicate with each other, unperceived by the outsider—or, if perceived, likely to be misinterpreted—are nevertheless the cues that make for effective communication. Their correct interpretation by black speakers adds greatly to their ability to communicate with black audiences.

PUBLIC
SPEAKING
BARRIERS

The potential communication barriers in the public speaking arena are numerous. For example, both perception and nonverbal behaviors can produce disruptive forces in a public speaking transaction. Another, perhaps more feared barrier in this arena is a speaker variable called stage fright. Fear of giving a speech is to be expected, but if uncontrolled it can destroy the entire transaction. Most of us can identify either directly or vicariously with "Unaccustomed As I Am," by Shana Alexander. Her account of stage fright, although humorous, is quite real. She also offers some hints for successful speech preparation that may be valuable to many readers.

SHANA ALEXANDER

UNACCUSTOMED

AS I AM . . . I am, God help me, about to do it for the fifth time.

My hands I know will be wet and my mouth dry. There will even be
an actual bumping inside my chest as I scrape back my chair and
walk unsteadily to the podium. "Thank you very much" (gulp . . .
weak smile), "and good evening, ladies and gentlemen."

My horror of stages, speeches, spotlights and footlights is old stuff.
I am a born spectator. My natural habitat is the audience. I know my
place and it is not in the spotlight. It is back up there in the snug
anonymous dark.

There is only one vantage point in the theater that is more de-
lectable to me than a box seat and that is a stool in the wings. From
that privileged back-stage perch, one can observe both the performance
taking place on stage and the response it draws forth from the audience. One is in touch with each, yet a part of neither. As a journalist,
I have been permitted to hang around a lot of back stages—at the
circus, in a turmoil of tinsel and shouts and beasts and satin and
feathers; at Broadway openings and Balinese dance concerts, at ballet
pandemoniums and gaudy Las Vegas girl shows. Wing-watching induces in me a scarily omnipotent feeling, akin to playing God.

I first emerged from the wings in a walnut shell towed by two
mice. It was a fourth-grade production of *Thumbelina*, and my morti-
fying costume was a leaf. Merciful obscurity closed in after that until
the time came to make a speech at my eighth-grade graduation. By
then I was burdened with 20 pounds of overweight, a mouthful of
braces and a broken leg. The event was so traumatic that for the next
20 years I stayed resolutely off the stage, refusing to take part in school
plays, team athletics, dance contests or campus politics. I even got my
college diploma by mail. Though my wedding took place in the relative privacy of my parents' living room, I would have preferred the
even greater anonymity of city hall.

For years I refused all invitations to participate in panel discussions, disk-jockey interviews, political rallies, awards ceremonies or
tree plantings. I never asked questions from the floor at lectures or
volunteered to help the magician in the nightclub. At raffffles, half of
me hoped I didn't have the lucky number.

The carrot that finally coaxed me out of the wings was of all things a journalism award. No acceptance speech, they said, no award. O vanity, vanity! I said I'd be there.

But there was something more to it than that. I really started speaking for the same reason that I stopped smoking. I was ashamed of myself. It was time to grow up. But the older one gets, it seems, the harder that is to do.

As my D-day approached, I retreated. Friends had rallied round with all sorts of advice, mostly contradictory. Don't be afraid to write it out. Read it. Memorize it. Put it on cards. Speak it off the cuff. Start funny. Start dull—an early joke lets them off the hook of curiosity. Turn from side to side so they can all see you. Find one nice face in the audience and tell it all to him. Get a new dress. Get a little drunk.

By the afternoon of the speech, trying to follow all this advice at once, I sat stupefied with terror in my room in the hotel where the banquet was to be held. My new gown hung on the back of the door, flowers and telegrams began to arrive. Were they condolences? Had I already died? Set out along the desk beside the typewriter were black coffee, tranquilizers, whiskey and an enormous dessert. I swallowed first one thing and then the other, striving for equilibrium like Alice nibbling from both sides of the mushroom. The black coffee fed the writer; the whisky nourished the coward; the ice cream was for the scared child and the tranquilizers—something new—were my hole card. I barely remember going downstairs to the hotel ballroom, or the dais, or the dinner, or anything at all until I felt my wet palms gripping the smooth sides of the lectern, and heard my own weird, oddly magnified voice rumble out over the crowd.

I was most unprepared for my own total unpreparedness: I didn't know where to look, where to put my hands, where to pitch my voice, when to pause, when to smile. To be *that* unknowing rarely happens to an adult; it gave me a giddy feeling; nothing to do but push on.

After a few moments I heard faint laughter. I was not quite conscious of it at first, but then it came again a bit stronger, until I was sure I heard it, and then as I was reading I began to wait for it, and to make spaces in sentences for it, to enjoy it, and finally to play with the words and with the audience, to swoop and glide and describe arabesques with all the nutty abandon of Donald Duck on ice skates.

Success. Triumph. Waves of applause. The night came to a kind of crescendo Andy Hardy finish that I have never been able to recapture. In the next three speeches I was nearly as scared as the first time, but not nearly as good. But I am going to try it again. I am getting to know the ropes.

A good speech must be written out. In speaking, the pen is still more important than the tongue. But the rules of speech-writing are different; a different sort of carpentry is required. Adjectives are more important in speaking than in writing. The very weakness of writing, which is adjectives, is the strength of speaking. Repetition is important too; the ear has a short memory. When you listen to a speech, the words literally go in one ear and out the other. So your main point ought to come early in the speech, and there should be continual reference back to it. Make jokes, but make them slowly; don't be afraid to stretch them out. Slowness followed by sudden acceleration is good, too. So is comedy juxtaposed to sudden solemnity, or vice versa. In speaking, you can really play an audience in a way a writer never can. A speech is not a lecture. The object is not to get points over; it is to try to make people feel something. That is a terribly interesting challenge for a writer—to try to intensify with voice and delivery what you used to try to accomplish merely with words.

I am becoming fascinated with the similarities and the differences between the two modes. Though speaking is still not fun. I want very much now to learn to do it better. And I enjoy the applause. Irving Berlin was right: there is no business like show business. Among other things, an occasional show-off trip to the podium turns out to be the perfect condiment to spice the introvert writer's life.

A speech course will not teach you
to get rid of the butterflies, but it may
help you get them to fly in formation.
L. Christensen

"Nervous About That Speech?" by Stephen S. Price provides us with additional understanding of the stage fright barrier. Again, Price makes it clear that stage fright is normal and, to a certain degree, desirable. He also offers some constructive suggestions for minimizing this significant public speaking arena barrier.

STEPHEN S. PRICE

NERVOUS ABOUT THAT SPEECH?

"Self-confidence is that wonderful, assured feeling you have—just before you fall flat on your face." That was how one of my new clients felt about public speaking. Oddly enough, he was confident in other speaking situations.

The pain and frustration connected with public speech is difficult to imagine by those who have never lived through the experience.

As a group, executives make brave attempts to conquer their speaking fears. Some succeed completely. Some appear to manage an outward calmness while suppressing inner tension, and some withdraw by refusing any promotion that requires public speaking.

There is a truism about speaking tensions: It only happens to the best people. Only the conscientious individual who is concerned about doing the perfect job suffers in anticipation of possible failure.

As Winston Churchill, himself an experienced speaker, once remarked, "The maxim 'nothing avails but perfection' may be spelled paralysis."

While I was working with Edward R. Murrow as a director on some of his CBS broadcasts, he once mentioned what was obvious —that he was always tense before going on the air. He called it "the sweat of perfection."

Conscientious people feel less capable than they really are. The reason: There is a great disparity between the ideal self-image and

Stephen S. Price, "Nervous About That Speech?," reprinted from Nation's Business, *June, 1967, pp. 84–88, by permission.*

that which is possible to accomplish. This criterion of self-evaluation makes any accomplishment seem small, and never good enough. It is a perfectionistic attitude which often inspires great deeds but also creates great frustration.

It is a false yardstick that depreciates any ability, however great. A review of past performances can sometimes bring a more realistic appraisal of what is expected and what is possible.

The circumstances and pressures that surround the speaking situation become a challenge to the ego. We are anxious about possible failure; we are nervous even about being nervous. Our normal reaction to all fear is either flight or fight. When we are giving a talk, we know that we are not going to fight the audience, and we are too responsible to run away.

Nevertheless, our system is prepared for violent physical action. We must find a way to release this nervous energy in constructive expression. If we do not, it tends to perpetuate the symptoms and sensations that bring distress and discomfort to the speaker.

The speaking pressures and tensions are released because our nervous system believes we need them. It is as if we set off a false fire alarm, and now we are stuck with the apparatus—energy that is seeking an outlet. Once it is given an outlet, we can return to a relatively normal physiological rhythm.

First, remember that every experience is different. The dissimilarities are greater than the similarities. What reminds us of the past is entirely different from the present. There are rarely, if ever, any situation in life which repeat themselves. There is always a difference: time, age, mood, audience, speaker, topic, results.

Next, we must remove the mystery labels of our feelings. Our feelings have no judgment. No matter how sophisticated we are, our feelings remain on "Primitive Standard Time." They respond when we need them, and when we *think* we need them. Poise and control comes with knowledge. The strange is fearful; the unknown brings apprehension. Conversely, with understanding comes control, with familiarity come comfort.

Shattering a Myth

One perfect example of how a psychological barrier kept people from accomplishment was the myth of the four-minute mile. For over a thousand years it was an accepted "fact" that it was humanly impossible to run a mile in less than four minutes. But in 1954 an Englishman, Roger Bannister, ran the mile in less than four minutes. Since that time, many other runners have run that mile and new records are being set.

Once we have understanding, we become selective and can choose to believe the reality and challenge the myth. We are then free to believe what is possible and to assume the attitude and the actions that help us change. We are ready to take on the outward manifestations attributed to a successful speaker.

There is a classic reference to this point written by William James: "Common sense says, we lose our fortune, are sorry and weep; we meet a bear, are frightened and run; we are insulted by a rival, are angry and strike . . . the more rational statement is that we feel sorry because we cry, angry because we strike, afraid because we tremble. . . .

"Everybody knows how panic is increased by flight, and how the giving way to the symptoms of grief or anger increases the passions themselves. . . . In rage, it is notorious how we 'work ourselves up' to a climax by repeated outbursts of expression. Refuse to express a passion and it dies. Count 10 before venting your anger, and its occasion seems ridiculous. Whistling to keep up courage is no mere figure of speech. On the other hand, sit all day in a moping posture, sigh, and reply to everything with a dismal voice, and your melancholy lingers.

"There is no more valuable precept in moral education than this . . . if we wish to conquer undesirable emotional tendencies in ourselves, we must assiduously, and in the first instance cold-bloodedly, go through the *outward movements* of those contrary dispositions which we prefer to cultivate. The reward of persistency will infallibly come, in the fading out of the sullenness or depression, and the advent of real cheerfulness and kindliness in their stead. . . ."

How can this approach be applied to the speaker?

Just recently I was called in to observe a speaker who was unusually lethargic in his speech and movements. He began with a molasses-paced, interminable walk to the speaker's stand. When he spoke, his pauses were so wide that the *Queen Mary* could have passed through with room to spare.

Since he was a comer for a top management position, his boss said to me, "He's a great marketing man, but as a speaker, he's a flop. The president wants him to do something about it."

When I interviewed the man, he admitted that he behaved as he did because he was very nervous about his speaking ability and

Practice every opportunity

wanted to hide it from the audience. He said, "I figured that if I could just slow myself down, I could lasso those shook-up feelings."

He had another talk to give in two months, so we went to work. First I got him to understand how unreleased tensions can create the impression of rigidity and immobility. During practice sessions he learned to put his nervous steam to work. He became familiar with the techniques of alert gestures, accelerated speech rhythms, energetic movements and lively expressions.

During his next talk, he amazed everyone, including himself. From the moment he stood up and walked to the platform, he was like a man electrified. He packed so much power into his enthusiastic movements and energetic speech delivery that everyone in the auditorium sat up and took notice. Since he used visual aids in his talk, the microphone bothered him because he had to return to it every time. Like an old pro, he confidently pushed it aside. He noticed that the room was hot, took his coat off and invited everyone else to do the same. He swept through his presentation with an aliveness that people are still talking about.

Following the meeting, he said, "I know I was supposed to force the energy at first, until I got going. But for a minute, I didn't believe it would ever happen. Then when I saw them sit up and open their eyes—that's meat to a marketing man!"

When Eddie Rickenbacker was a guest on a radio program that I was directing, we dramatized an incident in his life story. He told of

Release tension by action

the time when at 26 he returned to a hero's welcome as the "Ace of Aces" of the Ninety-fourth Flying Squadron of which he was the commander in World War I. An important banquet was given in his honor. He stood up to a great ovation, opened his mouth to speak, and was terrified.

He mumbled a few phrases in poor grammar and sat down. He decided right there and then that this would never happen to him again. The next day he hired a coach to teach him how to speak, he asked Damon Runyon to write him a speech, he studied grammar and arranged for a long lecture tour (at $1,000 a night) and thereby conquered his fear of speaking in public.

Mr. Rickenbacker learned that each specialty requires its own preparation. A hero in battle can be a coward at the banquet when he rises to speak, unless he is prepared.

If fear and tension do nothing else but stimulate the speaker to do his homework, they have performed their natural service.

Fear and tension should be considered a positive influence which sharpens our strategy so that we may do our best. We are always facing difficulties. We make progress by meeting the challenge and conquering our fears. In that way our emotions motivate greater effort—which invites growth and development.

Delivering a talk or a presentation does take time—time to prepare. Even the more experienced speaker, whether he admits it in public or not, profits from the perspiration of preparation.

Obviously, we cannot keep a secret from our nervous system. If our nerves are stirred up in anticipation of the event, they are more tranquilized by the very fact that we have done our best to make ready.

There is a military maxim which says, "When in doubt, attack." A prepared speaker never feels cornered. Whatever doubts he may have are swept aside when he behaves with the impetus of a man who knows what he is doing.

It is this knowledge which displaces his doubts with more confidence.

Ways to Reduce Physical Tensions

☐ Breathe in rhythm—slowly, deeply.
☐ Yawn several times.
☐ Gesture and move when possible.
☐ Relax throat, jaw, shoulders.
☐ Loosen arms.

Don't Be Perfect, Just Be Good

Most successful executives aim for perfection. Yet they know that perfection is its own worst enemy. So they balance the situation, not with sloppy effort, but by coming down a few notches from their highest ideals.

They know that only a few people can swim the English Channel, but short of that, many can learn to swim expertly.

Perfection is a state of mind; it is never a reality. So the best we can do is the most we can ask of ourselves. We can always do better next time.

When Maj. Edward Bowes, who was famous as the originator of the "Original Amateur Hour" during the 1930's, made his first speech, he told of an experience which illustrates this point.

"When I first came to New York, Mark Twain gave a dinner in my honor. There were many distinguished guests, and he noticed that I was getting panicky.

"When he asked, 'You feel all right?' I said, 'Frankly, I'm scared to death. I know that I will have to speak soon, and I don't know if I'll be able to get out of my chair. When I stand up, my mind sits down!'

"An experienced public speaker, Mark Twain replied, 'It might help you, Eddie, if you keep one thing in mind. Just remember they don't expect much!' "

When a man discusses his stress in anticipation of making a presentation, more often than not he will define his fears with such words as "I just don't want to make a fool of myself." All I can tell him is that a fool doesn't go through all he is going through in trying to deliver a good talk.

If he has properly researched his topic and prepared himself in the best way he knows how, then he should be able to ride out any tensions, however unpredictable.

For the rest, he must have faith in his audience, knowing that they will appreciate his effort. With every important venture we run a risk—a risk of making fools of ourselves. And if, by earnestly performing as we do, we are labeled fools, then that's a chance we must take.

For it is that very courage to meet what comes that is written on the speaker's face and is respected by the listeners. Perhaps the first lesson of wisdom is to be willing to risk being taken for a fool—a conscientious, hard-working fool, of course.

Speak Often, Keep Up the Momentum

To gain confidence, take up the challenge to speak at every opportunity. In that way you can develop a new tolerance for the stresses and toughen your reactions as muscles are toughened by activity. We all have a marvelous capacity to adapt to the external environment. Use it; speak often.

Throw away all your fine excuses.

When it comes to public speaking and presentations, use as a verbal talisman the potent words of Robert Frost, "The only way around is through."

Those who speak incessantly tend to
break down human relationships because
of their continual overloading and
jamming of listener's pathways.
D. Barbara

Audience members' attitudes
can be significant barriers in
public speaking transactions.
The following selection, "The
Audience as Individuals,"
from the book *Persuasion:
How Opinions and Attitudes
Are Changed* by Karlins and
Abelson, discusses a public
speaking barrier called
selective exposure. As you
read the selection, you will be
made aware of how your
current attitudes become
barriers for a speaker in a
public speaking situation—
barriers because they may
prevent you from even
exposing yourself to the
speaker's message. If your
current attitudes do not
prevent you from attending
the message, they will
probably influence you to
perceive selectively (or
distort) the message and
remember only those things
with which you agree.

MARVIN KARLINS
HERBERT I. ABELSON

THE AUDIENCE
AS INDIVIDUALS When you talk, who do you think is listening?

Who is more persuasible, a man or a woman?

In order to change someone's opinion, what must you know about his reasons for holding that opinion?

Does knowing about someone's personality help you determine his susceptibility to persuasive appeals?

THE PEOPLE YOU MAY WANT MOST IN YOUR AUDIENCE ARE OFTEN LEAST LIKELY TO BE THERE

Let us assume you were a political candidate running on the Republican ticket for office. During your campaign you decide to give a series of speeches presenting your platform. What segment of the voter constituency do you think will show up to hear your address? If you guessed "mostly Democrats" you'd be wrong. You would find mostly Republicans, not Democrats or Independents, listening to Republican campaign speeches. An early investigation designed to locate the influences which determine voter preferences showed that people read the papers and listen to the speeches that support their own points of view (Lazarsfeld, Berelson, & Gaudet, 1944).

This "selective exposure" hypothesis—that people tend to expose themselves only to persuasive appeals with which they already agree—has been repeatedly supported in a wide variety of experimental settings (as the following specimen studies indicate).

Specimen Studies

1. On April 7, 1965 Lyndon Johnson made a major foreign policy speech at Johns Hopkins University. It was widely known in advance that the address would be supportive of the government's military policy in Vietnam. Prior to the speech, 187 first-year psychology students filled out an opinion questionnaire designed to assess attitudes toward the government's military policy in Vietnam. Two days after the president's address the students filled out the questionnaire a second time. They were also asked if they: "(a) had actually seen or heard the president's speech, (b) knew indirectly about the speech, or (c) had neither heard the speech nor learned anything about it afterward." The experiments hypothesized that students who supported the government's position on Vietnam would have been more likely to attend President Johnson's speech (which was congruent with their beliefs) than those students who were less favorable toward such a stand.

> Findings: *The hypothesis was supported. "Among the females,**
> *those who were inclined to support a firm stand in Vietnam were*

---

* *Initial male attitudes on Vietnam were too homogeneous to allow for selective exposure to operate.*

more likely to expose themselves to a communication in which it was evident that such a policy would be defended. Those female subjects who were only lukewarm in their support of such a policy were less inclined to attend either directly or indirectly to the President's talk" (McGinnies & Rosenbaum, 1965).

2. Some cross-cultural validation for the "selective exposure" hypothesis is provided by Lutfy Diab in his study of 260 Arab students. Psychologist Diab suspected that an individual's political views would influence his exposure to the mass media, specifically, that a person would read newspapers and listen to radio stations that supported his point of view to the exclusion of media expressing opposite points of view.

To test his assumption Diab analyzed questionnaire data from his students which revealed: (a) the newspapers and radio stations they preferred; (b) their position regarding Arab unity. Prior to examining the questionnaires, Diab had a panel of judges categorize all Arab Middle East newspapers and radio stations according to their pro- or anti-position on Arab unity. With this information Diab was in a position to see if a person's attitude on Arab unity had a bearing on his approach to the mass media.

Findings: In general, the results support the selective exposure hypothesis. Subjects who were firmly pro- or anti-Arab unity showed preferences for newspapers and radio stations expressing points of view similar to their own. Thus, as in the McGinnies and Rosenbaum study (Specimen Study 1 on p. 84), individuals exposed themselves to sources of information congruent with their own beliefs (Diab, 1965).

3. It is reasonable to assume that most advertisers are at least as (if not more) interested in reaching people who do not use their products as they are in reaching those who do. Some information on whom the ads do reach came out of an experiment designed to test this hypothesis: that *after making a decision*, people tend to look for information that supports their decision and to avoid information that conflicts with it. The hypothesis was tested by studying the readership of automobile advertisements—owners of new cars and owners of older cars. Specifically, these three propositions on car ad readership were formulated:

1. New car owners will read advertisements for their own cars more often than ads for cars which they considered but did not buy, or ads for other cars which they did not consider at all.

2. New car owners will read ads for cars they considered seriously but did not buy even less often than ads for cars they did not consider at all. (This hypothesis is in line with the idea that, after making a decision, people avoid information that conflicts with their decision.)
3. Owners of old cars will not have these patterns of readership, because the effects of a decision wear off with time.

Names of men who had recently purchased new cars were taken from a state registration list. The same list provided names of owners of old cars, cars manufactured several years before the study was made. Interviews were conducted with 65 new car owners and 60 old car owners. The car owners were told that the survey had to do with advertising. There was no mention of the real purpose of the study. As part of the interview, the respondents were asked about the magazines they read, and how thoroughly they read each one. After remembering what they could about the ads they had seen, respondents went through actual copies of the magazines and indicated the extent to which they had read each of the automobile ads. There were a number of other questions in the same vein.

Findings: *New car owners read ads for their own make of car more often than ads for any other make (support for the first hypothesis). Old car owners did not read ads for their make of car any more often than they read ads for other cars (support for the third hypothesis). New car owners did not read fewer ads for cars which they considered seriously but did not buy as compared with cars that they did not consider at all (refutation of the second hypothesis). The authors offer a possible explanation for the result which was contrary to the second hypothesis. Perhaps new car owners read ads for cars which they considered and then rejected in order to look for disadvantages in these rejected cars and thus reassure themselves of the wisdom of their decisions (Ehrlich, Guttman, Schonbach & Mills, 1957).*

4. Before leaving the topic of "selective exposure," one related issue seems worthy of examination. We have established that a person tends to expose himself only to persuasive appeals with which he already agrees. However, what if an individual encounters a presentation where both his and an opposing point of view are aired?

A study by Hans Sebald (1962) gives us some insight into this question. In this investigation 152 Ohio State University students who had watched the 1960 Kennedy-Nixon presidential debates filled out questionnaires designed to "assess their attitudes or changes of attitudes toward the two presidential candidates before and after their . . . debates." Here, then, is a situation in which an individual is exposed to two different viewpoints, one of which he supports and the other of which he opposes. What happens?

> Findings: *According to the Sebald results, a form of "selective exposure" also occurs in these circumstances. The individual attends to those segments of the communication that support his views (selective perception); perceives and recalls information only if it reinforces his prior images (selective memory); and distorts statements to eliminate dissonant material (selective distortion). In short, the listener hears what he wants to hear, based on his prior attitudes and beliefs. In the Sebald investigation this meant that the TV viewer took from the Kennedy-Nixon debates information that preserved "(1) a favorable image of the candidate of the preferred party; and (2) an unfavorable image of the candidate of the opposing party" (Sebald, 1962).*

Discussion

It seems that persuasive appeals, before they can effect opinion change, must first overcome a host of individual defenses, including selective exposure, selective perception, selective memory and selective distortion. If the Red Cross advertised a free booklet telling about the blood donor program and what it has meant in time of emergency, many of the requests for it might be expected to come from the small fraction of our citizens who have already given their blood, whereas the Red Cross, of course, would be most interested in reaching non-donors. A frequent complaint in parent-teacher associations is that the meetings are attended by parents of good students. The parents of poor students, for whom the meetings are often planned, rarely attend. A large number of such illustrations could be found to show that people look for the programs, articles and news items that support their attitudes and beliefs, and tend not to expose themselves to communications which conflict with their own viewpoints. And the support, once found, need not be laced with too many facts! In the words of one author: ". . . many people may accept something they *want* to accept as 'proved' by the flimsiest of evidence: the mere invoking of emotional appeals ('Gentlemen of the jury, this woman is a mother'), the introduction of absolute irrelevancies ('Fascism is OK because Mussolini made the trains run on time') or the shallowest false logic or syllogistic reasoning ('No cat has eight tails. Every cat has one more tail than no cat. Every cat has nine tails')" (Miller, 1946).

SUGGESTED READINGS: SELECTIVE EXPOSURE

1. Diab, L. Studies in social attitudes: II. Selectivity in mass communication media as a function of attitude-medium discrepancy. *The Journal of Social Psychology*, 1965, 67, 297–302.
2. McGinnies, E. & Rosenbaum, L. A test of the selective-exposure hypothesis in persuasion. *The Journal of Social Psychology*, 1965, 61, 237–240.
3. Sebald, H. Limitations of communication: Mechanisms of image maintenance in form of selective perception, selective memory and selective distortion. *Journal of Communication*, 1962, 12, 142–149.

I heard a very profound statement last night. Unfortunately, I've forgotten it. J. Lair

---

In keeping with the general
notion of barriers to a
speaker's effectiveness in a
public speaking encounter, we
offer the following selection
from *Human Relations in
Teaching* by Howard Lane and
Mary Beauchamp. In the
preceding selection, Karlins
and Abelson addressed
themselves to individual
barriers to speaker influence.
In this selection, the authors
demonstrate how institutions
and organizations, as well as
individuals, have built-in
resistors to change.

HOWARD LANE
MARY BEAUCHAMP

CHANGE
AS CONTINUOUS
CREATION

Individuals and Institutions Find Advantage in Remaining Fixed

Always there are people and groups who find advantage in things as they are, and prefer them to remain unchanged. A little child, although liking to grow up, tends to cling to the advantages of his babyhood. The owner of slum property, getting profitable rentals with little expense, tends to oppose their replacement by public, non-profit housing. New Yorkers have long opposed strenuously the development of the St. Lawrence waterway which will make shipping more convenient and cheaper for much of America but will likely take business away from the Port of New York.

From Howard Lane and Mary Beauchamp, Human Relations in Teaching: The Dynamics of Helping Children Grow. *Copyright © 1955. Reprinted by permission of Prentice-Hall, Inc. Englewood Cliffs, New Jersey.*

When America was young it was organized politically into counties that had capitals or county seats to which every citizen could travel and return home in a day. This county was the citizen's government as he felt the need for and used it. Today the county system makes no sense. New York City includes five counties. Rural citizens can travel across a dozen counties in a day. Yet the numerous county officials and their friends and relatives would doubtless defeat any proposals to modernize their political organization. The workers of Chicago, Philadelphia, New York, Washington come from several states yet they cling to varied systems of taxation and oppose an over-all consistent system of state or national taxation.

One of man's favorite songs is "Rock of Ages." We like the security of the familiar. We tend to think well of the way we have lived. It is rather normal for us to believe that the kind of education that made us what we are is right for our children.

One of the authors of this book was one day exhorting a group of rural school teachers to stop aping the city schools and to take advantage of their informal, ungraded schools in the country. At the close of this exhortation a small elderly man rushed up to him and said emphatically, "That's a heck of a necktie you've got on." And followed in a moment with a query, "You didn't like that, did you? Well, let me tell you, folks likes their ideas even better than their neckties." He had been made uncomfortable by suggestions for making sharp changes in his ways of teaching. It was necessary for his self-esteem for him to believe that he was already doing pretty well.

An important source of maladjustment of the personality and of all social institutions is unevenness of change. Often the oversized child with normal mental development has a bad time of it with his elders because they expect him to act in accordance with his size. The youngster who becomes devoted to scholarship because of lack of adequate social development becomes increasingly a problem to himself, although teachers tend to applaud him. A great deal of harm

is done the world by men of substance who have not outgrown their adolescence and who have a tendency to throw their weight around. The adult who has never been able to free himself from the domination of his parents is often judged devoted and generous. *We deem it of great importance that teachers and parents shall value children in their own terms.*

Human institutions arise as groups endeavor to satisfy their needs. Daniel Boone was not a Boy Scout. Scouting arose with city life in recognition of the need of youngsters to go about in groups and keep relatively close to nature. At seventy-three Jefferson penned these words of wisdom which we record in bronze letters but often fail to heed:

> *But laws and institutions must go hand in hand with the progress of the human mind. As that becomes more developed, more enlightened, as new discoveries are made, new truths discovered and manners and opinions change, with the change of circumstances, institutions must advance also to keep pace with the times. We might as well require a man to wear still the coat which fitted him when a boy as civilized society to remain ever under the regimen of their barbarous ancestors.*[1]

It is interesting and rather sad to note how quickly institutions grow old. Originally they are set up to serve people. Soon they set down principles, develop ways of procedure that tend to become fixed. Soon they are appealing for the loyalty, conformity, devotion, and support of the persons they originally set out to serve. It appears that demands for loyalty are important early signs of decay of social in-

[1] *Thomas Jefferson in a letter to Samuel Kercheval from his home at Monticello, July 12, 1816. (Recorded in interior wall of Jefferson Memorial, Washington, D.C.)*

stitutions. Any institution finding it necessary to demand the loyalty of the people it presumes to serve must recognize the simple fact that it has failed to keep up with the times. Probably the most revolutionary statement in the history of human expression is, "Man was not made for the Sabbath; the Sabbath was made for man."

Failure to Change Brings Misery

But failure to change, to go along with creation, results in perversion, misery, degradation, violence, and untimely death. Enlightened Londoners knew long before Dickens' time that they should clear out their slums. Instead of doing it by deliberate, creative planning they left it to the bombs of the mad Hitler. The Congress of the United States cannot possibly function today as a calm, deliberate assembly of responsible representatives of the people as our constitutional fathers envisioned it. It has become a complex organization of committees, professional staff members, organized lobbying. A visitor to the Congress sees little of what was described in his civics book as the methodology of Congressional endeavor. Certainly we know that the attempt to seek security in things as they are whether it be for a person, an institution, or a nation is doomed to result in failure. Our only security lies in developing skills in anticipating and managing change.

Always there are those among us who seek to stem the tide of creation or to exert force contrary to it. These are the evil ones. Man's orderly progress toward cooperation has been constantly retarded by the beneficiaries of the *status quo*.

We might at this point illustrate some of the methods by which creative processes are thwarted. The personality needing to maintain its own integrity and security is exploited by threats of dire consequences that will result from change. The history of man's fears might be written in terms of the use of color words intended to inspire fear. Currently our genuine fear of some communists is being extended and exploited to the point that any person or idea can be discredited by the simple inquiry, "Isn't he, or isn't it, communistic?" Every age and region develops its opprobrious terms with which to oppose change. Change in the practices of schools has been markedly frustrated by making the term "progressive" a nasty one. We should look upon a *progressive educator* as we would a progressive physician or a progressive farmer—*one who does the best*

that he knows how in the light of up-to-date knowledge and facilities.
We know some individuals who deplore progress in education who
have already engaged the ministrations of progressive morticians.

Some of the processes of social relationships are being expertly
employed to prevent change. Influential legislators in our national and
state governments kill legislation by referral back to committee. Complex administrative structure often makes change so difficult to attain
that individuals desiring to change become weary and cease to bother.

---

*I have the choice of being right or
being human.*   H. Prather

From Hugh Prather, *Notes to Myself*. Reprinted
by permission of Real People Press.

The following selection offers
some good advice for overcoming a common com-
munication barrier in the
public speaking arena, namely,
poor listening. Although poor
listening habits are barriers to
communication in any arena,
they are especially problem-
atic in the public speaking
arena. An audience member
can feel much more secure in
his anonymity in the public
speaking arena than in interpersonal or public speaking
situations. As a result, the
speaker must attempt to cope
with poor listeners and
listeners must make special
efforts to overcome their poor
listening habits. In "Are You
Listening" by Stuart Chase,
we are given several specific
pointers for improving in this
area.

STUART CHASE

ARE YOU
LISTENING?
Listening is the other half of talking. If people stop
listening it is useless to talk—a point not always appreciated by
talkers.

Listening isn't the simple thing it seems to be. It involves interpretation of both the literal meaning of the words and the intention
of the speaker. If someone says, "Why, Jim, you old horse thief!" the
words are technically an insult; but the tone of voice probably indicates affection.

Americans are not very good listeners. In general they talk more than they listen. Competition in our culture puts a premium on self-expression even if the individual has nothing to express. What he lacks in knowledge he tries to make up for by talking fast or pounding the table. And many of us while ostensibly listening are inwardly preparing a statement to stun the company when we get the floor. Yet it really is not difficult to learn to listen—just unusual.

Listening is regarded as a passive thing, but it can be a very active process—something to challenge our intelligence. A stream of messages is coming in to be decoded: how close can we come to their real meaning? What is the speaker trying to say? . . . How does he know it? . . . What has he left out? . . . What are his motives?

Sometimes only about a quarter of an audience understands clearly what a speaker has said. To sharpen the ears of its members, the New York Adult Education Council has inaugurated "listening clinics." One member reads aloud while the others around the table concentrate on what he is saying. Later they summarize what they have heard and compare notes—often to find that the accounts differ widely. Gradually the listeners improve, and often they find themselves transferring the skill to business and home affairs. As one member said:

"I became aware of a new attitude. I found myself attempting to understand and interpret the remarks of my friends and associates from *their* viewpoint, and not from my own as I had done previously."

Some years ago Major Charles T. Estes of the Federal Conciliation Service was called in to help settle a long-term dispute between a corporation and its unions. The Major proceeded to invent a technique for listening that has since had wide application in the labor field. He asked delegates from both union and management to read aloud the annual contract which was in dispute. Each man read a section in his turn; then all discussed it. If a dispute began to develop, the clause was put aside for later examination.

In two days the delegates really knew what was in the contract, and were competent to go back and tell their fellow managers or fellow workers what it contained. "We had conditioned them to communicate," said the Major. The contract was not rewritten but has continued in force with very few changes for ten years. Good listening had transformed bad labor relations into good ones.

Carl R. Rogers, University of Chicago psychologist, suggests a game to be played at a party. Suppose a general discussion—say on the French elections—becomes acrimonious. At this point Rogers asks the company to try an experiment. Before Jones, who is on the edge of his chair, can reply to the statement just made by Smith, he must summarize what Smith has said in such a way that Smith accepts it. Any attempt to slant or distort is instantly corrected by the original speaker. This means careful listening, during which emotion is likely to cool.

The result is that everyone in the circle, by listening and rephrasing, acquires a working knowledge of the other fellow's point of view, even if he does not agree with it. The players are quite likely to increase their knowledge of the subject—something that rarely happens in the usual slam-bang argument. The experiment takes courage, says Rogers, because in restating the other man's position one runs the risk of changing one's own.

F. J. Roethlisberger of the Harvard Business School, in a recent study of training courses for supervisors, describes a significant contrast in listening. An executive calls foreman Bill to his office to tell him about a change in Bill's department. A casting will be substituted for a hand-forged job, and the executive tells Bill how to do it.

"Oh yeah?" says Bill.

Let us follow two steps which the boss might take at this point. First, suppose he assumes that "Oh yeah" means Bill does not see how to do the new job, and it is up to the boss to tell Bill. This he proceeds to do clearly and logically. Nevertheless, Bill is obviously freezing up, and presently things begin to happen inside the boss. "Can it be," he asks himself, "that I have lost my power to speak clearly? No, Bill just doesn't understand plain English; he's really pretty dumb." The look which accompanies this unspoken idea makes Bill freeze up even harder. The interview ends on a note of total misunderstanding.

But, says Roethlisberger, suppose the boss sees from the "Oh yeah" that Bill is disturbed, and he tries to find out why. He says: "What's your idea about how the change-over ought to be made, Bill? You've been in the department a long time. Let's have it. I'm listening."

Things now begin to happen inside Bill. The boss is not laying it on the line, he's willing to listen. So ideas come out, slowly at first, then faster. Some are excellent ideas and the boss becomes really interested in Bill's approach—"Smarter man than I thought!" A spiral reaction is set up, as Bill begins to realize that he never appreciated the boss before. The interview ends on a note of close harmony.

In the first case, the boss did not listen to Bill, he *told* Bill; and though the telling was clear enough the goal moved farther away. In the second case, the boss listened until he had located what was worrying Bill; then they went along together.

So far, we have been talking about sympathetic listening in face-to-face situations, to make sure we grasp the speaker's full meaning. But critical listening, too, is needed in a world full of propaganda and high-pressure advertisers. Here are some techniques which help to develop critical listening to a speech or a conversation, a sales talk at your door or the testimony of a witness before a jury:

Look for motives behind the words. Is the speaker talking chiefly in accepted, appealing symbols—Home, Mother, the Founding Fathers, Our Glorious Heritage, and so on—avoiding the need for thought, or is he really trying to think? Speeches are often solidly larded with symbols, and the well-trained ear can identify them a long way off.

Is the speaker dealing in facts or inferences? With practice you can train your ear to find this distinction in political and economic talk, and to follow the shifts from one level to the next.

The listener should also consider his own attitude toward the speaker. Is he prejudiced for or against him? Is he being fair, objective, sympathetic?

The sum of careful listening is to work actively to discover how the speaker feels about events, what his needs and drives appear to be, what kind of person he is. The appraisal can only be rough, but it can be a decided help in dealing with him, in giving him a fair answer.

One other thing: I find that careful listening also helps me to keep quiet rather than sound off foolishly. The best listeners listen alertly, expecting to learn something and to help create new ideas.

Are you listening?

I can listen to someone without hearing him. Listening is fixing my attention only on the other person. Hearing requires that I listen inside me as I listen to him. Hearing is a rhythm whereby I shuttle between his words and my experience. It includes hearing his entire posture: his eyes, his lips, the tilt of his head, the movement of his fingers. It includes hearing his tone of voice and his silences. And hearing also includes attending to my reactions, such as the "sinking feeling" I get when the other person has stopped hearing me. H. Prather

---

From Hugh Prather, *Notes to Myself.* Reprinted by permission of Real People Press.

PUBLIC
SPEAKING
SELF-DISCLOSURE

It is rather difficult to restrict any discussion of self-disclosure to the public speaking arena. One major reason for this is that the type of open and honest communication one normally classifies as self-disclosure is rarely heard in the public speaking arena. As we have indicated in the earlier treatments of this factor, self-disclosure is usually accompanied by personal risks. If self-disclosure is risky business in intrapersonal or interpersonal encounters, it is easy to understand why one rarely discloses in the public speaking arena.

The following reading, "The Search for Identity: Egocentric Speech," from the book *Speech and Man* by Charles Brown and Charles Van Riper presents us with unique insight into the personableness of communication in the public speaking arena.

CHARLES BROWN
CHARLES VAN RIPER

THE
SEARCH FOR IDENTITY:
EGOCENTRIC SPEECH

When, with an ear slightly askew so that it can truly listen, we scrutinize the torrent of talk that ebbs and flows about us, we note with some surprise that a very large portion of that speech is being employed for purposes other than the communication of information. All these people seem to be talking about themselves—sometimes almost *to* themselves. With this insight comes a second one: Much of our own speech is similarly egocentric. It is the thesis of this chapter that egocentric speech fulfills the deep human need to know who we are. If we can understand this immensely important power possessed by speech, we may be able to exercise it more effectively for our own fulfillment.

The perpendicular pronoun *I* is perhaps the most dominant, if not the most frequent, word in the speech of that mouthy mammal, man. Researchers Henle and Hubbel(1) recorded many samples of adult conversation, and they found that the egocentric pronouns, *I, me, my, mine,* and *myself,* occurred in from 30 to 40 per cent of all the remarks spoken by their subjects. Another researcher (who shall be nameless here) procured the data for his unpublished master's thesis by boring a hole in the floor of his apartment, inserting a microphone, and recording everything that was said in the apartment below. In this lower apartment lived a "typical American family," consisting of a father, mother, and two children—a son and a daughter. The researcher recorded everything that they said for a month and then spent a year analyzing his data. He concluded finally that most of what had been said (81.3 per cent) in that family during that time consisted of sentences about the self. Anyone with an analytical ear would not be surprised at his findings. As the poet Walt Whitman wrote, sounding his barbaric yawp over the roofs of the world, "I celebrate myself and sing myself."

Listen, if you will, to the staccato of the perpendicular pronoun in the speech about you: "And I said to him, I said. . . ." "I'm the kind of person who. . . ." "I think that. . . ." The *I*'s explode like popcorn in the conversational pan. Indeed, it is difficult to speak without them. To test this statement, we assigned some of our students the project of determining how long they could resist the use of one or another of the egocentric pronouns during an entire morning. Not a single one was able to prevent the occurrence of these pronouns for more than half an hour of conversation, and most of them slipped within five minutes. One girl plaintively protested that we'd almost made her mute, and another reported hesitant speech to a degree that resembled stuttering.

Egocentric speech pervades all ordinary communication; it is found in every mouth. Self-reference is the keynote to our verbal melody; we wander away from it on occasion, but over and over again we return to it. You will hear egocentricity in the casual conversation of the man on the street, in the shrill chatter of a cocktail party, and more softly in the murmuring of two lovers in the moonlight. Into the black cups of a million telephones go ten million *I*'s each day. In every store and business and school in the land we hear speech centered about the self. Surely something so universal must serve some basic purpose.

The Heart of the Matter

More than two thousand years ago, Socrates uttered a prescription for the ills of mankind that we still find fundamental, though difficult to fulfill. It was "Know thyself!" In every generation, the baby in the crib, exploring his fingers and toes, seeking to define the image of his body so that he can control it, is responding to that universal command. Since the dawn of history, man's progress has been measured by his mastery of the unknown. Yet the major mystery remains—man's own nature. Each of us in his own way must do what he can to understand who he is. Unfortunately, most of us are at least partial strangers to ourselves. We know what we look like because we have viewed ourselves in mirrors and photographs, but in large measure the person within the skin escapes us. Often we define ourselves only through the words with which other people have described us and those, as we have said earlier, may be distorted words. We must not know ourselves only through our reflection in *their* flawed mirrors. When our self-concepts are false, then troubles come. Across the barrier of two thousand years Socrates still speaks to each of us.

Speech and Self-Escape

Some speakers use their speech not to discover but to cover. They cannot bear to let others really know who they are, probably because they cannot bear the self-confrontation that comes by reflection. Some of these resemble magicians, deft and quick with their verbal sleight of hand, using their speech to conceal rather than to reveal themselves. Some of these speech magicians are tremendously glib. They seem to be able to speak fluently and copiously on any subject, in any situation, and for any length of time. When they have finished their almost compulsive logorrhea, however, it is very difficult to know what they have said. It is also difficult to know very much about them—which is why they speak that way. They are octopi, squirting a murky torrent of words to conceal themselves. They are not to be envied. An octopus is not usually a treasured companion.

There are also the verbal artists and offstage actors, those who do not dare be themselves and must paint pictures or play false roles instead. Some of these artists who paint pictures of themselves with words become very skillful, and their creations are often attractive. But they are not true. Sooner or later, the fraudulence will be exposed. We have nothing really to offer except ourselves. We are what we are, always with some flaws. Shall we be actors or persons? That is the question. We greatly admire the competence of skilled actors—but only on stage. We have known sad souls who have spent their lives and energies trying to sustain a false illusion about themselves. We have known a few who were able to so immerse themselves in false roles that they sounded completely sincere. But, as Wendell Johnson, the speech pathologist, once remarked, even a cockroach can be sincere. The place for an actor is on the stage, not on the platform or in the discussion group and certainly not in the normal verbal intercourse of living. Let us be ourselves when we speak! Security is the ability to tolerate liabilities and to do the best we can with what we have.

The Exploratory Function of Egocentric Speech

We have said that speech is introductory, that it is used to reveal the speaker. We must also make clear that it has another important function: to probe and test and reveal the listener. Speech, and we will develop this theme later, is a two-way process. There are always messages flowing both ways, even when the listener is silent. His facial expressions, his postures, and his body movements can be eloquent indeed. The speaker who attempts to ignore this feedback is most unwise. Not only will he be likely to lose his listeners in a hurry but, more important still, he loses another chance to know himself. In our search for identity we find it in the mirrors our listeners hold up to us.

The insect has antennae; we have speech. Every new audience, every new listener is an unknown, and the unknown often is colored more or less with threat. Accordingly, when the beginning speaker confronts such a situation he tends to recoil from the threatening audience contact, refusing to look at the listeners, and exposing as little of himself as possible. This is, of course, all wrong, as he will soon learn. What he must do is to use his speech to scan his audience, to explore the unknown, to seek the identification which will enable his message to be understood and accepted.

A skilled and experienced speaker knows this well. Even before he begins, he scrutinizes and listens to the hum of his audience; he learns as much as he can about its composition. Then, when he starts speaking, it is fascinating to watch his verbal radar at work, sending out his speech signals and scanning the feedback, hunting for the little cues that indicate that he and his listeners are in tune. And even after he has achieved this "fix," as the technicians call it, his radar never stops scanning for reduced impact, for rejection, for the first signs of listener loss. When he senses any of these reactions, he varies his output until once again the feedback indicates that he and his audience are one.

This same process can occur even in ordinary conversation. We watch our listeners and examine their verbal responses not only to find out if they understand us, but also to discover whether they accept us. If the aspect of the self we have exhibited in words evokes approval, then we realize that this feature is one that we can cherish. A little anecdote may illustrate this point. One of our students told us this tale:

> All my life I've been shy and mousy. I've been trained for years always to try to please, to hide my resentments, to be nice. Well, the other day I was talking to a boy who was needling me and teasing me, and suddenly, out of the blue, I just up and told him to go to hell. Why, I've never said anything like that in my whole life and I was just sick after I'd said it. But you know what happened? He looked at me with real interest and said, "Boy, I didn't know you had fire in you. Well, well, well." And I've got a date with him tonight!

Similarly, when the things we say create rejection, we learn from these rejecting responses the seamier sides of self, those that we should try to change or inhibit. The more we talk to people, the more we find out who we are. But we must scan our reflections in our listeners' mirrors if we hope to know.

One of the most effective ways of exploring an audience or a listener for these reflections of self is through the use of egocentric speech. People are interested in people. They prick up their ears and respond more visibly when they hear egocentric speech. The personal pronouns and statements about self are little gongs that ring for attention and arouse judgmental responses. The personal anecdote always seems to have some special power in this regard. In egocentric speech we have perhaps the most efficient tool that has been invented for scanning our listeners. By revealing one of our many sides of self and scrutinizing the feedback, we can explore not only our audience but ourselves. If the side of self we show is rejected or ignored, we at least know something very important about our listeners, and we can then show them other facets which they may accept.

Trail's End

Since we continue to change as long as life continues, the search for a fixed identity is probably doomed to failure. Yet at any given period of time we can hope to know the cluster of roles about our body images that we call the self. Such knowledge, with its attendant peace and security, is not won easily. There are many barriers and traps along the way. But the way is the speech way. We come to know who we are by knowing how we differ from others, and this means that we must talk to them. No one ever came to know himself by contemplating his silent navel. We need to identify with others to discern the discrepancies which add up to our own individuality. To find yourself you must lose yourself in others—an ancient paradox. Every time we speak to another person, seeking the identification that is so implicit in communication, we not only come to know the understandings and features and feelings we hold in common, but also those which we do not. We have to travel abroad to know what it means to be an American; we have to know a semi-saint to know the sinner side of self.

Thus, through speech we find the means to obey that ancient command of Socrates. We will find ourselves defined by the words which we speak to other people and those with which they answer, by revealing ourselves to them and having them revealed in turn to us. By knowing others we shall know ourselves. Truly this speech is a powerful magic.

Most everyone of us in one way or the other wants to be heard.   D. Barbara

---

"The Early Morning of the
Human Day" by Wendell
Johnson contains some of the
most profound statements
concerning self-disclosure in
the public speaking arena that
we have ever read. Johnson
provides us with an exciting
eavesdropping position from
which to listen to speakers.

WENDELL JOHNSON

THE EARLY MORNING OF THE HUMAN DAY

If we would understand a man by his words it is best that we listen to what he says when he is either in trouble or in love. For if we do, and if we are quiet and attentive, we will notice that no matter how fully he may be taken over by the illusion that it is to us he speaks, he talks at such times most surely to himself.

Pondering this, we come in time to realize that every speaker is his own most captive listener. And as we grasp the meaning of this more and more firmly, we are appalled by it. Because now we see something that had quite escaped our notice before. We had not often thought of speakers as their own listeners, and so we had not attended to them in a spirit of eavesdropping, as though listening in while they were talking to themselves. And now, in the spirit of eavesdropping, we can hardly help noticing that people talking about themselves and their private desperations are saying the most fantastic things to us, to themselves, that is. They are saying so much that is just not true, and much that is questionable at best, and they are saying it all as though it were to be taken for granted as wholly true, listening all the while quite unwonderingly to themselves saying these things. What is even more distressing, there is such a great deal that they might be saying to themselves that would be true and liberating, and we wait for them to say it, but they so seldom do, at least not in any very clear and self-informing fashion. So it is that, listening to themselves, there is so much they rarely hear that they should be hearing over and over again.

Watching all this going on in front of us, there are many things we call to mind. Blind men, for example. A blind man, we realize, has no way of knowing what precisely there is about a sunset that he doesn't see. We wonder whether he can even know that he is not seeing a sunset. Indeed, it would seem that a blind person who has never known what seeing itself is like could hardly know at all that he does not see—or, at least what he would understand by this must necessarily be quite different from what we who can see would understand by it.

And so we think of blind men and sunsets as we sit listening to people talking—to themselves—about their troubles, wondering whether they could possibly know what they are not saying, whether they could even be aware of the fact that they are not saying it. Listening, we can find no way to believe that they understand the difference it would make to them if they knew not only what they do not know but also that they do not know it.

Observing more closely—which means, most particularly with fewer preconceptions—we begin to see that what is still more important is the fact that they do not even realize that they are talking to themselves, that they are being affected by their own words. Most people, most of us, appear to believe that we shouldn't talk to ourselves, so far are we from knowing that we do in fact talk to ourselves—not usually aloud, of course—unceasingly and unavoidably all day long. And if we thought we did talk to ourselves we wouldn't admit that we do, so far are we from understanding that most of what we experience as thinking, wondering, "making up our minds," regretting, or longing, or being contented is a kind of talking we do to ourselves every day from morning till night—and on through the night in the free movies inside our heads that we call our dreams.

Pursuing such reflections, we come at last to feel strangely dumbfounded. Can it really be true, this deep unawareness that we seem to have of the unceasing symbolic processes inside our own heads? This great never-lifting mist of unconsciousness through which we appear to move so unsteadily—can this be real?

And can it be, as it surely seems, that this all-engulfing gray mist of unperceptiveness through which we grope is inhabited—is haunted? It appears to be haunted indeed, not only by the disembodied evil spirits and gods of our own unremembered creation, but also by the disfigurements of our fellows which we abundantly fashion from our private misunderstandings and discontents. It is haunted, as well, and thickly, by grotesque reflections of ourselves, as though we were moving through a shadowy hall of mirrors that we do not remember having entered and from which it does not occur to us to seek an exit.

Certainly all this is not something that we are able to capture, if only briefly, and to contemplate with wonder, and then fling carelessly away upon the unreturning wind. Above all, we feel driven to make quite sure that what we seem to see and hear is not, after all, illusion. For, certainly, if it is not illusion this can only mean that men—we, that is—are still wandering about in the early morning of the human day.

We have only begun to notice where we are and what we are about. What thinking we have done certainly has not been concerned primarily with ourselves. Most of us, if we can be honest, will admit that we have done precious little thinking of any systematic sort about the deeper reasons for our conduct and particularly about the process of thinking itself, especially our own. We have, however, done some thinking of other kinds—and it has been quite effective and suggests that we do have promising ability—we have done some thinking about such things as oil, coal, metals and the like. We have learned to process natural materials in most impressive ways, and even to create synthetic substances that nature forgot to contrive. We have made wheels and levers, invented engines, learned to fly, and put together enormous factories turning out products made wonderful by the amazing principle of interchangeable parts. We can send a message around the world before we can finish a sneeze. We are by no means stupid. In many ways we have shown that we are incomparably more clever than even the shrewdest primate or the most meticulous wasp.

It is our very cleverness, however, that we understand so dimly. The individuals among us who have been the most clever—the Galileos, Shakespeares, Einsteins—we don't pretend to understand very well. We say they are geniuses, which is a way of shrugging our shoulders, of saying nothing except something like, "It is His will," or, in common slang, "Search me!" So we express our feelings, wanting explanation. So far from understanding our "geniuses" we sometimes become greatly afraid and distrustful of them. We have killed a few, tortured many, and inconvenienced nearly all of them.

With respect to the dangers of man's destructiveness, it is later than we think—because with respect to the cultivation of man's constructive and co-operative tendencies, it is far earlier than most of us imagine. It is so early that there are men still living who were children when the world's first laboratory for the scientific study of human behavior was established by Wilhelm Wundt at Leipzig, Germany, in

1879. And this was a very small laboratory. Even so, with few exceptions, there was nothing like it in the United States until the present century. The first institute in America devoted to the scientific investigation of normal children, the Child Welfare Research Station at Iowa City, was not established until 1916.

It seems likely that few of today's leaders in government and public affairs in this and other countries have more than a freshman-course knowledge of the science of human behavior and its imperfections. And these imperfections are all too often those from which, in various forms and degrees, they themselves suffer—with consequences from which we all suffer. Moreover, most commentators and historians seem not to be properly trained to note or evaluate this crucial circumstance.

Surely no other single fact could have more important effects in relation to public affairs, and so ultimately in relation to our private affairs. Listening to men of state talking about the national and world problems confronting them, we cannot help recalling ordinary people talking about their own personal problems. There are in some measure the same indications that the speakers are naïve with respect to the psychological and symbolic—and so the human—factors involved in the problems they are talking about. There is also a similar tendency to speak with a firmer tone of finality than the speakers' apparent knowledge and comprehension would appear to warrant. There is the same failure, more often than we would wish, to ask the needed questions and to say the more constructive things that might be said, and the same apparent lack of awareness of all that is not being said. And there is a like tendency for the speakers not to realize clearly that they are their own most affected listeners.

We think of blind men and sunsets.

We need greatly, as surely we all appreciate, to have in high places men capable of speaking to themselves in public with wholesome effects on themselves and on the people who listen to them. We need leaders who realize, at the very least, that they are in fact talking to themselves as well as to others, and who are disposed to listen thoughtfully to their own voices with the welfare of all their other listeners constantly in mind. In the meantime we can protect ourselves against either cultivated or witless persuasiveness, most especially our own, only if we are trained to listen alertly, not only to others but to ourselves as well. Sound is so much with us that we perform the wonder of listening with very nearly the innocence of the beasties afield. We listen, save in our keener moments, as artlessly as we breathe. But, while under practically all circumstances Nature and the medulla oblongata will attend to our breathing for us, we can entrust our listening to our reflexes only at the risk of losing our birthrights.

The art of talking to ourselves is an auditory art as much as it is a vocal one. Its cultivation requires us to listen well through all the hours of day upon day to what we tell ourselves as we give the only answers we can fashion to the questions we are driven to design.

We ask ourselves. . . . We say unto ourselves. . . . And, listening in, we come, if we are watchful and reflective, to know shade by shade, though never wholly, the persons we have been and are and are becoming.

No matter what we talk about, we are talking about ourselves.   H. Prather

---

From Hugh Prather, *Notes to Myself.* Reprinted by permission of Real People Press.

PUBLIC
SPEAKING
EFFECTS

. . . as we make in our throats the
sounds of language, we are blown by
winds of our own blowing.
W. Johnson

It is difficult to understand or predict the specific effects of per-suasive attempts in the public speaking arena. We often exaggerate the potential effects and imagine ourselves at the mercy of skillful public speaking manipulators. It is fairly established, however, that few significant individual, group, or societal changes occur solely as the result of exposure to one public speech. It is more reasonable to compare single speeches to single conversations in terms of probable effects. Actually, the public speaking arena is usually not the most effective arena in which to persuade. A per-son is normally much more susceptible to persuasive attempts in the more personal interpersonal and small group arenas.

"The Art of Persuasion" by Gilbert Highet describes the persuasive effects of public speaking quite realistically. One of the major conclusions advanced by Highet is that the effects are gradual.

GILBERT HIGHET

THE ART
OF PERSUASION A strange enterprise, persuasion.

What makes us think that we can change another man's mind,
simply by talking to him? Surely it argues a great deal of confidence in
our own powers, in his malleability, and ultimately in the force of
speech, or reason, or both. It is tricky enough to try to persuade an
individual—a wife or husband, a friend or partner, a business prospect,
a rebellious daughter, an angry policeman. But how difficult is it to
influence a group of people—a hall full of wildcat strikers, a meeting
of creditors, a mutinous crew, or a jury?

Hard it is, surely. Yet it is done, and done constantly. When it is
well done, the patient scarcely feels it. Usually he thinks that he has
made his own decision, or that he has, through his own perspicacity,
managed to discover the truth. Once when Lord Brougham, the brilliant nineteenth-century lawyer, had won a difficult case, one of his
juniors fell into conversation with a juryman leaving the courtroom.
"Heavens," said the juryman, "what a wonderful lawyer that Mr. Savage is, to be sure! He does make a noble speech!" Brougham's assistant
heard this with astonishment, for Savage had appeared on the losing
side. "Well now," he said, "I should have thought Lord Brougham was
the better lawyer. Didn't he win the verdict?" "Oh yes," said the juryman, "but then you see it was easy enough for him, he had all the
right on his side."

That was a perfect example of persuasion, smoothly applied and
painlessly concluded. As long as he lived, that juror would be convinced that he and his peers had merely looked at the facts on both
sides and assessed their weight. He would never realize that Lord
Brougham had persuaded him to think one set of facts heavier than
the other.

Very few of us can have such power as that. Yet we all spend
much of our lives *trying* to persuade other people to do things for our
sake. Parents attempt to influence children; young men woo girls and
vice versa; husbands and wives are continually endeavoring to persuade each other, although a lot of their effort is wasted and some of
it backfires. And what is business but persuading the public to buy?
What is politics but persuading the public to vote for this and support
that and endure these for the promise of those?

If that is so, then how is persuasion, really skillful and effective

Appeared originally in the January 1951 issue of Vogue. *Copyright* © *1951 by*
The Condé Nast Publications, Inc.

persuasion, managed? If it is a fundamental activity, it must have a few basic principles.

It looks as though there were two different types of persuasion. One is the ordinary type, which we all try to do. The other is more mysterious and less logical, hard to resist and hard to understand. Suppose we look at the ordinary type first.

Anyone who wishes to win over an individual or a group must have something to offer. He can not bargain unless he has something to bargain with. Therefore, before starting, he should be quite clear what inducement he intends to put before his victim. It need not be large. It need not be lasting. But it must be attractive. The biggest and simplest mistakes are usually made at this stage. Sometimes the operator starts talking without having an exact idea of the size and scope of his own offer. He may realize too late that he hasn't offered enough, and then try to increase the bid, and meet a resistance which has grown inflexible. Sometimes he talks himself into offering far too much, and loses on the deal. (This is Reverse Persuasion.) Often he attempts to negotiate without offering anything tangible or interesting, and thinks he has been unjustly treated when the persuadee refuses.

An even commoner mistake is made by those unfortunates who choose the wrong inducement. A hook baited with clam will catch a sea bass, but if you drop it into a trout stream, you will get no trout. So, first, you should make up your mind about the nature of your inducement. And, second, you should think about it in connection with your patient, until you are quite sure it will really attract him. If it leaves him cold, you lose. If it repels him, the result may be disastrous.

For instance, when husbands and wives try to persuade each other, the chief consideration they have to offer is continued happiness in marriage. "You ought to do this, darling, because it will make us both happy—even happier than we are now." That is the standard married argument, and it is most effective when it is put like that. But there are difficult points in marriage at which such inducements have no real meaning. A wife or a husband sometimes begins to reflect that marriage is no good anyhow so that is useless to go on tinkering with it. At this point, bad persuasion will cause an explosion. A wife will say to her young husband, "If you go out drinking again next Saturday, I'll leave you and take the baby." The husband inwardly shouts, "Good, that's exactly what I wanted." What started him drinking was the new discomfort of home with a baby in it, and the new responsibilities. Now he is presented with a new escape from them all.

The abruptness and violence of these failures always surprise both parties. There is another reason for the failures. It is *hurry*. No important job of persuasion can be done quickly. Few important jobs of persuasion can be done in one stage. To be effective, persuasion must be slow, gradual, easy, patient.

That is how the best propagandists work—those who get lasting results. Think of the many Christian ministers who have converted ferocious savages, world-weary Chinese mandarins, fanatical Communist officials, glum peasants, and vain, flippant young noblemen. One of St. Teresa's operational rules was "Much can be done by patience." The most remarkable conversions of the Jesuit missionaries were planned years in advance and took many years to execute. It is the chief mistake made by American publicists, teachers, and statesmen, to think that if they point out the right course, everyone will at once follow it. Here is Democracy, we say. Look at it. It's good, isn't it? Well, adopt it. But . . . no. Without preparation, no conversion will last. Rapid-fire persuasion is almost sure to fail.

The second rule of persuasion, then, is that it must be gradual. And the third rule develops out of that. The third rule is that it must work on the emotions as well as on the mind. Human beings were suffering fear and anger, enjoying hope and pleasure, long before they were able to think clearly. Their emotions still lie deeper than their reason, sometimes work against their reason, and, for satisfactory action, should always be harmonized with their reason. Persuasion will be most effective when it begins with the emotions. Therefore we ought to start persuading—before introducing any arguments—by calming and smoothing, pleasing and flattering the patient. Surgery never begins until the patient is anaesthetized. Persuasion should never start until the patient has been made receptive.

This, then, is the technique of the ordinary type of persuasion. First, select the inducement. Second, establish a welcoming atmosphere. Third, argue gently, and slowly, and gradually.

We can all do that. But there is a much more difficult type of persuasion which seems to have no rules at all. Yet, when it works, it is far more effective. We often hear of a man who has been able to persuade hardheaded businessmen or wary old hardhearted dowagers that he is in direct communication with God, that he knows the hiding place of Kubla Khan's treasure, that he can foretell the stock market through magnetic rays, that he is the child of a multimillionaire, kidnapped in infancy, or the reincarnation of Paracelsus, or the Master of the Elements. Vast sums of money, limitless trust and adoration are lavished on these persuaders by their victims. And yet they have no real inducement to offer. Often they do not argue. Their emotional appeal is strong, but it is so absurd that we, standing outside, can scarcely understand how anyone could succumb to it. Casanova persuaded the Duchess d'Urfé that he could help her to be reborn as a male child, after a mystical marriage presided over by the Sylphs and the Moon. She was to appoint him guardian of her new baby-self and leave him all her money in trust; the operation failed only at the last moment through a slip of Casanova's roving attention. Saint-Germain persuaded numbers of experienced statesmen that he was two thousand years old and knew the Secrets of the Spheres. The Tichborne claimant persuaded Lady Tichborne that she was his mother.

Of the same order, though in a different group, are the great diplomats. We know their names—Bismarck, Disraeli, Richelieu, Franklin—but we do not know their methods. The biographies tell us the facts of their careers, but seldom explain *how* they contrived their marvellous successes. For instance, how did Bismarck persuade the king of the German states to accept the King of Prussia as German Emperor, and to stand behind his throne while he was crowned? Not just by pointing the guns of the Prussian Army at them. It was a long process, so tortuous, so varied and made of so many subtle touches that it has never been adequately described; but one thing is sure about it, that it was mainly the work of persuasion. Yet it was persuasion of a special type, depending little on the ordinary methods, something far more like the art of the man who holds three deuces and persuades his opponent, with a 5–6–7–8–9 straight, to throw in his hand.

It would be easier to understand the art of persuasion if these geniuses did not exist. But they do, and most of us are at their mercy. And they have no technique that we can describe, no rules, no—on the contrary, they are always incalculable, bold and random, could it be "inspired"?

Yet they do have a few traits in common, which are basic. The chief of these is will-power and concentration. If you really want to persuade people that you are St. John the Baptist returned to life, or the future ruler of Europe, you must be 1000% determined to do so. You need not believe it yourself. But you must concentrate on making others believe it. Every act, every word, every gesture must serve that purpose. Most people have weak wills and wandering minds. If they meet someone with concentrated conviction, they believe he is what he appears to be. If they meet someone with a strong will, they feel they must sooner or later give way to him; and sooner or later most of them do.

Another trait of many great persuaders (outside diplomacy) is this. They are not logical. They do not make clear, reasonable plans and enlist their victims in carrying them out. Often they talk nonsense.

They make dreams more real than daily life. Why they should do so is a hard question. Perhaps the cold truth about daily life is so grim that few of us can face it; we welcome a myth, if it is only strong enough. But the great top-level persuaders have usually been Quixotes who could make us, like poor Sancho Panza, ride on behind them, simply because they seemed to know where they were going, even if it was towards the Kingdom of Micomicon. A splendid example of this has recently appeared in the United States: the Armenian mystic Gurdjieff's *All and Everything,* twelve hundred pages of absolute nonsense, which looks from time to time as though it were about to make some kind of higher sense, and then shoots off into the circum-ambient gas.

But on this level one essential technique of persuasion remains valid. It is that persuasion must be gradual. People will believe anything, however absurd. But they will shallow it only in small doses. When Alice told the White Queen "One can't believe impossible things," the Queen replied "I daresay you haven't had much practice. When I was your age I always did it for half an hour a day. Why, sometimes I've believed as many as six impossible things before breakfast."

Therefore a high-level persuader will begin by hints, and rich stimulating morsels, and tantalizing glimpses into the Luminous Void. Slowly, slowly, almost reluctantly, he will lead his Sanchos further into the Impossible. Soon they will be pushing bravely ahead, jumping the chasms between Inexplicables, swinging freely across the ravines of the Incomprehensible, glissading upwards on the slopes of the Unutterable. Sometimes, dizzy with the thin air, they will pull their master gaily ahead into the unknown, and even if he tries to restrain them they will link arms and swing him out over the edge of sanity. Yet even then, the adventure of persuasion began slowly, slowly; patiently; quietly; slowly.

These, then, are the two kinds of persuasion. One is simple and reasonable. The other is weird and incalculable. Many can do the first, few the second. Just once or twice in our lives we may be able to exercise persuasion of the second type—once or twice at a tremendous crisis, when we feel that everything, *every thing* depends on what the girl will answer, or when we see the crowd warming up and a chance sentence seems to draw it together and make it our instrument, or when the tough old man asks us what we have to offer, and sits back and listens. At such times, with luck, we feel the flood flowing through us; we guide it and master it and see the others carried away by it.

Such a triumph may come only once. If it comes again, if we can recall it and strengthen it, we may become masters of persuasion. (Madame Pompadour began by being a girl who found she could twist one man round her little finger, and then a second man, and then. . . .)

But if not, we can do what is calmer and safer: we can settle for reason. We want not opposition, but harmony. Not conflict, but control. The friendly face, the calm voice. Quietness, gentleness, cheerfulness to relieve the tension. And then, slowly, the persuasion should begin. Kindness, real or imitated. Then reason, real or imitated. Even the imitation of kindness and of reason will draw people together, and will help, in time, to create the real virtues.

---

*You don't like people you change and
you don't change people you like.*
J. Kavanaugh

In "The Persistence of Opinion Change," Marvin Karlins and Herbert I. Abelson describe how and why persuasive effects that are generated in the public speaking arena tend to wear off. Also, they give some recommendations for countering the fickle nature of the effects. They rely on empirical data for their conclusions and provide us with a credible understanding of the nature of effects in the public speaking arena.

MARVIN KARLINS
HERBERT I. ABELSON

THE PERSISTENCE OF OPINION CHANGE

Does propaganda have a lasting influence on opinions?

Is opinion change at its highest point right after the persuasive communication has ended?

Are there any ways to make the impact of a persuasive appeal last longer?

IN TIME THE EFFECTS OF A PERSUASIVE COMMUNICATION TEND TO WEAR OFF.

In the typical attitude change study, an individual's opinion on a specific topic is assessed. This assessment is then followed by his exposure to a persuasive communication designed to change that opinion. Finally, the subject's opinion is re-assessed to see if the persuasive appeal has had any effect. Oftentimes it has. But for how long? Will a man persuaded today remain persuaded tomorrow? Do the effects of persuasive appeals wear off with passing time? These questions were asked by two investigators, William Watts and William McGuire, in 1964.

Specimen Studies

1. In their experiment Watts and McGuire measured persistence of induced opinion change and retention of persuasive communications in 191 undergraduates. Exery subject was exposed to four persuasive appeals, each pre-tested to determine in advance what student opinion on the topic would be. The four issues selected were: "Puerto Rico should be admitted to the union as the 51st state"; "Courts should deal more leniently with juvenile delinquents"; "The Secretary of State should be elected by the people, not appointed by the President"; and "The state sales tax should be abolished." Opinion change was measured on a 15-point scale where subjects could register their level of agreement-disagreement with the contents of the persuasive communications. Recall was assessed by ascertaining the subject's ability to recollect and recognize various aspects of the four persuasive appeals. The total experiment lasted six weeks, with subjects attending four separate sessions. Recall and opinion change measures were administered once during the study—at the conclusion of the fourth experimental session. What were the results of the investigation?

Findings: *There were three major findings of interest: (1) Opinion change was most evident immediately after exposure to the persuasive appeal. With the passage of time the impact of the communication steadily decreased, as reflected in the decay of the initial opinion change; (2) The subject's ability to recall and recognize the contents of persuasive appeals also decreased with the passage of time; (3) At first, opinion change was positively related to recollection of the persuasive communications: the more remembered, the more the change. With the passage of time, however, this relationship weakened to a point where sometimes message recall was negatively related to opinion change (the less one recalled of the persuasive appeal the more he was persuaded!). Thus, it seems that the effects of a persuasive appeal "wear off" with passing time, as does the individual's ability to recall and recognize the contents of that appeal (Watts & McGuire, 1964).*

2. In a cross-cultural study, James Whittaker and Robert Meade (1968) examined the longevity of opinion change in university students from Brazil, Hong Kong, Lebanon, Rhodesia, and India. In

the first phase of the study all subjects filled out an opinion questionnaire designed to assess their opinions on certain issues (they were
asked to express the extent of their agreement or disagreement with
such statements as: "We should continue supporting the United
Nations" and "A cancer cure will be found within the next five
years"). The students were also asked to select from a list containing
"classes of people" (e.g., lawyers, ministers, engineers, professors, etc.)
those they thought to be "authority groups" whose opinions they
would most respect and those groups whose opinions they would
least respect. The second phase of the investigation involved deception
by the experimenter. Each subject was readministered the opinion
questionnaire. This time, however, he was provided with a "comparison set of answers" for each issue. Unknown to the subject, these
"comparison answers" were determined by the experimenter, based
on the subject's response to the first opinion questionnaire. Each comparison answer was divergent from the subject's initial position.
Further, on one-third of the issues, the comparison answers were attributed to members of the subject's "high authority" group; on
another third to "low authority group" members; and on the remaining third, the responses were credited to the "majority of students at
this college."

In the final phase of the study (one month later) students filled
out the opinion questionnaire for a third time. This time no authority
groups were indicated. Of interest in this investigation was the longevity of opinion change as a function of source credibility (the impact of "high" and "low" authority references on subject's opinions).

Findings: *The results indicate that "differential source credibility
produces differences in opinion change regardless of the culture involved. High credible sources in general produce greater opinion
change than low credible sources."* Further, change decayed over
time regardless of whether a high or low credible source was involved. *In other words, there was less opinion change on the
third questionnaire than on the second no matter which credibility condition the subject experienced (Whittaker & Meade, 1968).**

3. Both affirmative and negative speeches were prepared on two
propositions: (1) the federal government should make medical care
available to all people; (2) the government should require federal

---

* *See also: Cook, T., & Insko, C. Persistence of attitude change as a function of
conclusion reexposure: A laboratory-field experiment.* Journal of Personality
and Social Psychology, 1968, 9, 322–328.

arbitration of labor disputes. The speeches were judged for effectiveness by speech professors, and then rewritten until they were all rated equally effective. The final form of each speech was tape-recorded for later use.

Over a thousand students in several groups took part in the experiment. First, they indicated their attitudes on one of the propositions on a questionnaire form. Then they listened to either the affirmative or the negative speech on that proposition, and then answered more attitude questions. Thirty days later, they filled out a third attitude questionnaire on the topic. A control group also filled out questionnaires when the other students did, but were not exposed to any of the recorded speeches.

Findings: *Each speech had a strong, immediate effect on the students' attitudes in the expected direction. The negative speeches produced a greater change than the positive speeches.*

After thirty days, the attitudes of all of the students had moved back toward their original positions. But the influence of the speeches was still evident. About one-third of the effect of the affirmative speeches was still measurable, as was about two-thirds of the effect of the negative speeches. The author drew two conclusions from his data: (1) after thirty days the influence of a message is weaker than right after its presentation, but there still is some influence; (2) the stronger the immediate effectiveness of the message, the greater will be its influence after thirty days (Cromwell, 1955).

4. The question of how long a communication will be remembered has something to do with whether or not the audience believes it and is favorably disposed toward it. One social scientists started with these hypotheses: The stronger the belief that a statement is true, the longer it will be remembered; the stronger the belief that it is false, the sooner it will be forgotten. The more highly approved a statement is, the longer it will be remembered; the more disapproved it is, the sooner it will be forgotten.

A group of 200 college students were handed a list of pro-Russian and anti-Russian statements. For example, one statement was "Equality is given to all racial and minority groups in Russia." The students indicated on a questionnaire whether they believed each statement to be true or false. They also showed whether they approved or disapproved of the general idea of the statement. For example, should all racial and minority groups in any country be accorded equal treatment with everyone else.

The statements in the questionnaire were woven into an essay, "Russia Today." Starting a week after the initial questionnaires were filled out, the essay was read to the students once every other day for a total of five readings. Memory tests on the essay were given immediately after the last reading, and every two weeks thereafter for two months.

> Findings: *Believing statements to be true increases the chance that they will be remembered; but believing that they are false does not seem to make them more easily forgotten. Attitudes seem to work the same way: approving a statement increased the chance that it would be remembered, but disapproving it did not have much effect in the other direction. When a person both believes and approves of something, it has the best chance of being remembered. When both disbelief and disapproval are working at the same time, the chances of forgetting are greatest. Finally, when a person believes something but does not approve of it, or approves of it but does not believe it, stronger influence on remembering is exerted by the degree of approval, rather than by the degree of belief (Garber, 1955).*

Discussion

There is no conclusive evidence on how long a changed opinion stays that way. Some investigators have reported examples of opinion change that lasted for years. Others are more likely to agree with an authority who wrote: "In those rare instances when educators, propagandists, advertisers, and others who want to influence large numbers of people have bothered to make an objective evaluation of the enduring changes produced by their efforts, they have been able to demonstrate only the most negligible effects" (Cartwright, 1951).

Why the disagreement between authorities on the longevity of changed opinions? Actually, the "short-term" and "long-term" advocates are both right—sometimes changed opinions are short-lived, other times, seemingly indestructible: the problem lies in distinguishing the types of opinions that are changed and the procedures for changing them. Generally, opinions that are meaningful (important) to the individual and/or have been established through long-term (or intensive) persuasive efforts are relatively stable and unlikely to change; opinions that are not of central concern to the person and/or have been changed in the course of "one-shot" or limited persuasive appeals are relatively unstable and open to modification. In the typical laboratory manipulation of opinions, where the subject matter is not often involving to subjects and the persuasive appeals are not emphatic, long-term attitude change should be the *exception*, not the rule. On the other hand, opinions are quite resistant to decay when they have been formed through extensive persuasive efforts (e.g., Carron, 1964). Such is often the case with opinions established during long-term psychotherapy.

SUGGESTED READINGS: PERSISTENCE OF OPINION CHANGE

1. Watts, W. A., & McGuire, W. J. Persistence of induced opinion change and retention of the inducing message contents. *Journal of Abnormal and Social Psychology*, 1964, 68, 233–241.
2. Whittaker, J., & Meade, R. Retention of opinion change as a function of differential source credibility: A cross-cultural study. *International Journal of Psychology*, 1968, 3, 103–108.

**MORE OF THE DESIRED
OPINION CHANGE
MAY BE MEASURABLE
SOME TIME AFTER
EXPOSURE TO THE
COMMUNICATION
THAN RIGHT AFTER
EXPOSURE (THE
"SLEEPER EFFECT").**

Specimen Studies

1. One in the series of *Why We Fight* movies used during World War II was called the "Battle of Britain," made to give U.S. troops confidence in our British ally. A questionnaire asking for opinions about Britain was completed by ten infantry training companies, after which five of them saw the film, and five of them were used as a control group and did not see the film. Five days after the picture was shown, about half of the men who saw it, and half of those who did not, filled out a questionnaire containing both opinion items and factual questions about Britain. Nine weeks later, the other half of

each group filled out the same questionnaire. In the results, the responses after five days were compared with the responses after nine weeks.

Findings: *The factual material suffered with time. More was forgotten after nine weeks than after five days. But interestingly enough, some of the opinion responses were more in the desired direction after nine weeks than after five days, while the rest of the opinion responses showed the expected decrease in desired change. The authors named their special finding "the sleeper effect" (Hovland, Lumsdaine & Sheffield, 1949).*

2. The sleeper effect was studied in an experiment on some high school students who were exposed to a communication on the effects of smoking. A feature of this experiment was a discounting statement: after the communication, one of the groups was told that evidence on the effects of smoking is by no means complete, and we are learning new facts every day. The experimenter's hypothesis was that the group that heard this discounting treatment should show less of the intended opinion change right after exposure than the other group, but show the *same* amount of change in the long run, after the discounting effect had worn off. Opinion measurements were made before exposure, right after exposure, and three and again six weeks later.

Findings: *The group that heard the discounting statement and the group that did not were more alike in extent of opinion change later on than they were immediately after exposure. Thus, the sleeper effect showed itself again, even though the results were not quite as marked as they were in the earlier experiments (Weiss, 1953).*

Discussion

A sleeper effect is said to occur when there is more measurable opinion change in the desired direction some time following exposure compared with that immediately following exposure. Several experiments have turned up sleeper effects in different situations. In addition to the two reported here, we can include those described in the chapter on characteristics of the communicator (persuader). These experiments made use of high and low credibility communicators, and their results indicate that opinion right after exposure favors the high credibility source, but that these effects wear off in a few weeks. Eventually there was almost the same amount of opinion change regardless of whether the subjects were initially exposed to the high or the low credibility communicator (Hovland & Weiss, 1951; Kelman & Hovland, 1953).

The authors of the first experiment reported here (the one on the Battle of Britain film) concluded that changes of opinion of a general rather than a specific nature may be more likely to show a sleeper effect. They feel that a sleeper effect is more likely to occur among people who are already predisposed to accept an opinion; possibly because their motivation for wanting to change their opinions will have something to feed on after they have been exposed to the communication (Hovland, Lumsdaine & Sheffield, 1949). Related to this is another very real possibility: Once the topic has been presented, the audience pays more attention to what is said about it in the mass media. This heightened awareness may lead to more reading and listening and thinking about it, until an opinion has been formed (Hovland, Janis & Kelley, 1953).

There are some concepts in the psychology of memory that were useful to the author of the second experiment reported here (the one on the effects of smoking). His hypothesis, which the data supported, was that the "discounting" statement would wear off some time after the audience was exposed to the communication. What is implied is that immediately after exposure, the emergence of an opinion change would be *actively prevented* by the effects of the discounting statement. But because so much more emphasis was given to the presentation on smoking than to the discounting statement (about the incompleteness of the evidence on smoking), the struggle between the emerging opinion and the inhibiting discounting statement would eventually be resolved in favor of the opinion change. These ideas tie in with the concept that forgetting is an active process: something else interferes with a thing learned. Forgetting is not always just the disappearance of a thought from the mind.

This concept of the sleeper effect, even before it is fully explored, may have significant implications for anyone who is interested in estimating the effects of a particular communication. The elapsed time between the actual communication and the measuring of its effects takes on a new meaning. In summary, it is safe to say that something like a sleeper effect has been repeatedly demonstrated. Finding out more about how it works and how to interpret data in the light of the relationships it implies is a task which is still being explored.

1. Weiss, W. A "sleeper" effect in opinion change. *Journal of Abnormal and Social Psychology*, 1953, 48, 173–180.

**OPINION CHANGE IS
MORE PERSISTENT
OVER A PERIOD OF
TIME IF THE
PERSUASIVE APPEAL IS:
(1) REPEATED AND/OR
(2) REQUIRES ACTIVE
(RATHER THAN
PASSIVE) LISTENER
PARTICIPATION.**

How to prolong the impact of a persuasive appeal: now there's a problem Madison Avenue can appreciate! Convincing Jane Doe to purchase a "Brand X" refrigerator is useless if, by the time she visits the store, the effect of the persuasive appeal has worn off. Advertisers have employed many types of persuasive appeals in an effort to sustain changed opinions. They have discovered, long before psychologists, that repeating a communication tends to prolong its influence. Specimen Studies 1 and 2 below attest to the effectiveness of message repetition for prolonging opinion change and lend credence to an old advertising motto: "To keep selling, keep reminding." Or, brought up to date: "Repetition sells good; like an ad campaign should."

Specimen Studies

1. Let us assume you were bent on discovering a way to prolong the impact of a persuasive communication. You enlist the aid of several hundred undergraduates and expose them to a persuasive appeal arguing for election of the President by Congress instead of by the voters. Later you send the students postcards requesting their attendance at a second session. On one-half of the postcards you also mention the topic of the earlier persuasive appeal (congressional election of the President). During the second session you examine the success of your persuasive appeal by asking the subjects to indicate on an 11-point scale: "How much do you agree or disagree that the President should

be elected by Congress?" You are interested in discovering whether subjects given communication reexposure (postcards stating the topic of the persuasive appeal) will exhibit more opinion change (favorably toward Congressional election of the President) than subjects receiving no such communication repetition. What would you find? Well—for a starter—that the experiment had already been performed by Thomas Cook and Chester Insko in 1968! What, then, did they discover?

> Findings: *Although the impact of the persuasive appeal decreased for all subjects with the passage of time—reexposure produced a greater persistence effect than did no reexposure (Cook & Insko, 1968).*

2. Affirmative and negative speeches were prepared on the topics of socialized medicine and federal aid to education. The two versions of each speech were submitted to speech professors who judged them for effectiveness. The speeches were rewritten and rejudged a number of times until they were all rated as about equally effective. Each speech was then tape-recorded for later use.

Several groups of students, over 200 in all, took part in the experiment. They were told that a study was being made of some of the problems of public speaking and audience reactions to speeches. The students then answered a number of questions to determine their attitudes on socialized medicine and federal aid to education. As soon as the questionnaires had been collected, each group of students heard one of the tape-recorded speeches (either pro or con on one of the two topics). Lastly, they filled out another form of the attitude questionnaire on the same two topics. Thirty days later, exactly the same procedure was followed with the same students: attitude questionnaire, same speech they heard before, alternate form of questionnaire.

> Findings: *The questionnaires administered directly after each speech showed a shift in opinion in the expected direction. The attitude questionnaire that was administered just before the second exposure to the speech showed that after thirty days had passed, some of the opinion change caused by the first exposure to the speech had worn off. The measurement made following the second exposure to the speech revealed two things: (1) students were not*

---

* See also: *Wilson, W., & Miller, H. Repetition, order of presentation, timing of arguments and measures as determinants of opinion change.* Journal of Personality and Social Psychology, 1968, 9, 184–188.

*influenced as much by the speech the second time they heard it
as they had been the first time; (2) the second presentation brought
the level of attitude change up to what it had been immediately
after the first presentation, thirty days previously (Cromwell &
Kunkel, 1952).*

Discussion

Early in the history of modern psychology, just as today, there was
much experimental activity directed to the study of human memory
and forgetting. Some of the findings of those earlier psychologists
about the processes of forgetting are valid to this day. One is that
people do not forget what they read or hear in equal increments. An
audience that has been exposed to a persuasive message will not
forget 10% of what they heard each week for ten weeks until they
have forgotten the message. Instead, the audience will forget most of
what they heard after two or three days. Then, the little they still
retain gradually dwindles down to a few fragments of what they had
originally heard. Interestingly enough, these last bits of material are
often remembered for quite some time.

Advertisers can make use of the known pattern of forgetting. For
instance, a direct mail campaign whose timing is one mailing a week
for six weeks might not have the impact of a campaign which consists of three mailings in close succession. When the follow-ups are
sent soon after the first mailing, the advertiser is catching his audience before they have forgotten most of what they read in the preceding mailing. The impact of the first mailing is being strengthened
before nearly all of it is forgotten.

We do not have to look far—about as far as the living room TV
set—for evidence that persuasion by repetition has an army of proponents. But what about the use of "active participation" to prolong
the impact of a persuasive appeal? We have encountered "active participation" in two earlier contexts and are already familiar with its
role in changing opinions. On pages 19–21 we observed that the impact of a persuasive appeal is enhanced by requiring active, rather
than passive, participation by the listener. Then, on pages 62–67 we
concluded that active audience participation (group discussion and
decision-making) helps to overcome resistance. Thus, it has already
been determined that active participation can enhance the effectiveness of persuasive appeals. What will be documented here is the long-
term impact (persistence) of that effectiveness.

One of the best examples of how active participation can maintain an opinion once it has been formed or changed was provided by Watts in 1967. In his experiment, 140 university students were divided into six experimental groups that either read (passive participation) or wrote (active participation) about one of three possible issues. A questionnaire designed to assess opinions on the three topics was administered to students just after they had read or written about the issues and again six weeks later. In the second testing session student involvement with, and recall of, the issues was also tested.

In examining his data, Watts found that initially both active and passive participation led to significant opinion change. Thus, students who either read or wrote a persuasive appeal favoring a specified issue changed their opinions in the desired direction. But what about persistence of opinion change? In the follow-up testing session six weeks later, subjects who had composed persuasive appeals (active participation) displayed significantly greater persistence of the initially induced opinion change than students who had read the persuasive communication (passive participation). In this study, active participation was clearly superior to passive participation in long-term opinion change (Watts, 1967).*

The knowledge that active participation prolongs opinion change finds practical application in psychotherapy. The increasing popularity and success of the newer "role playing" and "psychodrama" therapies with their emphasis on active patient involvement in the treatment processes is their way of recognizing the doctrine of "active participation."

The importance of active participation in long-range opinion change has also been documented with T-groups (Carron, 1964) and reference groups (Newcomb, 1963). Currently, active participation is being emphasized and practiced by an ever widening circle of individuals and groups in this society. VISTA, Peace Corps, Black Panthers, Peace Marchers, campus demonstrators, sensitivity training groups—all emphasize activities that center on participation. The implications of these movements for society have yet to be determined— possibly the study of active participation might provide us with some insights.

---

* For another example of how active participation affects the persistence of attitude change see: Mitnick, L. & McGinnies, E. Influencing ethnocentrism in small discussion groups through a film communication. Journal of Abnormal and Social Psychology, 1958, 56, 82–90.

1. Carron, T. Human relations training and attitude change: A vector analysis. *Personal Psychology*, 1964, *17*, 403–424.

2. Cook, T., & Insko, C. Persistence of attitude change as a function of conclusion reexposure: A laboratory-field experiment. *Journal of Personality and Social Psychology*, 1968, *9*, 322–328.

3. Newcomb, T. Persistence and regression of changed attitudes: Long-range studies. *Journal of Social Issues*, 1963, *19*, 3–14.

4. Watts, W. Relative persistence of opinion change induced by active compared to passive participation. *Journal of Personality and Social Psychology*, 1967, *5*, 4–15.

6

MASS COMMUNICATION:
TRANSACTING WITH SOCIETY

We refer to mass communication as those communication situations in which the senders and receivers of messages are separated by time or space. Many different types of communication encounters qualify as mass communication from this perspective. For example, movies or recorded television programs represent mass communication situations in which the participants (actors and audience members) are separated by both time and space. Live television or radio productions are mass situations in which the participants are separated by space. Notice that from this perspective, the key criteria are time or space separations—not the size of the audience. Although we usually think of mass communication encounters as involving large numbers of people, this is not necessarily the case.

Of all the communication arenas, the mass communication arena is the most unique. In other words, it is the arena that is most different from all the others. The characteristic that distinguishes it most sharply from the others is the separation of the participants by time or space. This quality affects the very nature of the communication transactions. As you recall, we noted that "transaction" calls for simultaneous encoding and decoding of the participants. Although all participants in a mass communication situation meet the criterion of simultaneous encoding and decoding, the transaction is at best indirect rather than direct. The separated participants cannot immediately share in each other's encoding and decoding activities. Although a skilled mass communicator will lead you to perceive that you are engaged in a direct transactional relationship with each other, the encounter is an indirect transaction. For example, if an author of a book talks with you in the interpersonal, small group, or public speaking arenas, you and the author will have the opportunity to partially share in each other's immediate transactional experience. The author can observe and thereby experience some of your encoding and decoding activities, and you can share his. Also, you will experience an immediate reciprocal influence, each effecting the other. When you read the author's book, however, the two of you are separated by time and space. The author was encoding and decoding simultaneously when he wrote the book, and you are doing the same as you read it. The two of you, however, were not able to directly share in each other's immediate experience when you read the book. Thus, we classify mass communication encounters as indirect transactions. The participants do encode and decode simultaneously, but cannot share or experience a direct reciprocal bond. Even though you will be directly affected by reading a book or watching a television program, you will probably not have a direct effect on the source. You may provide him with feedback by writing to him, but your chances of having much of an impact on him are very slim. The nature of these indirect transactions make influence in this arena more of a one-way happening as opposed to the two-way, reciprocal type of influence that is possible in direct transactions. Again, audiences do exert some influence on mass communication sources, but that influence is, at best, delayed.

Perhaps it is because of the one-way influence nature of the mass arena that many have grown to fear the potential power of the mass media. It used to be widely accepted that mass communication sources could manipulate the populace quite easily. Express an opinion on television, for example, and people would automatically believe it. Although the exact impact of mass communication influence has not been determined, we know that it is not all powerful. As you will discover in the following readings, people can and do resist mass communication influences.

Thus we can see that the nature of human communication in this arena is somewhat unique—the transactions are indirect. Also, from our perspective, large numbers of people do not necessarily have to be involved for the situation to be classified as mass communication. We have, however, included some selections in this unit that deal with the topic of the collective behavior of the masses because so much of a mass communicator's concern is with large groups of people. Finally, the effects of mass communication are probably not as great as many of us have been led to believe. Careful study of this unit should help you to become more aware of the role of mass media in your life and in society in general. Also, you may better understand your role in relation to others and the collective behavior of masses.

MASS
COMMUNICATION
PERCEPTION

*Every man has his own eyes to choose
the world with.* J. Lair

When we are consumers of mass messages presented through television, radio, newspapers, books and similar media, the communication variable of perception is fully operable. Just as the perception of others in arenas ranging from interpersonal to public speaking is important, so it is in mass contexts. Whenever a television program is aired, for example, the viewer's perceptions are quite varied. An exciting detective story to one person may be seen as a brutal display of violence to another. A tender love scene to one may be an overly dramatic "soap opera" to another. The message presented on the screen may have many different meanings for each of us.

The electronic media (especially movies and television) have a unique quality in that they can present very complete representations of human events and sometimes spark intense involvement. A good portion of the subtle cues we attach meaning to—tone of voice, eye contact, and the like—are often vividly portrayed on the screen. We get the opportunity to perceive a fairly good representation of a person. Whatever the medium, however, perception of others is constantly in operation.

The following satire by John Steinbeck presents a picture of how media use stereotyping to affect the perceptions of viewers. Although the picture is exaggerated, it is quite revealing. An interesting question to ponder while reading the selection is, "Do the media establish the stereotypes, or do they just use them?" In other words, do they use your own stereotyping habits to reinforce your perceptions? How about you, what type of "boxes" or stereotypes do you use to evaluate others—to "tell the good guys from the bad guys"?

JOHN STEINBECK

HOW TO TELL GOOD GUYS FROM BAD GUYS

Television has crept upon us so gradually in America that we have not yet become aware of the extent of its impact for good or bad. I myself do not look at it very often except for its coverage of sporting events, news, and politics. Indeed, I get most of my impressions of the medium from my young sons.

Whether for good or bad, television has taken the place of the sugartit, soothing syrups, and the mild narcotics parents in other days used to reduce their children to semiconsciousness and consequently to seminoisiness. In the past, a harassed parent would say, "Go sit in a chair!" or "Go outside and play!" or "If you don't stop that noise, I'm going to beat your dear little brains out!" The present-day parent suggests, "Why don't you go look at television?" From that moment the screams, shouts, revolver shots, and crashes of motor accidents come from the loudspeaker, not from the child. For some reason, this is presumed to be more relaxing to the parent. The effect on the child has yet to be determined.

I have observed the physical symptoms of television-looking on children as well as on adults. The mouth grows slack and the lips hang open; the eyes take on a hypnotized or doped look; the nose runs rather more than usual; the backbone turns to water and the fingers slowly and methodically pick the designs out of brocade furniture. Such is the appearance of semiconsciousness that one wonders how much of the "message" of television is getting through to the brain. This wonder is further strengthened by the fact that a television-looker will look at anything at all and for hours. Recently I came into a room to find my eight-year-old son Catbird sprawled in a chair, idiot slackness on his face, with the doped eyes of an opium smoker. On the television screen stood a young woman of mammary distinction with ice-cream hair listening to a man in thick glasses and a doctor's smock.

"What's happening?" I asked.

Catbird answered in the monotone of the sleeptalker which is known as television voice, "She is asking if she should dye her hair."

"What is the doctor's reaction?"

"If she uses Trutone's it's all right," said Catbird. "But if she uses ordinary or adulterated products, her hair will split and lose its golden natural sheen. The big economy size is two dollars and ninety-cents if you act now," said Catbird.

You see, something was getting through to him. He looked punch-drunk, but he was absorbing. I did not feel it fair to interject a fact I have observed—that natural golden sheen does not exist in nature. But I did think of my friend Elia Kazan's cry of despair, and although it is a digression I shall put it down.

We were having dinner in a lovely little restaurant in California. At the table next to us were six beautiful, young, well-dressed American girls of the age and appearance of magazine advertisements. There was only one difficulty with their perfection. You couldn't tell them apart. Kazan, who is a primitive of a species once known as men, regarded the little beauties with distaste, and finally in more sorrow than anger cried, "It's years since I've seen or smelled a dame! It's all products, Golden Glint, l'Eau d'Eau, Butisan, Elyn's puff-adder cream —I remember I used to like how women smelled. Nowadays it's all products!"

End of digression.

Just when the parent becomes convinced that his child's brain is rotting away from television, he is jerked up in another direction.

Catbird has corrected me in the Museum of Natural History when I directed his attention to the mounted skeleton of a tyrannosaur. He said it was a brontosaurus but observed kindly that many people made the same error. He argued with his ten-year-old brother about the relative cleanness of the line in Praxiteles and Phidias. He knows the weight a llama will bear before lying down in protest, and his knowledge of entomology is embarrassing to a parent who likes to impart information to his children. And these things he also got from television. I knew that he was picking up masses of unrelated and probably worthless information from television, incidentally the kind of information I also like best, but I did not know that television was preparing him in criticism and politics, and that is what this piece is really about.

I will have to go back a bit in preparation. When television in America first began to be a threat to the motion-picture industry, that industry fought back by refusing to allow its films to be shown on the home screens. One never saw new pictures, but there were whole blocks of the films called Westerns which were owned by independents, and these were released to the television stations. The result is that at nearly any time of the day or night you can find a Western being shown on some television station. It is not only the children who see them. All of America sees them. They are a typically American conception, the cowboy picture. The story never varies and the conventions are savagely adhered to. The hero never kisses a girl. He loves his horse and he stands for right and justice. Any change in the story or the conventions would be taken as an outrage. Out of these films folk heroes have grown up—Hopalong Cassidy, the Lone Ranger, Roy Rogers, and Gene Autry. These are more than great men. They are symbols of courage, purity, simplicity, honesty, and right. You must understand that nearly every American is drenched in the tradition of the Western, which is, of course, the celebration of a whole pattern of American life that never existed. It is also as set in its form as the *commedia dell' arte.*

End of preparation.

One afternoon, hearing gunfire from the room where our television set is installed, I went in with that losing intention of fraternizing with my son for a little while. There sat Catbird with the cretinous expression I have learned to recognize. A Western was in progress.

"What's going on?" I asked.

He looked at me in wonder. "What do you mean, what's going on? Don't you know?"

"Well, no. Tell me!"

He was kind to me. Explained as though I were the child.

"Well, the Bad Guy is trying to steal Her father's ranch. But the Good Guy won't let him. Bullet figured out the plot."

"Who is Bullet?"

"Why, the Good Guy's horse." He didn't add "You dope," but his tone implied it.

"Now wait," I said, "which one is the Good Guy?"

"The one with the white hat."

"Then the one with the black hat is the Bad Guy?"

"Anybody knows that," said Catbird.

For a time I watched the picture, and I realized that I had been ignoring a part of our life that everybody knows. I was interested in the characterizations. The girl, known as Her or She, was a blonde, very pretty but completely unvoluptuous because these are Family Pictures. Sometimes she wore a simple gingham dress and sometimes a leather skirt and boots, but always she had a bit of a bow in her hair and her face was untroubled with emotion or, one might almost say, intelligence. This also is part of the convention. She is a symbol, and any acting would get her thrown out of the picture by popular acclaim.

The Good Guy not only wore a white hat but light-colored clothes, shining boots, tight riding pants, and a shirt embroidered with scrolls and flowers. In my young days I used to work with cattle, and our costume was blue jeans, a leather jacket, and boots with run-over heals. The cleaning bill alone of this gorgeous screen cowboy would have been four times what our pay was in a year.

The Good Guy had very little change of facial expression. He went through his fantastic set of adventures with no show of emotion. This is another convention and proves that he is very brave and very pure. He is also scrubbed and has an immaculate shave.

I turned my attention to the Bad Guy. He wore a black hat and dark clothing, but his clothing was definitely not only unclean but unpressed. He had a stubble of beard but the greatest contrast was in his face. His was not an immobile face. He leered, he sneered, he had a nasty laugh. He bullied and shouted. He looked evil. While he did not swear, because this is a Family Picture, he said things like "Wall dog it" and "You rat" and "I'll cut off your ears and eat 'em," which would indicate that his language was not only coarse but might, off screen, be vulgar. He was, in a word, a Bad Guy. I found a certain interest in the Bad Guy which was lacking in the Good Guy.

"Which one do you like best?" I asked.

Catbird removed his anaesthetized eyes from the screen. "What do you mean?"

"Do you like the Good Guy or the Bad Guy?"

He sighed at my ignorance and looked back at the screen. "Are you kidding?" he asked. "The Good Guy, of course."

Now a new character began to emerge. He puzzled me because he wore a gray hat. I felt a little embarrassed about asking my son, the expert, but I gathered my courage. "Catbird," I asked shyly, "what kind of a guy is that, the one in the gray hat?"

He was sweet to me then. I think until that moment he had not understood the abysmal extent of my ignorance. "He's the In-Between Guy," Catbird explained kindly. "If he starts bad he ends good and if he starts good he ends bad."

"What's this one going to do?"

"See how he's sneering and needs a shave?" my son asked.

"Yes."

"Well, the picture's just started, so that guy is going to end good and help the Good Guy get Her father's ranch back."

"How can you be sure?" I asked.

Catbird gave me a cold look. "He's got a gray hat, hasn't he? Now don't talk. It's about time for the chase."

There it was, not only a tight, true criticism of a whole art form but to a certain extent of life itself. I was deeply impressed because this simple explanation seemed to mean something to me more profound than television or Westerns.

Several nights later I told the Catbird criticism to a friend who is a producer. He has produced many successful musical comedies. My friend has an uncanny perception for the public mind and also for its like and dislikes. You have to have if you produce musical shows. He listened and nodded and didn't think it was a cute child story. He said, "It's not kid stuff at all. There's a whole generation in this country that makes its judgments pretty much on that basis."

"Give me an example," I asked.

"I'll have to think about it," he said.

Well, that was in March. Soon afterward my wife and I went to Spain and then to Paris and rented a little house. As soon as school was out in New York, my boys flew over to join us in Paris.

In July, my producer friend dropped in to see us. He was going to take an English show to New York, and he had been in London making arrangements.

He told us all of the happenings at home, the gossip and the new jokes and the new songs. Finally I asked him about the McCarthy hearings. "Was it as great a show as we heard?" I asked.

"I couldn't let it alone," he said. "I never saw anything like it. I wonder whether those people knew how they were putting themselves on the screen."

"Well, what do you think will happen?"

"In my opinion, McCarthy is finished," he said, and then he grinned. "I base my opinion on your story about Catbird and the Westerns."

"I don't follow you."

"Have you ever seen McCarthy on television?"

"Sure."

"Just remember," said my friend. "He sneers. He bullies, he has a nasty laugh and he always looks as though he needs a shave. The only thing he lacks is a black hat. McCarthy is the Bad Guy. Everybody who saw him has got it pegged. He's the Bad Guy and people don't like the Bad Guy. I may be wrong but that's what I think. He's finished."

The next morning at breakfast I watched Catbird put butter and two kinds of jam and a little honey on a croissant, then eat the treacherous thing, then lick the jam from the inside of his elbow to his fingers. He took a peach from the basket in the center of the table.

"Catbird," I asked, "did you see any of the McCarthy stuff on television?"

"Sure," he said.

"Was he a Good Guy or a Bad Guy?" I asked.

"Bad Guy," said Catbird, and he bit into the peach.

And do you know, I suspect it is just that simple.

I have always regretted I am not as wise as the day I was born.
H. D. Thoreau

Notice in Hawley's short piece
how the originator of a mass
message, in this case, film, has
little control over the perceptions of others. The
message they "sent" is not the
one "received." Others may
not perceive our messages the
same way we meant them.

CAMERON HAWLEY

EXECUTIVE
SUITE
Look at what we did this last year with what we called a
"communications program." We put out a movie that analyzed our
financial report and had meetings in all the plants. The men weren't
much interested in our financial report—we knew that to begin with,
it was the premise we started from—so what did we do? We tried to
force them into being interested. We disguised the dollars as cartoons—
little cartoon dollars that jumped into workers' pocketbooks—other
little cartoon dollars that dragged in piles of lumber and built factories
—and a big fat dollar that took a trip to Washington and was gobbled
up by Uncle Sam. Oh, it was all very clever—even won some kind of
an award as an outstanding example of how to promote industrial
understanding. Understanding? Do you know what it forced our men
to understand? Only one thing—the terrible, soul-killing fact that
dollars were all that mattered to the management of this company
—dollars—dollars—and nothing else.

Selected from Executive Suite. *Copyright* © *1952 by the Houghton Mifflin*
380 *Company, Boston. Reprinted with permission.*

MASS
COMMUNICATION
NONVERBAL BEHAVIOR

It is only with the heart that one can
see rightly; what is essential is invisible
to the eye.   A. De Saint-Exupery

The preceding units in this book have developed the aspects of nonverbal behavior in communication contexts quite fully. In the mass communication arena the same nonverbal elements are, of course, present. Instead of providing readings similar to those presented earlier, this section will highlight nonverbal behavior that is unique to mass behavior.

Mass communication is closely connected to the notions of collective behavior because important collective behaviors such as demonstrations, riots, and parades are usually extensively covered by the media. Whether the media are portraying collective behavior or not, social movements, such as women's liberation, develop specific nonverbal components. Our 13 original colonies are heralded by the earliest American flag, black power brought us the clenched fist, and the beginnings of women's liberation introduced bra burning. Obviously, any mass movement can bring with it salient nonverbal aspects.

In "Style Rebellion and Identity Crisis," Orrin E. Klapp presents a comprehensive view of several significant factors of collective behavior. We have included this selection at this particular point in the book because when the mass media examine their potential mass audiences, they have to recognize the behavior and attitude trends that characterize society at that time. Also, Klapp discusses the importance of nonverbal signs and identifying ceremonies to the individuals who collectively constitute the masses. Individual identity is crucial to everyone and nonverbal symbols and practices are often necessary to help one maintain a feeling of individual worth. As you read this selection, try to view yourself as a member of the "great mass audience." What factors, nonverbal or otherwise, help you in your attempts to maintain individual identity?

ORRIN E. KLAPP

STYLE
REBELLION AND
IDENTITY
CRISIS

Visiting Russia recently, I was interested to see a band of hippies—about ten long-haired, beard-wearing, unkempt young men and women—marching down the Moscow subway, strumming guitars, and singing "Flower Power Will Overcome." It was a jolly good tune and smart tempo. They seemed American and English. The Russians were amused and did not bother them. I asked a Russian if the USSR had any hippies of its own. He said, "We had one, but they made him cut his hair." The wave had hit Russia, but it wasn't breaking very high.

Something odd is going on in the world—a rebellion which doesn't fit into the usual categories of political protest. There is a wide range of upheaval in styles of clothing, art, music, tastes, morals, and ways of living. Strange slogans like "flower power" and "turn on, tune in, drop out" don't really explain what people are doing; the slogans are as puzzling as the behavior itself. We should not, however, think only of hippies. There is a panorama of rebellion in style in all classes and most of the arts.

We see examples in the mod fashions of Carnaby Street; mini-skirts, mini-miniskirts, and nuns wearing minihabits; bikinis, nokinis, topless and peekaboo dresses; Castro-style beards on university students; fezzes, Moslem and tribal African garb on American Negroes; and black leather jackets, chains, knives, swastikas, and death's head insignia on boys riding motorcycles.

In entertainment, too, something odd is happening: beat music, loud, strident caterwauling, shocking in themes and lyrics, shattering the ears and producing deafness in some. Folksingers like Joan Baez and Bob Dylan are not celebrating the days of "Tom Dooley" nostalgically. They are bitterly protesting what's happening now. A Broadway play *Hair* features nude people cavorting while facing the audience.

Art is producing incomprehensible products, neither meaningful nor pretty: op and pop styles; put ons like Robert Rauschenberg's famous goat—stuffed, with an automobile tire about its middle; underground movies on such interesting subjects as a patch of human skin; multimedia happenings such as men breaking up an automobile with

From Tamotsu Shibutani editor, **Human Nature And Collective Behavior:** **Papers In Honor Of Herbert Blumer.** *Copyright © 1970 by Prentice-Hall, Inc. Reprinted by permission of Orrin E. Klapp, Professor of Anthropology, The University of Western Ontario, London, Ontario, Canada.*

axes. Everybody seems to be trying to be more sensational or incomprehensible, to shock and outshock, in escalation.

In the midst of this seeming pandemonium Bob Dylan plunks on his guitar and sings, "Something is happening, and you don't know what it is, do you, Mr. Jones?" Who is Mr. Jones? He is ordinary like you and me—the conventional person who works regular hours, dresses conservatively, doesn't spend his nights attending love-ins, be-ins, and happenings, and thinks a cigarette is something that gives you only lung cancer, not a trip to self-realization. Dylan implies there is a secret of some kind that Jones doesn't understand because he's square, straight —that is, accepts things as they are. Perhaps Dylan is right. We should examine this odd behavior carefully to see if it is saying anything to us.

It used to be that when a person disarranged his costume, let himself go, became dirty and unkempt, and made strange noises, he was locked up. Now he is a style leader or creative artist. The difference is that what would formerly have been regarded as sheer insanity is now being imitated widely and has authority for some. Why is this so? It seems to me that it is because more people now feel an urgent need for self-expression; so it is recognized as legitimate to "let go." A romantic right is growing to express oneself as one pleases.

With this new romanticism, we seem to be entering a new era, not just of science, technology and material progress, but of enlarged awareness, delighted acceptance and search for new experiences, seeing things and oneself in new ways by travel, scientific discovery, moon shots and undersea exploration, art, religion, sensitivity training, psychotherapy, and mind expansion, even by drugs like LSD.

The most startling aspect of this search is style rebellion in the ways people dress and live. That rebellion is more than a mere expression of taste in new and creative ways. It is protest which opposes a style with a different style that attacks, rebukes, shocks—puts down— prevailing standards. It is aggressive; it makes people angry; it has a flaunting, flouting, defiant quality. It is not simply aesthetic; indeed, it may be shockingly ugly and in bad taste. Its shock value contrasts with smooth fashion in which good taste reflects conformity. Rudi Gernreich, the fashion designer, gives the secret away: "Clothes are not status symbols any longer. . . . Style today is a kind of flaunting of one's personality."

Style rebellion is essentially an attack not on style itself but on the underlying values of the status quo—middle class morality, the hard work ethic, the success image, and conventional religion. We can see this attack in hippie style. Their uncouthness offends middle class cleanliness and respectability. Their scrounging, carefree existence as free riders and parasites offends the belief that it is good to work hard for one's own living (an idea which kept their forefathers going). Flower power is a flippant rebuke to militarism and the authority of state. Free love is a threat to the monogamous ideal and parental responsibility. The use of drugs seems an unpardonable, selfish, sensual indulgence, threatening morality and perhaps the entire work structure of productive society. Finally, their hair is unkempt, dirty, long in males, indistinguishable from that of females. As much trouble today seems to be caused by hair as by politics and ideology. For some reason people get excited about too much or too little hair, hair in the wrong places, hair curled or straightened, dyed or natural. Psychologists and anthropologists say hair is a sexual symbol; maybe that is why people get excited. Except on priests, long hair on males seems to be regarded as an attack on masculinity.

However, besides the attack on prevailing values, another feature of style rebellion should be noted. I call it ego screaming—behavior which says "look at me," "please pay attention to me." This shows the need for recognition. It indicates that such people feel ego deprivation, which is a significant symptom of modern times.

From this we can see that more is going on in fashion these days than the usual demand of people for something a little newer and better. Style rebellion is a protest of serious dimensions, not just a normal expression of freedom. It is a sign, I think, of social malaise. Something is wrong that people don't like and want changed. What, then, is wrong? What is the protest about?

When we ask what is wrong with the world, naturally we start looking for injustices, and we have no trouble finding them all over the world—displaced Arabs, starved Biafrans, suppressed Czechoslovakians, cheated sharecroppers, and crowded ghetto dwellers everywhere. But oddly this is not where style rebellion and protest are found. Style rebellion is characteristic of rather prosperous people, who enjoy freedom and have money for many indulgences. The middle class provides a large output of rebels; New Left activists, mods, beat musicians, folk singers, and hippies are well educated and have been raised with the "good" things of life. Only a fraction of the style rebels of today are poor and disprivileged. Nor is there among style rebels (as distinguished from the New Left) an ideology or radical program for remedying economic and civil injustice.

Style rebels appear on the same scene with New Left activists, and there is some collusion between them; but they are not identical and should be distinguished. The distinction seems to be as follows: members of the New Left are action oriented and concerned with public affairs, while style rebels are expression oriented and concerned with their own lives. The New Left attacks the Establishment and often attempts to seize power. Style rebels evade responsibility and drop out of the Establishment and its politics; they are not basically interested in politics. True, style rebellion sometimes verges on political protest when its activities clash with the police and regulations. Incidents such as the "filthy speech" rebellion at Berkeley or a man smoking marijuana cigarettes on the steps of a court building express disgust at laws which limit liberty. But, looking at activists of the extreme right and left, as one sees them in news photos or on television, one notes that most are conventionally dressed and do not fit the hippie or extreme mod or beat categories. What brings them together so often and confuses them in the public mind is their common antagonism to what they call the Establishment.

But we must ask what is this Establishment that they are protesting against? Is it capitalism? A certain government or party? Here we see that it is not so much protest against a political or economic system considered to be unfair as against such things as technology and bureaucracy in general, against standardization and impersonal treatment of human beings. The Establishment is not so much a class in Marxian terms as a way of life that restricts and denies full life for man, as Herbert Marcuse has pointed out. The Establishment is set of middle class values that college students see in their own teachers and parents—in their own class, not an enemy class.

There is, then, a definite attack on the middle class these days, but the odd thing is that much of it is coming from the middle class itself. It is not a proletarian uprising. Two kinds of protest should be distinguished: Lower class protest reflects the feeling of being cut off from middle class values (as we see it when mobs drag television sets from stores). Middle class protest reflects alienation from such values already experienced or seen firsthand. The lower middle class stands appalled at middle class protest. What's the matter with them? How possibly can one not want to be a business executive or a highly paid white collar worker, have two cars, three television sets, and live in a nice suburban neighborhood with a patio, barbecue, and swimming pool? Yet, there it is; the prevailing image of success has been rejected by many educated young middle class intellectuals, especially university students, by the artistic and literary crowd (outside Madison Avenue), and by entertainers. The songs of the Beattles—"When I'm 64" and "She's Leaving Home," for example—are full of dismal pictures of middle class life. We have heard again and again the familiar charges against this way of life. It is described as being materialistic, hypocritical, immoral, square, dull, and lacking challenge. And there is also the constant complaint about neglect of the individual—"Don't fold, spindle, or mutilate."

What I am suggesting is that style rebels are protesting not against the injustices of the world but against the meaninglessness (to them) of a set of values and a style of life (identity) offered by "successful" people in current society. They want to strike out and forge a new identity for themselves. They experiment wildly, sometimes desperately, even pathetically, to find something new. In this reaction there is a swing away from the styles of the hard worker, the businessman, the white and blue collar workers, the bureaucrat toward a more expressive life— toward, in Marcuse's terms, not "one dimensional" but many dimensional man. It is a reaction of boredom against the prevailing image of success and the comfortable life of suburbia.

This, then, is what I would call a meaning problem, which, expressed in terms of the individual, is an identity problem. We have to ask why modern technological societies, which can distribute goods adequately, so often fail to give meaning and satisfactory identity to their members. In prosperous societies troubles seem to shift to the meaning (or, if you prefer, spiritual) sphere.

We are asking, then, why it is that identity problems break out in societies which are materially prosperous, highly modernized and technologized, many of which have philosophies emphasizing the importance of the individual. Unrest is understandable among Rhodesian blacks or overcrowded starving Indians. But it is a paradox that the have nations, such as England, France, the United States, Switzerland, West Germany, and Japan should have abundant identity problems in the middle classes. These are countries with well developed economic and welfare systems, and many of them have constitutions emphasizing civil rights. The paradox seems to be that an individual can get what he wants in terms of material abundance and civil rights and still have a feeling that he doesn't count.

I can illustrate this with an anecdote about university graduation. The senior class of a California university was rehearsing in the open air theatre for the graduation ceremony that afternoon. The sun was already high, and the prospect was that it would be warm that afternoon. A proposal was made to the class president to speed up the ceremony by dropping the calling of names, thus saving about forty minutes. After discussion the class voted to eliminate the calling of names. At this point a student in one of the upper rows rose and threw his folding chair down into the arena, narrowly missing the kettle drum of the orchestra. He said, "I have waited four years for this, and I am damned if I will graduate without having my name called." Then he walked out. There was a moment of stunned silence. Then came a new motion from a member of the class that names be called. The motion was passed unanimously.

Here we see how easy it is to forget, to lose the individual in the midst of a system designed to educate him for opportunities and give him the good things of life. What had they forgotten? They had forgotten that there is more to education than facts, skills, and a job. Being appreciated as a person by others is an essential experience. Every human being needs periodic recognition, to stand out from the mass as somebody who counts, to have people care emotionally, to know that one's friends and relatives are proud. College graduation is a ceremony that gives meaning to a person. It has a sentimental purpose, not a practical one. Abolish it and the individual loses meaning. There is no efficiency in education which ignores identity.

The meaning of an individual—his identity—can be analyzed into two parts: (1) his purpose, the significance of his work and goals; and (2) his self conception, his sense of his own importance, his feeling that he is somebody who counts and that people care about him. Lack of these things creates an identity problem.

The odd thing is that counting people does not make them count; votes and statistics have little value for identity. Identity is provided by certain kinds of experiences which others must give. An individual cannot invent or generate his own importance (unless, of course, he is insane).

We can here briefly indicate some kinds of things that give identity and the ways in which modern society often fails to provide these. I would like to point out briefly six sociological factors disturbing identity all over the world, more in some places than in others—hardly at all, for example, in a village in Crete or a kibbutz in Israel but very much in modern society characterized by advanced technology, urbanism, and mobility. All over the world disturbances of identity are beginning. But in advanced societies they are often farthest under way because of cumulative effects and rapid changes. These identity disturbances feed unrest; they add bitterness to the demands of the "have nots" and make middle class life seem unsatisfactory to many.

The most obviously technological disturbance to identity, perhaps, is *destruction of environment,* of places which constitute home. All over the world we hear the sound of bulldozers and jack hammers wiping away familiar landmarks and the homes of people. Symbolically, a home is a place where a child is raised, a place rich with childhood and ancestral memories. New housing usually does not replace home psychologically, for it has no memories. Sometimes the rich move in where the poor have lived and create an entirely new environment. New towns, suburban tracts, and old people's communities (with names like "Sun Villa") rarely create home psychologically. Likewise, social succession, i.e., turnover of people, in urban neighborhoods brings in waves of new dwellers even when the buildings remain the same. In five or ten years an entire population can change, as has happened in Knottinghill Gate, London. The English are appalled to see a village as they knew it destroyed by migrants from the West Indies and Pakistan.

It is becoming a universal phenomenon for people to find that they cannot go back where they were raised to renew themselves through familiar sights and the folks back home. Often a man returns to his old neighborhood to find a high rise building and a parking lot. Even landmarks may be gone—hills flattened, skylines altered, rivers filled. Strange faces look out from the windows of his old home. The neighbor's children—his former friends—are gone. Such a man, having lost his home, has lost one of the strands of his identity. He cannot meaningfully refer to himself the way a Greek does who says, "I'm a Cretan," and thinks of his village. So, symbolically, masses of modern people, however well housed in material terms, are a homeless generation psychologically. As the adage says, "A house is not a home."

A factor equally disturbing to identity is *loss of contact with the past and tradition*. People are forgetting what kind of people their ancestors were and are becoming people without a past. Ethnic and tribal identities are being abandoned; old customs and ceremonies are being forgotten (though people like Dora Stratou are trying to preserve them); and ancestors and genealogies are losing importance. Cleveland Amory's well-known story about the Bostonian who applied to a Chicago firm for a job illustrates this. The young man brought with him a letter of recommendation stressing the quality of his ancestry in Boston. But the Chicago office replied that, though they were very impressed with Mr. X's pedigree, they were not interested in using him for breeding purposes. This reply expresses the modern feeling of the practical irrelevance of the past. Old ways are viewed as obsolete, corny. Modernism is rampant. The motto is "away with the old and in with the new."

History is becoming abstract knowledge about the past rather than the story of our people and our heroes. There has been a loss of the heroic view of history and of the "chosen people" concept. The record of the past has become dead history rather than living tradition. Folklore, folk dance, and song, when revived, are not living tradition but quaint historical study, danced and sung by people who did not learn these from their grandmothers. Hence folk today is modern fad, not really living tradition. As the sense of continuity with the past is weakened, man loses another thread of identity. He cannot locate himself as a link in a chain of ancestors; he often doesn't even know who his people were. He is an ambiguous man who must be what he makes of himself and is dealt with not as a respresentative of his people but statistically in the mass.

But it is not just what a man does or makes of himself but how society recognizes him that creates identity. A third factor is *loss of identifying ceremony*. As already illustrated by the story about the college graduation, there is less emphasis today than in the past on ceremonies that recognize the individual—his status, achievements, importance as a person. A whole range of ceremonies do this: baptism, birthdays, name days, religious confirmations, anniversaries, initiations, graduations, honors, retirements, funerals. Some families, institutions, and communities still do most of these things. But somehow—for reasons of efficiency or because there are too many people or we don't know people as individuals—we find less time for this sort of thing nowadays. Ceremonies of identity are becoming privatized—you do it on your own, the community rarely participates unless it is a man of distinction; each Joseph, George, and Peter is on his own. Or the ceremonies are so impersonal that the individual is lost. Even a funeral— that last of all recognitions—may be a quick and efficient disposal procedure with little satisfaction to the community (if they bother to come). Personal eulogies of the deceased are more and more rare. Today it is a fact that the average person doesn't have nearly enough ceremonies of recognition, and some don't have any at all. So it is not surprising to see a yearning for celebrities (who get what the average man doesn't), ego screaming in costume and faddism. Some people even commit crimes to get their name in the papers.

A fourth identity-disturbing factor, perhaps most important of all, is the relationship of mobility and numbers of people to *loss of social concern* in day-to-day relationships. We all know people are moving more and more these days, leaving their homes, crowding into cities, riding around in cars, airplanes, busses, vans, and scooters; homes are being built on wheels. The amount, speed, and radius of movement are increasing rapidly. Contracts with other people are increasing geometrically, accentuated by mass communication. We can easily see this means less time and attention for any *one* person, group, or locality. At the same time institutions are being redesigned for greater efficiency in handling masses of people. But that does not serve anybody in particular. It is not surprising, then, as sociologists have pointed out, that in the midst of social services people develop a sense of aloneness—the "lonely crowd" phenomenon, the feeling that nobody pays any attention to me. It is very hard to get anyone to take an interest in someone else, as is often seen in today's doctor-patient relationships. Old people, especially those whose children have moved away, feel neglected. Machinery and efficient services are used to replace social concern, but they fail. They arouse resentment by their red tape and cold professional manner. The production line, payroll number, and bureaucratic rubber stamps are all seen as enemies, as devices for denying identity.

Nor does increase of the number of friends with more contacts really remedy the problem. We know acquaintances cannot really take the place of friends, let alone kinfolk. Dale Carnegieism is a good political tactic but no substitute for concern. What I am saying is that, as mobility and number of contacts increase, life becomes more like a cocktail party and less like a birthday party; relationships shift toward the casual. This means that the chances become good that large numbers of people will suffer lack of social concern most of the time. As sociologists might say, there is an insufficient rate of meaningful interaction, man-to-man, day-to-day. The sheer amount of interaction is not the question. You can see a thousand people and not relate to anybody, but one phone call or letter can make your day complete. Most people, however, need more than a letter; most people require a matrix of frequent affection, support, emotional sharing, and genuine concern from a sufficient number of people outside their family, especially the approval of superiors and peers as confidants and buddies. The paradox, however, is that a buzzing extraverted society can suffer a lack of concern and not know it. This lack of concern is masked by what sociologists call false personalization or role-playing—for example, the pretense of concern by an insurance salesman. Associations and memberships may not mean anything beyond a membership card or being a member of an audience-crowd at meetings. How can one tell if there is genuine concern? Statistics of participation (for example, church attendance) are usually worthless. Some indices, however, can show it, such as the number of personal calls on a person who is sick. Few such calls invite the conclusion "I wasn't *that* important." Another sign of lack of concern is that people feel they can't get through to others, that they talk but nobody listens. There is a growth of psychotherapeutic programs devoted to breaking through emotional walls in modern society. This indicates inadequate feedback of emotional support, sincere affection, self-expression (to which others listen, as distinguished from ego screaming), and real information needed for personal guidance.

I have tried to explain how modern society can have a high level of involvement along with a low level of concern. Sociologists since Ferdinand Toennies and Emile Durkheim have pointed out that mass society suffers a chronically low level of social concern and that the break up of small groups which are the natural focus of concern (extended family, clan, tribe, village, parish) has not been replaced by associations of modern times like labor union, party, church, or social set. A vacuum persists. So rebels scream and say, "Look at me!", "Pay attention to me!"

It is not surprising that lack of concern goes with a fifth element in the context of modern identity problems: *shallowness of feeling*, inability to feel sentiments strongly or to sense that one is living fully. Many writers have noted various signs of emotional shallowness, such as violence and sensation in movies increasing without corresponding shock and depth of tragic feeling, and the passing away of romantic—strictly sentimental old-fashioned—love. Emotion is privatized. Everyone is trying to be cool; it is becoming embarrassing to express feelings openly, "wave the flag," be homesick, "wear one's heart on one's sleeve." Perhaps a reason is lack of emotional support; one sees evidence that others do not really feel what they say; and some say nothing at all—play it cool. In the background is the fact that our modern society continually overstresses reason, facts, and machinery at the expense of feeling, impulse, and intuition—the entire inner life. Objectivity is a fetish of science. One is apologetic for poetry, religious faith, artistic sensibility, premonitions, dreams, scruples, and prejudices of all kinds. I do not know all the reasons, but I think that the whole feedback network of emotion has become unplugged. So the batteries of sentiment do not get charged often enough. If this is so, then it is not surprising to see style rebellion and activism offsetting emotional shallowness with flamboyance, irrational extremes, search for intense experience even through drugs, a wish to feel oneself deeply, genuinely, even painfully.

Finally, we must consider the effect of entertainers, stars, recordings, films, and television on the success image. What does the current worship of celebrities do for identity? It seems plain that mass communication has a strong but confusing impact. It is confusing aspiration among the young by putting up dubious and unworthy ideals in place of the standard success image which has deteriorated. We can easily see that young people have been offered a variety of models in mass communication today which their parents never heard of and are very doubtful about approving. Some are downright alarming—rock musicians and their birds, playboys and playgirls, etc.

Many are glamorous successes, such as the four unwashed boys who with one recording made a million dollars in a week.

Contrasting with such exciting possibilities is the standard success image, which has become tarnished. I refer to the ideal of the' hard working Horatio Alger hero. Two reasons for the drabness of the standard success image can be mentioned. One is that literature has dismally depicted the mediocrity of the organization man and the bureaucrat in writings like William F. Whyte's *The Organization Man*, C. Wright Mills' *White Collar*, Sloan Wilson's *Man in the Grey Flannel Suit*. James Thurber's *Secret Life of Walter Mitty* and films like *The Graduate* present a similar picture. The white-collar worker's career is thus seen as unheroic, boring, restricted, a dreary shuttling between the rat race of business and the tame existence of suburbia. Material possessions do not compensate for such restriction; advertisements say "happy life" but that is not what the young see. The other reason for drabness of the standard success image is that the pileup of irrelevant information in a technological-scientific society has become an overload in education—boring and irrelevant school studies which discourage students and kill interest. One can almost hear a student say, "Look what you have to go through to get a job in bureaucracy and a fifty-foot lot in suburbia!" The college student feels acutely that he has to memorize and regurgitate at examination time (the phrase speaks of his attitude) the enormous pile of facts that he feels have no relation to his own life. But if he leaves the lecture hall and goes to the rest of life—television, community affairs, and all that—he finds the same irrelevance unless he restricts his attention to a narrow band of stimuli, such as rock and roll music, skin diving, or some sport or hobby which for him means intense and meaningful life—"where the action is," "What's happening *now*, baby."

So, putting all this together, we see young people caught in a dilemma between a rather drab career outlook and unrealistic, inappropriate, sometimes demoralizing career goals offered by celebrities as models in mass communication. This I call the Mitty Syndrome, dreaming of being glamorous TV stars or jet setters but unable to attain this in fact, wanting to be what one cannot be and not wanting to be what one is and has a realistic expectation of being. When such an explosion of wishes stimulated by mass communication is not met by realistic career opportunities, frustration follows. It is a formula for unhappiness, for dissatisfaction with oneself.

These six factors—destruction of the home environment, loss of contact with tradition, lack of ceremonies recognizing the individual, lack of social concern, weakening sentiments, and confusion of aspiration—add up to identity frustrations of the middle class in mass society. They are symbolic disturbances, breakdowns in the meaning of various symbols of the environment and in the meaning of success. No amount of pile up of wealth and welfare services is going to solve these problems unless focused on improving meaningful relationships of people to each other and to their home environments, thus reducing psychological and spiritual frustrations.

Once the problem is seen in these terms, the natural question is: What can be done to provide more identifying experiences in a mass society? I teach at a university of 23,000 students, of which I face 200 every week. It is a challenge to me to think of how to focus more on the student's identity as a person—not on new facts in the curriculum but on how to make them more relevant to his life. Not by nonacademic substitutes, such as football games and riots, but by something going on in the curriculum which the student will regard as too important to be disturbed by football games and riots. If he lets his hair grow long, I hope it will be because he is so interested in his studies that he hasn't time for a haircut, not because he wishes to defy society.

But how to produce such an academic miracle? It is the duty of educators to find out what techniques will do this. There is a clear difference between devices that increase efficiency of education (defined as number of students reached times amount of information transmitted) and devices that will identify students as persons and help them find what they need to grow as persons. Many highly efficient methods—large lecture halls, computerized learning, TV courses, films, machine scored examinations which call for no more achievement than a check in the right place—do practically nothing for identity. On the other hand, many methods accentuate identity. These include debate, creative writing and art, producing and acting dramas, solo performances and competitions, first name relationships, frank and open discussions, the cluster principle of living together in small groups, self-directed groups not dominated by the authority of instructors, and cathartic group sessions and other kinds of group therapy.

I trust that many will be studying the same problem in the factory, bureaucracy, community, church, hospital, welfare agency, and psychotherapy. Sensitivity training today is seeking a kind of interaction that will help people get through to others, solve emotional problems, and find themselves. New things are being discovered every day. There is reason to hope that we are on the verge of discoveries about how to make the individual important again even in a mass society. Already new forms of welfare are appearing whose motto is, significantly, not material benefit but pride. And we must get over the idea that the focus of social welfare is entirely in the lower classes. In my opinion, universities are just as much in need of identity programs as slums.

We need to develop youth programs which will put back into growing up, family life, and school experience as many as possible of the identity-giving features which have been lost by the mass society. These features include a home environment, contact with tradition and pride in the past and ancestors, ceremonies of recognition, genuine social concern, strong sentiments, and clear and satisfying models of aspiration. The difficulty of this need not discourage us from searching for levers of constructive change.

If we can do this with any real success, in my opinion, style rebellion and hippieism will disappear.

MASS
COMMUNICATION
BARRIERS

The nonconformists on campuses are
beginning to look so much alike I can't
tell them apart.   J. Lair

The mass media used to be viewed as conveyors of opinions that
were injected wholesale into the audience. Radio, television, and
print media supposedly propagandized us into believing almost
anything. We now know that such a view of the media is
extremely simplified and inaccurate.

As in the other communication arenas, the mass arena is
plagued by several communication barriers. To begin with, people
do not receive messages in total isolation. They often hear about
a message from others, watch it in the presence of others, and
discuss the message after having seen it. If your message is inaccurate, comes on too strongly, or you otherwise misjudge the
audience, its effectiveness will probably be diminished. The degree
to which the mass message relates to our own individual situation
is crucial. In the following essay, Marvin Karlins and Herbert I.
Abelson summarize research that demonstrates that successful
persuasion adapts to our reasons for believing certain things. They
also show how individual personality traits can impede or enhance persuasive attempts. Anyone who wishes to influence
others in the mass communication arena should be aware of how
individual habits and interests can be communication barriers.
Awareness of this information can also help one understand why
he responds to public or mass appeals the way he does.

MARVIN KARLINS
HERBERT I. ABELSON

THE
AUDIENCE AS
INDIVIDUALS

SUCCESSFUL
PERSUASION TAKES
INTO ACCOUNT THE
REASONS UNDER-
LYING ATTITUDES AS
WELL AS THE
ATTITUDES
THEMSELVES.

Because much of our behavior can be related to our attitudes, attitudes themselves are sometimes mistaken for the fundamental causes of behavior. Some remarks of social scientists in this regard are worth summarizing (Katz, 1960; Sarnoff & Katz, 1954). Identical attitudes may have different motivational bases. Successful propaganda comes from knowing what is *behind* the attitude. For example, we might find three people who all say they are against private ownership of industry. One of them feels that way because he has only been exposed to one side of the story and has nothing else on which to base his opinion. The way to change this man's opinion may be to expose him to facts, take him to visit some factories, meet some workers and supervisors. A second person is against private ownership because that is the prevailing norm or social climate in the circles in which he finds himself. His attitudes are caused by his being a part of a group and conforming to its standards. You cannot change this fellow just by showing him facts. The facts must be presented in an atmosphere which suggests a social reward for changing his opinion. Some kind of status appeal might be a start in that direction. A third person may have negative attitudes toward private industry because by making business the scapegoat for all his troubles, he can unload his pent-up feelings of bitterness and disappointment at the world for not giving him a better break. Attitudes often exist because they give people somebody or something to blame, instead of having to blame themselves for their own failures and shortcomings. Trying to change this third person with facts may actually do more harm than good. The more the evidence shows him how wrong he is, the more he looks for good reasons to support his beliefs. This kind of person can sometimes be influenced by helping him understand why he has a particular attitude. Once he realizes that his attitudes are protective devices for his personality, he may not hang on to them as tenaciously as before and may begin to see things in proper perspective.

In summary, three of the reasons why a man may have a particular set of attitudes are these:

1. Factual—the attitudes help give meaning to many otherwise unrelated bits of information. These attitudes should be especially susceptible to change by exposing the individual to new facts so that he can see things in a different light.

2. Social—having the attitudes makes it possible for a man to feel himself acceptable to the groups of people with whom he wants to associate. He may never actually be a part of these desirable groups, but he feels closer to them by having something in common with them. Buying a certain brand of whiskey may be the only link that an individual has with men of distinction, but he may regard it as better than no link at all. Likewise, our feelings of kinship with certain social groups often underlie our attitudes toward labor unions, the United Nations, scandal magazines and so on. Attempts at changing socially derived attitudes should be most successful when they are made with reference to the acceptability of the new attitudes to the groups that are important to the audience.

3. Personal—the attitudes provide a rationalization for an individual's shortcomings, and make it possible for him to face the world and himself. The employee who craves recognition for his achievements but doesn't receive it often cannot admit to himself that perhaps his achievements are not worthy of recognition. It may be much more satisfying for him to believe that other people are not intelligent enough to appreciate his worth. This kind of attitude is ego-defensive in function.

Specimen Studies

1. A test of the hypothesis that the motivations underlying attitudes are factual, social, or personal (ego-defensive) would involve (1) being able to identify these motivations in people; (2) attempting to change

some attitudes by techniques which appeal to one or more of these underlying motivations; (3) seeing if an appeal that is geared to a specific motivation works better than an appeal that is not related to the individual's motivations. Some experiments along this line have been conducted.

On experiment by Katz, Sarnoff and McClintock (1956) studied attitudes toward Negroes. A major hypothesis was that people's anti-Negro attitudes which have a personal (ego-defensive) basis can be influenced by showing that the attitudes exist to protect the personality rather than because the facts about Negroes logically support such attitudes. Another side of the hypothesis is that people whose anti-Negro prejudice does *not* have a personal (ego-defensive) basis can be influenced more readily by presenting them with factual information about Negroes.

Accordingly, the experimenters prepared two kinds of influence materials. One was for the ego-defensive group. It explained how scapegoating works, and how anti-minority attitudes are often the result of personality conflicts that have nothing to do with the attitudes themselves. This explanation was followed by a case history of a college girl which showed the connection between her prejudices and her personality. The other kind of influence material was for the non-ego-defensive group: a resume of the achievements of Negroes in America and how they have made good whenever opportunities were available to them.

Nearly 250 college students participated in the study. At a first session, they filled out questionnaires designed to reveal their attitudes toward Negroes and took some psychological tests which helped categorize the motivations underlying their attitudes as personal (ego-defensive) or factual.

For the second session, held a week later, the students were assigned to three groups, without regard to the answers they had given the previous week. One group read the material which explained the relationship between attitudes and personality. A second group read the informational material. The third group was a control group and read nothing. After exposure to their respective reading matter, the first two groups filled out the attitude questionnaires again. The control group did likewise. Six weeks later, all three groups once more answered an attitude-toward-Negroes questionnaire.

Findings: *The ego-defensive people in general did respond better to the material that attempted to help them understand themselves than to the purely informational material. But as the experimenters had predicted, the individuals who were* extremely *ego-defensive did not respond well to this kind of influence attempt. The reason advanced was that for these people, the attitudes they held were so crucial to the maintenance of their personalities that some kind of psychiatric treatment would be a necessary forerunner of successful persuasion (Katz, Sarnoff & McClintock, 1956).**

Discussion

There is a valuable lesson in these experiments and in the reasoning of the researchers responsible for them. The findings show that when the factors underlying attitudes are taken into account, persuasion is more likely to be successful. Successful persuasion depends on an understanding of why an audience should want to accept your point of view or buy your product.

Within the last two decades research on people's buying habits has undergone a considerable change. The change reflects an awareness on the part of advertising and marketing men of the need to know more about the personal factors underlying consumer brand preferences. This research emphasis has been named motivation research.** The justification for motivation research lies in the assumption that people often are attracted to or repelled by a particular brand of product for reasons that the purchaser himself may be unaware of, or unwilling to discuss with an interviewer.

Here is an illustration. Some clothing made from synthetic fibers is washable, and dries relatively free of wrinkles. It might be supposed that such "wash and wear" clothing would have immediate appeal to housewives as it requires little if any ironing before being worn. It is not very helpful for a manufacturer of such wash and wear garments to learn that some women refuse to buy them. But a con-

---

* *This experiment, with some modifications, was repeated at another time with another group of subjects. The results were substantially the same as those already reported (Katz, McClintock & Sarnoff, 1957).*

** *For an example of how one investigator describes the motivations underlying man's purchasing behavior see: Kotler, P. Behavioral models for analyzing buyers. Journal of Marketing, 1965, 29, 37–45. Nondemographic analyses, "psychographics," psychological or attitudinal market segmentation are all concepts that have evolved out of the motivation research idea; all attempt to relate personal or social characteristics of consumers with their buying behavior.*

sumer research study which attempts to discover the reasons underlying resistance to buying such clothing might reveal that (1) some women are still unaware of the no-ironing feature of the fabrics; (2) some women feel their neighbors might be critical of them for turning out a family in clothes that were not ironed; (3) some women might think they are not fulfilling their roles as housewives if they attempted to cut out any of the key household chores, such as ironing. These reasons correspond to the factual, social and personal bases for attitudes which were discussed earlier. Each of these reasons requires a somewhat different advertising and promotional effort. Women who do not yet know of the no-ironing feature may be persuaded to buy if the facts about the fabrics are presented to them. Women who fear the criticism of their neighbors might be persuaded by advertisements which show people like themselves enjoying the advantages of wash and wear clothing. And women who feel that to fulfill their roles as housewives requires a certain amount of ironing drudgery, might be persuaded by an insight approach: helping them understand why it is so important to them to play the part of housewife in such a particular and inflexible way.*

SUGGESTED READINGS: MOTIVATIONS UNDERLYING ATTITUDES

1. Katz, D. The functional approach to the study of attitudes. *Public Opinion Quarterly*, 1960, *24*, 163–204.
2. Katz, D., Sarnoff, I., & McClintock, C. Ego-defense and attitude change. *Human Relations*, 1956, *9*, 27–45.
3. Kotler, P. Behavioral models for analyzing buyers. *Journal of Marketing*, 1965, *29*, 37–45.

THE INDIVIDUAL'S PERSONALITY TRAITS AFFECT HIS SUSCEPTIBILITY TO PERSUASION

Thus far we have spent most of our time writing about persuasive appeals without paying much attention to personality differences

---

* *This example, though somewhat dated, has been retained for its illustrative value.*

among individuals exposed to those appeals. Some persuaders choose to ignore personality differences altogether—thinking the impact of their message will be the same on all their listeners regardless of any individual differences between them. Such reasoning, of course, is fallacious; there is ample evidence to indicate that the same appeal is received and acted upon differently by different listeners due to variations in their personality characteristics. Three such characteristics—intelligence, authoritarianism and integrative complexity—are examined in this section.

During the past decade an increasing number of investigators have become interested in exploring the relationship between personality traits and persuasibility—an interest kindled in large part by publication of the Hovland and Janis *Personality and Persuasibility* volume in 1959. Today there are literally hundreds of studies on the topic—enough information to fill several books. Obviously we cannot do justice to the area in the space of a few pages; what we will try to do is give the reader a feeling for the type of research being conducted in this domain and also show how personality does influence an individual's susceptibility to persuasion.

Intelligence and Persuasion

SPECIMEN STUDIES

1. In an experiment by Carment, Miles and Cervin (1965) 248 undergraduates were given a battery of tests designed to determine: (1) intelligence; (2) introversion-extroversion (see Eysenck, 1957); (3) opinions on several topics (e.g., the quality of products manufactured in America). From this initial sample of students a final subject selection was made, based on individual responses to the three tests. These remaining subjects were then divided into pairs to discuss one of the opinion topics they had disagreed on. Subject pairings pitted: (1) high intelligent-extroverted vs high intelligent-extroverted; (2) high intelligent-extroverted vs high intelligent-introverted; and (3) high intelligent-extroverted vs low intelligent-extroverted.

Subjects were judged on their *persuasiveness* and *persuasibility*. Persuasiveness was defined as: (1) the tendency to speak first and (2) speak the greatest amount during the discussion. Persuasibility was defined as the "tendency to change or not to change opinion when placed in a persuasion situation which requires arguing a topic with an individual who holds an opposing opinion."

Findings: *Results indicate that the more intelligent and extro-verted subjects are more persuasive (talk first and most) and less persuasible (change their opinion less frequently) in arguing their point of view with a disagreeing opponent (Carment, Miles & Cervin, 1965).*

2. One experimenter had a group of high school students in-dicate how they felt about various national groups, religious sects, political parties, etc. Some time later the students were exposed to a communication containing crudely propagandistic statements about each of the groups they had rated. The intelligence of the group was estimated from their scores on a standard intelligence test.

Findings: *The most intelligent students were the least influenced by this kind of propaganda (Wegrocki, 1934).*

3. During World War II, many experiments were carried on to test the effectiveness of the *Why We Fight* films which were produced for troop indoctrination. Opinions on the subject of a film were ascertained by the use of a questionnaire, both before and after the showing. The measure of intelligence which the investigators used was years of schooling completed.

Findings: *The films were in general more effective on the soldiers of higher intelligence. There were reversals in this trend, however, especially on opinion questions, but not so much for factual questions (Hovland, Janis & Kelley, 1953).*

Discussion

An examination of data from the *Why We Fight* films led to the conclusion that an over-all score for general intelligence is made up of separate components, each of which helps to explain the experi-mental results: (1) learning ability—the brighter people learn and re-member more; (2) critical ability—the brighter people can sort out the reasonable arguments from the specious ones; (3) inference-drawing ability—the brighter people can see the implications behind the facts.

From this kind of reasoning about intelligence and susceptibility to persuasion, two hypotheses were formulated (Hovland, Janis & Kelley, 1953):

1. "Persons with high intelligence will tend—mainly because of their ability to draw valid inferences—to be *more* influenced than those with low intellectual ability when exposed to per-

suasive communications which rely primarily on impressive logical arguments."

2. "Persons with high intelligence will tend—mainly because of their superior critical ability—to be *less* influenced than those with low intelligence when exposed to persuasive communications which rely primarily on unsupported generalities or false, illogical, irrelevant argumentation."

SUGGESTED READINGS: INTELLIGENCE AND PERSUASION

1. Carment, D., Miles, C., & Cervin, V. Persuasiveness and persuasibility as related to intelligence and extraversion. *British Journal of Social and Clinical Psychology*, 1965, 4, 1–7.

MASS
COMMUNICATION
SELF-DISCLOSURE

The person that each of us is—is unique.
J. Powell

Open and honest communication with oneself and others is the keystone to self-disclosure. In the mass arena, open and honest self-disclosure is not impossible, but it is very difficult. An announcer may reveal things about himself in disclosing to an audience, but such events are rare. In addition, we as consumers of mass messages cannot all self-disclose to the media. If you get angry with a TV program or newspaper you can shout and write a letter, but no truly open and honest communication can continue between you and the media.

We do need, however, some mechanism open for the disclosure of mass numbers of people. Many are fortunate to find friends and relatives to talk with, but others of us must seek other alternatives. Services such as Dial-A-Listener provide a partial channel for one to use for self-disclosure in the mass communication arena. Does the need for a Dial-A-Listener service tell you anything about the need for communication involvement in contemporary society?

THE
LISTENERS
In Davenport, Iowa, telephone number 323-1819 rang. The call was answered by a 71-year-old woman, a retired schoolteacher. "Hello," she said pleasantly. "This is your listener." Her caller said "Hello" back, but there was uncertainty in her voice. "Is this your first call to us?" the schoolteacher prompted gently. "Yes," came the reply. The subsequent conversation between two strangers went like this:

I'm a widow living in this house alone. I was so lonesome tonight I had to talk to someone. What bothers me is the loneliness, not talking to anyone.

I'm glad you thought of us. I hope you call any time you want to visit. You're only the second caller I've had tonight. I was getting lonesome too.

I like to sit out on the porch when there's a breeze. But there's not a breath of air moving. The air's so heavy.

It certainly is.

I guess I know why I'm so lonely. It was just about this time of year my husband died. We would have been married 45 years next Christmas.

It must be an especially difficult time for you.

The talk ranged over a variety of personal concerns—the shading elm tree in the front yard that had to come down, a son who seldom came to visit, all the small but vital concerns of an old woman in a house and a life that for many years had been too empty. In content, it was very little different from the 150 calls a month received by 323-1819, which is the number of a service known as Dial-a-Listener. At the receiving end is a rotating staff of ten volunteers—including the schoolteacher, a nurse, an author, a civil engineer—who keep the number open around the clock. At the other end are the lonely people of Davenport who hunger for the sound of a sympathetic human voice.

Although intended primarily to serve the aged, Dial-a-Listener occasionally gets calls from the young. One eleven-year-old boy, whose parents work, phones nearly every day after school, and sometimes

Drawing by O'Brian: © 1961 The New Yorker Magazine, Inc.

late at night when he can't get to sleep. "I think I'm a homosexual," began another youthful caller. "Where can I get help?" He was referred to a social agency. Crank calls are rare. One high school girl rang up to ask how to divide 182 by 9; her listener, no arithmetician, was stumped.

Sympathetic Voice

This modest effort in human relations was begun last March by the Senior Citizens' Pilot Project under the sponsorship of the Scott County Commission on Aging. Unlike the numerous Dial-a-Prayer switchboards and suicide-prevention centers, its purpose is neither to deliver canned messages of hope nor to cope with life-and-death crises, but to offer lonely callers a simple human connection. The service costs almost nothing: less than $700 a year for telephone equipment and a few office supplies. Not everyone can be a listener. "We're very selective about our volunteers," says Clayton Moore, the project director. They are screened for the qualities that will survive the impersonality of the telephone: a warm, sympathetic voice and, above all, the willingness to listen.

Anonymity is scrupulously observed. No one ever knows who the other person is, and no one ever asks. "People feel free to talk when they know their friends or family will never know what's being said," observes Director Moore. "They tell us things they can't talk about to someone they know." If Dial-a-Listener works, it is because there is loneliness at both ends of the line. The listeners seem to get as much out of it as their callers. But many of the calls are like un-finished stories that have a beginning but no end. "It's like reading only a little way into a book," said one listener rather wistfully. "You don't always know how things work out."

To reveal myself openly and honestly takes the rawest kind of courage.
J. Powell

One factor that impedes self-
disclosure in the mass arena
is that our attitudes serve
important functions for us.
Our attitudes are sometimes
"frozen" and serve to protect
us from persuasive attempts.
Those attitudes also then
prevent open and honest
communication. George W.
Howells spells out some of the
important functions our
attitudes serve for us. As you
read the selection, think of
how disclosure is prevented
or facilitated by such attitudes.

GEORGE W. HOWELLS

DIFFERENCES BETWEEN PEOPLE— HOW IMPORTANT ARE FEELINGS?

Resistance to Change

So here we find ourselves face to face with one of the thorniest of problems, the problem of resistance to change. You probably know, from experience, of examples in industry where some change has been proposed, change which seems obviously to be of advantage to all concerned, but which has been strenuously resisted, with little apparent reason, or for stated reasons which obviously have little to do with the situation. Two theories are sometimes advanced to account for this common type of situation. The first is that people are often too stupid to see where their best interests lie. The other is that man is instinctively reluctant to change his ways. Neither of these theories even begin to hold water. In resisting change, people often reveal high intelligence and skill in justifying their stand, and

From George W. Howells, Human Aspects of Management. *Reprinted by permission William Heinemann Ltd., London.*

resistance to change is found in all levels of the community. With regard to so-called instinctive conservatism, we know enough about instincts to realize that man has remarkably few of them; as stated above, man is essentially a learning animal, which means he does not have to rely on instincts. Indeed, it can usually be seen that, once change *has* been accepted, people become enthusiastic about the new ways of doing things. The source of the problem is that changes in methods of working, changes in techniques, changes in almost any part of the job, represent changes in the kinds of pressure under which people live. Most people have, perhaps not without difficulty, built up a system of attitudes which enables them to adjust to pressures with which they have become familiar. It must be recognized that it is asking a lot if, in response to changing circumstances and resulting different pressures, we have to ask people to try to change their attitudes. When they persist in resisting change it is as well to understand that people are not showing their stupidity; neither are they behaving instinctively. They are behaving in a very characteristic human way; only very unstable people are likely to change their attitudes easily.

However, the fact that we can, and must, understand the problems associated with people's attitudes, does not alter the fact that supervisors are often on the spot when changes are afoot. The supervisor is probably at the receiving end of most of the resistances. Being understanding may be very desirable, but in itself it does not solve any problems. If one is to get change accepted, and if one is aware of the existence of resistant attitudes, what does one do? The cliché answer, again, is better communication; but what sort of communication? Have you ever noticed how, when details of changes, with the reasons, are communicated to people who are opposed to the idea, they seem to remain remarkably unconvinced? It often seems that the result of such communication even hardens the resistant attitudes. Even worse, it can often happen that your argument is thrown back at you, having been given a twist which seems to suggest that the reasons given *for* change are really reasons *against* change. How is this possible? We have only to refer to the last chapter to see the process all too quickly. "Facts" always involve interpretation. Interpretation depends on background. Attitudes form a very insistent background to the interpretation of data, and, particularly if the data seem to threaten the attitudes, they can usually be interpreted in a way which ensures that the data fit into the pattern of attitudes. A well-known story illustrates the process.

The children in a certain school held very negative attitudes towards foreigners. The head teacher, to improve the attitudes, provided a lot of material, films, posters, leaflets, to provide information about foreigners. One teacher gave his class an essay to write, to see what changes had occurred. The brightest boy, Spinks, ended with the following: "In my opinion, all foreigners are bastards." Disappointed but not downhearted, the teacher gave a series of lessons on the great achievements of foreigners. Marconi, Röntgen, Curie, and so on. These, he thought, would be conclusive facts. A further essay was set, and Spinks now concluded: "In my opinion, all foreigners are cunning bastards."

It can be seen that communication does not necessarily change attitudes; it can often have the reverse effect. The problem, of course, arises from the fact that we often have a too-narrow concept of communication. Communication does not automatically mean giving information; it can also mean receiving information; it can also mean expressing feelings; it can also mean listening to other people expressing their feelings. One person can never change another person's attitudes. Attitudes are entirely a matter of personal adjustment. The only person who can change a person's attitudes is that person himself. How does it happen?

How Attitudes Change

Attitudes change in three ways. First, although we have stressed that attitudes resist change, this is not the same as saying that attitudes do not change at all. Most attitudes in most people are changing gradually and almost imperceptibly, by a sort of evolutionary process. When one studies the history of past periods, even of the last century, one can see how attitudes towards, for example, the punishment of criminals, or cruelty to animals, have changed. The hanging of common thieves, the baiting of bears, were accepted as commonplace not so very long ago. The change of attitude in such matters is quite apparent, though the transition seems to have been gradual. Similarly, attitudes to conditions of employment have shown a fairly gradual change. Our problem, however, in modern times, is one of almost explosive change in technological and economic fields; undoubtedly attitudes to these changes would change slowly if the evolutionary processes were allowed their chance. Unfortunately, the very gradualness of these processes is something we cannot afford. If people are to reap the advantages of these changes their attitudes to them must adapt at a more rapid pace than the evolutionary process permits.

Second, attitudes can change as a result of a person's having experienced a severe shock, or intense pressure. Battle neurosis, or shell-shock, is an extreme example of the effects of severe shock. "Brainwashing" is an example of the effects of intense pressure. These are mentioned only for the record. It is not anticipated that supervisors will feel inclined either to shock, or to brain-wash, their subordinates! Even if, in despair, you were so inclined, you would be faced with the problem that, although such methods can undoubtedly lead to attitude change, the nature of the change is very unpredictable and could lead to most unwelcome results.

Third, attitudes can change in a fairly rapid, yet fairly controlled way, if people are permitted, even encouraged, to give expression to their attitudes. To see why this is so, let us briefly recapitulate the nature of attitudes. Remember that they are essentially emotional in their origin. The existence of an attitude implies that a lot of emotional energy, which might otherwise go to waste in impulsive reactions, is being held in reserve, for more controlled uses. This emotional pressure maintains the attitude in its usually inflexible form; this is why, if facts are shot at it, they often bounce back, distorted. But if a person gives expression to his attitude, by describing, explaining, and justifying his feelings, it will be found that the process involves the release of emotional tension. It is one of the most consistent patterns in human behaviour, that unexpressed attitudes seem to harden. It will be found that, when a person is encouraged to express his attitudes, he often starts off very dogmatically, even explosively. Sometimes, of course, this can be very discouraging for those trying to get acceptance of new ideas, but it would be very short-sighted to try to stifle the objections. Rather, further expression should be encouraged. It is very likely that, when the initial dogmatic resistance has subsided, the emotional tension having been reduced, one will find that the resistant attitude gradually becomes more flexible: "I wouldn't like it to be thought that I am prejudiced. I'm always prepared to hear what anyone has to say. What are you suggesting, anyhow?" This is probably an over-optimistic example. It is not often as easy as that, but nevertheless this type of reaction, in a more complex and extended form, is quite characteristic. Quite apart from the fact that one can frequently observe this sort of thing happening in everyday affairs, a large number of controlled investigations by social psychologists have confirmed that this sort of pattern, in which emotions are gradually released by the expression of attitudes, does lead to greater flexibility of attitudes. Once attitudes, embodying preconceived resistances, have been loosened up, people are usually prepared to look at facts more objectively and interpret them in a more detached way. One such psychologist, Kurt Lewin, coined a descriptive way of describing the process. He talked about the "unfreezing–refreezing" process. It is as though attitudes represent a pattern of frozen emotions. Expression of the attitudes generates warmth which causes the emotions to thaw. They are then reshaped in the light of the new facts and finally refreeze in a new and more appropriate form.

Interaction of Ideas and Attitudes

The distinction we have been making between the rational and irrational bases of human differences is to some extent artificial, since they interact to such an extent. We are now in a position to see where this interaction occurs. We saw that ideas are the abstract, generalized form of our perception of experience, used as the basis of interpretation of new experience, and for the solving of problems. We also saw that attitudes are the habitual patterns of control of our emotions, developed to enable us to cope with the pressures of life without too much stress. It is easy to see that these are connected. Ideas organize our knowledge; attitudes organize our feelings. Every time we have a new experience, our ideas and attitudes are brought into action jointly. We talked in the last chapter about value ideas and said that conflicts about values occur very easily and are not easy to reconcile.

Let us think of an example. In this country's delicately balanced economy, credit squeezes are an all-too-familiar experience. If the squeeze is tight enough it leads to redundancy. The word redundancy refers to an idea. The idea refers to the process of dismissing employees because there is insufficient work for them. In basic English these people are now unemployed. We could make use of the word "dismissal"; we could also use the phrase "unemployed." But instead we use the words "made redundant" for the process of dismissal, and "redundant" for unemployed. It will be noticed that, in terms of the actual event, "dismissed" and "made redundant" mean the same; the employee is given notice that his services are no longer required. But there are values attached to the event. "Dismissed" suggests that the reason for the notice may be some shortcoming on the part of the employee; "made redundant" suggests that the reason lies entirely in the shortage of work. "Redundant" suggests out-of-work through no fault of one's own; "unemployed" suggests the rather hopeless situation of millions in the 'thirties. What we are saying, in other words, is that an idea like "redundancy" cannot be separated from certain attitudes that go with it.

At the time this book is being written, there is severe conflict in the motor-car industry concerning redundancy as the result of yet another credit squeeze. The conflict, superficially, is about avoiding redundancy by work-sharing. It is said that, if the men are being made redundant because of work shortage, it would be fairer and more acceptable to the men to share out the available work. But there is another side to the conflict. By implication the men are saying that the real issue is not redundancy but dismissal. The fear is widely expressed that many of the "redundant" men will never get their jobs back, because the management will use the opportunity to adapt their methods to enable future production to expand with the reduced labour force. The outcome of this serious conflict lies very much in the future, at the time of writing, but it is clear that the conflict is just as much about values as it is about the "factual" events. Any final resolution will have to take account of the combined differences in ideas and attitudes involved. This example shows how careful one must be in trying to unravel the true nature of a conflict situation. It may well happen that the words used to describe what is happening have these two kinds of meaning, and we must try to disentangle the events to which the words refer from the values which get attached. No one gets very far if one side thinks the conflict concerns certain *events*, while the other side is preoccupied with *values*.

People were not created for institutions.
Institutions were created for people.
People were not created to travel on
railroads, airplanes, and ships. These
were created to serve people. People
were not born to use hotels, houses,
offices, and stores. These were built to
serve people. Business is for people;
people are not just for business.
L. Appley

MASS
COMMUNICATION
EFFECTS

If the media do not lead us like lemmings to the sea, what kinds of effects do they have? This section will examine some of these effects and help place them into perspective.

The media can be assessed from many points of view. We can study whether the media changes votes, alters our attitudes, induces us to violent acts, or simply changes our general outlook on life. Whatever area we wish to pursue, the same general principle holds true: change comes in small doses and rarely from one message. Our attitudes and behaviors usually do change, but slowly over time.

There are many reasons why the mass media only produce gradual changes in us. Most important, as noted earlier, our interpersonal communication with others alters the effects of media messages. Then, too, we usually do not respond favorably to messages that are greatly opposed to our own attitudes. The most successful messages are those that are somewhat close to our own attitudes. And media messages cannot be put in irresistible "packages" or appeal to hidden motivations. They have no magic power over us, but can, in time exert small amounts of influence.

Raymond Bauer's classic essay "Limits of Persuasion" gives us a detailed account of the power of mass messages. If you are concerned that the mass media have far-reaching effects on you because they can appeal to your unconscious motives, you need not be too concerned. Bauer helps us to see clearly that presently there are limits to mass persuasion and that we all have the power to resist persuasive attempts.

RAYMOND A. BAUER

LIMITS OF PERSUASION

Man seems to live in perpetual hope and horror that infallible means have been developed whereby one man can control another's behavior. As usual, the hope and the horror are opposite sides of the same coin:

☐ On the hopeful side, some selfishly see the possibility of advantage for themselves in gaining control over their fellow men. Others, more idealistically, look to a "science of man" as the basis for establishing a Utopia which will be optimally efficient in the production of both material goods and human happiness.

☐ On the side of horror, some fear that they themselves will be "manipulated" to the advantage of someone else. Others fear the motives for their own relations to their fellow men. The image of a potential Utopia gets turned inside out, and we see that the reverse image is that of *1984*—the totalitarian state of George Orwell's novel—in which the best qualities of man are lost.

Recent developments in the science of psychology, and the publicity given to some of its more sensational applications—such as "subliminal advertising" or "brainwashing"—have strengthened our anxiety. The significance of these developments is of particular concern to businessmen, for they, along with politicians, will be responsible for the use of the new techniques. But there is no reason for panic. Anxiety stems, in part, from ignorance of the causal relations between the "persuaders" and the "persuaded." To show this relationship, and the limitations it imposes on the techniques, we must consider three broad areas of application:

☐ Propaganda and human relations.
☐ Appeals to "noneconomic" motives.
☐ Appeals to "unconscious" motives.

With a better understanding of the functioning of these techniques, we will be in a stronger position to evaluate them realistically.

New Fear or Old Scare?

The specter of "manipulation" and "hidden persuasion" has stalked all the lands that man has ever inhabited. The most primitive manifestation of the deep anxiety which we feel on this issue is represented by Nightmare Alice, the witch of Li'l Abner Land. From time to time, Nightmare Alice makes an effigy of one of the "good people" of Dogpatch and places this person under her hidden control. Black magic is found among most nonliterate peoples, and the fear of it persists. In the Middle Ages, people were "possessed by the devil"; in our own colonial times we went back to "witches."

In recent decades, to be sure, we have done away with such superstitions and become more "scientific." Or have we simply dressed up our old fears in modern fashions? Remember how during the 1920's and 1930's we worried about the mysterious powers of the mass media, particularly as manipulated by such practitioners as George Creel and Ivy L. Lee? My point is that although this century has led to tremendous progress in our knowledge of the human mind, our fear that this knowledge will be misused is as old as the history of man.

But what are the facts? Does modern psychology give us the tools to control each other? The full range of considerations is, of course, beyond our purview here. Moreover, any discussion of psychological techniques of persuasion and manipulation must, of course, be done without knowing what new knowledge may be developed. It is my belief, however, that what I have to say must hold in principle for almost any conceivable situation that may develop.

Ratio of Resistance

Let me begin my positive assertions with what may seem like a paradoxical statement. Without doubt we have, largely on the basis of improved social science knowledge in the fields of psychology, sociology, and anthropology, developed increasingly refined and effective means of persuasion. It does not follow, however, that even in the field of advertising we are able to effect more persuasion. How can this be? Simply because the increased knowledge benefits not only the persuader but also the target of persuasion. As the persuaders become more sophisticated, so do the people to be persuaded.

One way of reading the history of the development of techniques of persuasion is that the persuaders have been in a race to keep abreast of the developing resistance of the people to be persuaded. Thus:

☐ In the decades following World War I, we were very excited about the power of propaganda. We came close to saying that if it were possible to get a story in the newspapers or on the radio, people would automatically believe it and act on it. But what happened? Many people became so suspicious of propaganda that they would scarcely believe the news on the sports page.

☐ As a result, World War II propaganda in the Western countries was markedly different from that of World War I. Propagandists—that is, "persuaders"—were scrupulously careful not to test the credulity of their readers and listeners; they also avoided more blatant emotional appeals.

Why? People had become more sophisticated, and more resistant to "persuasion." Social science research on the effects of communications, by the beginning of World War II, had pretty well destroyed the myth of propaganda's omnipotence.

☐ We see today similar developments in advertising. There is still some advertising that is reminiscent of the old-fashioned pitchman selling snake oil. However, the development of the "soft sell" seems to me a tacit acknowledgment of the developing resistance of the potential consumer.

MANIPULATION MORE DIFFICULT

Within business and industry we have witnessed the evolving concern with human relations and communication. These events also have been viewed with horror as evidence of the growth of manipulation. But the viewers-with-horror naively assume that the knowledge on which this presumed manipulation is based is limited to the manipulators. Without in any way depreciating the desirability of the human relations approach—I not only favor it but even try to practice it—I doubt if it has produced any increase in manipulation.

As a matter of fact, all this new concern must have made the process of interpersonal communications more complicated. It is traditional that, as people become more diplomatic, their communications become more subtle. Perhaps we are all reaching the point of the diplomat who, on being informed of the death of his opposite number, queried: "I wonder what he meant by that." So in the absence of any long-run trend statistics on the number of effective persuasive and manipulative acts in business and industry, I shall remain content with pointing to the obvious mechanisms of resistance to persuasion; noting that manipulation has become more difficult; and suggesting there is no more reason to believe that the actual practice of manipulation has increased than that it has lessened. The data to prove me wrong are unobtainable.

Hidden Persuaders?

Our main fear, however, is not that we will be taken in by the persuasive logic of a Madison Avenue salesman but that, through appeals to deep, unconscious motives, we can be manipulated without even knowing it.

A book such as Vance Packard's *Hidden Persuaders*[1] generates a good deal of soul searching, both among the general public and within professional circles. This book, for the benefit of the fortunate few who are not familiar with it, tells *a* story, though certainly not *the* story, of how psychology has been applied in market research. By determining people's unconscious motives "via the principles of modern dynamic psychology," researchers are able to devise methods whereby mysterious and miraculous marketing results are produced. The consumer is powerless to resist these techniques, and he just buys and buys without knowing why. From this it is, of course, only one step to applying these techniques in politics, and *1984* will arrive at least twenty years ahead of schedule. Packard's picture, needless to say, is a trifle stylized.

Packard wrote his book to warn the public. The net impact of the volume is that there has been a complete revolution in market research in the form of motivation research, the term for the intensive explora-

[1] *New York, David McKay Company, Inc., 1957.*

tion of the psychological factors involved in consumer behavior and product usage. But it is only the *intensity of concern* that is new. So far as I can see, the major practical result has been—as one might expect —an increased and unrealistic demand for motivation research. Packard succeeded in painting the picture of psychological demonology so persuasively that motivation researchers are now concerned with giving their clients a more realistic notion of what they can do.

But Packard also succeeded in creating again the primitive anxiety that we are on the verge of being able to establish complete control over human behavior to the extent that the victims of this control will not have a chance to resist it because they do not realize it is there.

NONECONOMIC MOTIVES

In the first place, people *do* have some chance to resist the motives associated with the new techniques. People buy many things for *noneconomic* reasons, but such motives are not necessarily *unconscious*. It is a serious mistake to equate the two; and the use of the term *irrational* makes the confusion even worse. Once you label noneconomic motives irrational, you imply they are unreasonable, and you are well on the way to assuming they are unconscious.

When I say that people do things for noneconomic reasons (what others might call "irrational"), I am talking about the fact that people may buy a particular automobile because they desire status, the esteem of themselves and others; because they like products which fit their own self-image; or even because a man likes the feeling of potency which comes from driving an overhorsepowered vehicle. But I can see no reason to say a man is more "rational" to want transportation than to want self-respect and the esteem of others—though if it helps you to understand why he is doing what he is doing, you can say he is being less economic.

It is true that most of the motives I have just mentioned are not usually cited in response to the direct question: "Why did you buy that product?" In our culture, the accepted reasons for buying a product bear on its primary economic function: for instance, the cost of transportation provided by the car, the cleaning effectiveness of a soap, and so on. Accordingly, we are not as likely to think of the noneconomic motives as reasons for buying, bearing as they do on the secondary functions (or "added value") of products. Or, if we do, perhaps we feel a little ashamed and so are reticent about them. But in no meaningful sense are these motives unconscious. With a little stimulation almost every one of us recognizes their existence.

PRACTICAL CONSEQUENCES

This is no mere quibble. The fact that people can and do acknowledge the existence of these motives has considerable practical consequence. The use of appeals directed to such motives—as well as the widespread discussion, which we have already witnessed, of the concern given such motives in product design and merchandising—is bringing them into the center of consciousness as buying motives even if they were not there before. Some people will come to accept these as proper buying motives, and will probably learn to shop as astutely for the product that gives them the most prestige as for the product that has the lowest price, best mechanical qualities, and so on. Other people will resist these appeals, not accepting the secondary functions as a legitimate reason for buying.

Appeal to such motives may still serve, as in the past, to win the merchandiser a temporary advantage. However, as such appeals become customary and the public becomes generally aware of them, they will leave the merchandiser just about where he was to start with as far as his "persuasive advantage" is concerned.

Just because marketing and product design are based increasingly on psychologically oriented market research, it does not follow that products will continue to be sold increasingly on the basis of their secondary functions or "added value." At this time merchandisers are becoming more and more alert to the power of the secondary characteristics of products to satisfy consumer wants. As a psychologist I can have no conceivable objection in principle to people's noneconomic wants being satisfied. But we must look seriously at the possibility that this trend may reach the point of saturation.

Even now, the "irrationality"—a word I detest—of the consumer may be grossly overestimated. In few, if any, of the discussions of consumer motivation is there any mention of the growth of such consumer information services as Consumer's Research and Consumer's Union. The notion that people are not concerned with and do not understand the technical aspects of the products they buy may have to be tempered in the future. Today's consumers are almost certainly more interested and better informed on the technical features of products than they have been in the past.

There is something ironical in depicting the housewife shopping in the supermart as being indifferent to economy, being cozened by hidden persuaders into spending 15% more for her market basket than some stringent criterion says is necessary. Remember, the corner grocery store offers the housewife psychological rewards that the supermart does not. Yet in the interests of economy housewives have deserted the corner grocery store for the more impersonal, but more economical, supermart. This very same group of housewives has patronized discount houses, which scarcely give them the same psychological satisfactions as do department and high-class specialty stores.

One of the established arguments for stressing the secondary functions of a product is that all products in a given line are virtually identical with respect to their primary economic function. But suppose all automobiles in a given price range become virtually identical with regard to their symbolic value: this might drive the manufacturers to strive again for differentiation on the basis of the primary function of transportation. This notion is far from facetious. While Chrysler may indeed have gotten into difficulty a few years ago by de-emphasizing styling, today it is the small economical car—American Rambler or a foreign make—that is making inroads into the market, not the cars with "sex appeal."

This is not to brush aside the importance of the motives that the motivation researchers have stressed. I am merely suggesting that we keep our image of the consumer in somewhat clearer perspective. The merchandiser who concentrates too much on the secondary characteristics of products will find himself in as much difficulty as the one who ignores them completely. Motivation research may indeed become indispensable *because* of the very trends in the population I have been describing. The merchandiser will probably need increasingly detailed psychological knowledge of consumers as the years go on, if only to know what difficulties he is up against and how far he must stay away from noneconomic appeals.

Unconscious Motives

This is not the whole picture. All that I have said to this point is that many of the motives with which motivation research deals are *not* unconscious *in any meaningful sense;* and that, as these particular motives are appealed to, the consumer recognizes them more explicitly as motives linked to consumer behavior, and develops the capacity for a critical appraisal of appeals to such motives.

But there *are* some truly unconscious motives—that is, motives which the individual would not acknowledge consciously *to himself* even if, or especially if, they are called explicitly to his attention. To illustrate:

One of the most spectacular of the claims for the exploitation of unconscious motives is the development of the hardtop convertible. The hardtop is labeled as a compromise between the male buyer's dual attachment to the stable, reliable wife, symbolized by the sedan, and the flashy, unreliable mistress, symbolized by the convertible.

Certainly, in psychoanalytic thinking, it is accepted that the male child has conflict over thinking of his mother as a sexual object, and develops a split image of women. But I cannot conceivably take a stand on whether or not this is the complete story of the hardtop, or what substantial portion of the story it may comprise. I use it only as an example of appealing to a motive that is meaningfully referred to as unconscious.

There is something very plausible in the notion that if we understand another person's unconscious motivation, then we can appeal to his motives and get him to do something without his knowing why he did it. Certainly, he ought to be powerless to resist. To some extent this is true. But the entire picture is more complicated. Remember that there is a reason for certain motives remaining unconscious; in general, conscious acknowledgment of these motives would produce intolerable anxiety. Hence, appeal to such motives may backfire, and backfire violently. Thus, on an *a priori* basis, combining the "mistress and the wife" in the form of the hardtop convertible *could* have aroused anxiety and caused people to stay away from this model in droves.

My concern is not hypothetical. Research projects give us evidence that this happens, as in the following cases:

☐ One of the most deep-seated motives that is postulated in Freudian psychology is fear of castration. Furthermore, our anxiety over dental work is asserted to be due to a displacement of this castration anxiety. Again, I ask you to take this interpretation on its face value. It is only if you take it seriously that there is any issue at all. Presumably any message directed at relieving this anxiety ought to be met with prompt and vigorous positive response. Thus, instructions on oral hygiene ought to be listened to attentively, remembered, and acted on. However, experiments at Yale show that highly emotional messages on oral hygiene are less effective than detached, less emotional ones in conveying information on proper methods of preserving teeth.[2] Furthermore, the persons who heard the more

---

[2] *Carl I. Hovland, Irving L. Janis, and Harold H. Kelley,* Communication and Persuasion *(New Haven, Yale University Press, 1953), pp. 56–98.*

emotionally charged lectures were *less* resistant to counterpropaganda.

While the psychologists who did this work have been conservative in interpreting these results, in the context of this discussion I am willing to put myself out on a speculative limb. I would argue that this finding suggests that what I have already indicated may be true, that strong appeals to unconscious motives *may* evoke a great deal of anxiety, with resultant strong resistance to the message directed at the person. Thus, appeal to unconscious motives is a subtle and complex business which may well backfire.

☐ Much has been made of the possibilities of subliminal advertising—the presentation of messages at an intensity low enough so that the individual at whom they are directed is not aware of their presence. Work on subliminal perception is extremely controversial within the profession of psychology, and the particular data on which subliminal advertising was promoted are more questionable than most. However, what is significant is that Professor George Klein of New York University, on whose basic research subliminal advertising was built, reported in the public press that his own experiments gave evidence that some people responded *negatively* to the purportedly unseen stimuli.

There are innumerable difficult technical problems involved in subliminal advertising, and I do not want to pass judgment one way or another on the effectiveness of this phenomenon—although I have some profound doubts. All I want to point out is that to the extent we have firm knowledge in this area, some of that knowledge at least suggests that the individual may resist even "unperceived" messages. My guess would be that extensive use of subliminal advertising—again begging the technical question of what it is and whether it could be pulled off—would increase the strength and pervasiveness of resistance.

Power to Resist

I am not arguing for or against the effectiveness of any of these techniques of persuasion. I have merely indicated that individuals have the capacity to resist even on the unconscious level. I *am* arguing that the individual's resistance to persuasion probably increases in proportion to the efforts made to persuade him against his own perceived interest. We may even go further than that. Our primitive anxiety concerning the possibility of being manipulated leads us to resist persuasion by others, even in some instances where it may be *in our own interest.* Thus we have the automatic response, "Nobody's going to tell me what's good for me."

My guess is that over the years the American people have developed resistance to manipulation at about the same rate that our techniques of persuasion have become more sophisticated and effective. I mean, of course, that *if the audience had remained the same,* our new techniques would be more effective than our old ones. But the audience has not remained the same. The pace of the race has grown swifter, but it is difficult to say who has gained on whom.

Another point to remember is that merchandising is a competitive activity, and any technique of research or persuasion is about equally available to anyone who wants to make use of it. Even the vaunted subliminal advertisements would tend to cancel out each other if all refrigerator manufacturers, for example, were to use them on television. Competition among persuaders, indeed, is very much like that between the persuader and the object of his persuasion. Adoption of a new technique may well give a momentary competitive advantage, but this advantage lasts only until competitors have also adopted that technique. As long as there is a multiplicity of advertisers, it is difficult to see how the public at large can become the passive puppets of "hidden persuaders."

OMNIPOTENT CONTROL?

But there is still one other dread possibility to dispose of, if we can. Let us consider what might happen if there were *no* competition—if the tools of manipulation were in one group's hands. This would be *1984,* the society in which an elite group will direct the behavior of everyone else, in so subtle a way that no one is aware that it is happening. Perhaps it has already happened? How could we tell when it began?

I would not say for a moment that there are no situations in which one person can exercise absolute control over another. Give one man a gun (known in the vernacular as a "persuader"), and he can do a pretty good job of directing the activities of an unarmed man. True, some people in such a situation have escaped, taken the gun from the man, or got themselves shot. But I would not like to quibble about such a small minority, particularly in view of the fact that the effectiveness of this persuader depends on its presence being known, not hidden.

Accounts of brainwashing and similar phenomena indicate that— with a considerable expenditure of effort, careful control of a man's environment (which includes isolating him and getting him in a state of fatigue), good intuitive psychological insight, and a great deal of patience—it *is* possible to change the beliefs of a large proportion of one's victims. There is even some threat in the offing that the use of drugs and of electrodes implanted in the brain may make such procedures more effective.

Although I have some modicum of competence on such subjects, I frankly do not know exactly how far one can go now or in the immediate future with such procedures of influencing people. But look at how remote this is from the notion of controlling *a large society* via psychological techniques. Not only is it doubtful if strictly psychological practices would effect a considerable amount of brainwashing in the absence of all the other factors of control over the individual's environment, but there is the very practical matter that the amount of time and energy expended on each individual must be at least equal to his own time and energy. In short, the influencing of a single individual in a confined situation and by a large number of people is an entirely different case from that of a small number of people influencing a large number of people on a societal level. The Soviet Union is the closest approximation to this latter circumstance that we have seen, and I can say from my own studies of that society that the persuasion was far from hidden, far from total, and, possibly, far from desirable for the efficient functioning of the society.[3]

To be quite realistic, I do not see how anyone who has observed or operated any large-scale organization can take seriously the notion of complete control of behavior. In particular, social science has taught us at least as much about the *necessity* of permitting initiative—which a *1984* society by definition cannot do—as it has taught us about directing behavior.

Conclusion

In sum, I am skeptical about the extreme pictures of "hidden persuasion" that have been drawn for either the present or future of business or politics. This does not mean I am indifferent to the prospects of individual instances of the unscrupulous use of psychological or other social science knowledge. What I have been attacking is the notion of

[3] *See, for example, Raymond A. Bauer, "Brainwashing, Psychology or Demonology," Journal of Social Issues, Vol. 13, No. 3, 1957, p. 41.*

the possibility of omnipotent control over the behavior of large numbers of human beings. That such a notion rears its head repeatedly comes, I believe, from our primitive anxiety over manipulation. This anxiety is caused, on the one hand, by our fear that other people may be doing it to *us*, and therefore that we have lost control over our own destiny. It comes, on the other hand, from the notion that *we* may be doing it to others; and here we have a sense of guilt concerning our own motives and behavior toward those others.

I may be fighting a straw man in the sense that this particular *object* of people's fears is not real. But the *fears* exist; they are real. To date most people have not recognized that the threat of omnipotent control over man's behavior *is* a straw man. It may be that my contribution here is that of pointing out that the "hidden persuaders" in their exaggerated form are, in fact, made of straw.

---

*The process of controlling behavior has
an outstanding characteristic: When it's
effective, you can't tell who is controlling
whom.*   J. Lair

Eric Hoffer, the insightful
longshoreman, gives us a view
of the effects due to mass
behavior. He notes that mass
movements do not attain
converts solely by using
persuasion. The most influential mass movements have
utilized coercion as a
necessary partner to
persuasive attempts.

ERIC HOFFER

PERSUASION
AND COERCION

83

We tend today to exaggerate the effectiveness of persuasion as a
means of inculcating opinion and shaping behavior. We see in propaganda a formidable instrument. To its skillful use we attribute many
of the startling successes of the mass movements of our time, and we
have come to fear the word as much as the sword.

Actually the fabulous effects ascribed to propaganda have no
greater foundation in fact than the fall of the walls of Jericho ascribed
to the blast of Joshua's trumpets. Were propaganda by itself one-tenth
as potent as it is made out to be, the totalitarian regimes of Russia,
Germany, Italy and Spain would have been mild affairs. They would
have been blatant and brazen but without the ghastly brutality of
secret police, concentration camps and mass extermination.

The truth seems to be that propaganda on its own cannot force its
way into unwilling minds; neither can it inculcate something wholly
new; nor can it keep people persuaded once they have ceased to believe it. It penetrates only into minds already open, and rather than
instill opinion it articulates and justifies opinions already present in
the minds of its recipients. The gifted propagandist brings to a boil

ideas and passions already simmering in the minds of his hearers. He echoes their innermost feelings. Where opinion is not coerced, people can be made to believe only in what they already "know."

Propaganda by itself succeeds mainly with the frustrated. Their throbbing fears, hopes and passions crowd at the portals of their senses and get between them and the outside world. They cannot see but what they have already imagined, and it is the music of their own souls they hear in the impassioned words of the propagandist. Indeed, it is easier for the frustrated to detect their own imaginings and hear the echo of their own musings in impassioned double-talk and sonorous refrains than in precise words joined together with faultless logic.

Propaganda by itself, however skillful, cannot keep people persuaded once they have ceased to believe. To maintain itself, a mass movement has to order things so that when the people no longer believe, they can be made to believe by force.[1]

As we shall see later, words are an essential instrument in preparing the ground for a mass movement. But once the movement is realized, words, though still useful, cease to play a decisive role. So acknowledged a master of propaganda as Dr. Goebbels admits in an unguarded moment that "A sharp sword must always stand behind propaganda if it is to be really effective."[2] He also sounds apologetic when he claims that "it cannot be denied that more can be done with good propaganda than by no propaganda at all."[3]

84

Contrary to what one would expect, propaganda becomes more fervent and importunate when it operates in conjunction with coercion than when it has to rely solely on its own effectiveness.

Both they who convert and they who are converted by coercion need the fervent conviction that the faith they impose or are forced to adopt is the only true one. Without this conviction, the proselytizing terrorist, if he is not vicious to begin with, is likely to feel a criminal, and the coerced convert see himself as a coward who prostituted his soul to live.

[1] *Niccolo Machiavelli*, The Prince, *Chap. VI.*

[2] The Goebbels Diaries *(Garden City: Doubleday & Company, Inc., 1948), p. 460.*

[3] Ibid., p. 298.

Propaganda thus serves more to justify ourselves than to convince others; and the more reason we have to feel guilty, the more fervent our propaganda.

85

It is probably as true that violence breeds fanaticism as that fanaticism begets violence. It is often impossible to tell which came first. Both those who employ violence and those subject to it are likely to develop a fanatical state of mind. Ferrero says of the terrorists of the French Revolution that the more blood they "shed the more they needed to believe in their principles as absolutes. Only the absolute might still absolve them in their own eyes and sustain their desperate energy. [They] did not spill all that blood because they believed in popular sovereignty as a religious truth; they tried to believe in popular sovereignty as a religious truth because their fear made them spill so much blood."[4] The practice of terror serves the true believer not only to cow and crush his opponents but also to invigorate and intensify his own faith. Every lynching in our South not only intimidates the Negro but also invigorates the fanatical conviction of white supremacy.

In the case of the coerced, too, violence can beget fanaticism. There is evidence that the coerced convert is often as fanatical in his adherence to the new faith as the persuaded convert, and sometimes even more so. It is not always true that "He who complies against his will is of his own opinion still." Islam imposed its faith by force, yet the coerced Muslims displayed a devotion to the new faith more ardent than that of the first Arabs engaged in the movement. According to Renan, Islam obtained from its coerced converts "a faith ever tending to grow stronger."[5] Fanatical orthodoxy is in all movements a late development. It comes when the movement is in full possession of power and can impose its faith by force as well as by persuasion.

Thus coercion when implacable and persistent has an unequaled persuasiveness, and this not only with simple souls but also with those who pride themselves on the strength and integrity of their intellect. When an arbitrary decree from the Kremlin forces scientists, writers, and artists to recant their convictions and confess their errors, the chances are that such recantations and confessions represent genuine

[4] *Guglielmo Ferrero*, Principles of Power *(New York: G. P. Putnam's Sons, 1942),* p. 100.

[5] *Ernest Renan*, The Poetry of the Celtic Races *(London: W. Scott, Ltd., 1896),* essay of Islamism, p. 97.

conversions rather than lip service. It needs fanatical faith to rationalize our cowardice.

86

There is hardly an example of a mass movement achieving vast proportions and a durable organization solely by persuasion. Professor K. S. Latourette, a very Christian historian, has to admit that "However incompatible the spirit of Jesus and armed force may be, and however unpleasant it may be to acknowledge the fact, as a matter of plain history the latter has often made it possible for the former to survive."[6] It was the temporal sword that made Christianity a world religion. Conquest and conversion went hand in hand, the latter often serving as a justification and a tool for the former. Where Christianity failed to gain or retain the backing of state power, it achieved neither a wide nor a permanent hold. "In Persia . . . Christianity confronted a state religion sustained by the crown and never became the faith of more than a minority."[7] In the phenomenal spread of Islam, conquest was a primary factor and conversion a by-product. "The most flourishing periods for Mohammedanism have been at the times of its greatest political ascendancy; and it is at those times that it has received its largest accession from without."[8] The Reformation made headway only where it gained the backing of the ruling prince or the local government. Said Melanchthon, Luther's wisest lieutenant: "Without the intervention of the civil authority what would our precepts become?—Platonic laws."[9] Where, as in France, the state power was against it, it was drowned in blood and never rose again. In the case of the French Revolution, "It was the armies of the Revolution, not its ideas, that penetrated throughout the whole of Europe."[10] There was no question of intellectual contagion. Dumouriez protested that the French proclaimed the sacred law of liberty "like the Koran, sword in hand."[11]

---

[6] *Kenneth Scott Latourette*, A History of the Expansion of Christianity *(New York: Harper & Brothers, 1937), Vol. I, p. 164.*

[7] *Kenneth Scott Latourette*, The Unquenchable Light *(New York: Harper & Brothers, 1941), p. 33.*

[8] *Charles Reginald Haines*, Islam as a Missionary Religion *(London: Society for Promoting Christian Knowledge, 1889), p. 206.*

[9] *Quoted by Frantz Funck-Brentano, op. cit., p. 260.*

[10] *Guglielmo Ferrero*, The Gamble *(Toronto: Oxford University Press, 1939), p. 297.*

[11] *Crane Brinton*, A Decade of Revolution *(New York: Harper & Brothers, 1934), p. 168.*

The threat of communism at present does not come from the forceful-
ness of its preaching but from the fact that it is backed by one of the
mightiest armies on earth.

It also seems that, where a mass movement can either persuade or
coerce, it usually chooses the latter. Persuasion is clumsy and its results uncertain. Said the Spaniard St. Dominic to the heretical Albi-
genses: "For many years I have exhorted you in vain, with gentleness,
preaching, praying and weeping. But according to the proverb of my
country, 'where blessing can accomplish nothing, blows may avail.' We
shall rouse against you princes and prelates, who, alas, will arm nations
and kingdoms against this land . . . and thus blows will avail where
blessings and gentleness have been powerless."[12]

[12] "Dominic," Encyclopaedia Britannica.

One way to test the effects of
a mass medium is to do
without it for a length of time.
Could you, for example, not
read books, watch movies, or
listen to radio or television?
"Life Without the Tube"
presents some interesting
information on the effects of
television. Are you addicted
to your TV set?

___

TIME

LIFE
WITHOUT THE
TUBE

That addicts deprived of drugs suffer physical pain has been known for centuries. That human beings denied TV can experience psychological withdrawal symptoms has just been discovered. The finding was reported by the Society for Rational Psychology in Munich. Kicking TV cold turkey, says the German firm, can lead to moodiness, child spanking, wife beating, extramarital affairs and, at home, decreased interest in sex along with fewer orgasms.

The society asked 184 habitual viewers to renounce the tube for a year. At first they seemed happy to be free of it. They went to the movies three times as frequently as before, visited relatives and friends twice as often, and spent twice as much time reading and playing games. Before long, however, they felt a renewed urge to watch TV. Though the subjects were paid for every day of self-denial, one man resumed his habit after only three weeks. No one held out for more than five months.

What drove them back to the tube was mounting tension at work, at home and in bed. Quarreling and physical aggression increased. Before the sets were switched off, only 2% of the husbands had ever beaten their wives and only 58% of the parents had disciplined their children by slapping them. Afterward, however, the percentages rose to 5 and 66. With the TV on again, aggression decreased and sexual habits went back to normal—except that for a while, husbands and wives had a few more orgasms than they were used to and single people masturbated more than before.

None of this means that TV is either a tranquilizer or an aphrodisiac, cautions Psychologist Henner Ertel. In fact, the tube might well foster tension and dull sensuality in those who are unaccustomed to it. But among devotees, it may mask conflicts and even provide a last link between otherwise estranged couples. "With people who watch regularly," Ertel explains, "many behavior patterns become so closely related to TV that they are negatively influenced if one takes the set away. The problem is that of addiction."

One small little girl, in a few words, has the power to personalize relations between nations at war.

JOHN GLIDEWELL

ON FIGHT AND FLIGHT

When my older daughter was a girl of four or five, I was on active duty in the Korean War. Once at dinner she asked me, "Do Air Force planes drop bombs on real cities?"

"In wartime they do."

"Do any people get killed?"

"Yes, some get killed." By now I was hopelessly caught in the impossible task of explaining the cruel folly of war to a trusting child.

"Why do we kill people?"

"They are our enemies. They are trying to kill us or our friends. That makes them our enemies."

"Do any little children get killed?"

"Yes, sometimes."

"Are they our enemies?"

All my adult wrappings fell off, and I stood exposed to my child in all my foolishness. I spoke through the shame in my heart and the hot tears in my eyes.

"No, they are not our enemies."

I paused to regain my composure.

"The world can be a cruel place. But I promise you that I will do all I can in my time to help build a world in which little children will be safe. It's a solemn promise."

I'll never forget the promise. But I haven't had much effect on the world in trying to keep it.

The wise man knows what the questions are.   W. Johnson

Reprinted from Choice Points, *by John Glidewell by permission of The M. I. T. Press, Cambridge, Massachusetts. Copyright © 1970 Massachusetts Institute of Technology.*

437